BOUND FOR FREEDOM

BOUND FOR FREEDOM

*The Book of Exodus in Jewish and
Christian Traditions*

GÖRAN LARSSON

HENDRICKSON PUBLISHERS

© 1999 by Hendrickson Publishers, Inc.
P. O. Box 3473
Peabody, Massachusetts 01961-3473
Printed in the United States of America

Third Printing, Softcover Edition — June 2006

ISBN-13: 978-1-56563-975-1
ISBN-10: 1-56563-975-8

Original edition: *Uppbrottet: Bibelteologisk kommentar till Andra Moseboken.*
©Verbum Förlag, Stockholm, 1993.

Library of Congress Cataloging-in-Publication Data

Larsson, Göran.
    [Uppbrottet. English]
    Bound for freedom: the Book of Exodus in Jewish and Christian
traditions / Göran Larsson.
    Includes bibliographical references and indexes.
    ISBN-13: 978-1-56563-975-1
    ISBN-10: 1-56563-975-8
    1. Bible. O.T. Exodus—Commentaries. I. Title.
BS1245.3.L3713   1999
224′.1207—dc21   98-52685
                                                         CIP

Images used on pages 5, 16, 26, 40, 53, 80, 96, 112, 126, 156, 184, 207,
and 245 are adapted from the *Erlangen Haggadah*, an illuminated MS produced in 1747 and held at Universitätsbibliothek Erlangen, Germany. Its
miniature illustrations depict each section of the Passover seder service.
Used by permission.

Cover art:
Chagall, Marc (1887–1985). "Moses Receiving the Tablets of the Law."
1950–52. Oil on canvas, 1.94 x 1.30 m. Coll. Ida Meyer-Chagall, Basel,
Switzerland.
© 1999 Artists Rights Society (ARS), New York/ADAGP, Paris.
Photo credit, Giraudon/Art Resource, New York

To my mother and to the memory of my father

Table of Contents

A Word from the Author

*T*his commentary is primarily for Bible readers, teachers, and ministers who wish to include all of Scripture in their studies and sermons. Its point of departure is the text as transmitted to us, rather than the prehistory of the text—that is, the text as we have it now rather than the process that led to its formation. Many scholarly works have focused on the formation of the various books of the Bible, and biblical studies has thoroughly analyzed their transmission through different periods into their final literary form.

No matter how important the study of this prehistory of the Bible may be, it must be followed up by a serious study of the final product as a whole. This is, after all, the only text that is available to us; the assumed sources are mostly scholarly reconstructions, the extent and shape of which are subject to ongoing academic debate.

Furthermore, it is the completed book that has been handed down from generation to generation. We must ask what factors made this text so important that over the centuries people have found it worth reading, interpreting, and diligently applying to their everyday lives, even at the risk of martyrdom. How could the Bible have achieved such tremendous power and influence? In this respect, the Bible differs from all other contemporaneous documents, which today attract the interest of only a few scholars. In a sense, these other ancient texts can be said to have died, while the Bible lives and continues to make a positive impact on peoples' thinking, transforming their lives.

The people of Israel were the first to receive, preserve, and constantly revive the book of books. They became the tool by which God gave the biblical revelation to the world. The people of Israel saw to it that the Bible never became just one of many obscure Near Eastern texts. Through Israel's unique gift to humanity, the Bible, we have received a heritage that is still a formative factor of paramount value in today's society.

Needless to say, the sages of Israel were the first interpreters of the Bible. If not for a constant interpretation and application of the biblical text, the Bible would not have survived. Every Bible commentary presenting the text as God's living word accepts responsibility for bridging the distance between the text and the contemporary reader. Such a commentary will necessarily attempt to do justice to the text itself, trying to understand its language, frame of reference, and historical, cultural, and religious contexts.

This, however, simply does not suffice. The Bible is much more than a collection of documents and a history book. The stories recounted and the commandments given serve to elucidate God's will and purpose for humankind. History is viewed as proceeding from within God's plan; from beginning to end the Bible is interpreted history. Therefore, the historical questions, When? Where? What? and How? must be accompanied by the even more basic questions, Why? and To what purpose?

A commentary that purports to construct a bridge between the world of the Bible and contemporary reality must take seriously the fact that we stand at the far end of that bridge. What questions emerge when we are addressed by this voice from the distant past? What response to today's questions can this voice provide? Where am I in the context of the eternally divine and human story of the exodus? What divine message do I find transmitted to me through the text I am reading?

Biblical authors were convinced that this message stands above and beyond time and space. The subsequent interpretations of the text as God's voice to us were therefore designed to make it alive to people of every age, in every time. Consequently, in order to understand the text better, it is imperative to consult these interpretations, particularly the most ancient. To adequately comment on the original book dealing with the exodus from Egypt, one needs to learn from the ancient Jewish commentaries. Historically, culturally, and, above all, religiously, these commentaries come closest to the people whose liberation is there described.

It is for these reasons that my commentary on the book of Exodus employs Jewish traditions of interpretation. As a Christian, I also share in this tradition, not only because the book of Exodus is part of our Bible but specifically because Christianity emerged from the framework of Judaism. The New Testament's message is constantly illuminated by stories and commandments from the five books of Moses, not least of all from the book of Exodus. Furthermore, these sources were vigorously studied within the early church.

Thus, it is not my intent to provide a critical discussion of textual and historical questions that involve the book of Exodus. These, of course, are important, but I will leave the detailed discussion of them to others. In this commentary, I will treat Exodus as an integrated narrative, a story of Moses in Egypt and at Sinai, leading God's people from slavery. For so it was read by the early interpreters who have left us theological insights that also deserve to be heard and heeded. They do not stand against historical inquiry. They stand alongside it.

What is more, a commentary stressing the history of interpretation must include the Christian traditions of interpretation, even when they are in conflict with Jewish ones. In this respect, the Bible has led to a lively, healthy debate resulting in unavoidable dividing lines among various possibilities of textual interpretation. Yet, instead of serving as a tool to penetrate deeper into the endless depths of God's revelation and to build bridges between people of different faiths, the texts have often been sharpened into weapons not only to defend oneself but also to hurt and wound others.

When it comes to Jewish-Christian relations, this is a tragic theme with recurrent variations throughout history. In light thereof, I regard it as highly relevant, nay essential, to deal with theological questions relating the book of Exodus to current Jewish-Christian dialogue. Therefore, the discussion of words and concepts, like "law," "election," and "holy people," as well as single texts (like "eye for eye, tooth for tooth," so often misunderstood in the Christian tradition), and theological questions (like "To what extent are the biblical commandments still binding?") perhaps receive a disproportionately large space in my commentary. The reason is indicated in the subtitle, *The Book of Exodus in Jewish and Christian Traditions;* hopefully needless stumbling blocks between Christians and

Jews may be removed through the knowledge and understanding of how each other reads the text.

With these principal points of departure, my commentary does not set forth each detail in the text. Instead of a
verse-by-verse commentary, I discuss larger units, arranged
according to their major themes. The biblical text commented
on is rarely quoted. However, there are constant references to
the verses dealt with and to pertinent parallel texts. I take for
granted that the reader will first open the Bible, study the sections referred to in the chapter headings, and then keep the
Bible open for ongoing reference.

When the Bible is quoted, the translation is the New Revised Standard Version (NRSV). Other translations are indicated in the notes, except the Talmud and the *Midrash Rabbah,*
which are usually quoted according to the Soncino editions,
and the translations of Philo and Josephus, which follow the
standard editions of the Loeb Classical Library. Other translations are mine.

References to chapters and verses without indication of a
specific biblical book always refer to the book of Exodus. Hebrew and Greek words have been transliterated in a simplified
way that seeks to facilitate correct pronunciation. For the sake
of clarity, I have retained the classical usage "Old Testament,"
even though I realize the anti-Jewish connotations of this term
(see pp. 130, n. 2, 169, 198).

For those interested in further studies, references are
provided in the notes. I have tried to keep them to a minimum,
aware of the large number of scholarly commentaries available
for advanced students and scholars. This also applies to the
bibliography, which contains only a limited number of basic
books that are referred to in an abbreviated way in the notes.
Works appearing in the bibliography that are mentioned in
this commentary will be cited with a shortened title. For extensive bibliographies, see, for example, the commentaries of
Childs *(The Book of Exodus)* and Sarna *(Exploring Exodus).*

Bound for Freedom has undergone a long delivery process.
It was first published in Sweden in 1993 after I was privileged
to spend the academic year of 1991–1992 at the University of
Chicago Divinity School as a visiting scholar. At that time I
had behind me twelve years of teaching Hebrew, Bible, and
rabbinic literature at the Swedish Theological Institute in Jerusalem. Numerous Passover meals, during which the exodus
story is vividly dramatized and commented on, and discus-

sions with sages, scholars, students, and friends, have been a constant source of knowledge and inspiration.

Among the many teachers of mine throughout the years, four names stand out: Professor Gillis Gerleman of blessed memory, and his successor Tryggve N. D. Mettinger, my esteemed teachers of Old Testament studies at Lund University; Professor Shaul Lieberman of blessed memory, a Ga'on of this century who graciously shared his precious time with me in Jerusalem; and Professor Haim M. I. Gevaryahu of blessed memory, scholar and Tzaddik, who opened the door for me not only to his home but to the most distinguished scholars and sages of Israel.

Some people have been directly involved in the creation of this book. Reverend Gillis Simonsson, the director of Verbum Publishing House in Sweden, asked me to write it and was very supportive during the work. Dr. John Kutsko, senior editor at Hendrickson Publishers, enthusiastically received my English book proposal. The collaboration with him and other staff members has been pleasant and inspiring, and their professional input is felt throughout the book. Professor Frank H. Seilhamer, former president of Hamma School of Theology, Springfield, Ohio, and professor of Old Testament at Trinity Lutheran Seminary, Columbus, Ohio, read a part of the manuscript and gave me helpful suggestions for improvement. Attorney Lisa A. Runquist, who went through the entire book and pointed out several matters that ought to be changed, was also very helpful.

Last but not least I want to particularly thank Dr. Charles Abraham, linguist, translator, scholar, and friend, who has spared no efforts in bringing my Swedish-influenced English into a readable vernacular and also provided me with many invaluable comments regarding the content. His wife Lu Ellen has unstintingly participated in the work and provided editorial proofing so crucial to an author.

As I deliver this manuscript, I pray that the published work will result in a partial fulfillment of the prophecy of Isaiah, "For out of Zion shall go forth the law *(Torah),* and the word of the LORD from Jerusalem" (Isa. 2:3).

Göran Larsson
San Diego

Abbreviations

GENERAL ABBREVIATIONS

AB	Anchor Bible
ANET	*Ancient Near Eastern Texts Relating to the Old Testament* (ed. J. B. Pritchard; Princeton: Princeton University Press, 1969)
AOAT	Alter Orient und Altes Testament
ASOR	American Schools of Oriental Research
ASTI	*Annual of the Swedish Theological Institute*
b.	Babylonian Talmud *(Talmud Bavli),* followed by name of tractate
BA	*Biblical Archaeologist*
BAR	*Biblical Archaeology Review*
BASOR	*Bulletin of the American Schools of Oriental Research*
BR	*Bible Review*
CBQ	*Catholic Biblical Quarterly*
cf.	compare
ch(s).	chapter(s)
CSCO	Corpus Scriptorum Christianorum Orientalium
CTA	*Corpus des tablettes en cunéiformes alphabétiques découvertes à Ras Shamra-Ugarit de 1929 à 1939,* ed. A. Herdner (Mission de Ras Shamra 10; Paris: Geuthner, 1963).
ed.	editor; edited by; edition
EncJud	*Encyclopaedia Judaica* (Jerusalem: Keter Publishing House, 1972)

f(f.)	and the following one(s)
HUCA	*Hebrew Union College Annual*
JAOS	*Journal of the American Oriental Society*
JBL	*Journal of Biblical Literature*
JJS	*Journal of Jewish Studies*
JNES	*Journal of Near Eastern Studies*
JPS	Jewish Publication Society
JQR	*Jewish Quarterly Review*
JSOTSup	Journal for the Study of the Old Testament: Supplement Series
m.	Mishnah, followed by name of tractate
n.	note
NRSV	The New Revised Standard Version
NovTSup	Novum Testamentum Supplements
PG	*Patrologia Graeca* (ed. J. P. Migne; Paris, 1844-)
PEQ	*Palestine Exploration Quarterly*
SBS	Stuttgarter Bibelstudien
t.	Tosefta, followed by name of tractate
TDOT	*Theological Dictionary of the Old Testament* (ed. G. J. Botterweck, H. Ringgren, and H. J. Fabry; trans. J. T. Willis, G. W. Bromiley, and D. E. Green; Grand Rapids, Mich.: Eerdmans, 1974-)
trans.	translator; translated by
v(v).	verse(s)
VT	*Vetus Testamentum*
y.	Palestinian Talmud *(Talmud Yerushalmi),* followed by name of tractate
ZAW	*Zeitschrift für die alttestamentliche Wissenschaft*

BIBLICAL ABBREVIATIONS

Gen.	Genesis	2 Sam.	2 Samuel
Exod.	Exodus	1 Kgs.	1 Kings
Lev.	Leviticus	2 Kgs.	2 Kings
Num.	Numbers	1 Chron.	1 Chronicles
Deut.	Deuteronomy	2 Chron.	2 Chronicles
Josh.	Joshua	Ezra	Ezra
Judg.	Judges	Neh.	Nehemiah
Ruth	Ruth	Esth.	Esther
1 Sam.	1 Samuel	Job	Job

Ps.	Psalms	John	John
Prov.	Proverbs	Acts	Acts
Song	Song of Songs	Rom.	Romans
Eccl.	Ecclesiastes	1 Cor.	1 Corinthians
Isa.	Isaiah	2 Cor.	2 Corinthians
Jer.	Jeremiah	Gal.	Galatians
Lam.	Lamentations	Eph.	Ephesians
Ezek.	Ezekiel	Phil.	Philippians
Dan.	Daniel	Col.	Colossians
Hos.	Hosea	1 Thess.	1 Thessalonians
Joel	Joel	2 Thess.	2 Thessalonians
Amos	Amos	1 Tim.	1 Timothy
Obad.	Obadiah	2 Tim.	2 Timothy
Jon.	Jonah	Titus	Titus
Mic.	Micah	Phlm.	Philemon
Nah.	Nahum	Heb.	Hebrews
Hab.	Habakkuk	James	James
Zeph.	Zephaniah	1 Pet.	1 Peter
Hag.	Haggai	2 Pet.	2 Peter
Zech.	Zechariah	1 John	1 John
Mal.	Malachi	2 John	2 John
Matt.	Matthew	3 John	3 John
Mark	Mark	Jude	Jude
Luke	Luke	Rev.	Revelation

For there is no freedom without the learning of the Torah (*Pirqe Avot* 6:2)

Introduction

$\mathcal{T}$he Bible is the book of liberation and freedom. Miracles of redemption are recorded there in overflowing abundance, but at the center of everything is the deliverance of Israel from Egypt, a theme resounding throughout the entire Bible. We are about to open the book of this miracle, the book of Exodus, the great book of freedom, which embodies God's vow and declaration of eternal love to his people, "When Israel was a child, I loved him, and out of Egypt I called my son" (Hos. 11:1).

This relationship of love, however, sets out on a long walk toward freedom, a walk often circuitous and at times on the wrong road. We now join the Israelites on their arduous path to freedom, and it is easy to relate personally to them or to acknowledge the unchanging God who again and again shows himself the great Liberator: "I am the LORD[1] your God, who brought you out of the land of Egypt, out of the house of slavery" (20:2). This statement can be regarded as God's signature throughout the ages (see pp. 140ff.), for the God of the past is also the God of the present and the future, "the same yesterday today and forever."

The house of bondage is here as well, even though it may appear under a different guise in various places and times. Reading the book of Exodus, we can equally participate in the words of the Jewish *Passover Haggadah,* "In every generation it is everyone's duty to look upon himself as if he came out of Egypt, as it is said: 'And you shall tell your son on that day: It is because of what the Lord did for me when I came out of Egypt' " (Exod. 13:8).[2]

This perspective makes the book of Exodus alive. Those who have transmitted the holy texts from generation to generation have done so out of the same ardent faith. More than just history, this book deals with us as well! Exodus is not a closed chapter in human history. Its message is alive and vibrant. That is why we can continue reading, contemplating, and learning from this book. In this way, history meets the present and the experience of a nation in the past merges into our own present realities, yearnings, and hopes.

The slaves in America rightly comprehended Moses' demand, "Let my people go!" as universal. With the same insight, poor and oppressed people all over the world find inspiration, encouragement, and strength in these words. Typically, a "theology of hope" has emerged from the book of Exodus, for the liberation from Egypt deals not just with the past and the present; what is recounted there provides the basis for our future hope as well.

In the Old Testament, the theme of liberation is repeated at least 120 times. Often the references are made to a renewed exodus, a complete liberation, which once and for all will put an end to darkness, slavery, and bondage of any kind. Our hope looks to a redemption destined to embrace not just one oppressed people but all humankind. It includes not only liberation from darkness and pain but from everything that now causes distress on earth.

The title *Bound for Freedom* is deliberately ambiguous. It expresses the fundamental biblical message that there is no freedom without boundaries. As we will see, the real act of liberation takes place at Sinai with the giving of the Torah. Exodus is not about unconditional freedom, which, in fact, would only have meant exchanging one oppressor for another and one exile for another. The ancient sages of Israel repeatedly express this profound biblical and experiential wisdom. For example, "Whoever takes upon himself the yoke of the Torah, from him the yoke of the government and worldly futility will be removed. But whoever casts off the yoke of the Torah, upon him will be laid the yoke of government and worldly futility. . . . There is no freedom without the learning of the Torah."[3] Only the liberating word of God can set people free and bring them to the promised land and eventually to authentic freedom.

Eventually, yes. But it will take time. The way to freedom is long. Its final goal still lies ahead of us. This is the second message transmitted through the title *Bound for Freedom*. The full liberation is to take place when the long way to freedom is finally accomplished. The exodus from Egypt is but the beginning. It merely sets the agenda for future events. It constitutes a prophetic pattern for all subsequent liberations.

Thus, the exodus from Egypt opens a gate of hope toward the future. In Jewish tradition, 14 Nisan, Passover night, is also the time of the final redemption. When Revelation, the last book of the New Testament, momentarily raises the veil and allows us a glimpse into the ultimate promised land, we see that all pain will pass and that the threatening waters will forever freeze into a crystal sea. Significantly, the rescuer and liberator of Israel appears in this vision, where the people of God sing the song of eternal liberty and victory, "the song of Moses, the servant of God, and the song of the Lamb" (Rev. 15:3).

But we are not there yet. When Jews celebrate the Sabbath and the other great feasts in memory of the deliverance from Egypt (Deut. 5:15), these are also days of hope that provide a foretaste of the final Sabbath rest still to come (Heb. 4:9). While preparing ourselves for this day, the book of Exodus gives our faith deep roots in the past, solid confidence in the present, and bright hope for the future.

1

The Prelude

*J*f the Bible is a book about a series of exiles and homecomings, it is also a book of many promises and fulfillments. It speaks of a divine plan for history in general and for individual peoples and nations. But God's history is not a marionette theater, where dolls without willpower are forced to act according to the manipulation of strings from above. It is also not a matter of blind improvisation, where the outcome is decided by the actors. The final scene is envisioned from the first act. So are the main points in the drama. However, the Lord not only supervises the development of the events but also actively interacts with the players throughout the drama.

On the biblical scene, the people of Israel appear in the limelight. It is their particular liberation that we will soon witness. The first seven verses in the book of Exodus contain a condensed description of an exodus and a homecoming, a promise and its fulfillment. The children of Israel, who had to leave their land and depart for Egypt, have been blessed and have found a second homeland in Egypt. But as always in this world, something fragile and imperfect immediately opens the perspective toward new exiles and renewed promises of a return home. It is merely the beginning of a long way to freedom.

A PEOPLE IS BORN

This long journey actually began hundreds of years before with God's calling of Abraham to leave his country and people, relying on the promises of a new land and a great nation emanating from his offspring (Gen. 12:1–3). When we enter the book of Exodus, the prediction given to Abraham in Gen. 15:13 has already been realized: "Know this for certain, that your offspring shall be aliens in a land that is not theirs." The beginning of the next act is therefore only to be expected: "And they shall be slaves there, and they shall be oppressed for four hundred years."

Before this dark scene is played out, we get a hint of the great liberation the oppressed people anticipated. The very first letter of the book of Exodus actually expresses the profound link between what we should yet expect and what has happened before—the little word "and": "And these are the names of the sons of Israel."[1] When the sons of Jacob are listed in the first verses of the book of Exodus, this in itself is a reminder of the beginning of the miraculous fulfillment of the promise to Abraham, Isaac, and Jacob in the book of Genesis: that God would bless them and make them "a great and mighty nation" (Gen. 18:18; cf. Gen. 12:2; 15:5; 22:17; 26:4; 28:14; 46:3; 48:4). The beginning of Exodus echoes Gen. 46:8–27 (cf. Gen. 35:23ff.). However, we now witness a further step toward the fulfillment of this promise in the description of the enormous growth of the people (v. 7). From the very beginning, there is every reason to trust in the fulfillment of the promised liberation (Gen. 15:14; 28:15; 46:4; 48:21). The scene is thereby set for the unfolding drama.

When Pharaoh complains to the Egyptians that "the Israelite people are more numerous and more powerful than we" (v. 9), he is expressing God's own plan, although he is in open defiance of it. His statement does not necessarily mean that they indeed were numerous. Antisemitic paranoia has expressed itself in a similar way throughout the ages. For example, in no way did the Jews pose any real threat to Hitler. Yet he depicted them as a mortal danger not only to Germany but to the whole world. The classical antisemitic accusation of double loyalties is also voiced by Pharaoh, namely, that the Israelites may "in the event of war, join our enemies and fight against us" (v. 10).[2]

Ironically, the oppressor of Israel is the first to proclaim Israel as a *people*. In the book of Genesis we follow the history of several *families* who are promised that they will some day become a great people; in the book of Exodus, we witness the birth of this people.

The fact that it is their archenemy who makes them aware of their identity as a people is something that has been repeated throughout history. In the book of Esther, Haman selects the Jews for extermination. In modern times, many assimilated Jews in Germany only became aware of their Jewish ancestry through the laws and policies instituted under Hitler's dictatorship. The same pattern was evident through the antisemitism in the former Soviet Union and in other parts of the world.

Even in another respect Pharaoh expresses a prophetic perspective on the long way toward freedom for the now enslaved people of Israel. Again, Pharaoh is the first human indirectly and unwittingly to proclaim the exodus event!

His fear that they may "escape from the land" (v. 10) ought to be rendered literally "*go up from* the land." The Hebrew verb used, ʿalah, is prophetically used by Joseph in the prediction: "I am about to die; but God will surely come to you, and bring you up out of the land that he swore to Abraham, to Isaac, and to Jacob" (Gen. 50:24). It will soon be echoed in God's promise: "I have come down to deliver them from the Egyptians, and to *bring them up* out of that land" (3:8).

The promise was certainly fulfilled a generation later, when the people entered the promised land under the leadership of Joshua. But again, it was only the beginning of a long way to freedom, which would continue throughout the centuries. For the last two thousand years, it remained the dream and hope of the dispersed Jewish people. Only during the last hundred years and particularly in our generation was it brought to a renewed fulfillment with the immigration to the land of Israel and the creation of the modern state. Significantly, the technical term for "immigration" in modern Hebrew is ʿaliyah, derived from the same verb, ʿalah, which is used here by Pharaoh (and earlier by Joseph). This derivation marks it as a kind of fulfillment of ancient prophecies (cf. pp. 179f.).

PHARAOH

Very often the tyrants of this world fear anyone who might pose a threat to their position. They desire to strengthen their own power and fame by oppressing others. Pharaoh is an outstanding example of these evils.

In the 1950s, when Egypt's President Nasser moved a huge statue of Rameses II to Cairo and named the place after him, one of Nasser's motivations was that the oppressor of Israel should be honored. He probably chose the right pharaoh.

Rameses II ruled over Egypt during the greater part of the thirteenth century B.C.E., probably 1290–1224.[3] During his long and powerful reign, Egypt became a huge empire that extended from Nubia, at the border of today's Sudan in the south, to Syria in the north. Rameses transferred the administrative center from Upper Egypt to the fertile northeastern delta of the Nile and the land of Goshen where the Israelites had received permission to reside (Gen. 47).

Here he made his capital the city of Rameses, which was located somewhere east of today's Ismailia. As in other parts of his huge empire, this area experienced a time of great prosperity. It is not surprising that the whole province was named after him, "the land of Rameses" (Gen. 47:11).[4]

It is, in fact, hard to find another Pharaoh who fits the biblical record so well. He had to rule for a long period, matching the statement "After a long time the king of Egypt died" (2:23). Finally, Rameses II not only moved the administrative center to the north but also lived there himself, in proximity to the Hebrews in Goshen, which might be why the daughter of Pharaoh is said to have found Moses in the Nile and brought him to the royal palace (ch. 2).[5]

Through inscriptions and archaeological finds, the city of Pithom can be traced. The name is linked to Atum, the sun-god, who was worshiped in a splendid temple in the middle of the city. Both Pithom and Rameses were centers of prosperous governmental districts, complete with Pharaoh's palaces, temples, administrative buildings of exceeding beauty, and huge storehouses. Intensive building activities probably went on here during his entire reign.

Papyrus texts from the thirteenth century have been found that describe the impressive dimensions, splendor, and glory of Pithom: "His Majesty—life, prosperity, health!—has built himself a castle, the name of which is 'Great of Victories.' . . . The sun rises in its horizon, and sets within it."[6] The borders of the city were marked by four temples in each corner, Amon in the west, Seth in the south, the goddess of Uto in the north, and the temple of her Semitic colleague, Astarte, in the east (Astarte is mentioned in the Old Testament in 1 Sam. 31:10 and 1 Kgs. 11:5). In the midst of the city,

Rameses himself sat enthroned like a god in a castle, "like the horizon of heaven."[7]

Anyone who has seen some of the colossal temples and burial monuments in Egypt can easily translate this description into reality. Many of these elaborate and gigantic edifices carry the signature of Rameses II. Abu Simbel in the south boasts four enormous statues of Rameses directly hewn in the rock and a countless number of statues and reliefs in the tomb chambers. There are impressive monuments in the Valley of the Kings at Luxor, where a statue of Rameses weighing at least one thousand tons has fallen down, crushing its face. These architectural treasures bear witness to a creativity that has few counterparts in world history.

A ruler of such prominence has, of course, evoked numerous legends both in the early history of Egypt and in later literature. A classical historian who lived just before our era called him "king of kings and despot of despots,"[8] and scholars of today often add the epithet, "the Great." Another powerful and power-seeking tyrant inevitably comes to mind who is also known as one of the greatest builders in history, King Herod (37–4 B.C.E.), who also bore the epithet, "the Great."

SLAVERY

A cultural explosion of such dimensions could hardly have taken place without sacrifices and victims. Many documents give evidence of large-scale slavery during Rameses's reign. Even if slaves could work for private masters, slavery was above all a state institution. Inscriptions and illustrations from the period indicate that slaves were considered to be the property of Pharaoh. They were tattooed with his seal and marked like cattle. The system was given divine sanction. For example, in the temple of Edfu an inscription from Rameses's reign depicts a god registering slaves for Pharaoh. There are also several reliefs that show how Pharaoh delivers the subjugated nations to the gods.[9] As we know, even in recent times slavery and oppression have been defended by people who believed it to be part of the divine order.

Many different peoples thus suffered as slaves in Egypt. The people of Israel, however, became the target of something new and unique. Slavery was no longer just a matter of exploiting their labor. More and more it became a tool of

keeping them downtrodden and preventing them from pro-
creating (vv. 10–11).[10] It was the first of three measures taken
by Pharaoh to subjugate and control the Israelites as a nation.

How could Pharaoh have imagined that this subjugation
would prevent their natural increase? A Jewish commentary
assumes that he commanded the taskmasters to establish
daily working quotas so high that the Israelites would not be
able to return home in the evening and would have to spend
the night at the work site.[11]

In light of the rich documentation regarding slavery in
ancient Egypt, this assumption is not unrealistic. Besides
sowing and harvesting, the slaves also had to break up the
fertile mud when the waters of the Nile dried at the shores.
Slaves extended the numerous canal systems that led the
water into the fields, and the quarries and brickyards required hard labor. The grim reality behind "taskmasters"
(v. 11) and "mortar and bricks and all kinds of work in the
field" (v. 14) are reflected in the following contemporary report on the hard lives of the working people at the hands of
their harsh supervisors:

> Now the scribe lands on the shore. He surveys the harvest. Attendants
> are behind him with staffs, Nubians with clubs. One says (to him):
> "Give grain." "There is none." He is beaten savagely. He is bound,
> thrown in the well, submerged head down. His wife is bound in his
> presence. His children are in fetters.[12]

At the Jewish Passover meal, a hard-boiled egg is always served (see p. 89). One explanation of this tradition is
based on the fact that the egg gets harder the longer it is
boiled. This is indeed an apt illustration of the words in
verse 12: "But the more they were oppressed, the more they
multiplied and spread." The original plan of Pharaoh completely failed. Therefore, the next phase of oppression was
initiated, posing a deadly danger to the people.

GENOCIDE

The previously mentioned similarity between Rameses II
and Herod the Great is no less obvious when we read what
Josephus and an ancient rabbinic tradition tell about the tragedy that was now to occur. According to this tradition, Pharaoh's astrologers prophesied that the liberator of Israel was to

be born. If he survived, he would humiliate Egypt and gain
eternal fame (cf. Matt. 2). As in the case of Herod, this prediction would explain why Pharaoh ordered only the boys to be
murdered.[13]

Pharaoh had to prevent the freeing of the slaves at any
price. Like his kindred soul twelve hundred years later, the
mighty despotic Pharaoh would not refrain even from genocide in order to protect his position. Like so many tyrants, he
now looked for collaborators among the ordinary people to
execute his murderous plans (vv. 15–16). He had to resort to
underhanded methods since the whole of the people would
probably not be ready for such a heinous crime, at least not
yet. Thus, Pharaoh took the second step to subdue the Hebrews and moved from slavery to secret slaughter.

When even this plan failed, perhaps Pharaoh first polled
the people regarding their attitudes toward the Hebrews before he ventured to issue the atrocious decree to "all his
people" that makes up the final chord in the first chapter:
"Every boy that is born to the Hebrews you shall throw into
the Nile." By this the third and last step was taken. Now it was
no longer a matter of secret negotiations with enticed collaborators but of a public, unambiguous command aimed at
genocide.

The gradual escalation in Nazi Germany from hate
propaganda to trade boycott, the banning of Jews from certain occupations, the steps toward racial segregation, the
open violence of *Kristallnacht,* the ghettos, the labor camps,
and finally Auschwitz and the so-called final solution, are
certainly unique in their ghastly dimensions. However, the
basic pattern can be discerned in the tragic drama enacted
three thousand years earlier.

Even here we find exceptional heroes to look up to and
emulate.

TWO WOMEN

In seven verses they dominate the scene—these dignified
examples of courage and fear of God, with its noble fruit, love
of one's fellow human beings. In the history of human liberation, they deserve to be remembered forever.

It is typical of the biblical standard of measure that one
of the most despotic rulers in world history, the pharaoh of

Egypt, is never once mentioned by name. However, Shiphrah and Puah, two midwives in the service of life, who had the bravery and integrity to follow their conscience and to defy this tyrant, are mentioned by name—names still used by representatives of the people they tried to save.[14]

Nothing would have been easier than giving in to the legalized barbarism, hiding behind blind obedience, and repeating what so many in similar situations have said to justify their inaction, "We had to obey orders." But these two women chose to obey God rather than persons. Those who indeed fear and love God more than anything else will also necessarily love their neighbors as themselves. They will intervene in an active and meaningful way, rather than merely feeling sympathy and compassion from a distance. When encountering Shiphrah and Puah, the heroines of these verses, we are reminded of Elie Wiesel's unforgettable words:

> The age of hypocrisy has been succeeded by that of indifference, which is worse, for indifference corrupts and appeases; it kills the spirit before it kills the body. It has been stated before, it bears repeating: the opposite of love is not hate, but indifference.[15]

In this context even something as noble as telling the truth can express the same kind of indifference as blind obedience. It can hardly be doubted that Shiphrah and Puah were lying to Pharaoh in verse 19 (cf. pp. 153f.).[16] But they did so in the service of life and love! In so doing, they saved many human lives, and perhaps they even saved the one destined to become the savior of Israel.

Who, then, is my neighbor? This age-old question finds a clear-cut answer in the actions of the midwives, particularly if it is strangers they have endeavored to help. Here I tend to follow an interpretation that is contrary to the majority of translations, which designate Shiphrah and Puah "the Hebrew midwives." The Hebrew expression *lammeyalledoth ha῾ivriyyoth* should rather be understood as an abridgment of *lammeyalledoth ᾿eth ha῾ivriyyoth;* that is, verse 15 should be translated, "And the king of Egypt said to *those who delivered the Hebrew women.*" Another possibility, leading to the same conclusion, would be to change the vowels to *limeyalledoth ha῾ivriyyoth,* which would then be a genitive construction and translated "the midwives of the Hebrews." Even here nothing would be explicitly stated about the nationality of the midwives.

As a matter of fact, this is obviously the understanding of the Hebrew text as translated in the Greek of the Septuagint and the Latin of the Vulgate; Josephus and several Jewish commentators after him interpreted the text in the same way.[17] This reading consequently allows the possibility that the midwives were Egyptian women, a possibility that strengthens inasmuch as it seems unlikely that Pharaoh would have asked Hebrew women to murder their own kin. Furthermore, in the rest of this chapter he only addresses Egyptians.

My neighbor is the person whom I encounter along life's path, no matter who he or she is. Every person is created in the image of God. Neither nationality nor religion nor any other factor can erase this indelible attribute of humanity. According to Jewish as well as Christian ethics, the commandment of love transcends all borders and differences. To be sure, the commandment, "You shall love your neighbor as yourself," is clarified by the verse, "The alien who resides with you shall be to you as the citizen among you; you shall love the alien as yourself" (Lev. 19:34). It is sad that nationalism and religious blindness have often limited how far love of one's neighbor should reach.

The reason behind the courageous deeds of Shiphrah and Puah is fear of God. They have to obey God more than any human being on earth, even if this person is the most powerful leader, generally considered to be divine. The rationale for spurning Pharaoh is not that the midwives purport to help a special people, God's people, or that they have to see to it that God's promises regarding this people are fulfilled. All these facts were concealed from them. Rather, the fear of God and the respect and love of his creation were enough to make them act as they did. They were simply human, wonderfully human. The commandment of love and the identification with the outsider and stranger is something universal, which people among all cultures and religions in one way or another include as one of the highest ethical standards.[18]

To achieve one's highest human potential is not easy. Had it been easy, Pharaoh would have had to give up his evil plans. In that case, there would have been more than two mentioned in this chapter who had the courage to be human. But, as usual, there were too few like them in those days, just as there were too few Raoul Wallenbergs to stand against the

Nazi evil. When evil triumphs, there are usually more idle accomplices than champions of justice. As a matter of fact, all that evil needs to succeed is a sufficient number of "respectable" people who remain passive and indifferent.

USURPING GOD'S DOMINION

Chapter 1 introduces a theme which will recur throughout the first act of the exodus drama: a line is drawn between God's and humanity's dominion. The theme works itself out in three interactions: between Pharaoh and the people, the women and the people, and the women and Pharaoh.

Pharaoh's transgressing into the realm of God's dominion is directly expressed through his claim of authority over life and death. Indirectly, it is also expressed through the fear he is obviously able to instill into his people to make them all accomplices in his murderous crime against the enslaved Hebrews (v. 22). He exploits their fear of the Israelites (v. 12). The verb "fear" hides more than it immediately expresses. In the deepest sense, it is a prerogative of God to be feared, as is obvious from Joseph's address to his brothers when they weep and say, "We are here as your slaves" (Gen. 50:18). Joseph's reaction is this: "Do not be afraid! Am I in the place of God?"

Fear of God is the reason the midwives avoid participating in the slaughter. They acknowledge God as the ruler over life and death and as the utmost object worthy of our reverance. "Do not fear those who kill the body but cannot kill the soul," Jesus would later admonish (Matt. 10:28), and the apostles testify, "We must obey God rather than any human authority" (Acts 5:29). This reaction ought to be natural before God—sincere obedience, utmost reverence, overwhelming awe.[19] No human being, not even the most powerful rulers of this world, can claim the same, unless they assume the role of God. This, however, is a prominent characteristic of Pharaoh. He wants to be feared. He wants what Joseph refused, to be "in the place of God."

Joseph also used the same expression when he refused to enslave his brothers—that he was not God (Gen. 50:18–19). In Hebrew the same verb, ʿavad, is used for "to toil, work, serve, and worship," and the same noun, ʿeved, is used both for a slave and a servant. Not surprisingly, the noun ʿavodah means both slavery and service, work and worship.[20] In verses 13–14 these words appear no fewer than five times to describe what the Egyptians did to the Hebrew slaves.

Slavery is yet another example of usurping God's domain. God is the sole rightful owner of a human being. As creator, God is not only the source of life but uniquely the one who can claim what we consider to be ours, whether property or human effort. All human beings without exception are created in the image of God (Gen. 1:26–27). This implies that every human being is ultimately employed by none but God, being God's servant and even partner in the service of humankind. Slavery negates this fundamental calling and dignity of every human being. The slave owner enters the domain of the creator when he falsely claims ownership of another's life, whose owner is God alone. It is therefore not surprising that slavery and homicide, at times even genocide, often go hand in hand.

God's objective in liberating his people is to change them from slaves to servants so that they might serve him alone where they are now laboring under the self-proclaimed god-king Pharaoh. This theme is recurrent throughout the following chapters: 4:23; 7:16; 8:1; 9:1, 13; 10:3, 26; and 14:12 (see pp. 17, 55, 71, 76–79, 127).

The midwives withstand the temptation of directing their fear and service toward the wrong object. Obviously, their example finds few parallels among the people. Therefore, Pharaoh is able to proclaim openly his decree of death in the hope of being obeyed. As we begin the next chapter, the shadow of death hovers over the people of Israel.

2

The Discovery

*T*he discovery of Moses in the Nile and Moses' discovery of his people and their plight are the two focal points in this chapter. Both shed light upon the character of the leader of the liberation. The first discovery is the prerequisite to the second, and both are necessary stages on the road that leads Moses to the great commission assigned to him in the next chapter. At the same time, what happens here is shaped by Pharaoh's decree at the end of chapter 1.

DELIVERED FROM THE WATER—
THE DELIVERER FROM THE WATER

Water plays a crucial role in creation: it is the precondition for every living thing. On the other hand, it poses a threat with its ability to extinguish life. In the Bible, too, we see water's role in both destruction and salvation. When God creates the world, he separates water from water and builds a firm foundation in the midst of the waters. Later, the waters of the flood drown most of creation, a kind of reversal of creation by returning it to primordial chaos. Only in an ark that floats on the water is the future of the world preserved.

It is probably not by accident that the same Hebrew word for Noah's ark, *tevah,* is used for the little papyrus basket in the water of the Nile where Moses is laid (v. 3). This "ark" not only cradles a little child, but also the hopes of a people chosen by God to be the special instrument for the salvation of the world. The rescue of the small and particular encompasses the rescue of the many and universal.

There is, consequently, a constant parallel between Israel and the world.[1] For example, the number of Israelites mentioned in the introduction to the book of Exodus, seventy, is the same number as "the descendants of Noah's sons" in Gen. 10 who form the origin of all the nations of the world.[2] The same allusion to the universal number of seventy may be included even in this story. As has been observed,[3] this section (2:1–10) in the Hebrew text consists of 141 words. The word in the middle is the word "child" (2:6), referring to Moses, who is thus surrounded by seventy words. Even if this striking fact should be sheer accident, the message is clear. When Moses is threatened with being drowned in the waters of the Nile but is rescued through the "ark" in order to become the deliverer of Israel, it is an event that will have far-reaching consequences.[4]

First, however, Israel's liberation is at stake. The very name given to Moses expresses, as is so often the case in the Bible, what his mission in life will be (cf. Matt. 1:21; 16:18). The name "Moses" is a common element in Egyptian names.[5] It is derived from a word with the basic meaning of "being born" and appears frequently together with names of Egyptian gods, such as Rameses and Thutmoses, common names of pharaohs. Thutmoses means "the god Thut is born," and Rameses means "The sun-god Re^c has given birth to him," that is, he is the son of Re^c.

When the daughter of Pharaoh gives her adoptive son this Egyptian name, the text explains the name as deriving from a Hebrew verb *mashah,* meaning "to draw out of" (v. 10). Modern rules of comparative linguistics cannot, of course, be applied to the text in this case. In the Bible it is primarily the sound of a word and its associations that are the basis of such word derivations. The name Moses (Hebrew *Mosheh*) is undeniably reminiscent of the Hebrew verb *mashah.*

More important, however, is the fact that the princess unwittingly gives a name to the baby that expresses what will become of him. The Hebrew grammatical form *mosheh* is an active participle. Therefore, the literal meaning of Moses is "he who draws out of." The one who has been delivered out of the water will himself become the deliverer from the dangers of the water. Maybe this deeper meaning of the name Moses was in the mind of the prophet when he wrote, "Then he

remembered the days of old, of Moses his servant. Where is
the one who brought them up out of the sea?" (Isa. 63:11; cf.
2 Sam. 22:17 and Ps. 18:17).

THREE WOMEN

Again in this story, women play the leading role in the
preparations for the liberation. In fact, no fewer than twelve
women are mentioned in the first two chapters of the book
of Exodus: the two midwives, Moses' mother, "daughter of
Levi," and sister and Pharaoh's daughter, whom we are to
encounter next, and finally the seven daughters of Jethro
(see further below). Is there a correspondence intended between the twelve sons of Israel, listed in the beginning of
Exodus, and these twelve daughters, who had such an active
part in the rescue of Israel, represented by these sons?
Drastically expressed, can we say that "the twelve tribes owe
their deliverance to twelve daughters"?[6] The midwives tem-
porarily altered the destiny of the doomed sons. In this
chapter, one particular son, bearer of the future destiny of
the nation, is rescued by other women, whose actions are
decisive for all of history.

Like the authors of several ancient commentaries, we
may wonder how Moses' mother, Jochebed (6:20; Num. 26:59),
could possibly have abandoned her son the way she did. According to one Jewish tradition, the Egyptians knew that she
had given birth to a son, and she expected them to come at
any moment to take her son away. She had to choose between
his certain death and his uncertain destiny. At the last moment, she carefully placed him in the river and told the Egyptians he was already in the Nile.

Whatever the actual circumstances were, the text makes
one thing clear: the Egyptian people cooperated with Pharaoh
to implement his murderous decree. Evil requires human
hands to succeed, but God's will is also carried out by human
agency. The next woman who in this way embodies God's will
is Moses' sister, Miriam (15:20–21; Num. 26:59; Mic. 6:4). She
does not let her brother out of her sight. Through her imagination and boldness, Moses is returned to his own mother
(vv. 7–9). This is a vital connection, since it allows Moses to be
nurtured by his own family and gain a sense of identity with
his own people during the early years of his life. It is unclear

what age verse 10 envisions for the return of Moses to what would be his adoptive mother, but we may assume that it occurred around the age of three, the usual age of weaning. As we will soon witness, these first years with his mother and people left their indelible imprint on Moses—as did certainly the years with the next woman to be considered.

Let us not forget the third woman in these verses, again a Gentile woman, Pharaoh's own daughter. Assuming that Rameses II was the pharaoh of the Exodus, it is striking that among his six wives and 200 children, of whom 111 sons and 59 daughters are known to us,[7] this is the only child who, through determination and mercy, acted as an instrument to fulfill God's plan. She was perhaps not of the caliber of Puah and Shiphrah, who were both merciful and brave. They, unlike the princess, had much to fear from Pharaoh, for he held their lives in his hands. Notwithstanding this, the daughter of Pharaoh proved to be a noble person because of her compassion, thoughtfulness, and sense of justice. She defies her own father and even adopts the despised and doomed Hebrew child as her own. Additionally, a touching proof of her character is the little noticed fact that she offered wages to the wet nurse, Moses' mother (v. 9). She did not exploit her position of authority over the enslaved and despised people who were entirely at the mercy of the Egyptians.

In this way, a remarkable thing happened: Moses' mother was paid to bring up her own son. Even more remarkably, this boy, who would become the deliverer of Israel from Egypt, entered the royal court of Pharaoh precisely because of Pharaoh's own decree, according to which Moses had no right to live! Here Moses could have used the same words in relation to Pharaoh that Joseph spoke to his brothers, "Even though you intended to do harm to me, God intended it for good, in order to preserve a numerous people" (Gen. 50:20).

All three attempts of Pharaoh to repress the people of Israel failed. The oppression had the opposite effect and led to an even greater increase of the population (1:12). The first murderous effort had the same result (1:20), and the official genocidal decree led to the rescue of the one to liberate Israel and to his preparation for a great mission.[8]

As a result, Moses is now ready to fulfill the task that God has in store for him. The next discovery will bring Moses a step further along that path.

OUT TO HIS BROTHERS—THE FIRST EXODUS

Let us first see more precisely what is written in the beginning of verse 11. Each word is replete with meaning. Three statements in particular sum up what Moses was experiencing.

He Grew Up

What is here described took place years after Moses had left his mother. He had spent many years at the court of Pharaoh. Nothing is said in the text of Exodus about his age, but according to Jewish tradition, he was forty years old. In a deeper sense, he had certainly matured in knowledge, wisdom, and power. After the daughter of Pharaoh had adopted him as her son, he had received an education befitting a royal prince.

Even though the Bible is silent on this point, Jewish tradition speculated at length on what this education entailed. Luke states, "Moses was instructed in all the wisdom of the Egyptians, and he was mighty in his words and deeds" (Acts 7:22). Philo of Alexandria gives more details in his description of the world of the young Moses. His teachers were the most renowned of their times. Like a student in Philo's time, Moses studied literature, logic, rhetoric, and astronomy with Greek teachers. Assyrian teachers led him into the secrets of cuneiform writing, and Chaldeans taught him astrology. Other subjects mentioned by Philo are rhythm, harmony, and instrumental music, as well as various aspects of the Egyptian religion: mythology, symbolics, and the holy animals (see pp. 54f., 60f., 63f., 143, n. 28). According to Philo, Moses soon surpassed the insights of all his teachers!

Sources for Philo's account of Moses remain lost to us, but they were numerous and varied in their reliability. Many papyrus documents have been preserved throughout thousands of years in the dry climate of Egypt, among them teaching materials and school exercises. A textbook from Rameses's time presents "teaching transmitting skill and instruction to the ignorant, knowledge of everything extant, what Ptah has created and Thoth has written—the heaven with its stars, the earth and what it contains, what the mountains provide and what swarms in the sea, all things enlightened by the sun and everything that grows on the earth."[14] In it we find, among other information, the names of ninety-six cities, forty-two kinds of buildings with their different sections, forty-eight kinds of meat, and twenty-four different kinds of drinks! It is obvious that the discipline was strict. A pupil confesses: "I am lazy and careless and deserve a hundred blows." And a teacher complains: "My heart is sick of giving you further teaching. . . . I may give you an hundred blows, and yet you cast them all off."[15]

Among these documents one category of educational materials is particularly conspicuous, namely, texts that express a deep contempt of manual labor while stressing the value of study. Studies lead to a life far away from dust, dirt, and toil under harsh taskmasters. These texts emphasize the extremely low status of the working class in ancient Egyptian society: "Behold there is no profession which is not governed, it is only the learned man who rules himself. . . . The poor ignorant man, whose name is unknown, is like a heavily-laden donkey, he is driven by the scribe."[16] It is even stated that a subordinate, who "must work till the sun sets" and then cannot sleep for hunger, "is dead while he yet lives."[17]

The situation of foreign slaves was certainly even worse. One example is sufficient to make the point clear:

> The maker of pots is smeared with soil, like one whose relations have died. His hands, his feet are full of clay; he is like one who lives in the bog. . . . The carpenter who is in the shipyard carries the timber and stacks it. If he gives today the output of yesterday, woe to his limbs! The shipwright stands behind him to tell him evil things. His outworker who is in the fields, his is the toughest of all the jobs. He spends the day loaded with his tools, tied to his toolbox.[18]

This misery is contrasted to the luxurious life of the educated: "Set your sight to be a scribe; a fine profession that suits you. You call for one; a thousand answer you. You stride freely on the road. You will not be like a hired ox. You are in front of others."[19]

Moses' instructors probably implanted this contempt for the lower classes in Moses, who would not have become a mere official. His future insured that he would be one of the most prominent figures of the empire, with all the perquisites that position would entail: might, wealth, and glory. With this background the expression in verse 11 is much more powerful.

He Went Out

The letter to the Hebrews 11:24–25 states: "By faith Moses, when he was grown up, refused to be called a son of Pharaoh's daughter, choosing rather to share ill-treatment with the people of God than to enjoy the fleeting pleasures of sin." Since it is literally stated that Moses went out "to his brethren," we are also reminded of another statement in a different context from the letter to the Hebrews, "For this reason Jesus is not ashamed to call them brethren" (2:11).

No, Moses has definitely not forgotten whence he came, and he is not ashamed of his origins. Instead, he identifies totally with the suffering of his people. The years at Pharaoh's court have provided him with the necessary background to be able to liberate his afflicted people. First of all, he has contacts at the highest echelons of government. He has an impressive education and experiences that will be of great importance in accomplishing the difficult tasks that lie ahead. He has achieved a stature that brings him respect both among the Egyptians and his own people.

Another aspect, however, is at least as important. A verse from Proverbs may serve as an illustration: "Under three things the earth trembles; under four it cannot bear up: a slave when he becomes king" (Prov. 30:21–22). This statement indeed reflects a deep experience and a profound insight in human psychology. Contrary to what has often been stated, the initiative for a liberation movement should come from the top rather than from the bottom. It is usually best led by people who have been in power but have chosen to abandon their privileged position when they become aware of the system's injustices. History has witnessed more than enough "slaves who have become kings," under whom the earth has trembled when they have become intoxicated with power. Upstarts are prone to become cruel leaders. On the other hand, nobody is better suited for leadership than the one who has already tasted the sweetness of privilege and position but relinquished a high station to follow an inner calling to serve others. The lowly who ambitiously climb often step on others, while the highborn who humbly descend are frequently suited to lift others. Salvation first comes from above, then from below!

Christians see the most clear example of this in Christ himself, "who, though he was in the form of God, did not regard equality with God as something to be exploited, but emptied himself, taking the form of a slave, being born in human likeness" (Phil. 2:6–7). To a certain extent, the Hebrew slaves could have applied similar terms to the high official from Pharaoh's house who came to their assistance. In order to become a mediator between the Egyptians and his people, it was not enough to know only one side from within. Moses also had to become like one of the oppressed himself. Even in this respect the words from the letter to the Hebrews are relevant, "Therefore he had to become like his brethren in every respect" (2:17).

Only among his own people and later in the land of Midian (v. 15) could Moses really become familiar with the God who is the liberator of the captives and the helper of the afflicted, the God of the desert and of the valley of death. Therefore, Moses went out to the Israelite slaves, yet not merely to inspect them or the world outside his own refined life. What happened to him was a personal exodus that led him to a discovery from which there was no return.

He Saw

The Hebrew expression used here for "saw," *ra'ah,* plus the preposition *be,* indicates a deep emotional involvement on the part of the observer. The same expression appears in Gen. 21:16 and 44:34. We ought to translate it "look into," meaning that one sees and understands the inner meaning, the depth beyond the surface. In this case, the expression means that Moses did not distance himself from the Israelite slaves, but rather regarded them as his brethren and identified with them and their burdens.

Unable to remain passive when he witnessed the brutal beating of the Israelite slave, Moses killed the Egyptian taskmaster. Yet Moses is the same man who eventually would transmit the commandment, "You shall not murder," to Israel and the world! How is this moral dilemma to be explained? One thing is clear, this story cannot be used to justify bloodshed for noble aims, for example, liberating an oppressed people. The point of the story is to express Moses' deep devotion to his people and not to legitimize homicide in that situation.

Moses' killing of the taskmaster is not depicted as a heroic deed. The Jewish commentaries struggle intensely with the question regarding Moses' guilt and do not exonerate him out of hand. One midrash claims that this homicide is one reason why Moses was not allowed to enter the promised land.[20] Another tradition views his action in a more favorable light, stressing that the slave would have been beaten to death had Moses not intervened. In such a situation it is not only permitted but obligatory to kill the attacker in order to save a human life (see further 20:13, pp. 150f.).[21]

Verse 12 states that Moses killed the Egyptian only when "seeing no one." According to one interpretation, it is not to be understood that Moses was afraid or had a bad conscience. Instead, the text should be read in light of Isa. 59:15–16, where exactly the same Hebrew expression appears, "The Lord saw it, and it displeased him that there was no justice. He saw that there was no one, and was appalled that there was no one to intervene; so his own arm brought him victory." Moses was not indifferent; he intervened when he saw that no one cared for justice.[22] Moses realized the depth of the suffering of his people, not only from their outward oppression but also their inner distress. While this interpretation may not do justice to the context, it is nevertheless thought-provoking and instructive.

Strengthened by his compassion and zeal for justice, Moses could not remain in his comfortable world any longer. He returned to the slaves the following day (v. 13) and immediately became embroiled in a new conflict. This time the problem was a confrontation between two Hebrews. Here it becomes obvious that the previous action of Moses was not directed against the Egyptians as a people. He proved that he would not only take action against the enemies of his people, he would also intervene to bring peace and unity among his own.

In a third "exodus" to his people, Moses proved he was ready to intervene wherever injustice appeared and whoever its victims were. Fleeing for his life, he was now among total strangers in the land of Midian (v. 15). By a well he witnessed some women who were humiliated and wronged by the local shepherds. Again he stood up for the weak, and he saw to it that justice was done and even helped the women water their flocks. Moses, who himself had been rescued by women, became a champion on behalf of women. In the three expressions in verse 11, we discern the features of a future leader and liberator: an Egyptian aristocrat who has left his high position, identified with the oppressed, and is now ready to intervene and translate his convictions into action.

The last verses of this chapter tell us that many years pass, silent years that Moses spent with the bedouin in the wilderness. The name he gave to his son, Gershom (v. 22; the verse cites a folk etymology, Hebrew *ger* = "stranger"), indicates, however, that he did not forget the land of Egypt, and that he would not stay in the wilderness forever. The name also links him to the prophecy given to Abraham, according to which his seed would "be aliens *[ger]* in a land that is not theirs" but would eventually "come out with great possessions" (Gen. 15:13–14). A signal to return came with the news that Pharaoh had died (v. 23). Rameses probably died in 1224 after a long reign of sixty-six years. He survived thirteen sons and was succeeded by his son, Merneptah, who died ten years later after a number of misfortunes.

The decisive signal to return came from above. Strangely enough, at this point in the book of Exodus, God has only been mentioned once, in connection with "fear of God" by the midwives. He has been silent, but not passive. His hand has secretly and invisibly linked one event to the next. Now the time has come to make himself known to his servant Moses and to his people Israel, whose lament he hears and whose pain he feels. His covenant with their forefathers is irrevocable and the fulfillment of his promises has drawn near.

Here we have reached a remarkable turning point in the exodus drama. Now is the time for God to interfere. Like a resounding peal, the liberty bell is heard in the concluding words of the chapter: "God heard," "God remembered,"[23] "God looked upon,"[24] and "God took notice."[25]

3

The Master, the Mission, and the Means

Exodus 3:1–4:17

The character of Exodus changes significantly beginning with chapter 3. So far we have only seen the stage set and heard the overture to the great drama that we now follow in detail, act by act. The first two chapters paint the scenes with sweeping brush strokes. Chapter 1 covers more than four generations; chapter 2 covers over two-thirds of Moses' 120-year life span (cf. 7:7). The remaining thirty-eight chapters focus on events that take place within a single year, the decisive year of the liberation. It is only now that we begin to follow a series of events, where each little step is measured. But the pace constantly increases and the steps become ever bigger and more dramatic until the liberation (ch. 14) and its sequel (ch. 15).

The first two chapters have made one thing perfectly clear: without God's active interference, the enslaved people would be doomed. However, it is equally clear that God interferes by using human beings. Through these instruments God prepares and carries out the drama of liberation to its glorious end.

THE MASTER AND THE MISSION (3:1–17)

Up until the end of the last chapter, God has remained silently in the background. Now he appears on the scene as the principal character. The place he chooses is the silent wilderness, more precisely "Horeb, the mountain of God" (that is, Mount Sinai), where he will later reveal himself to all of Israel. Although originally the names come from different sources, the Bible in its final form makes no distinction between Horeb and Sinai. Horeb may focus more on the area, while Sinai describes the mountain itself (cf. 19:1ff.).[1]

Here God reveals himself in a burning bush. The sight of a bush in flames is in itself nothing very peculiar in a dry desert, but normally the bush would be instantly turned into ashes. What makes Moses linger and approach the place is the duration of the burning. The bush is hosting the fire, but the fire is nourished by something other than the wood of the bush. Moses is not kept in suspense very long as to what the fire signifies. The sight he watches is followed by something even more dramatic, words he can hear. His name is pronounced. When he realizes who is calling him, he has to take off his sandals out of reverence and cover his face, for nobody can see God and remain alive (33:18–23).

God's warning in 3:5, "Come no closer," given at his first appearance to Moses, will then be repeated in various ways and is finally sounded in the concluding chord of the book of Exodus, at the same time marking the prelude to the book of Leviticus (see 40:34–35). The same attitude of reverence that characterizes Moses is evident when Isaiah faces God in the temple (Isa. 6:5).

We certainly need this reminder of God's holiness. The closer we come to the Lord, the more we experience the huge distance between ourselves and God. We realize how small and impure we are. In several cultures, footwear symbolizes both power and impurity, precisely what we have to take off before God. In many places in the world, the worshipers respond to an outward reminder of God's holiness by removing their shoes. This applies not only to Islam. Christians in India, among others, regard it as disrespectful to enter a chapel with shoes on. In the temple of Jerusalem everyone had to be barefoot. At the reading of the Aaronite blessing (Num. 6:22–26; cf. p. 92, n. 23) in the synagogue, the priests *(kohanim)* still remove their shoes. In some Yemenite synagogues, the participants are barefoot during the whole service.

The Fire and the Bush

Both the fire and the bush in which God reveals himself to Moses express something about God's character. Fire burns and purifies. When God is compared to a "devouring fire," the statement serves as a strong warning not to break the commandments (Deut. 4:23–24; cf. Ps. 79:5). Fire is also God's robe, marking his presence. In fire Abraham encountered God (Gen. 15:17). Soon a pillar of fire will lead Israel during the night (13:21–22; 14:24), and God will descend in fire on the same mountain where Moses has his vision (19:18; 20:18; 24:17; see pp. 135ff.). Just like the bush, the whole mountain will burn with fire (Deut. 5:23). Fire is not only a decisive element in the first act of the exodus drama, but it also delivers a message of hope in the last scene of the book (40:38).

God's self-revelation in fire is a powerful expression of divine holiness. This aspect of God is visible throughout the Bible. God is the elevated and holy one, the sovereign monarch who cares for the whole world as well as every creature. God reveals his will and character to the world while remaining the unfathomable one whose essence nobody can comprehend. At the same time, God is the merciful and compassionate parent. In many prayers in the Jewish prayer book, these two aspects of God's character are kept together in an exemplary way; God is invoked both as "Our Father" (ʾavinu) and "Our King" (malkenu).[2] In a similar way, Christian prayer models these two aspects of God.

This chapter reveals both of these aspects of God. As soon as Moses has become aware of the holy one in the fire, he also encounters the merciful one possessing compassion and care. This love, empathy, and total identification with an afflicted people is expressed in God's choosing a bush as the place for his revelation: "God said to Moses: 'Do you not realize that I live in trouble just as Israel lives in trouble? Know from the place whence I speak unto you— from a thornbush—that I am, as it were, a partner in their trouble.' "[3]

The rabbis ask, Why did God not choose another place, for example, "from the peaks of the mountains, from the elevations of the world and from the cedars of Lebanon?" The answer is found in God's self-humiliation while speaking from a bush: "On him the words of Solomon can be applied, 'One who is lowly in spirit will obtain honor' (Prov. 29:23). . . . And it is written, 'For though the Lord is high, he regards the lowly' (Ps. 138:6)."[4] The revelation consequently implies that no place is too lowly for the presence of the Lord.

These thoughts have inspired an early Christian allegorical interpretation connecting the bush with Mary, Jesus'
mother. According to this interpretation, the bush where the
Lord was revealed refers to Mary and the words of her praise:
"My soul magnifies the Lord, and my spirit rejoices in God my
Savior, for he has looked with favor on the lowliness of his servant" (Luke 1:46ff.).[5]

These interpretations certainly do justice to the concluding verses in chapter 2 as well as to the verses immediately
following the story (3:7–10), where God again acknowledges
that he is very close to the people in their distress. Not indifferent, God does not sleep or slumber, even in times of divine
silence. All the time God watches, listens, feels, and suffers
when they suffer.[6] Finally God intervenes in keeping with the
promises to their fathers. Now this time has drawn near. The
very way in which God approaches Moses tells a great deal
about the divine nature and plan for the people of Israel.

The God of Your Fathers

"I am the God of your father, the God of Abraham, the
God of Isaac, and the God of Jacob." By this presentation God
begins to speak with Moses (3:6). Then the expression "the
God of your fathers" appears no fewer than three times in chapter 3 (vv. 13, 15, and 16). God tells Moses to introduce his address to the people with these words, and he is to refer to the
"God of the Hebrews" when he speaks to Pharaoh (3:18; 5:3).

Obviously this way of referring to God is supposed to
help Moses and the people to believe in the salvation that God
promises to give. They will be liberated from slavery in Egypt.
They will leave the house of bondage and be provided with
property (3:21–22; see further 11:2–3; 12:35–36 and pp. 94f.).
Eventually they will inherit "a good and broad land, a land
flowing with milk and honey" (3:8; cf. Num. 13:27), that is, a
land offering rich possibilities and suitable both for cattle
breeding (milk) and farming (honey).[7]

This was precisely what God had promised Abraham
and later repeated in various ways to Isaac and Jacob (Gen.
15:13–16; 50:24). This promise was not abandoned even
when it was contradicted by an ordeal that seemed to be hopeless, as was the case for Moses' own father, who faced Pharaoh's decree to throw every newborn male into the Nile
(1:22)! Then the people were threatened by extermination,

and it certainly could seem as though God had forgotten what he had promised. Maybe it is precisely then that God first addresses Moses as "the God of your father" (3:6). God's presence even in those dark days was the cause of Moses' survival. Therefore, Moses now had reason to believe that God would fulfill all his promises to previous generations as well, the promise made to Abraham, Isaac, and Jacob.

God as the God of our ancestors thus gives a guarantee on which we can rely. Since God did not abandon them, there is a firm basis for our hope. And what remained unfulfilled during their lives, and maybe even during ours, still remains as a firm promise for the future. God is faithful! The One who has been our help in ages past is our hope for days to come. This is the deep meaning behind the words, "I am the God of your father, the God of Abraham, the God of Isaac, and the God of Jacob."

In this way, the liberation of Israel from slavery in Egypt provides a foundation even for our faith. God's eternal faithfulness toward Israel from generation to generation gives us reason to hope for something similar. If he has not revoked his gifts and call to the Jewish people (Rom. 11:29), we boldly believe that this applies even to us, in spite of a long and largely gloomy church history, which in no way appears more glorious than the history of Israel.

A replacement theology that claims that God has withdrawn promises from the Jewish people in favor of new promises made to the church, and that God has replaced an allegedly old covenant with a new one implies nothing less than sawing off the branch on which we ourselves sit! Paul would say that we sever the very root of the tree into which we have been grafted (Rom. 11:18; see pp. 198ff.).

Your God

In many passages in the Bible and in later Jewish tradition, we find a phrase that combines two ways of speaking about God and to God, "Our God and the God of our fathers." In the Jewish prayer book, this is one of the most common phrases indicating how God is approached. With this phraseology a bridge is built between past generations and our own times and between the present and the future, which we have stressed as so important for our faith. Just as he has finished recounting his promise to the fathers, he asks Moses to become his messenger. When Moses is hesitant about his ability, God focuses on him alone, "I will be with you; and this will be the sign for you that it is I who sent you" (3:12).

You as an individual do not disappear among the multitudes! You are not reduced to just a link in a chain of generations following previous ones! The God of your fathers is your God! Which one of these aspects of God is the most important one is impossible to say. They must be kept together and must not be separated. Otherwise, God will be either a God of the past who does not affect us in our present life, or a God whom we create in our own image according to our own thoughts, desires, and needs.

In the name of God, which is now revealed at the request of Moses, the past and the present are linked in an eternal now. The name *'ehyeh 'asher 'ehyeh* (I AM WHO I AM or "I am the One who is") describes the God of the fathers, who gave the promises and set the goals for our history. God is the God of the present, who is with us every day fulfilling promises, and the God of the future, who will finally lead his people home to the promised land. It has already been introduced in verse 12, "I will be with you" (Hebrew *'ehyeh 'immakh*), and it will appear again in the assertion of God's faithfulness to his promises (4:12, 15).

Another way of expressing the meaning of God's name is the use of formulations such as "I am the first and I am the last; besides me there is no god" (Isa. 44:6) or " 'I am the Alpha and the Omega,' says the Lord God, 'who is and who was and who is to come, the Almighty' " (Rev. 1:8). This latter formulation is an effort at expressing in Greek a rabbinic way of speaking about God, which is actually possible only in Hebrew. God is the first, which is paralleled to the first letter of the Hebrew alphabet *('aleph)*. He is further the present one, which is paralleled with the middle letter *(mem)*. Finally, he is the last one, compared to the last letter *(tav)*. When these three letters are combined, we get the word *'emet,* which means "truth."[8] By keeping what he has promised, God proves to be the very personification of truth, the one whom we can therefore rely on totally.

YHWH—*The* LORD

Many scholarly works have been written on the interpretation of the name of God in 3:14 without reaching any consensus. The name I AM in Hebrew (²ehyeh), alludes to the name consisting of four letters, *YHWH,* which is usually translated as "the LORD" (v. 15). These consonants are written without vowels, and there is no tradition preserving their original pronunciation. According to the Jewish tradition, this name should not be pronounced (see p. 145). Instead, the name *²Adonay* (in the Septuagint *Kyrios*), which means "the Lord," is read.[9] We find, however, parts of the name of God in the praise "Halleluj*ah*" and in such names as Judas (Hebrew *Yehu*dah), Jonathan (Hebrew *Yeho*nathan), and Elijah (Hebrew Eli*yahu*).[10] However, how the whole divine name should be pronounced is unknown.

Most scholars agree that *YHWH* is a form of the verb "to be" *(hayah),* in the third person masculine singular, that is, "He who is," meaning "the eternal." In this case, there would then be a parallel between God's own proclamation of his name as "I AM" (v. 14) and the same name proclaimed by humans as "HE IS" (v. 15). Instead of being a form of the verb *hayah* in the indicative form Qal, it could also be derived from the verb in the form Hiphil, which is used to express causation (meaning one who causes something to happen). In that case, the meaning would then be "He who causes (things) to come into being." Thus the targum comments: "He who spoke and the world came into being, who spoke and the universe existed" (Ps. 33:9).[11]

In the Bible and in the ancient Near East, a name often expressed the character or mission of its bearer, as we see in the cases of Abram (Gen. 17:5), Jacob (Gen. 32:28), and Moses (see p. 17). The prohibition against pronouncing God's name is founded on the humble realization that a human being can only partly grasp God's essence and plans. However much we may have comprehended, still we have only discerned dim reflections of reality (cf. Isa. 55:8–9 and 1 Cor. 13:12). The unmentionable is the unfathomable. Lack of realization of this inescapable fact leads to idolatry. The prohibitions against pronouncing God's name and making an image of God therefore have the same basis (see 20:4, pp. 143f.).

Nevertheless, God's name is now revealed to Moses, thereby obviously revealing something essential about the divine nature. To understand the meaning of God's name, the obscure grammatical form is not decisive. The linking of the name with the God of the fathers, on one hand (3:15), and with the promise of help, "I will be with you" (3:12),[12] on the other, provides the best framework for the meaning of the name. The name sums up the unbroken line between what God has done and promised in the past and the prospective liberation. God is what God does (cf. Matt. 11:2–5).

"I AM" is not a philosophical concept, but rather a historical one. It does not deal primarily with the essence of the supreme being. It testifies of one who is active in history, constantly intervening to realize a plan with the world in general and with a particular instrument, the people of Israel (see further p. 49.)

When the Lord and Moses meet at God's mountain, Israel and the world have arrived at a decisive crossroad. The choice of direction that Moses faces entails a mission that has few parallels in world history. Thus, for this weighty mission God provides the means.

THE MISSION AND THE MEANS (3:9–4:17)

The first two chapters show how when God fulfills his promises, he does so through human beings who, willingly or unwillingly, consciously or unconsciously, prove to be divine agents. Evil plans finally come to naught but nevertheless serve God's purpose. Above all, God needs servants who wholeheartedly adhere to the divine calling and faithfully take upon themselves the tasks with which they are entrusted.

Such a heavenly and overwhelming calling is now given to Moses: to go to Pharaoh and negotiate with him and finally liberate the people (3:10). No wonder that Moses despairs and exclaims (3:11): "Who am I that I should go to Pharaoh, and bring the Israelites out of Egypt?" He who speaks in this way is the one who was rightly characterized as "very humble, more so than anyone else on the face of the earth" (Num. 12:3).

Meek and Merciful

The humility of Moses is, of course, a precondition for his being able to fulfill his mission and is one explanation of why God would entrust him with this great task. Another quality that Moses demonstrates is his compassion. According to 3:1 he is keeping the flock of his father-in-law Jethro when he encounters God and receives his calling.

One rabbinic tradition makes a connection between these two events. Just as God took David from the flock "to be the shepherd of his people Jacob" (Ps. 78:70–71; cf. Amos 7:15), God now tests Moses by watching how he tends the sheep. The midrash tells how once when a sheep went astray Moses went after it until he found it, laid it on his shoulders, and carried it back to the flock. "Thereupon God said: 'Because you have mercy in leading the flock of a mortal, you will for sure tend my flock Israel.' "[13]

"I Will Be with You"

In his own eyes, Moses lacks the qualifications required for such a great commission. Therefore, God has to help him focus in a different direction. Moving away from Moses' question ("Who am I?"), God reminds him of a question far more important, "Who am I, your God?" The liberation does not depend on you, but ʾehyeh ʿimmakh ("I will be with you"; 3:12). Again, the name of God, promising his faithfulness, appears in this statement.

God also offers Moses a "sign" as a confirmation of this promise: "When you have brought the people out of Egypt, you shall worship God on this mountain." Moses will return to this place, but the next time he will be accompanied by his people. Then the yoke of slavery will be changed to the yoke of heaven and the slavery of Pharaoh to the service of the king of kings (cf. p. 127)! When this mission is over, it will be clearer what is the content of the enigmatic name of the great Lord (Deut. 4:32ff.).

Usually signs are given as an instant confirmation of what they are supposed to signify—in this case a sign that God is indeed with Moses. We would certainly expect the sign to precede the fulfillment and equip Moses with the needed assurance to be instrumental in this. The burning bush is a powerful sign to Moses, as are the signs in 4:1–9. However, the final confirmation of God's authority and faithfulness in keeping with promises comes only after completion of the mission, when again God's fire will descend at this mountain. Then Moses will see that what is promised has now indeed come true. Then he will realize that these promises were not empty.

Until then he will have to learn to trust the Lord, go where he is sent, carried by his promises and by his presence: "I will be with you." One day Moses will see how true this is—here at the same place![14]

Exodus 3:11–12 contain a summary of both the mission given to Moses and the means to fulfill it. It is no surprise that Moses is still perplexed by how all this will be carried through. He returns four times to God, asking him to be more specific or even release him from the seemingly impossible mission (3:13; 4:1, 10, 13). Each time, he receives an answer that is a variation of this basic theme, "I will be with you," followed by yet another promise that he will be equipped with all the means needed to fulfill the mission.

First, Moses wants to know what he should say when the children of Israel ask him about God's name. The next time, Moses expresses doubt that the people will listen to him and believe that God has indeed revealed himself to him (4:1). His anxiety is certainly not unfounded. Many have falsely claimed to speak by God's command. It is therefore not only legitimate, but mandatory to scrutinize those who speak in the name of God.

Signs and Wonders

God takes Moses' objections seriously and equips him with the ability to perform miracles. Moses is able to transform his rod into a snake. His hand can become leprous and immediately be healed. Finally, he can turn the water of the Nile into blood.

These three signs have one thing in common that makes them different from the signs that the Egyptian priests could perform. "Magic" was a main element in the Egyptian religion at this time, and those who mastered these powers were held in high esteem. The priests, belonging to the highest officials of Pharaoh, possessed secret knowledge and were skilled in all sorts of mysterious rites. By casting spells, they could allegedly overpower humans and control gods and thereby attain dominion over the world of nature and the world of the gods, realms which could not be separated since some animals were regarded as divine. Through magical formulas, the magicians claimed to exercise the power of the gods. The master of magic therefore became a player in the world of the gods.[15]

Against this background, Moses appears in total contrast to the Egyptian magicians. According to the text, Moses does not perform the miracles, but it is God who works through Moses. Neither particular skills nor mysterious formulas or properties are required, and when the wonders take place nobody is more surprised than Moses himself!

This is precisely the kind of intervention that Moses needs; everything points to the power of God, while Moses senses his own impotence. What Moses needs to demonstrate to his people in order to be believed is not his own excellence. He realizes that the people of Israel will not believe in him at all and fears that they will say, "*The* LORD did not appear to you" (4:1). The purpose of these signs and wonders is consequently to make the people realize that it is the Lord and nobody else who has sent him.

But even to the Egyptians these signs will give a clear message. As we know, both Pharaoh and the Nile were regarded as divine.[16] The cobra represented in particular the national god of Lower Egypt and was the foremost symbol of Pharaoh, reflecting his claim to divine royalty, sovereignty, and power.[17] Therefore, it constantly appears on his crown or helmet, as depicted in reliefs, paintings, and statues. His scepter is often a stylized cobra. Even the Egyptian gods are frequently depicted with a scepter in the form of a snake. We are safe in concluding that the transformation of the rod to a snake is a sign aimed precisely at the very symbol of Pharaoh's alleged power. It demonstrates so clearly who is the true King and God (7:8ff.). The sign of the Nile turning to blood, where the rod is again used, also emphasizes God's power over humans and the earth (7:14ff.; see further pp. 59ff.).

It is not equally clear whether there is a similar symbolism behind the wonder of the leprous hand. The number of different interpretations indicates the problem of understanding why such a sign is chosen. One example may be sufficient; the hand symbolizes the people of Israel, who previously were free. Soon they were plagued by slavery, symbolized by leprosy. Now the time of healing has drawn near—the liberation![18]

God's Words in Moses' Mouth

By now Moses has indeed been assured that his anxiety is unfounded and that he should have no further reservations.

The servants of God, however, are rarely heroes. Once again Moses questions the wisdom of God in selecting him as his spokesperson. In order to carry out the mission, one would certainly have to be able to speak eloquently and convincingly, especially since he must address no less a personage than Pharaoh himself. "I am slow of speech and slow of tongue," Moses complains and stresses that this impediment had not been cured by God's revelation to him (4:10).

Moses says literally that he has a "heavy mouth and a heavy tongue," which probably expresses some kind of verbal deficiency (cf. p. 56). The rabbis speculate as to whether his poor speaking ability was due to a general inability of formulating speech, or was due to his absence from Egypt for at least forty years. Unlike Aaron, Moses could not adequately express himself in the Egyptian language. It is also not clear whether he asks for a particular skill or simply tries to escape a superhuman task. Probably the latter is the case.

God's answer in 4:12 follows the same course as the previous. He varies the phrase, "I will be with you" (3:12) by adding some specificity, "I will be with your mouth" (ʾehyeh ʿim pikha). He reminds Moses, have you already forgotten what I told you when I revealed my name to you? Have you not already experienced how I dictated my message to you (see 3:16–17)? I do not need excellent speakers but rather people who listen to my voice. You shall not speak your own words but only mine, and I will put them in your mouth when you need them!

We recognize this situation in other passages in the Bible. When Jeremiah received his calling, he exclaimed: "Ah, Lord GOD! Truly I do not know how to speak, for I am only a boy." The answer once given to Moses was repeated to Jeremiah, "Do not be afraid of them, for I am with you to deliver you, says the LORD. . . . Now I have put my words in your mouth" (Jer. 1:4–9; cf. Judg. 6:14–16; Isa. 6:5ff.; Ezek. 2:4–3:11). When Jesus sent out the disciples, he told them, "Do not worry about how you are to speak or what you are to say; for what you are to say will be given to you at that time; for it is not you who speak, but the Spirit of your Father speaking through you" (Matt. 10:19–20). Moses' fear proves that he had the humility that enables God to speak through him.

"O LORD, you have enticed me, and I was enticed; you have overpowered me, and you have prevailed" (Jer. 20:7).

These words bear witness to struggle and resistance. Such a struggle now takes place between God and Moses. In his fifth objection, Moses openly reveals his inner doubts and shouts desperately, "O, my Lord, please send someone else" (4:13). It does not help that God has promised him all the means requested for his mission. He wants to withdraw from his calling, and it almost seems as though the result hangs in the balance as to who will finally be victorious in this struggle between his obstinate messenger and the Master.

Moses' Words in Aaron's Mouth

As in the previous encounters, God offers Moses more help. Not only does Moses have God at his side, he will also get human support—his own brother Aaron (4:14). Aaron is depicted as quite the opposite of Moses. It is as if God is saying to Moses, "Aaron, unlike you, can really speak, and Aaron, again unlike you, is ready and willing to accept his task."

Two brothers will accordingly support and complement each other in a difficult task. To be sent out two by two is certainly not a bad start of a hard mission. The decisive factor, however, is that God repeats a promise using the key words from 3:12, 14 and 4:12: "I will be with your mouth and with his mouth" (ʾehyeh ʿim pikha we-ʿim pihu; 4:15). Just as God puts his words in Moses' mouth, Moses will be to Aaron "as God," putting his words in his brother's mouth (v. 16; cf. 7:1–2).

It is possible that this distribution of responsibility alludes to the situation at Pharaoh's court, where one of the highest officials had the title ra, which means "mouth." He acted as a liaison between Pharaoh and the other officials. Some texts indicate that he was second to Pharaoh, as when the title is given to the pretender to the throne.[19] Since Pharaoh is regarded as being like god, the odd way of viewing Moses as God and Aaron as a mouth may be explained as a parallel to the relationship of Pharaoh and his deputy.

The call of Moses in these chapters is unique in the entire Bible. It is by far the largest and most detailed one of its kind. It is also unique in its description of the intimate communication between God and Moses. Already at this early stage it becomes obvious that Moses is exceptional among all the prophets (cf. Num. 12:6–8; Deut. 18:18 and 34:10). At the same time this story is universal. It demonstrates human weaknesses and inability to trust in the Lord. It also focuses on the truth behind the encouraging words of what a merciful and gracious God we have, "For he knows how we were made; he remembers that we are dust" (Ps. 103:14).

God does not dismiss Moses, but rather patiently listens to him until he has poured out his heart. He allows Moses to express fully his doubts and misgivings and accepts him as he is. Again and again he repeats his promises and gives Moses confirmation of their veracity. Even in moments of anger over Moses' stubbornness, he continues helping him to believe. He treats Moses as a partner, not as an automaton. We will see even later—in Exod. 32—that this intimate relationship with God creates for Moses a place above all other prophets.

4

The Return

Exodus 4:18–6:30

*T*he expression "to return" (Hebrew *shuv*), is crucial in this section. In the first five verses alone it appears five times. First, Moses returns to Jethro in order to ask permission to return to his people (4:18). At the same time, God commands him to return to Egypt (4:19). What happens to him there, both among his own people and among their oppressors, returns him to the Lord again (5:22), who in turn returns to his promises to Israel and to his calling to Moses (ch. 6). In this portion, we find constant flashbacks to the oppression, despair, and budding hope hitherto described and a foretaste of what is prepared for the next stage. It seems to be a huge deployment before the intense battle launched in the following chapter.

THE RETURN TO THE ISRAELITES (4:18–31)

In the few concentrated verses concluding chapter 4, Moses returns after the long absence that began in 2:15. After the many years in exile, his situation is now totally different from the one he left. A new generation has grown up. Moses is no longer the wanted criminal, but neither is he the grandson of Pharaoh. In the meantime, he has acquired a family—his wife Zipporah and his sons Gershom and Eliezer (see 18:2–4). Together with them he returns in obedience to the calling he had received to bring the message of the Lord to Pharaoh. Now it will become clear whether the fears he expressed to God or the help he has been promised will become reality.

The return begins in a strange and terrifying way (4:24–26). The account of the perilous revelation of God can certainly be counted among the most enigmatic in the entire Bible, as indicated by the numerous interpretations it has elicited.

The original meaning of the story is problematic in itself. Contextually, the key to understanding it appears in the preceding verses. There Pharaoh is threatened with the death of his firstborn son unless he releases Israel, God's firstborn. The threat refers, of course, to the tenth plague, from which the firstborn of Israel are saved (ch. 12; pp. 93ff.). We have already followed Moses through his first exodus out of Egypt. He has also experienced his first revelation of God at Sinai. In a similar way, this story gives a foretaste of the subsequent visitation of "the destroyer" to the houses of the Egyptians, while the blood on the doorposts of Israelite homes protects them (12:23).

Here, however, it is the blood of the circumcision that protects. In an analogous way, the Israelites will later smear the doorposts with the blood from the lambs as a protecting sign. Zipporah now puts a sign on her son with the blood shed at the circumcision. She touches his feet with the foreskin (4:25).[1] This probably means that she makes a sign on him so that the blood is clearly visible. Through this act, the protecting sign of blood is anticipated, the sign saving the firstborn of Israel during the last plague. Through the circumcision, the firstborn son—probably Gershom   is grafted into Israel, thus becoming one with the people, God's own firstborn son (4:22). The circumcision signifies the act of adoption by the Lord.

The protective power of the circumcision is stressed in another story strikingly similar in its message. Not surprisingly, the book of Joshua demonstrates many parallels to the exodus story, the blueprint of salvation, and Joshua's career parallels Moses' (cf. Josh. 1:1–5; 3:7–17; 4:14–24; 24).[2] In Josh. 5:2–12 the people of Israel, born in the desert, are circumcised before the celebration of the first Passover in the promised land. Immediately after this event, Joshua encounters a man with a drawn sword (Josh. 5:13–15). This encounter ends well, probably because Joshua has fulfilled the obligation of circumcising the people. Similarly, the threat in Exod. 4:24–26 is averted only after the circumcision is performed.[3]

Zipporah's designation of her son as a "bridegroom of blood" in 4:25–26 is also problematic.[4] There may be an indication that this strange expression was no longer used when the text was finally edited, since it requires explanation. Verse 26 should literally be translated: "Then she said 'bridegroom of blood' about the uncircumcised," that is, she said so at that time, which may indicate that this expression is odd and was later no longer used for the uncircumcised.[5]

It is possible that the Gentile woman Zipporah by using the expression "bridegroom of blood" implies that she, by circumcising her son, has entered the covenant herself and become a daughter of Israel. Another option is to read the text as if Zipporah were addressing the Lord himself as the "bridegroom of blood." By adopting her son, the Lord in a deeper sense also becomes her own bridegroom.[6]

Here we encounter another courageous woman who plays a decisive role in the exodus drama. Through her resolute action, she not only saves the life of the firstborn but of her people as well, since this event anticipates the rescue of the entire nation in another fateful night soon to come. In this way, the event demonstrates, again, how the saving of the one entails the saving of the many (cf. pp. 16f., 76).

The Blood of the Covenant

Although it is difficult to resolve all the problems contained in this text, its main message is sufficiently clear. The text wants to stress the necessity of circumcision and the saving significance of blood. The circumcision signifies kinship with the covenant people who are to be saved when the firstborn of Egypt are slain. Circumcision is required for partaking of the paschal lamb (12:48). There is even a Jewish folkloric tradition according to which all males were circumcised before the exodus, allowing the blood from the circumcision to be mixed with the blood from the lambs.[7] In this story, the firstborn is protected in a similar way by the blood of the circumcision. One tradition also regards this blood as atonement for the sin of Moses when he did not circumcise his son earlier.[8]

After this event Moses' entire family becomes an integral part of the people of Israel, and through this event the approaching liberation is foreshadowed. Just as the Lord promised, Moses and Aaron meet in joy and together return to their people in obedience to God's command (4:27ff.). In accordance with God's promise (3:18; 4:8–9), their glad tidings are received with joy and confidence.

In the last scene of the chapter we see the entire people bowed to the ground, not pressed by heavy burdens, but filled with faith and thankfulness, worshiping the Lord (4:31). After a long sequence of fateful events ahead, this beautiful vision will be repeated (14:31).

The first goal has been attained. In his dialogue with God, Moses had been at least as anxious about how his own people might receive him as he was about his meeting with Pharaoh. Even later we will be able to follow this war on two fronts, the first phase of which Moses has successfully won. When the curtain is lifted again (ch. 5), we are in the palace of Pharaoh—the next battlefield!

THE RETURN TO THE EGYPTIANS (5:1–21)

We can only imagine what this return must have been like for Moses. Here he had played as a little child. Here all his memories of childhood were hidden. This time, however, there was no pause for nostalgia, and Moses and Aaron launch an immediate attack: "Thus says the LORD, the God of Israel, 'Let my people go, so that they may celebrate a festival to me in the wilderness.'"

Pharaoh's answer comes without further delay: "Who is the LORD, that I should heed him and let Israel go? I do not know the LORD, and I will not let Israel go" (5:2). This answer is an outright declaration of war, not against Moses and Aaron who were just messengers, but against the people of Israel and above all against the Lord, in whose name they had spoken. Pharaoh thought himself to be a manifestation of the divine in his own right and certainly contended that he was able to take up the fight against other gods, particularly the god of a despicable people of slaves.

Compromise or Test?

In accordance with the instructions in 3:18 and 4:23, Moses and Aaron only request permission for a minor journey into the wilderness to sacrifice to the Lord (5:1, 3). The rabbinic commentaries discuss whether it was right to present such a compromising demand when, in fact, the purpose was to leave the country for good. Why did they not use plain language to express what they wanted?

Answers vary. Some try to avoid the problem by caviling at words: Moses does not actually claim that they intend to return. However, since he only mentions the celebration of a feast, Pharaoh could hardly have understood otherwise than that they had asked for a merely temporary liberation. Moses does not lie, but neither does he tell the truth. On the other hand, it is not difficult to defend Moses, since negotiations with unscrupulous oppressors can hardly follow common ethical rules.

The interpretation most appealing to me is on another plane. When God instructs Moses about what to say, he intends to put Pharaoh up for a test. It is a biblical theme that God tests the righteous through heavy burdens (Abraham, Job, Daniel, etc.) which reveal their faithfulness and strength and make God's name great and glorified. The evil ones, on the other hand, are tested by something easy, which, notwithstanding, leads them to fall. That way their evil thoughts and deeds are even more apparent. Pharaoh is tested through a modest request from a tormented people for a few days of rest and celebration. When he refuses, he displays his true face and acknowledges beforehand what is to follow. Hereafter there are no more references to the three-day journey into the wilderness.

This interpretation leaves a hypothetical question open: What might have happened should Pharaoh indeed have granted them brief vacations? It is certainly possible to imagine that they would have returned and continued the negotiations for a later liberation. It is even possible to speculate about a peaceful settlement between the Hebrews and the Egyptians. But history would then have taken a different course.

The Grip Tightens

Pharaoh's answer to Moses and Aaron expresses his contempt of the Lord by increasing the oppression further. He thus accuses Moses and Aaron of taking the people away from their work (5:4) and gives instructions to increase their work load. Not only must they deliver the same amount of bricks as before but even gather the straw required to strengthen bricks—a method of brick production still used in the Middle East.

The barbarous slavery here described can be richly illustrated by the numerous descriptions in words and pictures surviving from this period of Egyptian art. From these documents, strongly confirming the accuracy of the biblical record, we get a clear impression of institutionalized slavery linked to a developed bureaucracy with officials and a reporting system documenting every working team and even every single brick.

In a letter from the thirteenth century B.C.E., a supervisor complains of the miserable working conditions in an area infested with poisonous insects and wild beasts:

> I am staying at Kenkenento, unequipped, and there are neither men to make bricks nor straw in the neighborhood. . . . There is the gnat at sunset and the midge at noon; the sand-fly stings and sucks at every vein. . . . The heat which is here does not subside.[9]

A very telling document is a leather scroll, dated to the fifth year of Rameses II, displayed in the Louvre in Paris. It contains a register in which the superior of a particular area has listed his supervisors and the number of bricks each one had to deliver. Beside the requested amount the actual delivery is registered, for example, "Yupa, Urhiya's son: 2,000 bricks requested; delivered 660, 410, 560; total 1,630; missing 370."[10]

A certain report sheds light upon Pharaoh's accusation that the request of the Hebrews to go and sacrifice to their God is due to laziness and only a pretext to escape work (5:8, 17). On a limestone tablet, dated to the fortieth year of Rameses, a supervisor has written the names of his forty-three slaves together with the days they have been absent in a month. At each one he has noted the reason for their absence with red ink, for example, "sick," "bitten by a scorpion," but also "has sacrificed to the god," or simply "lazy."[11] When Pharaoh linked the two latter reasons, he probably expressed a common accusation against the slaves. The fact that the Hebrews wanted to worship a god whom Pharaoh did not recognize certainly makes their request singularly detestable.

The Egyptian hierarchy of superiors and underlings is well documented. It is typical under such oppressive systems that those who rank just above the slaves are recruited from among the slaves themselves. The "kapos" of the Nazi concentration camps have their early predecessors in "the supervisors of the Israelites, whom Pharaoh's taskmasters had set over them" (5:14). The temporary ease of their own agony that their dubious "promotion" meant led to a double contempt from both their superiors and from those whom they were forced to oppress. When they finally complain to Pharaoh, they encounter only disdain and continued hardship (5:17ff.).

Two phrases sum up the irreconcilable starting points of the negotiations and bloody battle ahead: "Thus says the LORD, the God of Israel" (v. 1), and "Thus says Pharaoh" (v. 10). The expression "Thus says" in biblical language usually introduces the prophetic declaration of God's will. Even in ancient Near Eastern texts the formula is used to proclaim the word of the ultimate divine authority. Through his deeds Pharaoh has already demonstrated his ambition of usurping God's dominion (see pp. 76ff.). Now he is referred to in the same terms as God himself. The critical issue to be settled is nothing less than who is in charge, who has the authority over the people of Israel and ultimately over all nations and all of creation: the God of Israel or the gods of Egypt, manifest in Pharaoh.

We have now reached a dark chapter in the humiliation of the Israelites, even labeled "the lowest point in the story of redemption."[12] The most degrading aspect is probably the despair that characterizes the bitter reaction of the people when they turn their anger against Moses and Aaron. They obviously prefer a hopeless *status quo* with continued oppression to belief in and a struggle for their liberation (5:20–21). The situation looks yet more gloomy when even Moses is filled with wrath and returns to God, who is ultimately behind their profound distress.

THE RETURN TO THE LORD (5:22–23)

Moses now in turn accuses God himself: "O LORD, why have you mistreated this people?" It is true that he repeats the same words in the following verse, with Pharaoh as the subject. The Lord has not yet saved the people from Pharaoh. Therefore, he is responsible for the agony of the people. Sins of omission cannot be excused by comparing sins of trans-

gression! The old excuse, "I have done nothing!" rings as hollow as "I only obeyed orders!"

Nevertheless, how can Moses possibly step into the presence of the King of kings and the Lord of lords in such a way?
Has he not himself tried to escape from his calling? What can
a little human creature put forward before the creator and
ruler of the entire universe? Moreover, had the Lord not predicted that precisely this would happen (3:19; 4:21)? What
else could Moses have expected?

His bitter protest raises many questions. The most critical ancient commentaries regard Moses' reaction as expressing lack of faith and as explaining why he was not allowed to
enter the promised land.[13] Others want to see extenuating circumstances in that Moses certainly was prepared for Pharaoh's refusal of their petition but not that he would tighten
the grip in such a dreadful way.[14]

I like best those efforts to defend Moses that stress his
love for his people as the key to understanding his protest.[15]
To put it bluntly: he just did his job! He just followed his calling! Just as he did when he once "went out to his people"
(2:11; see p. 22), even this time he totally identified with
the suffering Hebrews. He pled their cause, just as he was
called to do.

Three focal points converge in this plea: God, Pharaoh,
and the people. Moses had earlier carried out his task before
Pharaoh and then had spoken in the name of the Lord. Now
he actually does the same thing before God but speaking in
the name of the people. We will hereafter follow Moses in his
hard task as a mediator, wherein his most difficult test will
be to plead the cause of his people before the Lord himself
(chs. 32–33).

THE LORD RETURNS TO MOSES (6:1–30)

Even now we see that God patiently listens to his servant
and takes his protest seriously. This time there is no hint of
anger or even of rebuke in his answer. One has the impression, instead, that God approves of and appreciates the deep
engagement and love that Moses' protest expresses. Therefore
he not only accepts him but also once again compassionately
repeats what he has already promised. He makes it clear to

Moses that the fulfillment of these promises is not far away:
"Now you shall see what I will do to Pharaoh" (6:1).

No Shortcut to Freedom

This headline summarizes well God's words to Moses
here and throughout the book of Exodus. It is a message
that is difficult to digest but full of promise. At one point the
Lord is patently clear: The promises are irrevocable. The
timetable for their realization, however, entails several long
delays. The patriarchs had experienced this fact. They received the promise of the land and yet had to live there as
strangers and even abandon it for hundreds of years. Abraham even had to buy the tiny plot of land needed to bury his
wife Sarah (Gen. 23).

This is the bitter reality behind the surprising statement
in verse 3 that Abraham, Isaac, and Jacob did not know the
name "the LORD" *(YHWH)*. We know that this name is actually very common in the stories of the patriarchs. Most modern Bible scholars explain this contradiction as emanating
from different sources, which later merged. However we consider the history of the Pentateuch, it is improbable that the
final "editor(s)" could have been unaware of such an apparent
contradiction between the sources. We are rather to assume
that the text was earlier read in a way differing from the one
most natural to us. So how could the difficulty possibly be
resolved?

Jewish commentators stressed that a literal reading of the
text elucidated by the verses immediately following indicates
that it does not actually state that the patriarchs did not know
the name of the Lord, or that he had not revealed his name to
them. God rather says: "By my name *YHWH* I was not known
to them."[16]

What is the difference? In chapter 3 we dealt with the
rich cluster of meanings linked to the name of the Lord. It was
the content of the name that was unknown to the patriarchs.
How could it be otherwise? They had not seen the promises
fulfilled. It is when the Lord carries out what he has promised
that the meaning of his name becomes clear. We saw this in
chapter 3, where the immediate fulfillment of the promises
was proclaimed after the Lord revealed his name to Moses
(see pp. 31ff.).

Similarly, verse 3 is followed by a reference to the covenant and its promise of the land, which the patriarch had not seen fulfilled, but which Moses and the people of Israel are now indeed gradually to see materialize. God is known through actions. When Ezekiel is alluding to this text in Ezek. 20:5–6, it is precisely this aspect of his name that he focuses on: "Thus says the Lord GOD: On the day when I chose Israel, I swore to the offspring of the house of Jacob—making myself known to them in the land of Egypt—I swore to them, saying, I am the LORD your God. On that day I swore to them that I would bring them out of the land of Egypt into a land that I had searched out for them."[17]

What the patriarchs, on the other hand, experienced of God's essence had more to do with the content of the name "God Almighty"—ʾEl Shadday. In the patriarchal narratives, this name is above all linked to God's blessing them through making them fruitful and multiplying their descendants (Gen. 17:1–2; 28:3–4; 35:11; 43:14; 48:3–4; 49:25–26). They received a blessing for themselves and their families, while the national aspects of the remaining promises referred to a future fulfillment (see pp. 5f.). For this reason, that aspect of God's character contained in the name "the LORD" remained unknown to the patriarchs. What this fulfillment will entail is now further revealed and confirmed to Moses. Even though this explanation may not measure up to modern scholarly standards, it is certainly a worthy effort of wrestling with the biblical story as transmitted to us, based on a firm belief that contraditions in the text are to be resolved from within.[18]

Five Stages

The fulfillment takes place in stages. It is not a matter of one liberation only, followed by one immediate homecoming once and for all. Because of constantly fulfilled promises, Israel will be a people of constant liberations, a people bound for freedom, yet enjoying that freedom only gradually and partially. Not least, the four wearisome decades in the wilderness will become a prolonged practical exercise of the lesson now taught to Moses. There is no shortcut to the promised land. In 6:6–8 God indicates five stages that the people will have to pass on that road.

(1) "I am the LORD, and I will free you [Hebrew *hotsiʾ*] from under the burdens of the Egyptians." Slavery will soon fade into memory. In this first act of liberation, Moses will become the instrument according to the calling he has received: "I will send you to Pharaoh to bring [Hebrew *hotsiʾ*] my people, the Israelites, out of Egypt" (3:10). No human force, however, can fulfill the promises. Therefore the Lord is always the ultimate subject.

(2) "I will deliver you [Hebrew *hitsil*] from their bondage." Rabbinic tradition regards every expression in the Bible as having a deeper meaning. There are consequently no real parallelisms, that is, two expressions alongside one another repeating the same idea in different words. This statement appears to be very similar to the previous one. Notwithstanding, the rabbis want to see an intensification in God's actions toward his people. It might here, for instance, be a matter of the liberation from the "spiritual Egypt," which only the Lord can accomplish, while the previous one focuses more on the physical liberation. In support of such an interpretation the verb "to bring out" in 3:10 has Moses as the subject, while the verb "to deliver" in verse 8 appears with the Lord as subject.

(3) "I will redeem you [Hebrew *gaʾal*] with an outstretched arm and with great acts of judgment." According to one Jewish tradition, this statement refers to the miracle at the sea, which climaxes the liberation of both the Israelites and the Egyptians (see 14:16 and Isa. 63:12).

(4) "I will take you for my people [Hebrew *lakah li leʿam*], and I will be your God [Hebrew *hayah lakhem leʾohim*]." The liberation does not merely imply divestment of something. It is not an aim in itself, but does have a clear purpose. The service to the King of kings will replace the slavery under Pharaoh. The people will change owners. Their true lord is the one who says: "Israel is my firstborn son. . . . Let my son go that he may worship me" (4:22–23).[19] Only when this takes place has the liberation achieved its highest goal.

One commentator stresses a development in the four statements above, from mere justice (liberation of slaves) to compassion and finally to love.[20] The fourth stage clearly points forward to the revelation at Sinai (cf. 19:4–6), God's great declaration of love to a people, or to use another image, God's ultimate adoption of the people called to be firstborn (see p. 41).

The fourth promise is followed by an important corollary: "You shall know that I am the LORD your God, who has freed you from the burdens of the Egyptians." This connection between what God does and what the people perceive points to two significant aspects of the liberation: one objective, the other subjective. One is what God has done. If the saved people do not perceive what God has done, then they will never reach a living relationship with God, which is the purpose of the liberation and the goal of the way toward Sinai. They will miss the greatest blessing. Only there will they become personally aware of what God has done for them, and only there will the divine liberation set conditions for their continued walk.[21]

It is significant, then, that the revelation at Sinai is placed exactly in the middle of the book of Exodus, thus serving as its climax (see pp. 126ff.). Moreover, Sinai is also located between the way out of Egypt and the homecoming. Therefore yet another promise remains to be fulfilled.

(5) "I will bring you into the land [Hebrew *havi*ʾ *ʾethkhem ʾel haʾarets*] which I swore to give to Abraham, to Isaac, and to Jacob." Even though this promise has already been realized—in the past as well as in modern times—its final fulfillment belongs to the future. At the Jewish Passover meal (see pp. 87ff.), four cups of wine are drunk, symbolizing the first four promises above. A fifth cup is poured but not drunk, since it symbolizes the salvation that the people bound for freedom are still under way to attain.

Every Passover meal is concluded by the words "Next year in Jerusalem!" This wish may seem irrelevant to those who have seen the promise of the land fulfilled and now celebrate Passover in Jerusalem. But even there the same words are pronounced, only with a modest addition: "Next year in rebuilt Jerusalem!" They are very much aware of the fact that the fifth promise is not a concluded chapter. Jerusalem is not yet the realm of peace expressed in its name. As long as there are still people in the world who struggle against poverty and oppression, physical and spiritual, there is every reason to continue longing, hoping, working, and praying for a next year in a rebuilt Jerusalem (see p. 90).

Back to Reality

Immediately after hearing these heavenly promises, Moses becomes painfully aware that this day is still far away. When he hurries away to his people to deliver the rich words just heard, the reaction is quite different from the one at his first visit (cf. 4:31): "But they would not listen to Moses, because of their broken spirit and their cruel slavery" (6:9).

We could have expected that the people might have rejoiced and that Moses, carried away by the wonderful promises and firm support of the people and strengthened in his faith, should have undertaken his great mission. Instead the reaction of the people is summarized in this sad statement: They did not listen. They did not even protest. They had reached the lowest stage: indifference and resignation. Next we hear that even Moses was at the point of despair (v. 12).

The Bible is not composed of heroic stories from a glorious past. It deals with reality and depicts ordinary people of flesh and blood. The genealogy in 6:14–26 is an important reminder. The people are presented as they are, in noncensored form, with all their failures and shortcomings. That is why they come so close to us today, and we can easily identify with what they teach us.

Such is the gloomy starting point as we approach the next chapter: a people without further strength, ready to surrender; a leader in despair; an oppressor who is more determined than ever to continue his intransigence. But standing before them—and us—is a God who hears, sees, remembers, and keeps promises. The real battle now begins—on all fronts!

5

Ten Strikes Less One

Exodus 7–11

*T*he battlefield in this section is the palace of Pharaoh, even though the effects of this war will be felt all over Egypt. The battle is between the Lord of Hosts on one hand and the Egyptian gods with their earthly representative on the other. The representatives of the Lord are two brothers who have been equipped to plead his cause. The outcome of the battle is announced even before it has begun. The victory is granted but it will be hard earned. Not even after the ten strikes that we are going to witness is the struggle over. It will only initiate a final, decisive phase.

THE WARNING

To Moses and Aaron the power balance seems uneven in spite of all the promises they have received. The Lord, therefore, gives them a description of the situation and sets forth the order of command: In relation to the mighty leader of the superpower, Moses is like God (7:1). The same expression is used in 4:16 to characterize the relation between Moses and Aaron (see pp. 38f.). In this context, however, Aaron is called a prophet, for it is now Pharaoh, not Aaron, who is the focus. As God speaks to the prophets, so Moses is to speak to Aaron. Moses directs God's words to Pharaoh through Aaron. This means that Moses can confidently forget the anxiety he expressed at the end of the last chapter. His "uncircumcised lips" do not affect the outcome of the battle.

This does not necessarily imply that Pharaoh will listen and obey. However, this is not to become a reason for Moses

to despair as he has done hitherto. To this end God gives to
Moses, Aaron, Pharaoh, and his spiritual leaders an unambiguous forewarning of to whom the final victory belongs: The
rod of Aaron swallows the rods of the Egyptian magicians
after they have been turned into snakes (7:9ff.). Even though
most translations use the same word for the reptile that Moses' rod (4:3) and Aaron's rod (7:9) were transformed into,
"serpent," the Hebrew text uses two different words: *nahash*
and *tannin,* respectively. The latter word actually does not
mean "serpent" but a kind of sea animal. In other texts it is
often translated "dragon," for example, in Ezek. 29:3 and
32:2, which are particularly interesting in this context. In
those passages it is precisely Pharaoh who is compared to a
dragon that is destroyed. In all likelihood it is a crocodile that
is being referred to. (This is the meaning given to the word in
modern Hebrew.) The reason *tannin* is translated "serpent" in
this context most likely arises from the assumption that the
rods of Moses and Aaron are transformed in a similar way.

Lexicographically and substantively there are reasons
that mitigate against such a harmonization in the translation.
The central role ascribed to the crocodile in Egyptian mythology makes it probable that the crocodile as well as the snake
was intended when the Lord demonstrates his power over
Pharaoh. The god depicted as a crocodile—Sobek or Suchos—
was "The Powerful Ruler of the Nile" and was worshiped in
temples along the Nile, not least in the delta, where the palace
of Pharaoh was located. This god was regarded as a patron
deity and a protector against all sorts of dangers. He was more
than just another figure in the enormous pantheon of Egyptian gods. He often appeared together with the sun-god Re͑
and was revered as the creator and even as the father of the
gods, the god-begetter. He was also depicted as the judge who
defeated evil, yet was called "great in grace" by the faithful.[1]

In the light of these characteristics, the words in Ezek.
29:3 become very significant: "I am against you, Pharaoh king
of Egypt, the great dragon sprawling in the midst of its chan-
nels, saying, 'My Nile is my own; I made it for myself.' " It is
beyond any doubt that the god of the Nile, namely, the god of
creation, is referred to. Here Pharaoh is manifestly identified
with the god depicted as the crocodile-god who ascribes to
himself the power of creation.

God transforms Aaron's rod into a crocodile, which in
turn swallows the crocodiles when brought forth by Pharaoh's

magicians. It is not just a marvelous miracle. In a deeper sense it is a sign that even the god of the huge waters and his earthly representative are like a rod in the hand of the Lord. Moreover, we will soon see how the Lord demonstrates his power over the Nile (7:17ff.).

Nevertheless, it is not certain that our text depicts the crocodile-god as an evil god who is defeated. The situation here is notably different from the one in 4:2ff. There Moses performed a sign before his own people. Unlike the crocodile, the snake is consistently given negative characteristics in Egyptian mythology. This god, Apophis, often represents the power of darkness, the archenemy of the god of heaven, and rebels against the sun-god, Re^c, but who is defeated every time the sun rises and spreads its light over the world.[2] As viewed against this obvious difference between the deities represented by the snake and the crocodile, respectively, there is reason to assume that the symbolism behind the two miracles in 4:2ff. and 7:8ff. differs as well.

Before his own people Moses demonstrates that all the evil that the snake, represented by Pharaoh, symbolizes will be destroyed by the God of Israel (4:2ff.). *Before Pharaoh* Moses and Aaron give a sign that purports to legitimize their request (cf. Pharaoh's words "perform a wonder" in 7:9). In this context Aaron symbolically expresses that all the good that the Egyptians link with Sobek/Suchos, which Pharaoh ascribes to himself, comes in reality from the great God of the Hebrews and from no other god. In this respect God can be compared to a crocodile that swallows the other crocodiles. All through the book of Exodus, a great familiarity with the culture and religion of Egypt can be detected. Here we see how the message, dressed in a robe taken from Egyptian mythology, is made comprehensible to Pharaoh and his counselors.

If not before, at least now, Pharaoh ought to realize how overdue his attention is to the message brought by the two ambassadors of the slaves from their God. However, the reality is quite different.

THE HARDENING OF PHARAOH'S HEART

The first time Moses and Aaron appeared before Pharaoh in the name of the Lord to petition for freedom, Pharaoh had answered: "I do not know the LORD, and I will not let Israel go" (5:2). Now the first part of this answer ought to be different. Exodus 7:13 states that his heart was "hardened" and that he refused to listen to Moses and Aaron. The Hebrew text says literally that his heart "became strong" (Hebrew *hazaq*).[3] In the following verse Pharaoh is said to be "heavy-hearted" (Hebrew *kaved lev*) as an explanation of his refusal to let the people go. These two expressions may imply that he had now begun to know the Lord, but nevertheless chose to close his heart to him.

The adjective *kaved* related to parts of the human body may express that they do not function normally, as is the case with Moses' "heavy tongue" in 4:10 (see p. 37), the heavy eye in Gen. 48:10, and the heavy ear in Isa. 6:9–10 and 59:1.[4] A heavy heart would thus be a heart that has lost its sensitivity and receptivity.

However, it is also possible that the designation "heavy-hearted," used only in connection with Pharaoh and the Egyptians in the Bible, expresses an authentic Egyptian folk belief, according to which man's heart was weighed after death. Egyptian temples and tomb scenes have depictions of a heart placed on a scale. An evil heart is heavy and outweighs the scale of truth and righteousness, often represented by a feather. It is then thrown to a monster that devours it.[5]

A "strong" heart probably means that it is hardened. Such a heart withstands the emotions aroused in it. A person with such a heart is convinced that he absolutely does not have to change, whatever happens. The two expressions would thus focus, respectively, upon the objective and the subjective aspects of the hardening of Pharaoh's heart.

Whatever the specific cultural significance, the universal meaning is sufficiently clear, though bewildering to many Bible readers. Looking into their own hearts, they have wondered whether they too perhaps may have been struck down by such a hardening of the heart. It is particularly agonizing that the text states that it is God who hardens Pharaoh's heart. We have already come across this thought (4:21; 7:3; cf. 3:19), and we will encounter it again at short intervals (9:12; 10:1, 20, 27; 11:10; 14:4, 8, 17).

Everyone who takes the Bible seriously asks: how does this fit together with the biblical testimony that God does not desire the death of the sinner but wishes that he or she would turn from evil ways and live? If God reacts in this way in one case, how can anyone know that he or she has not already come under the same terrible judgment as Pharaoh? Moreover, how can we blame Pharaoh if it was God who so hardened his heart? What can a person do when confronting God? The fate of Judas Iscariot raises the identical question, as do other biblical narratives.

We are certainly not able to discern the secrets behind God's actions; nor do we need to. Again and again we need only the reminder given in Deut. 29:29, where a distinction is made between the secret things that belong to the Lord and the revealed ones that belong to us. However, to ignore the difficult passages in the Bible is more often a sign of superficiality than genuine humility. The difficult texts are an invitation to even deeper studies of the Scriptures, even to a struggle with these texts. Such a Jacoblike wrestling with the Word of God is usually followed by a blessing.

Several Jewish commentaries reflect such a wrestling. They have discovered a pattern in the relation between the ten verses stating that God hardens Pharaoh's heart (see above), and ten other passages claiming that *Pharaoh* himself hardens his heart (7:13, 14, 22; 8:15, 19, 32; 9:7, 34, 35; 13:15). Even a cursory survey makes it clear that Pharaoh's own intransigence comes first, above all in connection with the first five plagues. Only then is it stated that it is the Lord who hardens Pharaoh's heart.

From this we can conclude that Pharaoh is in full control over his decisions and willfully acts the way he does. At no time does the Bible teach that God sets human beings up to commit sins. This does not, however, preclude the possibility that a person can become entangled in his or her own evil thoughts and actions to such an extent as to be no longer able to change. One who knows a person well can sometimes predict how he will react in a given situation (cf. 3:19).

Maimonides explains in his commentary on repentance that persons are totally free when God presents the ethical choice between good and evil. As soon as a person has made the choice, he or she is no longer as free. One who would walk the way of life will automatically reject many alternatives that previously seemed to be real choices. Such a person also seeks God's help walking the right path (Ps. 27:11; 51:14). On the other hand, every step on the way of sin leads humans further astray from the ethical choice they first had. One becomes more and more entangled in the net of evil.[6]

However, this explanation insufficiently explains God's hardening of Pharaoh's heart. There almost seems to be an objective aspect implying that God made it impossible for Pharaoh to turn from his evil ways. When Pharaoh hardens his heart during the plagues, he eventually reaches a stage where he has lost his freedom of choice. He becomes so trapped in his own evil that finally there is no way back. After he has been tested a certain number of times, God, whose plan Pharaoh has set out to spurn, sets a limit—the hardening of his heart.

When was this limit reached? That belongs to the things hidden from us. In any case Pharaoh does not want to repent. Therefore, we can conclude that those anxious about having been punished by the hardening of their own hearts show precisely through this anxiety that they have not come under this punishment.

There is another peculiarity in the narrative of the plagues and the hardening of Pharaoh's heart. Contrary to what could have been expected, the plagues do not come as a punishment for Pharaoh's hardening of his own heart. It is rather the other way around: only after each plague is it is said that Pharaoh's heart remained closed. It would therefore seem that only when the plague has ceased does Pharaoh hold the choice in his hands—repentance or the hardening of his heart. Rabbinic commentaries explain that a human being in deep distress may seek to return to God. During his suffering, however, it is a matter of coercion, and not necessarily real repentance. Only when the person is back in his or her former situation does it become clear whether he or she was serious or not. Therefore, it is only when life has returned to normal and Pharaoh has peace that he is facing the great decision: to harden his heart or to flee to the Lord and fulfill what he had perhaps intended when in the midst of his sufferings.

One midrash appropriately applies the words in Prov. 27:22 to Pharaoh:

> Of him and of all like him it is written: "Crush a fool in a mortar with a pestle along with crushed grain, but the folly will not be driven out," which means: if you crush and chastise the fool with the strikes of afflictions and plagues, and you give him alleviation by lifting up the pestle from the mortar, his foolishness will not depart from him, since he forgets all the plagues. Such was the evil Pharaoh. When he experienced alleviation between each plague . . . , he forgot the plagues.[7]

The comparison is particularly apt, since the ten plagues are generally known as "the ten strikes" in Hebrew.[8]

The purpose of the heavy strikes that hit Pharaoh and the Egyptians is consequently to crush the heavy, hard heart of Pharaoh and to give him the knowledge of the Lord that would lead him to let God's people go (7:16–17). The battlefield of Pharaoh's heart is actually the central stage of the drama, as indicated by the fact that the hardening of his heart is the only motif recurrent in all the ten plagues we are now going to witness. It occurs no fewer than twenty times between 4:21 and 14:17.

Even another peculiarity puts the hardening of Pharaoh's heart in focus in the plague narrative: the Hebrew root *kaved* ("heavy") appears ten times—five times referring to Pharaoh's heart and five times referring to the plagues themselves. The heaviness of the plagues may thereby be viewed as the consequence of the hardening of Pharaoh's heart.[9]

In the light of Egyptian mythology and concepts about physiology, we can now more easily understand why the goal of the hardening of Pharaoh's heart is ultimately expressed as the glorification of the God of Israel: "I will harden Pharaoh's heart . . . so that I will gain glory for myself over Pharaoh and all his army; and the Egyptians shall know that I am the LORD" (14:4; cf. 14:17–18).

In both biblical and Egyptian ideas about physiology, the heart is the most important part of the human being, the center of the entire personality, including all mental, intellectual, and spiritual capacities. When God overpowers the heart of Pharaoh, the tyrant is doomed. He is an evil sinner in glaring contrast to the perfect image of the Divine, which he claimed to be and was believed to be. His heavy heart will certainly tip the scale against him. In other words, he is sentenced not only to destruction in this life, but also in the afterlife. Nothing could more clearly manifest who is in full charge than the hardening of Pharaoh's heart.

NINE STRIKES

1. Blood (7:14–25)

The first plague, directly linked to the miracle that Aaron performed with his rod, demonstrates who is the

Lord of life-giving—or death-bringing[10]—water. Both Moses' and Aaron's rods are used: Moses' rod when the plague is proclaimed, and Aaron's when it is executed. A rabbinic commentary explains this distinction by referring to Moses' own experience when he was first put into the Nile: "Why did not Moses smite it? He said: 'Because though I was cast into it, it did not injure me.' "[11]

The Egyptians, however, had used the river as a deadly instrument for carrying out genocide. Now, the same element is turned against them, and water will eventually give them the deadly blow that will seal their destiny (see ch. 14, pp. 100ff.). "For with the same device with which they planned to destroy Israel I am going to punish them. They planned to destroy My children by water, so I will likewise punish them only by water. For it is said: 'He hath digged a pit, and hollowed it, and is fallen into the ditch which he made' (Ps. 7:16)."[12]

Even after this strike Pharaoh remains unyielding. Psychologically this is understandable: his own magicians had repeated a similar miracle, explaining away the interference of the Lord (7:22–23).[13] Another explanation of Pharaoh's intransigence would be the fact that the Nile's turning into the color of blood was not an unknown phenomenon. We read in a text from around 2000 B.C.E.: "The River is blood. If one drinks of it, one rejects (it) as human and thirsts for water."[14] The description probably refers to a catastrophe sparked by unusually heavy rains in southern Egypt and Ethiopia, which caused the red soil to wash down to the Nile delta. A drastically increased amount of soil containing a large amount of microorganisms can change the balance of oxygen in the water, which may be fatal to the fish (cf. 7:18, 21 and pp. 74f.).

No natural explanations, however, do justice to the horrifying dimensions of the catastrophe and to the claim of the biblical story to describe the direct intervention by God. The Egyptians should have understood the event as a direct attack on their gods. As we know, many gods were linked to this source of life and fertility in Egypt, not only the god Sobek. One of the most prominent gods, Osiris, the ruler of the whole earth, was represented by the Nile as his bloodstream. There was also a special Nile-god, Hapy, who was a god of creation and fertility. In fact, the Nile itself was worshiped as a god: "Hail to thee, O Nile, that issues from the earth and comes to keep Egypt alive! Hidden in his form of appearance, a darkness by day, to whom minstrels have sung. He that waters the meadows which Re[c] created, in order to keep every kid alive."[15] The entire Egyptian pantheon is now challenged by the God of Israel as will be further demonstrated. "The LORD executed judgments even against their gods" (Num. 33:4). Notwithstanding, the heart of Pharaoh remains hardened, perhaps finding comfort from his own magicians, who are able to imitate the miracle.

2. Frogs (8:1–15)

Even this plague, which also hits the water of the Nile in a terrible way, was probably understood as another fierce attack on the Egyptian pantheon. Considering that the Egyptians had thrown the Hebrew children into the Nile, it may not be a coincidence that frogs are used as a means of God's punishment. The well-known and widely revered goddess, Hekt, who was considered a helper of women when they were delivered of their children, was represented precisely by a frog![16]

As for Pharaoh personally, this plague is more severe than the previous one, since it is impossible to prevent the frogs from entering the houses. They do not refrain from entering the palaces, and not even the very opposite of the moist element they prefer, the ovens and the kneading bowls (8:3)! Their tremendous multitude can hardly be more dramatically expressed. Even though frogs normally appear in great numbers along the shores of the river Nile, even an unusual natural phenomenon cannot explain what is described here.

Even this time, Pharaoh's own magicians are not at a loss for an answer (8:7). That they produce even more frogs, however, can hardly have impressed Pharaoh. If anything, he wanted to get rid of the torturous presence of the frogs. Therefore, he takes three remarkable steps. First, he gives in and asks Moses and Aaron to come. Then he asks them not only to stop the plague but—for the first time—to "pray to the LORD to take away the frogs." To be sure, he uses the very name of the Lord, *YHWH*. Thirdly, he gives his promise that is the consequence of knowing the Lord: "I will let the people go to sacrifice to the LORD" (8:8). We thus witness a total turnabout from the man who earlier had contemptuously declared: "I do not know the LORD, and I will not let Israel go" (5:2).

Moses agrees to negotiate, and, believing that God will help him, he even allows Pharaoh to decide how long he may have to terminate the plague (8:9). According to a midrash, the purpose of this suggestion is to make sure God's interference will be absolutely clear. Nobody can have a chance to claim that the plague ceased by accident.[17]

Not surprisingly, Pharaoh asks for the shortest delay possible. Moses accepts, referring to the power of the Lord (8:10). When this power is indeed revealed and while the land is still experiencing the terrible stench of decomposing frogs, Pharaoh proves that he has learned nothing: "But when Pharaoh saw that there was a respite, he hardened his heart, and would not listen to them, just as the LORD had said" (8:15). Thus he becomes the living example of the words in Prov. 27:22, quoted above. Consequently the pestle is raised for the next strike.

3. Gnats (8:16–19)

This time the Lord hits without prior warning. Aaron receives the command, "strike the dust of the earth,"[18] and huge swarms of gnats are produced, attacking both man and beast. It is not clear exactly what kind of gnats are referred to. In modern Hebrew the word *kinnim* means lice. The rapid spread of the insects, however, would indicate, rather, a kind of mosquito.

For the first time, the Egyptian magicians surrender. They now understand that they are witnessing something other than just magic. Quite a different power must lie behind what they are seeing: "This is the finger of God," they concede. Exactly what they mean by this statement is not quite clear. The expression is used in the Bible to refer to God's might (Ps. 8:3; Luke 11:20; cf. Exod. 31:18). It is also possible that the magicians have in mind a well-known motif in Egyptian mythology. The opponent of the gods, Seth, is at war with his brother Osiris and struggles with the god of heaven, Horus, over world dominion. Seth's finger constantly threatens to destroy Horus's eye. The expression also appears in connection with the attack of the moon-god, Thoth, against the Apophis snake.[19] If such beliefs were held by the magicians, it is probable that the expression "the finger of God" is to be understood against the background of Egyptian mythology.

Several Jewish commentaries contend that the Egyptian priests in using this expression want to diminish Moses' and Aaron's role in connection with this plague: it did not emanate from them, but was an insignificant "natural" catastrophe, an "act of God." In this way they would have attempted to explain why they were unable to perform anything similar.[20] Even the commentaries that understand the words of the magicians as a confession of God limit this confession to no more than a weak expression of faith, given the fact that they only mention the finger of God. In 3:20 God spoke of his hand, which will smite the Egyptians. In the fifth plague this hand is also to be discerned (9:3, 15). But above all, it is to be seen at the exodus itself as expressed in the words in 14:31: "And Israel saw the great hand."[21]

Whatever Pharaoh's magicians meant, one thing is clear: although earlier through their miracles they sought to strengthen Pharaoh in his determination not to let the people go, their confession of God does not influence Pharaoh, and his heart remains hardened.

4. Flies (8:20–32)

This plague is mentioned in Ps. 78:45: "He sent among them swarms of flies, which devoured them." This statement would make more sense if it referred to beasts of prey rather than insects. The Hebrew word ᶜarov is unclear. Its basic meaning is "mixture." A widely-attested rabbinic tradition claims that it refers to wild beasts of different kinds.[22] It is therefore very common to see beasts of prey in the pictures illustrating this plague in the *Passover Haggadah*. However, the context would rather support another common interpretation. The statement that "the houses of the Egyptians shall be filled" with these animals (8:21) points in the direction of an insect, maybe a kind of tropical bloodsucker with the ability of reproducing very rapidly. The Septuagint, the book of *Jubilees*, and Philo speak about "dog flies."[23]

This time it is obvious that these animals are tools in God's hand. For the first time, it is mentioned that the Israelites will escape. By making this distinction between his people and the Egyptians, God obviously demonstrates not only who is behind the plague but also who has the authority over the land. Moreover, the exact time for the plague—"tomorrow"—is predicted (8:29).

Pharaoh understands the message and makes Moses and Aaron a second offer: "Go, sacrifice to your God within the land" (8:25). The last words imply restriction. Pharaoh simply sticks to the letter of what God himself has said when he warned Pharaoh against the plague: "that you may know that I the LORD am in this land" (8:22). Then, why would the Israelites have to leave for the wilderness to sacrifice to their God, if he is present "in this land"? To quote God out of context in order to achieve one's own ends is the way of the serpent, whether in paradise, in Pharaoh's palace, or among us today.

Moses does not, however, retreat from his original request to sacrifice in the wilderness, and he explains that the Egyptians might stone them if they saw their offerings, which are "offensive to the Egyptians" (8:26). He is probably aware of the fact that the sacrificial animals represented gods to the Egyptians. Because of the holiness ascribed to animals, they were surrounded by a great number of taboos. Some animals could not even be touched. Traditions varied with the areas, since every place had its own patron god, often represented by a particular animal.

Moses' misapprehension before Pharaoh is excellently illustrated in a record by the Greek author Plutarch (46–120 C.E.). He describes a deep animosity and even acts of interregional war precisely because of the desecration of each other's holy animals. The following statement is particularly illustrative as a background for Moses' words: "Even today the inhabitants of Lycopolis are the only people among the Egyptians who eat a sheep; for the wolf, whom they hold to be a god, also eats it."[24] The Roman historian Tacitus (55–120 C.E.) similarly claims:

> Moses introduced new religious practices, quite opposed to those of all other religions. The Jews regard as profane all that we hold sacred; on the other hand, they permit all that we abhor. They dedicated, in a shrine, a statue of that creature whose guidance enabled them to put an end to their wandering and thirst,[25] sacrificing a ram, apparently in derision of Ammon.[26] They likewise offer the ox, because the Egyptians worship Apis.[27]

Tormented by the flies, Pharaoh eventually agrees to let the people go; "provided you do not go very far away," he adds (8:28). Surprisingly he also pleads for Moses' intercession: "Pray for me." Pharaoh now has begun to acknowledge the presence and power of the Lord. Therefore, he bears even greater responsibility after this when he disavows his promises and once again hardens his heart.

5. Pestilence (9:1–7)

Pestilence among cattle was probably not an unusual phenomenon in ancient Egypt. Yet it is as evident as before that it is the hand of God that also sends this plague: the time for its occurrence is indicated beforehand, and the cattle of the Israelites is spared. Pharaoh significantly "inquired and found that not one of the livestock of the Israelites was dead" (v. 7). He obviously begins to realize that no natural cause in the world can explain the pestilence, termed "heavy" (kaved).[28] He begins to acknowledge the tremendous power of the God announced by Moses. This power is manifested not only in the seriousness of the plague but also in the distinction made between the Israelites and the Egyptians. This dramatic turn, in fact, demonstrates that the God of Israel—and no other force—must be behind the tragedy. Thus the very people of Israel become a powerful sign of the presence and potency of the one true God. Throughout history the miraculous survival of the people of Israel remains a living testimony of the existence and faithfulness of the God of Israel, the creator of the universe (cf. Jer. 31:35ff.).[29]

It is possible that even this plague expresses the victory of Israel's God over Egyptian gods, since at least two distinguished gods were represented as animals now stricken: Hathor, the mighty sun-goddess, depicted as a cow bearing the solar disc between her horns, and Apis, the fertility god depicted as a bull. However, even if Pharaoh understands the message, he remains unshakably obstinate. Not even this strike can soften his heart of stone.

6. Boils (9:8–12)

The Egyptians were also familiar with epidemics of the kind here described. In Deut. 28:27 the expression "the boils of Egypt" is obviously a well-known concept, possibly referring back to this plague, but more likely describing a disease that was common in Egypt.

This time it strikes both man and beast with an unusual intensity. Every Egyptian is directly affected, and not only the cattle owners. The gradual increase in the severity of the plagues is also reflected in the role played by the Egyptian magicians. To begin with, they were able to imitate Moses and Aaron. During the third plague they are totally powerless, and they speak about "the finger of God." At the two subsequent plagues, they seem to be nothing but silent witnesses of what occurs. But this time, not only is their power gone; they have to suffer from the plague themselves: "The magicians could not stand before Moses because of the boils" (9:11).

A more profound motif may lie behind the text's stressing that this plague afflicted the magicians. According to Lev. 13:18–23 boils make a person unclean. Even in Egypt ritual purity was an essential precondition for access to the sanctuary. When even Pharaoh's own "court theologians" and priests are targeted by a disease barring them from fulfilling their religious duties, the message is probably comparable to the defeat suffered by the Egyptian gods in previous plagues.

Now it seems as though the fate of Pharaoh and the Egyptians is sealed. After the first five plagues we learn for the first time that "the LORD hardened the heart of Pharaoh" (9:12; cf. pp. 55ff.). Nonetheless, the Lord continues his efforts to move Pharaoh and gives him a long, intense warning before the next strike.

7. Hail (9:13–35)

Several rabbinic commentaries have noticed that the first nine plagues can be divided into three groups of three. The three plagues in the first group demonstrate similarities with the corresponding plagues in the other two groups (see further below, pp. 74ff.). The seventh plague is the first one in the third group. Like the first and fourth plagues (7:15; 8:20), this one is announced to Pharaoh early in the morning. More important than such external details is the fact that the plagues in this group are described as more severe and decisive than the previous ones. This already becomes clear in the more detailed description of the plague and in Pharaoh's reaction afterward, which will add a totally new feature. This time the people are not only afflicted, but some of them are even killed.

From now on, the plagues will also be more painful for Pharaoh personally: "For this time I will send all my plagues upon your heart" (9:14).[30] Pharaoh will not only witness desolation around him, his own life will be shaken from within by the strikes prepared for him. He now receives an even more powerful warning than he had before. Several of his own servants, "who feared the word of the LORD," take these warnings to heart and are given the possibility of escape (v. 20). Their behavior indicates a growing resistance against Pharaoh even within his closest ranks.

The enormous intensity of the following catastrophe is described in various ways. It is probably not by chance that the Hebrew word for "hail" (barad) appears no fewer than fourteen times within a few verses—twice the number of fullness! It is stated twice that the catastrophe was unheard of in the history of Egypt (vv. 18, 24).

As concerns the crops, above all, what has reached a certain ripeness and cannot be recovered is destroyed: the flax and barley, which ripen earlier than wheat and spelt (vv. 31–32). Since the barley harvest in Egypt normally takes place in February-March and wheat is harvested a month later, this and the following plague must have occurred at the very beginning of the year, that is, about two or three months before the exodus.

Even in this case Egyptian gods are probably targeted. The special patron of the crops, the fertility god Min, is rendered impotent, perhaps also the goddess of life, Isis, who is often depicted as preparing flax for clothes.

For the first time, we now hear a remarkable confession of sins from Pharaoh's own mouth: "This time I have sinned; the LORD is in the right, and I and my people are in the wrong" (9:27). Earlier, he had reluctantly acknowledged the power of the Lord and then promised to let the people go, at least for a certain time. Now he not only realizes the grandeur of God but also has become aware of his own evil, which is always the consequence of knowing the Lord. He also understands the consequences. Without any reservations whatsoever, he therefore promises to release the people and even asks Moses for intercession: "Pray to the LORD! Enough of God's thunder and hail! I will let you go; you need stay no longer" (9:28).

Though Moses, wise from experience, has hardly any confidence in Pharaoh's promise, he turns to God to terminate the plague. He actually goes out of the city before stretching out his hands to the Lord (9:33). According to Abrabanel, Moses had a special place outside the city where he used to pray, which Jews still regard as a holy place. Abrabanel probably had in mind the old synagogue in Cairo, where later the famous Cairo Genizah was discovered.[31] According to an ancient tradition, this was the place to which Moses went after he had spoken with Pharaoh. Still today there is an inscription with Moses' words in 9:29. Even though this site has not been authenticated, it is moving to see how Bible verses in this way have been kept alive through thousands of years in the same country and by the descendants of the same people to whom Moses was sent so long ago.

God hears Moses' prayer. Just as surely Pharaoh's heart remains hardened in spite of the plague he has personally experienced and the conviction he has sensed in his inner conscience. It will soon be clear that neither the fear of God nor the confession of sins penetrated to his innermost being. He has feared the pain and the punishment rather than God himself. Rather than a personal relationship with God, he sought a personal reprieve from God. His confession of sins is soon a repressed memory, as are his promises of a change of mind.

In his commentary on this passage, Rashi points out that Pharaoh's guilt is even greater now that he has become aware of his sin. Earlier, he had acted out of self-interest; now he becomes a conscious sinner, even more entangled in his own evil. The final chord in this chapter is therefore ominous and tragic. As soon as the pain of the plague has eased, he persists in his evil way and again closes his evil heart (9:34)—the hard and heavy heart that not even the heavy hailstorms of God's wrath have been able to soften.

8. Locusts (10:1–20)

In connection with the previous plague, we witnessed how Pharaoh's own servants began to take warning from God's word (9:20). After the proclamation of the next plague, it is they who try to make Pharaoh rethink his position. The opposition to Pharaoh's stubbornness is obviously growing among his closest advisers. They realize that Moses and Aaron have the welfare of Egypt in their hands (10:7).

The plague is severe. It blackens the land and leaves no life on its surface (cf. v. 17). Again this time it is twice described as being unique in Egyptian annals (vv. 6, 14). What was left of vegetation after the hail is now finally destroyed. The gods targeted by the previous plague are hit again.

This time Pharaoh seems to be more serious in his negotiations than before. Now he desires to know more precisely who exactly is applying for an "exit permit" (10:8). This question probably entails the same suspicion as his reservation in 8:28: "I will let you go . . . provided you do not go very far away." Deep down, he realizes that it is not a matter of a mere three days' journey into the wilderness for a sacrificial service, which only adult men are to perform (cf. 23:17). His suspicions are confirmed by Moses' undisguised answer in 10:9: "We will go with our young and our old; we will go with our sons and daughters and with our flocks and herds."

Finally, Pharaoh is ready to concede to Moses' original request, as he understands it, namely, only the men are to leave (10:11). Nothing beyond this! Consequent to Moses' latest demand, negotiations reach a deadlock, with Moses and Aaron driven out of the court. It is within this context that Pharaoh's enigmatic words in verse 10 must be understood. Outwardly they seem to consist of a blessing, literally: "The LORD be with you when I send you and your little ones away!" The real meaning, however, is the very opposite of a blessing: just as minimally as I intend to let you go, so may your god be minimally with you! Or he may simply be ironic, expressing contempt for the God of Israel.[32]

The following words point in this direction: "Plainly, you have some evil purpose in mind." A literal translation of the Hebrew text, however, would rather be, "You will see that evil is in front of your faces." These words can certainly be taken to mean "evil is, as it were, written on your faces!" But they may also be interpreted as a threat from Pharaoh: you will certainly encounter evil, if you pursue your intentions! The Hebrew word for "evil" (ra'ah) is, moreover, almost homophonous with the name of the Egyptian sun-god, Re', of whom Pharaoh was thought to be an incarnation. Therefore, we might actually understand his words to be yet another declaration of war from an Egyptian god against the God of Israel: my god is against your god![33] In any case, Pharaoh's answer is sufficiently clear to provoke the next heavy strike.

Locusts are a recurrent plague in the eastern parts of the Mediterranean and large areas of northern Africa. I remember that a few years ago in Israel we waited breathlessly as huge swarms of locusts advanced through Tunisia and Libya and left barren land behind. What we find in 10:12–15 fits very well with the events we watched on television. The wind conditions determined whether the locusts would reach us. Had the southwest wind blown a little stronger, we would probably also have been stricken by the plague.

Since locusts usually enter Egypt from the south or the west, it is difficult to interpret the expression "an east wind" *(ruah qadim)* in verse 13 literally. Naturally, the hot desert wind from the east can represent an unpleasant wind in general.[34] The strong wind, which finally terminates the plague by driving the locusts into the Red Sea, however, literally must have been a west wind.

With the land laid waste through hail and locusts, Pharaoh has every reason to ask for forgiveness once again. This time his confession of sins is directed toward both the Lord and Moses and Aaron: "I have sinned against the LORD your God, and against you" (10:16). It is also followed by an indirect commitment that no more plagues will be needed to induce him to let the people go: "Do forgive my sin just this once, and pray to the LORD your God that at the least he will remove this deadly thing from me."

Moses without a word now leaves Pharaoh (cf. 9:30). From bitter experience he knows how little Pharaoh's assurance is worth. At the same time he realizes more and more the meaning of the Lord's word about the hardening of Pharaoh's heart.

9. Darkness (10:21–29)

Anyone who has experienced the desert wind, the *hamsin,* at its worst can easily relate to the description of a darkness so intense it can be called "a darkness that can be felt." It is true that the darkness in the book of Exodus was unique both in its duration and in its intensity. But when the desert wind fills the air with dust, it results in a darkness not to be overcome by light. It is not a matter of darkness in negative terms—absence of light as at night—but a material darkness with the air filled with a substance rendering it hard to breathe and to move.[35] The *hamsin* is common in springtime and chronologically would fit in well after the two previous plagues.

Darkness like this is documented in ancient Egyptian sources: "The sun disc is covered over. It will not shine (so that) people may see. . . . No one knows when midday falls, for his shadow cannot be distinguished."[36] This darkness, however, defies all natural explanations, since it discriminates between the area where the Israelites lived and the rest of Egypt.

If Pharaoh in verse 10:10 (above p. 69) really wanted to threaten Moses and Aaron with the sun-god Re᷍, this plague could be understood as a direct reproof from the God of Israel. We have mentioned that the struggle between the power of darkness, Apophis, and the power of light, represented by the sun-god and the sustainer of the world, Re᷍, was a well-known motif in Egyptian mythology (p. 55). Every sunrise confirmed the continued superiority of the sun-god. The absence of the sun for three days must therefore have been interpreted as an ominous defeat of the god probably regarded as the highest deity.[37]

The three-days duration of this plague may also have a particular significance as related to the oppression of the Israelites under Egyptian slavery. Pharaoh did not even allow them three days' vacations to worship the Lord (3:18; 5:1–3). The three days of darkness may therefore be understood as sending a particularly concrete message to Pharaoh to listen to Moses and let the people go.[38]

The darkness must also have particularly shaken Pharaoh, given the fact that he claimed to be the son and representative of the sun-god as well as of other gods (see pp. 15, 17, 55).[39] A complimentary poem for Pharaoh Merneptah (see p. 25) yields an uncanny meaning when read against the background of this plague:

> Attend to me, O rising sun that illuminates the Two Lands with his comeliness; O solar disk of mankind that dispels darkness from Egypt. Thy nature is like unto thy father Re who arises in heaven. Thy rays penetrate into a cavern, and there is no place void of thy comeliness. Thou art told the condition of every country whilst thou art at rest in thy palace. Thou hearest the speech of all countries, thou possessest millions of ears. Thine eye is more radiant than the stars of heaven, thou canst see better than the solar disk. If one speaks, though the utterance be from a cavern, it comes down into thine ear. If aught is done that is hidden, yet will thine eye see it. O Binere-miamun, lord of mercy, creator of breath![40]

Such glorifying words of worship are certainly not limited to the god alone but are also extended to his earthly manifestation, Pharaoh:

> Worship King Ni-maat-Re, living forever, within your bodies and associate with his majesty in your hearts. He is Perception which is in

(men's) hearts, and his eyes search every body. He is Re, by whose beams one sees, he is one who illuminates the Two Lands more than the sun disc. He is one who makes the land greener than (does) a high Nile, for he has filled the Two Lands with strength and life.[41]

This sun is now darkened. The land of Egypt is witnessing a "twilight of the gods" which has gone down in world history. Pharaoh realizes who has sent the darkness and what this implies. Therefore he agrees to release the people—even the women and the children—and only conditions his release by insisting that the cattle must remain hostage (10:24). Moses rejects the compromise, and the struggle enters a new critical stage. Pharaoh arrogantly proclaims in a threatening way that the negotiations have come to an end. Should Moses again appear, he is to be terminated (10:28).

Yet, the decision-making power is no longer lodged in Pharaoh's hands. What he does not know is that the tables are about to be turned. He will have to entreat Moses and Aaron to come back (12:31), and then the Egyptians will beseech them to leave. Through his action he has signed his son's death warrant, as well as his own.

THE LAST STRIKE FORETOLD (11:1–10)

The dialogue between Moses and Pharaoh is not yet over. Moses has yet another matter to proclaim to Pharaoh—a terrible something that will overshadow all the plagues so far. A mortal blow will fall upon the land and upon the people of Egypt, leaving no house unaffected, from the royal palace to the working-class quarters. Only one distinction will be made: the people of Israel, the first-born of the Lord (4:22), will be spared when all other first-born male humans and beasts die. Then negotiations will no longer hinge on Pharaoh's caprice. He will not only allow the people to go, but he will urge them to do so and even drive them away (11:1).

A detail in the text should not be overlooked. In 11:6 "a loud cry throughout the whole land of Egypt, such as has never been or will ever be again," is predicted. There is hardly any doubt that this "loud cry" refers back to 3:7 where, concerning the enslaved and oppressed Israelites, the Lord asserts that he has "heard their cry on account of their taskmasters." Now the tables will turn. This time the

cry will be heard not from the slaves but from their taskmasters, in particular from the supreme taskmaster, Pharaoh himself.

With these ominous words of judgment echoing in the
halls of Pharaoh, Moses dramatically abandons him to his
fate (11:8). Moses no longer plays the role of a miserable
representative of the slaves. He appears as the apostle of the
author of all authority over heaven and earth.

The introductory words of chapter 11 may communi-
cate the impression that a new revelation has taken place in
the midst of the audience with Pharaoh. Until now we have
seen, however, that the Lord was revealed to Moses only
after he had left Pharaoh. From Moses' concluding words in
the previous chapter, we can further conclude that he is already fully aware of the content in the Lord's proclamation
given here. The first three verses can therefore be regarded
as a narrative parenthesis. They simply express what Moses
recollects before he announces his prophecy of doom to
Pharaoh.

As a matter of fact, the Lord has already revealed what
is said here. In 4:21–23 he has not only described Israel as a
firstborn son, but also contrasted this fact with Pharaoh's
firstborn—who will have to die (see pp. 40ff.). God has already proclaimed in 3:20 that Pharaoh finally will have to
release the people. In the verses immediately following God
says that he will make the Egyptians favorably disposed toward the Israelites, so that the latter will receive precious
gifts from the former (see 12:35–36). Through the interference of the Lord, Moses and the formerly despised
slaves have now achieved respect in the sight of the Egyptians, even up to the inner circle around Pharaoh himself
(11:2–3).

By this time, everything is prepared for the final strike.
The concluding words of chapter 11 clearly set forth that
the first great mission of Moses and Aaron is now complete.
They will not be sent to Pharaoh any more. The Lord will
settle with him. In contrast to the previous plagues, the
last one will need no external means or human emissary.
Instead, Moses and Aaron will hereafter serve as God's
mouthpiece toward their own people. What is now prepared
will not allow the people to sit on the grandstand. The stage
is set for the great departure. The preparations can wait no
longer!

THE STRUCTURE OF THE STRIKES

Many efforts have been made to systematize the strikes against Pharaoh and Egypt in these chapters. However they may or may not be interrelated, the message is clear: "so that you may know that the earth is the LORD's" (9:29). Notwithstanding this, it is tempting to look for a certain inner relation between them, which could shed some additional light on the message they convey.

As briefly mentioned above, the plagues have been divided into three groups of three, whereby numbers one, two, and three in each group are compared for similar features. The first ones in each group (the first, fourth, and seventh) are introduced by Moses coming before Pharaoh in the morning. The second ones (the second, fifth, and eighth) are introduced by the formula "Then the LORD said to Moses, 'Go to Pharaoh and say to him . . . ' " They are also preceded by a warning. The third ones, finally, are not preceded by any warning.[42]

Some see the plagues structured according to increasing severity: they begin with nature, causing nuisances but not necessarily disease and death. Then they affect cattle and crops, inflict bodily pain on human beings and finally even death. Such a crescendo can certainly be disputed, for example, when boils come after pestilence, or darkness marks the climax. The impotence of the Egyptian gods does become ever more obvious, and Pharaoh is gradually stripped of his divine ambitions, while God and his servants are ever more glorified, first in the eyes of Pharaoh's magicians and officials and then in the eyes of Pharaoh himself.

This is, in fact, the core of the narrative: the power struggle within the realm of the divine. It is therefore not too farfetched to assume a link between the order of the plagues and natural phenomena in Egypt, especially since nature in Egyptian mythology was personified by various gods.

Efforts have thus been made to understand the plagues as parallel to well-known natural phenomena that follow one after the other according to the order in the text. During late summer rains south of Egypt, the Nile may turn red, caused by clay and microorganisms brought down to the delta from

Upper Egypt. This phenomenon sparks a chain reaction, leading to subsequent plagues. The fish are choked (7:18, 21) and infected with disease, causing the frogs to leave the water and eventually to die. This creates an ideal breeding ground for insects, which become a nuisance in early fall, even causing pestilence and boils. "The boils of Egypt" was probably a well-known phenomenon even before the sixth plague (p. 65). Hail may possibly occur during the rainy season in winter, and locust plagues are known particularly in late winter and early spring. Finally, in early spring the desert wind bringing sand and dust may darken the skies dramatically.[43]

Such phenomena may certainly be linked not only to the single plagues but also to their sequence. As pointed out above, their intensity, duration, sudden appearance, and equally sudden disappearance, as well as the discriminatory targeting of the Egyptians and sparing of the Israelites, can, however, only be explained in one way: God's hand!

In the light of the divine battle reflected in the nine strikes, another link to creation is even more illuminating. This battle has already begun with the onset of slavery, which implies distorting God's order of creation and assuming God's lordship. It is indeed possible to discern a theological structure in this narrative, linking it to the motif underlying slavery: usurping the dominion of God (see pp. 14f.). Since slavery is a distortion of the divine order of creation and a denial of the divine dignity assigned to each human being, it would not be surprising if the plagues are related to the creation story.

The first strike is against the life-giving water, corresponding to the first act of creation, where the prime element is the water out of which creation emerges (Gen. 1:2ff.).

The second strike implies frogs "swarming" in the water. The corresponding act of creation would be the creatures "swarming" in the sea according to Gen. 1:21.

The third strike hits "the dust of the earth, so that it may become gnats." Is this, perhaps, reminiscent of Gen. 1:11–12, where the earth puts forth vegetation? If this is the case, even the eighth plague—locusts—may be a negative counterpart as well, targeting the vegetation of the earth.

The fourth strike may correspond to the creation of the flying creatures in Gen. 1:22. If the plague refers to beasts of prey rather than insects, it would affect another aspect of creation, expressed in Gen. 1:24–25, where the "cattle and creeping things and wild animals" are created. Even the fifth and sixth plagues affect these creatures.[44] By this point we have reached a reversal of humankind's divinely appointed authority over the creatures in the sea, in the air, and on the earth in Gen. 1:28. Now these animals have taken over the dominion over Egypt.[45]

The seventh strike signifies a removal of the separation, which God made between water and water, water and land (Gen. 1:6–10; cf. Gen. 7). Together with the eighth strike, it also ruins the vegetation (cf. Gen. 1:12).

The ninth strike, as it were, takes creation back to its ghastly beginning when the earth was "a formless void and darkness covered the face of the deep" (Gen. 1:2), by removing the separation between light and darkness (Gen. 1:4).

The last strike, finally, hits the very crown of creation, the image of God (Gen. 1:26; cf. pp. 15, 131, 150f.).

Why ten strikes? Is this number meant to correspond to "the ten divine utterances by which the world was created and ordered" (Gen. 1:3, 6, 9, 11, 14, 20, 24, 26, 28, 29)?[46]

This analysis does justice to the universal aspect of exodus connected with the rescue of Moses through the little "ark" (see pp. 16f.). Through the ark of Noah, creation was repaired and restored after a terrible distortion. In a parallel way, the liberation of Israel can be regarded as a renewed mending of creation in connection with a renewed corruption, as demonstrated by the enslavement and affliction of the people of Israel in Egypt. Not surprisingly, the Sabbath is associated with both the creation of the world and the redemption of Israel (see pp. 239f.). In this perspective, the ten plagues reflect a struggle, the objective of which goes far beyond what is immediately apparent.

THE BATTLE'S ULTIMATE OBJECTIVE

At the beginning of the conflict, Pharaoh had proudly and scornfully acknowledged: "I do not know the LORD, and I will not let Israel go" (5:2). Hereby, he actually summarizes the ultimate aim of the battle: (a) The Lord will be recognized as the One-Who-Alone-Is; and (b) God's people will be liberated in order to serve him.

At the first front line the battle is almost won: gradually Pharaoh has begun to acknowledge the God he at first denied so categorically. Still, this knowledge hitherto has had hardly any consequences. At the second frontline the battle therefore still remains to be fought. The people still await their unconditional liberation from Pharaoh. As long as this has not happened, Pharaoh proves in action that his awareness of the Lord is only a grudgingly theoretical knowledge. Moses expresses it in this way: "I know that you do not yet fear the LORD God" (9:30). We can say that Pharaoh knows of God without accepting God. What is ultimately at stake is who brokers the power, or equivalently, who is God—Pharaoh or the Lord. Believing in one God permits no compromise between these two antithetical alternatives.

The ultimate object of the battle is thus not only to reach a settlement between God and an obstinate human being. Pharaoh is both in his own and in the people's eyes—analogous to Moses—a representative of the divine. There exists, however, a fundamental difference between Pharaoh and Moses in this respect. In the case of Pharaoh, there is no distinct border between Pharaoh and his gods, while Moses is no more than a mortal messenger. The outcome of the battle between the two will, therefore, do no more than alter the destiny of an oppressed people. Ultimately, what is at stake is the knowledge and confession of the one true God.

The calling of Israel to move from the servitude under Pharaoh to the service of the one true God is also at stake. They are God's firstborn son, whom God offers to make a "priestly kingdom and a holy nation" (19:6; see pp. 132f.). Freedom from Pharaoh is not a goal in itself; for as Moses pleads in the name of the Lord, "Let my people go, so that they may worship me" (10:3). The verb used, ʿavad, means both "to worship" and "to serve/work" (cf. pp. 14f.). For the time being, the Israelites are still slaves, but soon they will exchange masters and only serve the King of kings—the ultimate objective of the negotiations.

It is important to keep these fundamental dimensions of the drama in mind in order to understand Moses' totally unqualified demand for an unconditional capitulation from Pharaoh. This is not a matter of prestige but of God's glory. Moses' uncompromising attitude toward Pharaoh constitutes a fitting background to another scene that we are soon to witness: the receiving of the tablets of the covenant with the first of all commandments, "You shall have no other gods before me" (ch. 20).

Because this decisive struggle, it is probably not by chance that a particular phrase with slight variations recurs exactly as many times as the plagues: "that you may know that I am the LORD." Even before Moses appeared in front of Pharaoh, God expressed his purpose for Moses' mission (7:5, 17). It is then reiterated at short intervals throughout the story of the plagues (8:10, 22; 9:14, 29; 10:2; 11:7) and again recapitulated twice more in connection with the extermination of Pharaoh's army in the Red Sea (14:4, 18).

To know and to acknowledge the power of the Lord, the God of Israel, is not merely a matter of experiencing the tremendous might, majesty, holiness, and presence of the divine. Only God can proclaim, "There is no one like me in all the earth" (9:14). Knowing God also implies that other gods are unmasked as the powerless icons they actually are. The miracles with the rods and with some of the plagues—the first, second, and ninth—were directly linked to central motifs and symbols, which must have immediately reminded the Egyptians of their own gods. The actions spoke for themselves: these "gods" are powerless in the face of the God of Israel. Even Pharaoh's own "court theologians" eventually had to admit their own impotence standing before the presence of this God.

The fact that it is not only Pharaoh and the Egyptians who are stricken by the Lord but, above all, their gods is remarked upon in both biblical and postbiblical tradition. As the Lord is crossing through the country on the first night of Passover, he executes judgment on "all the gods of Egypt" (12:12; Num. 33:4). The list of the ten plagues in the book of *Jubilees* 48:5 concludes in this way: "And upon all of their gods the LORD took vengeance and he burned them with fire." Even the *Dayyenu* hymn in the *Passover Haggadah* views the judgment on the gods of Egypt as a particularly important event, when it lists the most important milestones in the history of Israel.[47]

However, the consistent adversary in this life-and-death struggle is Pharaoh. Even though he claims to represent the gods, he remains a representative of humans, the old Adam who aspires to claim the throne of God. In his obstinate refusal to submit to the Lord and surrender to his innermost convictions, he is, in fact, most human. The inhuman cruelty and hardness that he demonstrates in the beginning gradually gives way to another feature that we more easily identify with ourselves. The unscrupulous mass murderer in the first chapter and the ruthless oppressor in the fifth chapter is inevitably crushed. At first he begged for relief of his pain. Then he confessed his sin. Finally, he acceded to negotiation, even yielding considerable concessions.

In conclusion, Pharaoh's resistance to the Lord can be summed up in one single point: he tried to hold onto the ultimate initiative. He wanted to be the one setting down the conditions. He persistently saw himself sovereign and supreme, owner of the land as well as the people. It is precisely at this point that no compromise is possible. "The earth is the LORD's," he is told (9:29). Nor does the people of Israel belong to Pharaoh, for "thus says the LORD, Israel is my firstborn son" (4:22)!

Ultimate ownership and sovereignty is the crucial issue. As long as Pharaoh withholds his own power and independence from God, the battle will continue. It can only end with a complete and unconditional capitulation to the Lord. Toward this goal, God tried to lead Pharaoh through nine stations of his *via dolorosa,* where each strike revealed a new dimension of God, as well as a new limitation of Pharaoh. At each of the stations God sought to bring Pharaoh understanding: stop here that you may understand that I am the Lord, unequaled in heaven and on earth, divine proprietor of everything, yet still loving every human being created in my image, even an insignificant and miserable people of slaves, whom nobody else cares for! I am the Lord!

So far, all God's efforts have led only to partial victories. The battle is consequently not yet over. In spite of all that has happened, the battle has yet to reach its culmination. Next time the curtain is lifted, we will witness the preparations for the final struggle.

6

The Liberation Prepared

Exodus 12:1–13:16

*T*he countdown for the liberation is now approaching its end. The last decisive battle remains. Before the dawn of freedom, however, lies a long, dark night. The birthpangs grow in intensity before the delivery of God's firstborn, Israel. There is no doubt that we are now facing both the final stage and a new beginning.

The Lord has henceforth and forever stopped talking to Pharaoh and is now attending exclusively to Israel in order to prepare them for the great miracle due to occur. First, God proclaims a new calendar. Because of the marvelous event they will soon witness, the month that the thin lunar crescent has just proclaimed will be regarded as the first of the months of the year (12:2).[1] After two weeks the moon will shine brightly over a people on its way toward freedom. In the light of this hope the last preparations can now begin.

The instructions God gives through Moses inaugurate a feast that for all future time will unite the nation that now stands between slavery and freedom, darkness and light, death and life, fear and hope. In this situation the preparations express a creed in action (cf. Heb. 11:28). These Passover preparations can be summarized under three key words: relationship, renewal, remembrance.

PASSOVER—THE FEAST OF RELATIONSHIP
(12:1–14, 21–28, 43–51)

The significance of the paschal lamb can be summed up in various ways. One feature seems to unite them all: the aim of unifying the people from the disruption and chaos that characterized the condition of slavery. Out of the divided tribes a united nation will emerge. A nation will be born to a new life. A new relationship will be the blessing of Passover for the days to come—a relationship with the Lord, interpersonal relationships, relationships with coming generations.

Like a reverberating echo, we hear expressions like "the whole congregation of Israel," "all the Israelites," "each family," "each household," and "throughout your generations." This is the first time the people of Israel have ever experienced, as a united body, relationship with one another before the Lord—the first "communion." The various prescriptions make this patently clear.

The Paschal Lamb, the Circumcision, and the First Supper

The sacrificial lambs are to be separated previously on the tenth day of the month but are to be slaughtered only on the fourteenth (12:3, 6). No reason for this interval is indicated. This ordinance is never mentioned again and is thus something unique for this first Passover in Egypt. Rabbinic tradition interprets it as a special "holy relationship" preparation that is to be related to the foremost sign of this holy relationship, circumcision.[2]

The paschal meal in Egypt is a real relationship meal—the first of its kind in the history of Israel. This explains why the ordinances regarding the circumcision are dealt with in connection with the paschal lambs (12:43–49). Only those who through circumcision had been accepted into Israel could therefore participate in the meal (cf. baptism and holy communion in Christianity).

During the chaotic conditions of slavery, circumcision had obviously not been fully observed. In addition to this, other peoples had joined Israel (a "mixed crowd"; 12:38). Therefore, many "communion guests" were still uncircumcised. The regulations in 12:43–49 indirectly imply that not only the lambs should be separated but also that all those who sought to participate in the relationship and in the meal should be circumcised.[3]

The same rule was equally applied at the end of the trek through the desert according to Josh. 4:19; 5:2–10: first circumcision, then the paschal meal. According to Jewish tradition, the most critical healing process occurs three days after a circumcision.[4] In order to have the lambs ready on the fourteenth of

the month, they were therefore separated already on the tenth
day, when the uncircumcised also enter the covenant of circumcision. In this way the new relationship was prepared and
then sealed through the communion meal.

The Paschal Lamb and the Blood Sign

The covenantal sign of the circumcision and the paschal
lamb are further linked by the ordinance to smear the door
lintels with the blood of the lambs (12:7, 22–23). In this way
the lamb becomes a relationship sign analogous to the circumcision. The sign of the blood points to "the blood of the
covenant" of 24:8, shed to seal the covenant at Sinai. There
the blood is sprinkled both upon the altar and upon the
people, and even this ceremony is concluded by a meal expressive of the relationship between the Lord and all the
people (24:6, 8, 11). In the Passover ritual, the door lintels of
the Israelites take the place of the altar. The blood of the lambs
powerfully symbolizes the bond between God and Israel and
between every member of the people, a bond later sealed
through the covenantal blood at Sinai.

Blood as such does not possess any magical power. God
does not need it. Therefore, it is specifically written: "The
blood shall be a sign *for you* on the houses where you live"
(12:13). Only through relationship with the Lord can blood
come to symbolize salvation. Analogous to the blood of the
circumcision (cf. 4:24ff.; pp. 41ff.), the blood on the Israelite
door lintels represents protection for the houses marked
with it.

"When I see the blood, I will pass over you," God says
(12:13).[5] This statement leads us to think of another story
where the word "see" (Hebrew *ra'ah*) plays a decisive role.
When Abraham is commanded to offer up his son Isaac,
he leaves for "the land of Moriah" (Gen. 22:2). The name
"Moriah" can be explained as a combination of the Hebrew
words for "the Lord" and "see." When Isaac asks, "Where is
the lamb for a burnt offering?" he receives the answer, "God
himself will provide the lamb" (Gen. 22:7–8, 14): literally,
"God will see [Hebrew *yir'eh*] for himself the lamb."

Not surprisingly the rabbis make the connection between this story and the blood that God sees in connection
with the paschal lambs. They interpret that God, when he saw
the blood at the door lintels, actually saw the blood of the

lamb that he had provided ("[fore]seen") for himself.[6] This bold interpretation undeniably does justice to the whole context in which the blood sign appears. In Gen. 22 the "only son" (v. 2) of Abraham is spared, and the ram is sacrificed in his place. Here Israel, God's firstborn, is spared when the lambs are sacrificed. Moreover, Israel is not only called God's "son" but also his "flock," liberated when the lambs are sacrificed in its place: "He struck all the firstborn in Egypt. . . . Then he led out his people like sheep, and guided them in the wilderness like a flock" (Ps. 78:51–52).

The Paschal Lamb and the Communion Meal

The Passover meal is an expression of the profound relationship among the people who will soon depart together. First, "the whole congregation of Israel" should participate. Second, they could only eat the lamb together with others (12:3–4, 21)—no private meals! The paschal lambs were to unite all the households of Israel around the same destiny. Rabbinic literature explains that there were never fewer than ten sharing one lamb.[7] As we know, there were thirteen at the last Passover meal of Jesus. The Samaritans who still continue this tradition on Mount Gerizim receive up to eighteen for one lamb.

The ordinance that the consumption of the lambs must take place during one and the same night and in one and the same house (12:8, 22, 46) stresses the relationship character of the meal. All the participants had to eat the lamb together at the same time. The table fellowship could not be broken. If anything was left until the morning it could not be eaten but had to be burned (v. 10; 34:25).

The very preparation of the lambs dynamically manifests the call to the new all-embracing relationship of the oppressed and disunited people at their first Passover. The lambs must not be cut up but should be roasted whole (12:9), nor should their bones be broken (12:46; cf. John 19:32–36). The bones symbolize a wholeness; the Hebrew word ʿetsem means "bone," "substance," and "person." Through this ordinance the lamb as a symbol of relationship and unity is emphasized. In this respect the theme of the paschal lamb in the New Testament is highly appropriate: It was slaughtered "to gather into one the dispersed children of God" (John 11:52).

PASSOVER—THE FEAST OF RENEWAL (12:15–20; 13:3–10)

The eating of unleavened bread is another expression of a profound relationship among the people. Here, however, the ordinances are more focused on another motif: purification and renewal. They contain one negative and one positive aspect: the prohibition against "leaven" (Hebrew *hamets* or *se'or*) and the commandment to eat "unleavened bread" (Hebrew *matsah*). These two aspects stand in juxtaposition. *Se'or* stands for the old dough used at baking, like yeast. The word *hamets* is defined in rabbinic tradition as all products containing any derivative of wheat, barley, oats, rye, and spelt, as soon as they have begun fermenting, for example, bread, beer, and whisky.[8]

According to the rabbinic definition, fermentation begins eighteen minutes after any liquid has been added.[9] Therefore, *matsah* has to be baked within this period of time. It contains only flour and water and is rolled out to a thin dough which is pricked to remove air, since air can precipitate fermentation. The crop must be kept under special supervision all the time from the harvest in order to prevent moisture from transforming it to *hamets*.

The prohibition against leaven at Passover is strict, and the penalty for violation is no less than being "cut off from Israel" (12:15, 19; on this punishment, see pp. 236f.). It is insufficient not to consume any leaven. It must not even "be seen" among the people (13:7). To obey this ordinance, kitchen and household utensils are carefully cleaned before Passover. In the evening before the fourteenth of Nisan a final symbolic search of the house is made (Hebrew *bediqath hamets*). Then at least a symbolic remnant of leaven is always found, which is burnt the following morning. This tradition expresses a central thought linked to the leaven. Since fermentation and decay are closely linked, the leaven symbolizes sin, that is, decay in an inner sense. This symbolism may also underlie the prohibition of leaven in connection with sacrifices (23:18; Lev. 2:11; 6:16–17).[10]

The removal of the leaven is a living proclamation intended to disavow the old and the sinful and to begin anew in faithfulness to the Lord and his commandments. Paul expresses this Jewish approach to the leaven in the following way (1 Cor. 5:6–8):

Do you not know that a little leaven[11] leavens the whole batch of
dough? Clean out the old leaven so that you may be a new batch, as
you really are unleavened. For our paschal lamb, Christ, has been sacrificed. Therefore, let us celebrate the festival, not with the old leaven,
the leaven of malice and evil, but with the unleavened bread of sincerity
and truth.[12]

This removal of all leaven and the eating of unleavened
bread is such a central motif that it has designated the name of
the entire feast—"the festival of unleavened bread" (12:17;
Lev. 23:5–6; 2 Chron. 30:13, 21; 35:17; Ezra 6:19–22). Since
the lamb was eaten only in the evening and night of the first
day of Passover, while unleavened bread was to be eaten seven
days (12:15, 17; 13:6–7), the latter observance dominated the
feast. When the cult was later centralized in the temple in Jerusalem, and Passover became a pilgrim festival (Deut. 16:2,
5ff.; see pp. 179f.), the slaughter of the lambs there and their
consumption were restricted within the walls of Jerusalem.
Jews unable to make the pilgrimage to Jerusalem were consequently precluded from eating the Passover lamb. To them,
the feast was above all "the festival of unleavened bread." After
the destruction of the temple and the cessation of the sacrifices, no paschal lambs could be slaughtered any longer.
Therefore, Passover today is very much centered around the
ordinances regarding *matsah* and *hamets*.

Even though we do not know how the commandment to
eat unleavened bread was understood from the very beginning,[13] it assumes a particular meaning in connection with
the liberation from Egypt. It reminds one of the harsh conditions of slavery—"the bread of affliction" (Deut. 16:3)—
and of the speedy departure (12:34, 39). The removal of the
leaven becomes a concrete admonition to the liberated people
to turn the outward transformation into an inner renewal
as well.

The liberation from slavery is no objective per se. The
real purpose will become clear when the miracle of Passover
continues with the miracle of Pentecost and its powerful proclamation of what it means to remove the leaven in an inner
sense (see below Chapter Nine). This deeper liberation and
renewal, however, will not be finished in this era. Therefore,
the festival of unleavened bread will never cease from the realm
of history: "This day shall be a day of remembrance for you.
You shall celebrate it as a festival to the LORD; throughout

your generations you shall observe it as a perpetual ordinance" (12:14, 17; 13:3; Deut. 16:3).

PASSOVER—THE FEAST OF REMEMBRANCE

To remember means to make the past present. It means to be united with both the people that then were saved and coming generations to whom the call for liberation and renewal will always be directed. Among all the ordinances for Passover, none is repeated as many times as the one to remember what the Lord has done and to celebrate it year after year, from generation to generation.

In the description of what happened in Egypt before the liberation, the laws for the future celebration of Passover are constantly intertwined in such a way that it is difficult to distinguish between history and future, story and ritual.

The people bound for freedom will survive as a nation only if the Passover miracle is continuously transmitted into the future as a living reality. This is one of the deepest secrets behind Passover as a feast of remembrance.

"And You Shall Tell . . ." (12:24–27; 13:8, 14)

The commandment to tell the children about the Passover miracle is repeated three times in this section. It is given again in Deut. 6:20–21 (cf. Deut 6:7). In Jewish tradition this fourfold repeated biblical commandment means that it is an important duty to share this miracle with, and make it alive to, future generations whatever their level and background may be. Children are obviously curious, which can be inferred from the formulation of the question: "What is the meaning of the decrees and the statutes and the ordinances which the LORD our God has commanded you?" (Deut. 6:20). Another poses his question in a simpler way: "What does this mean?" (13:14) To such a person, a simpler explanation should be given. In 13:8 there is not even a question, but simply a command to recount what the Lord has done. This refers, perhaps, to generations so alienated from knowledge that they are not even able to formulate a question on the matter; nor may they even care to know. In our days such an interpretation has become desperately pertinent.

However, everyone, even these latter, are to be told about God's miracle that they may be united with their people in a collective memory of Israel's liberation. It is not only a question of what God has done in the remote past, but each must understand, "It is because what the LORD did for me when I came out of Egypt" (13:8). Each must know, "By strength of hand the LORD brought us out of Egypt, from the house of slavery" (13:14). The miracle is about me! We are liberated! The miracle takes place now! Only if this reality becomes alive to each one can Passover become a feast of remembrance in the way God intends it to be.

"And you shall tell . . .": this is the translation of the Hebrew expression *we-higgadta* (the noun for "telling" or "story" is *haggadah*). Because of the central commandment to tell the Passover story, this word bears a special meaning. The whole ritual for the celebration of the Passover meal is called the *Passover Haggadah* (Hebrew *Haggadah shel Pesah*). In addition to meal instructions, it contains a collection of interpretations and explanations of Bible texts that are related to the exodus. There are psalms,[14] hymns, and stories that bridge centuries and even thousands of years, uniting the generations through what Passover has come to mean.

The *Haggadah* has been translated into most major languages in the world and has gone through over four thousand editions. Every year new ones are published, often with additions and interpretations focusing on oppression and liberation in our own time.[15] The *Haggadah* is a living book, and reading it becomes particularly vivid when combined with the Passover meal, the various dishes of which are symbolically linked to the liberation from Egypt. All takes place according to a special order. Therefore, this meal is called the *seder* meal.

The Seder *Meal*

The Hebrew word *seder* means "order." The whole meal is a sort of dramatization of the exodus. Some dishes follow the biblical ordinances; others are linked to Passover in another way. One aim is to arouse the curiosity of the children by stimulating them to ask questions and by attaching the Passover story to something concrete that has form, color, and taste. In a way, Psalm 34:8 provides a main theme for the *seder* meal: "Taste and see that the LORD is good!" In front of the host a special demonstration plate is put. The following discussion lists the various dishes according to the order in which they are explained in the *Haggadah.*

(1) *Zeroaᶜ*. After the destruction of the temple, the paschal lamb could no longer be slaughtered. It is therefore present only in a symbolic way, represented by a roasted bone, *zeroaᶜ*. Usually it is not a bone from a lamb, and most Jews do not eat lamb at all during Passover, since it is not regarded as proper to do things reminiscent of rituals that could only be carried out in the time of the temple (cf. p. 236). There is no lamb present, and so non-Jewish guests are welcome at the meal, since the prohibition in 12:43–48 is only mentioned in connection with the lamb.

(2) *Matsoth*. Three *matsoth* (unleavened bread) are placed one above the other beside the *seder* plate. They are used in connection with the blessing over bread and wine—which inaugurates every Jewish feast—in order to fulfill the commandment to eat unleavened bread at Passover. Additionally, the middle wafer has a particular function. At the beginning of the meal it is broken in two. One half is wrapped in a cloth, and then one of the children usually hides it somewhere. This bread, called ʾ*afikoman,* is a special reminder of the Passover lamb and is eaten as the last bite to conclude the meal. It is therefore important that this half be found again. The one who has hidden it thus has a key function at the end of the *seder* and often uses it to bargain a promise to get a special gift later. In this way the curiosity and tension among the children is kept alive until the very end of the meal.

(3) *Maror.* The bitter herbs (Hebrew *maror*) are the third ingredient of the meal and are directly ordained in the Bible (12:8). Usually horseradish or lettuce (Hebrew *hazereth*) is used. Lettuce is in itself not bitter, but the stem has a bitter aftertaste. This reminds one of how life for the Israelites in Egypt was sweet to begin with but eventually was made bitter by the Egyptians (1:14).

(4) *Karpas. Karpas* is a Hebrew loanword from the Greek *karpos* which means "fruit." It is usually parsley or a piece of potato dipped in salt water (cf. Matt. 26:23). Before it is eaten, a blessing is said, expressing thanks to the Lord "who creates the fruit of the ground." Most commentaries interpret this tra-

dition as a general reminder of the slavery and tears in Egypt. In reality, however, it is a reminder of the sacrificial cult in the temple. According to Deut. 26:1–11, "some of the first of all the fruit of the ground" should be taken "to the place that the LORD your God will choose as a dwelling for his name," that is, later, to the temple in Jerusalem. In this way, the people express their gratitude to God for having brought them to the promised land and having granted them permission to enjoy its fruit, something that took place in the time of the Passover (see Josh. 5:10ff.).

(5) *Haroseth. Haroseth* is a mixture of apples, nuts, almonds, cinnamon, and wine. The red color reminds one of the mortar and bricks at the time of the slavery (1:14). The bitter herbs are dipped into this mixture (cf. Matt. 26:23).

(6) *Egg.* A roasted or blackened egg is interpreted in various ways. It can symbolize the thank-offering that the pilgrims sacrificed in the temple on Passover day according to the commandment: "No one shall appear before me empty-handed" (23:15).[16] The egg is also the symbol of mourning and serves as a reminder of the temple, the destruction of which put an end to the Passover offerings. Others understand the egg to be a symbol of the rescue of the Jewish people from oppression and persecutions. Just as the egg gets harder the more it is boiled, Israel has become stronger the more it has been tested in the furnace of suffering.

(7) *Wine.* During the *seder* meal, four cups of wine are required. A common rabbinic tradition understands them as symbols of the four ways in which the Lord will save the people according to 6:6–7: "I will free you from under the burdens of the Egyptians, and I will deliver you from their bondage, and I will redeem you with an outstreched arm and with great acts of judgment, and I will take you for my people, and I will be your God" (see p. 50). Two cups are drunk before the main meal and two after. The third cup is called both the cup of salvation and the cup of blessing. It is drunk before "the hymn" (see p. 87, n. 14) and is the cup mentioned in connection with the Last Supper (see Matt. 26:27–30; Luke 22:20; 1 Cor. 10:16).

In the light of 6:8—"I will bring you into the land that I swore to give to Abraham, Isaac, and Jacob"—one could contend that even a fifth cup ought to be drunk. This has, indeed, been discussed in Jewish tradition. Eventually it became customary to pour a fifth cup without drinking it. It is called

Elijah's cup and is a reminder of the future salvation in connection with the coming of the Messiah (cf. Mal. 4:5–6).

Bound for Freedom implies a future tense. In this era, God's people will always look forward to the final redemption, since what God has done so far is no more than a beginning of something even greater to be fulfilled only on "that day." This is expressed in the concluding words of the *Haggadah:* "Next year in Jerusalem!" or, as is said by those who are celebrating Passover in Jerusalem, "Next year in rebuilt Jerusalem!"—the Jerusalem where all promises are realized (see p. 51). The remembrance of the past constantly supports this hope.

A Sign and a Memorial

The remembrance theme of Passover is further stressed by one commandment in particular. According to 13:9 and 13:16, the liberation from Egypt shall be a "sign" on your hand and a "reminder" between your eyes, in order that the law of the Lord may be in your mouth.[17] Mentioning these parts of the body underlines the remembrance as an activity that influences the whole personality. The miracle of liberation has to become a personal experience with consequences for life. If I truly remember that the Lord has brought me personally out of Egypt, then it must influence my thoughts and feelings, my words and deeds.

The admonition to let God's word be a sign on the hand and the forehead is repeated four times: 13:9, 16, Deut. 6:8, and 11:18. These passages stress the responsibility for transmitting tradition to coming generations. In a Jewish tradition that can be traced back at least to the third century B.C.E., this commandment is to be taken literally. That is, a visible sign shall actually be bound on the hand and arm and on the forehead.[18]

This understanding is in accord with the context in Deut. 6:8, where the following verse obviously deals with an actual inscription of something on the doorposts. The translations usually conceal this concrete meaning by saying that something shall be bound "as" a sign. The Hebrew text does not use this comparative word *(ke)* but the preposition "to" *(le),* which indicates that something shall indeed be bound "to be" a sign. Therefore, the passages are written on parchment that are put in two small leather boxes. One is bound on the upper left arm,[19] and the other is placed on the forehead just above the edge of the scalp. They are called *tefillin,* which means "sign" (see further p. 257, n. 13).

The binding of *tefillin* constitutes a visible creed. Through this sign, one acknowledges a desire to put one's body in the service of God and unite one's own weak arm with his strong one.   This is a proper response to the liberation from slavery to freedom and an appropriate expression of what it means to be bound for freedom. The *tefillin* are a sign of both freedom and obedience.

Like many other concrete commandments this is also a covenantal sign (see pp. 190f., 195, 238, 242ff.). The binding of *tefillin* is concluded by winding the strap around the middle finger like a wedding ring while the words from Hos. 2:19–20 are recited: "And I will take you for my wife forever; I will take you for my wife in righteousness and in justice, in steadfast love, and in mercy. I will take you for my wife in faithfulness; and you shall know the LORD" (see also pp. 131, n. 6, 151f., 254).

This mutuality of the covenant between the Lord and the people is also articulated very strongly in Isa. 49:16, where the Lord is said to carry the people as a sign: "See, I have inscribed you on the palms of my hands."

"Consecrate to Me All the Firstborn . . ." (13:1–2, 11–16)

Even consecrating the firstborn males of both humans and animals is an act of remembrance. The commandment is mentioned immediately before the question asked by the child in 13:14 and shall serve as a "sign" (v. 16). The meaning of this act is expressed in the answer to the child: "by strength of hand the LORD brought us out of Egypt, from the house of slavery." The thought is thus asserted that the firstborn males of humans and beasts are a living remembrance of the liberation. Therefore, the firstlings of cattle and people belong to the Lord, not because of inherent holiness, but solely through God's decision. God has the right to them, and therefore they shall be dedicated to their rightful owner. The firstfruits of the field (23:19; see pp. 174f.) and the clean animals shall be sacrificed, while the ass has to be redeemed with a lamb—or killed—since it is unclean (13:13; 34:20; cf. Lev. 27:27). To use the donkey would mean stealing it from the owner, the Lord himself.

As the firstborn, every male who "opens the womb" is counted. One who is born after a miscarriage or who is delivered through cesarean section is consequently not regarded as a firstborn even if the first child. Neither does a firstborn son whose mother or father is a descendant of a priest *(kohen)* or a Levite need to be redeemed, since he is already regarded as consecrated to the Lord.[22] All other firstborn males have to be redeemed. This is done on the thirty-first day by delivering them to a priest who gives them back after the payment of a particular ransom coin (Num. 18:15–16).[23] Since Jesus was a firstborn, Joseph and Mary observed this commandment (Luke 2:22–23).

When Israel consecrates the first to the Lord, the totality is symbolically delivered (cf. Rom. 11:16). In this way even this commandment became a reminder of the calling received by the people to be consecrated to God as a kingdom of priests and a holy nation (see 19:5–6). In other words, this is a covenantal act. All the people are God's firstborn and possession (see 4:22–23; Hos. 11:1), initially demonstrated by the Lord during the first Passover. Therefore, Passover is the feast of remembrance for all future generations.

The firstborn, however, also brings a reminder of a totally different kind, a painful reminder (see pp. 108ff.). God's firstborn son, Israel, is redeemed, as it were, through the firstborn of Egypt. Before God's firstborn can leave toward freedom and a new life, other firstborn sons have to pay a high price for their own or other peoples' evil. The house of bondage still keeps its doors obstinately closed for the people whose God can no longer be trifled with. The birth pangs therefore enter their final, decisive stage.

The connection between the consecration of the firstborn in Israel and the slaying of the firstborn in Egypt should not be overlooked. As a matter of fact, the Egyptians have prevented God's people from serving their God. Israel's firstborn will be spared and redeemed later when they are able to serve God according to their calling; the Egyptians do not have this option.

Therefore, the final strike is actually to be understood as God's demonstration of his sovereignty over Pharaoh and Egypt by collecting their unredeemed firstborn and firstlings.[24] Their rebellion against the God of Israel now transforms this collection of what rightfully belongs to God into a harvest of death.

THE FINAL STRIKE (12:29–36)

Only two verses are needed to describe the final, lethal strike (vv. 29–30), and after another two verses the unconditional capitulation of Pharaoh is a fact. The "loud cry" predicted by Moses (11:6) is like a whistle announcing that the war has come to an end, or at least to a halt. This tragic and yet wonderful unraveling of a long drama of liberation, however, should not have been surprising to any participant. After repeated warnings, God in nine painful plagues has proven who has all the power in heaven and earth. Moreover, this final strike has been announced in every detail (4:22–23; 11:4–8). Any further descriptions of the last plague are therefore superfluous. Since Pharaoh has defied all the warnings, the outcome is predictable.

In the middle of the night Pharaoh has to forget his ambitions for divinity and realize that he is no more than an ordinary mortal of flesh and blood, a father who has lost his beloved son, a human being with the same feelings of grief and fear of death as anybody else. Life and death are not in his hands but totally in the hands of the God who has struck the Egyptians with this fatal plague, while miraculously saving the Israelites.

The message is clear. This is the judgment against Pharaoh for having refused to let Israel leave. But it is, above all, judgment against "all the gods of Egypt." Finally, the reality behind the words "I am the LORD" (12:12) dawns on him. He realizes that the God of Israel has gained the victory. Therefore, he has to accede to the right of Israel to exist as a free nation, and for the first time he pronounces the word "Israel" (12:31).

He relinquishes the last condition to let the people go— "only your flocks and your herds shall remain behind" (10:24)—and says: "Take your flocks and your herds, as you said, and be gone" (12:32). He is also aware of the purpose of the liberation: "Go, worship the LORD, as you said" (12:31). Nothing is left of the previous conditions he had set up—first, that they could worship the Lord within the land of Egypt (8:25, 28), second, that only the males could leave (10:8ff.), and finally, that they had to leave the livestock behind (10:24). The unconditional capitulation is a fact. At last he indirectly confesses the might of the Lord by expressing his own dependence upon him as he petitions Moses and Aaron for a blessing (12:32).[25]

In yet another respect, God's promises are fulfilled on this night. Twice before, he has given a strange prediction to the people: they will not leave empty-handed but will receive silver, gold, and clothing from the Egyptians. Therefore, they shall not hesitate to ask their neighbors for such gifts (3:21–22; 11:2; cf. Ps. 105:37). A similar promise is actually given generations before. Already Abraham was told that his descendants would be slaves in a foreign country, but would finally come out "with great possessions" (Gen. 15:13–14).

Now we are told that the promise is being fulfilled (12:35–36). The conclusion, however, is enigmatic: "And so they plundered the Egyptians." This statement that the Israelites plundered the Egyptians is certainly not in accord with what is said before, that is, that they would ask their neighbors for gifts, which they would grant since "the LORD had given the people favor in the sight of the Egyptians, so that they let them have what they asked."

Obviously, the Egyptians sympathized with the Israelites, and in spite of the slavery the relations seem to have been good. This conclusion is confirmed by the notice that it was particularly the women who made the deal, and that the objects received should be put on the children (3:22). So, evidently, they were not spoils but gifts of friendship, which gives us reason to believe that the Egyptians and Israelites lived in proximity to each other in good neighborly relations.

If so, how do we understand the strange concluding remark in 12:36? The translation of the verb *natsal* in the Piel form by "despoiled" is far from irrefutable. It appears in this form only in two other passages (2 Chron. 20:25 and Ezek. 14:14). In the former verse it obviously means "plunder," while in the latter it means "deliver," or "save."[26] In medieval Hebrew sources, the verb means to "excuse somebody" and "free somebody from guilt," which is not very far from the meaning "save," that is, save somebody from guilt.[27] Probably later Jewish tradition has preserved a very old meaning of the verb, which indeed helps us to understand this text in a way that does justice to the context.

The concluding remark would then explain that the Israelites and the Egyptians finally reconciled with one another and parted in peace. The gifts expressed this reconciliation. In the midst of the darkness of oppression and death there is a glimpse of hope. And, again, women are the particular instruments to bring about this hope of a better world where forgiveness, rapprochement, and even friendship, defy the uttermost challenges.

The realization of the promise to Abraham in Gen. 15:14 is not depleted by these relatively modest gifts but rather by the cattle that the liberated people brought with them (12:38; cf. 10:25–26). Nonetheless, the gifts from the Egyptians would leave an indelible imprint on the memory of the Israelites for the future. They would even come to influence the laws of slavery. Since they did not leave empty-handed, it was indeed their duty to outfit their slaves at their departure (see Deut. 15:13ff.; pp. 158ff.).[28]

After a long and painful period of preparation, the liberty bell finally proclaims the hour of freedom, a new dawn for the enslaved and afflicted people: "The Israelites journeyed" (12:37). Hereafter we will follow the first dangerous steps of the liberated people, bound for freedom.

7

The Liberation

*T*he people of Israel will never be the same after the harrowing experience narrated in this portion of Exodus. The first tottering steps of the exodus are a tightrope walk between life and death, rescue and disaster. It is not just a miracle, a revelation among others. According to Jewish tradition no other prophetic revelation would surpass this miraculous event.[1] Emil Fackenheim similarly calls the divine deliverance from Egypt through the waters of the sea, as well as the revelation at Sinai later Israel's two "root experiences."[2] All the people witness these events simultaneously. Furthermore, they can never forget what they have experienced and will transmit it from generation to generation as something eternally relevant and ever present. This first liberation will foreshadow, or rather spotlight, all subsequent acts of salvation. The people of Israel become bearers of a collective memory, constantly fusing history and present time and even forming future hope.

Israel is saved, and born as a people, out of the sea. The rescue through the sea therefore becomes an indispensable part of Israel's "birth history" and even traces out the blueprint for the eschatological salvation of humankind. This miracle, soon to be witnessed, inaugurates a new era for Israel and in a wider sense for the entire world (see, for example, Isa. 11:10–16; 51:9–11).[3]

THE PATH OF LIBERATION (13:17–14:2)

From the very first verse a basic theme of Israel's exodus is highlighted: the way God has determined for them is not a convenient shortcut. It is a long, winding, and dangerous road. The ancient coastal route along the Mediterranean through the land of the Philistines could have been managed in two weeks![4]

As different as heaven is from earth (Isa. 55:8–9), however, so do God's ways differ from those of human beings. There is no shortcut from slavery to freedom. The newborn people must learn to walk, and this will take at least a generation under the Lord's guidance in the world's wilderness. The promised land is further away than human maps indicate. "God led the people by the roundabout way of the wilderness" (13:18) is a kind of divine manifesto, which God's people again and again will come to experience during their walk toward the fulfillment of their Lord's promises.

The reason for this roundabout route is said to be the immediate danger of war lying along the closest route. This reasoning fits well with ancient Egyptian sources that describe the road along the Mediterranean. The flat land made the northern border very vulnerable to attacks. Therefore, a line of fortresses was built to afford a northern defense against the enemy. The Israelites consequently would have encountered numerous well-trained soldiers had they chosen that way. Moreover, they would have quickly reached the land of Canaan only to confront the peoples living there. A newly liberated slave population would probably not have been ready for such an enormous challenge.

Therefore, they now head toward the "Red Sea," in Hebrew *Yam Suf.* This name refers to the common Egyptian reeds (Hebrew *suf;* see 2:3, 5). Even though so many places are recorded in connection with the exodus (see Num. 33:5–37), it is not clear exactly which route the people took and which area "the Reed Sea" refers to.[5]

The first place mentioned is Succoth, about one day's journey east of Rameses (see p. 8). The next place, Etham, was probably located further toward the east, "on the edge of the wilderness." But how did they then proceed? According to 14:2, they were to "turn back and encamp in front of Pi-ha-hiroth, between Migdol and the sea, in front of Baal-zephon."[6] None of these locations are now known. Therefore, several possibilities are left open. Obviously they returned to habitable areas again. Since Pharaoh understands their moves as if they were "entangled in the land," they have probably made a circuit before having encamped, waiting for the next dramatic phase of their departure. It is also obvious that they were now in close proximity to the "Reed Sea."

There are numerous theories locating this water, which can be summarized into three main groups.[7] One locates it as far to the north as possible, at the Mediterranean. A bay bends toward the southwest of today's Port Said, and another further to the east, halfway between Port Said and El-Arish. Papyrus grows in both of these bays. Strong east winds are common in the area (see 14:21), as are big alternations in the water level contingent on these winds and the tides.[8] Notwithstanding this, this theory seems less probable, since the Israelites are explicitly told to avoid the coastal road (see p. 112, n. 1).

A second theory suggests a location as far to the south as possible, at the Gulf of Suez. After the crossing, the route would have continued along the eastern shore toward the southern part of the Sinai peninsula. Mount Sinai is traditionally located at the site of St. Catherine's Monastery. This tradition, however, is late and cannot be traced further back than the fourth century C.E., when the first Christian church was built in the area. The great distance from Goshen in the northern Nile delta further speaks against this theory, as does the total lack of papyrus near the Red Sea.

More probable is the identification of the "Reed Sea" with the "Bitter Lakes," north of today's Suez and toward Ismailiya. Therefore, Mount Sinai is probably located further north in the Sinai peninsula than the common Christian tradition assumes. Jewish tradition was never particularly interested in pinpointing this mountain. The very thought that a particular place holds a lasting, inherent holiness is basically alien to the Bible. Geographic holiness occurs only when and where the Lord will "put his name." A place remains holy only while God is revealing himself there (see ch. 3).[9] Consequently, in Jewish tradition the what of the exodus has totally overshadowed the where of the exodus.

THE CHALLENGE OF LIBERATION (14:3–18)

The path toward liberation is paved with dangers and temptations. The liberated people immediately face major challenges. One comes from outside: Pharaoh and his army.

The second one is already there in their midst: doubt, distrust, and disbelief. The external enemies will change; the internal ones remain the same. Now comes the first great test.

Already while mourning the loss of his firstborn son, Pharaoh has begun to regret letting the people go (14:5). When the implications of the liberation dawn upon the people, they also regret that they have left. Facing the danger of the approaching Egyptian army, they are seized with fright and wish themselves back in the calm and irresponsible life of slavery (14:11, cf. 16:3; Num. 14:1–4). After all, degradation is better than destruction!

Even though both Pharaoh and the Israelites have clearly witnessed the strong hand of the Lord in action, it is now as if they had seen nothing. It is obvious that miracles are able neither to frighten nor to entice anyone to believe, at least not immediately. Both the Egyptians and the Israelites are, as it were, blindfolded. Neither of the two seriously counts on the God who holds both creation and history in his hands. Even if the intimidated people of Israel do cry out to the Lord (14:10), they expect destruction (v. 11). At the human level, the victory is Pharaoh's and the hope seemingly exhausted for Israel, fatally trapped between the Egyptian army and the sea. Their newly acquired freedom is shortly to be no more than a memory.

It is in this desperate situation that Moses must proclaim the comfort of the Lord: today you encounter the threat of Pharaoh for the last time. You will soon witness something totally different, the salvation of the Lord. "The LORD will fight for you, and you have only to keep still" (14:13–14). The same bright conviction is echoed as a basic theme throughout the Bible: "For not in my bow do I trust, nor can my sword save me. But you have saved us from our foes, and have put to confusion those who hate us" (Ps. 44:6–7); "Not by might, nor by power, but by my Spirit, says the LORD of hosts" (Zech. 4:6).

Nonetheless, "For everything there is a season, and a time for every matter under heaven" (Eccl. 3:1). In this hour of destiny, both preaching and prayer have to be short. Therefore, even Moses is challenged by the Lord: "Why do you cry out to me? Tell the Israelites to go forward" (v. 15). In plain language, now is not the proper time for prayer! Now is the time for action. Now is the time to leave. So desist from talking to me; talk to the people. Order them to proceed!

The almost reproachful words of God to Moses—
"Why do you cry to me?"—have naturally sparked many
observations in the rabbinic commentaries. "The Holy One,
blessed be He, said to Moses: 'Moses, My children are in
distress, the sea forming a bar and the enemy pursuing, and
you stand there reciting long prayers; wherefore criest thou
unto Me?' "[10]

The commentary then points out that "there is a time to
be brief in prayer and a time to be lengthy." We will find a good
example of the latter in Moses' intercession for his people,
when they have fallen in sin and it is too late to warn them
(chs. 32–33). But now is the time for action and to rely on the
enduring validity of the words in 2:24–25 (see p. 25). And even
more than that: "Before they call I will answer, while they are
yet speaking I will hear" (Isa. 65:24).[11]

THE MIRACLE OF LIBERATION (14:19–31)

What no eye has seen, nor ear heard, nor the heart of
man conceived, God has already prepared. He has already
outlined the plan (14:16–18). As an outward sign of the realization of this plan, the pillar of cloud moves behind so as to
form a protecting shield between the Israelites and the Egyptians (14:19–20).

What is now enacted before the eyes of both peoples, can
be given a natural explanation to a large extent. The partly
shallow Bitter Lakes as well as the equally shallow swamps
along the Mediterranean shores during low tide and under the
influence of "a strong east wind" (14:21) can be almost emptied of water. It is, however, senseless to speculate about how
much or how little can be explained through "normal" natural
phenomena. The story is in any case totally incomprehensible
unless the key word is taken seriously, a word appearing no
fewer than seven times in this chapter: "hand."

This word refers once to the Israelites. It is said in 14:8
that Pharaoh "pursued the Israelites, who were going out
boldly"; the Hebrew words translated by "boldly," *beyad ramah,*
literally mean "with raised hand." In 14:30 the word "hand"
refers to the Egyptians, literally "Thus the LORD saved Israel
that day from the hand of Egypt." In four cases (14:16, 21, 26,
27), it is Moses' hand that is at work.

Ultimately, the Lord is the one who works through Moses. Moses' hand is the glove in which God's hand works. When Moses raises his hand, God performs his miracles. The chapter concludes with the decisive statement, "Israel saw the great work that the LORD did against the Egyptians"; literally, they saw "the great hand that the Lord did with Egypt." All of nature rests in God's hand. He masters all its resources, and demonstrates through his servant how he takes the hand of a frail human being and performs with it what no human hand is otherwise able to accomplish.

Consequently, the natural and completely human in no way contrasts or diminishes the supernatural and divine. Here we witness how through Moses God achieves the objective of saving the firstborn son, Israel, the future tool for God's plan of salvation for the whole world. It is for this reason that the wind blows in the direction and with the necessary force at the precise moment for Israel to cross the sea, while their persecutors remain embedded in the mud and finally fall victim to the evil they have planned for others (cf. Ps. 7:14–16).

An Egyptian inscription describing the divine attributes of Pharaoh is remarkable when read in the light of what we have just witnessed. This inscription compares Pharaoh to a horrifying goddess called Sekhmet, who sends all kinds of diseases. Those who spurn Pharaoh will face a terrible end:

> He is Sekhmet against him who transgresses his command; he whom he hates will bear woes [or sickness]. Fight on behalf of his name, and be scrupulous in the oath to him, that ye may be free from a taint of disloyalty. He whom the king has loved will be a revered one, but there is no tomb for a rebel against his majesty, and his corpse is cast into the water.[12]

Pharaoh's house has been hit by the most dreadful disease, and there is no tomb for his mighty army. On the contrary, it is they who are "cast into the water,"[13] and it is Moses, the leader of the rebellion against him, who stands dry-shod on the other shore, together with his people. Now the tables are turned.

The secret behind this turn of events is drastically expressed in 12:41: "At the end of four hundred thirty years, on that very day, all the companies [or armies, divisions] of the LORD went out from the land of Egypt." The people bound for freedom is God's army, and Moses is God's commander (see also 6:26; 7:4; 12:17, 51). But above all, "the

LORD is a warrior; the LORD is his name. Pharaoh's chariots and his army he cast into the sea" (15:3–4; see below). The exact indication of the timing proclaims God's unswerving faithfulness and unfailing ability to carry out a strategy to the very end. Only the Lord can proclaim: "There is no one like me in all the earth" (9:14).

Therefore, yet another dimension of the miracle at the sea surfaces over the roaring waters in the soaring wind. Not surprisingly, virtually all elements recorded at the beginning of the creation story are present here: the water itself; the "wind," in the creation story usually translated "spirit;"[14] the dry land; the darkness (covering the Egyptians); and the light (leading Israel). Even the motif of dividing the sea is reminiscent of a similar process "in the beginning": God creates by dividing waters from waters (Gen. 1:6–7) and gathers the waters together so that the dry land might appear (Gen. 1:9; cf. 8:14).

In the miracle at the sea we recognize the features of the creator of the world in the savior of Israel. In a trembling moment, the world is brought back to the chaotic situation "in the beginning," when an act of divine creation is needed to overcome chaos. This is not the first time, nor will it be the last, that the motif of creation and salvation, as well as creation and revelation, are fused. It will resound in the mighty song of victory soon to be sung by the people bound for freedom (ch. 15). This miracle reveals the rescue of a group of slaves and marks a necessary act of reparation for all of creation as well as an act of preparation for universal redemption (cf. pp. 105ff.).

The Lord performs yet another miracle that is equally beyond human power: "Israel saw the great work that the LORD did against the Egyptians, and the people feared the LORD and believed in the LORD and in his servant Moses."[15] To witness a miracle does not necessarily lead to fear of God and faith. This has constantly been demonstrated both among the Egyptians and the Israelites until now. To realize and acknowledge the power of the Lord, which the Egyptians must finally do (14:25), is not the same as having faith. Neither is the fear of divine judgment and punishment that leads one to cry to God in distress, a fear demonstrated by Pharaoh (cf. 10:16–17), the same fear presented here.

No, to fear and believe in God results from a miracle of God, a miracle that transforms one's whole life. It means seeing God's great hand where others see only the blind forces of nature or destiny. But above all, it is to grasp that hand and make it the guide and support in every situation of life. Where this miracle occurs, a new song will be heard, a song glorifying God in a way similar to what we now hear the Israelites sing.

THE SONG OF LIBERATION (15:1–21)

This is the song of praise and victory sung by a people saved. This song intones the same refrain sung by the apostle centuries later: "By grace you have been saved through faith, and this is not your own doing; it is the gift of God, not the result of works, so that no one may boast" (Eph. 2:8–9).

There is no room for boasting about anything other than the Lord's gratuitous love for Israel. When the people are saved they lack even faith, not to mention deeds, upon which to build their hope. It is only after their rescue we find stated that they believed in the Lord (14:31). Amazed and astounded, they can only witness the unexpected miracle of God. A Jewish midrash focuses in particular on the words, "In your steadfast love you led the people whom you redeemed" (15:13), and states, "Thou hast shown us mercy, for we had no meritorious deeds to show, as it is said: 'I will make mention of the mercies of the Lord' (Isa. 63:7); 'I will sing of the mercies of the Lord for ever' " (Ps. 89:1).[16] Exultation, therefore, breaks forth like a powerful flood, a jubilant song made up of variations on one single theme.

Soli Deo Gloria—*Glory to God Alone!*

This song, "the Song of the Sea," is in this respect different from all similar songs of victory yet found among the surrounding peoples. In those, the king is the focus of the interest. Even though he may be supported by the gods, the purpose of the texts is to glorify the earthly ruler for the victory he has achieved.

Scholars have noticed the similarities between chapters 14 and 15 and stories dealing with the victories of Rameses II and his sons. They also consist of descriptive prose with a supplementary poetic song praising the victory.

When Rameses II had defeated the Hittites (ca. 1280 B.C.E.), a hymn was composed which begins in this way:

His majesty was a youthful lord,
Active and without his like;
His arms mighty, his heart stout,
His strength like Mont in his hour.
Of perfect form like Atum,
Hailed when his beauty is seen;
Victorious over all lands,
Wily in launching a fight.[17]

Once the song has described the beauty and boldness and multiple qualifications of Pharaoh, the ruler himself starts to talk. He lists all his good deeds before the god Amon, all the precious offerings he has given, the temples he has built, and the obelisks he has raised high in honor of the god. Based on this he hopes for the favor of the god in battle. The description of the victory is concluded by the following words: "My majesty overpowered them, I slew them without sparing them." Finally, the letter of capitulation of the defeated Hittite king is quoted. It begins with the words, "You are Seth, Baal in person."[18]

In the light of this and like songs of victory, the words in 15:9 become vivid and realistic: "The enemy said, 'I will pursue, I will overtake, I will divide the spoil, my desire shall have its fill of them. I will draw my sword, my hand shall destroy them.' " The following verses pose a glaring contrast between the "I" and "my" of the enemy and the "you" and "your" of the Lord: "You blew with your wind, the sea covered them; they sank like lead in the mighty waters. Who is like you, O LORD, among the gods? Who is like you, majestic in holiness, awesome in splendor, doing wonders?"

Despite Israel's total victory over the Egyptians, there is not a hint of any self-righteous and self-glorifying triumphalism. The introductory words set the tone for the whole hymn: "I will sing to the LORD, for he has triumphed gloriously; horse and rider he has thrown into the sea. The LORD is my strength and my might [or song], and he has become my salvation."

The words "the Lord," "God," "he," "you," and "your" reverberate from beginning to end and are the only ones to describe the victorious champion. It is his right hand, and not that of Moses, that has acted. Moses is not even mentioned in the song, which concludes with a jubilant credo: "The LORD will reign forever and ever."

This is the grand *Te Deum* of Israel, which models the song of praise in the Bible, in Jewish worship, and in Christian liturgy. There is no room for boasting of any human achievement. The motto is, "My soul makes its boast in the LORD; let the humble hear and be glad. O magnify the LORD with me, and let us exalt his name together" (Ps. 34:2–3). "Do not let the wise boast in their wisdom, do not let the mighty boast in their might; do not let the wealthy boast in their wealth; but let those who boast boast in this, that they understand and know me, that I am the LORD; I act with steadfast love, justice, and righteousness in the earth, for in these things I delight, says the LORD" (Jer. 9:23–24; cf. Luke 2:46–55; 1 Cor. 1:26–31).

Therefore, it is not surprising that this first song of Israel is rendered in the same humble spirit when it is later repeated in the Bible: The tragic destruction of the Egyptians as well as the role of Moses are downplayed, even ignored, while the power of the Lord is proclaimed with unabated intensity (see, e.g., Josh. 2:10; 4:22; 24:5ff.; Neh. 9:9ff.; Ps. 66:5ff.; 77:15ff.; 78:12ff.; 105:23ff.; 106:9ff.; 114; 136:13ff.; Isa. 51:10; 63:11ff.; cf. Deut. 32:48ff.).[19]

It is thus striking, but hardly surprising, that Moses is not mentioned even once in the Jewish *Passover Haggadah*, which contains so many texts and traditions related to the exodus out of Egypt! For even this book echoes the tone of the Song of the Sea with its basic theme, *Soli Deo Gloria*. This tone extinguishes every effort to elevate the human at the expense of the divine. The whole concept of the *Haggadah* can be summed up in the confession: "The LORD brought us forth from Egypt: not by the hands of an angel, and not by the hands of a seraph, and not by the hands of a messenger, but the Holy One, blessed be he, himself, in his own glory and in his own person."[20] The glory belongs to God, God alone!

A New Song

This song has gained a position in Jewish tradition, unique in the Bible.[21] Already artistically expressed when written in the Torah scrolls, it is recited in the synagogue as the congregation stands in adoration in a way done only at the reading of "the ten commandments." The Sabbath on which it is read is called "the Sabbath of Song" *(Shabbath Shirah)* and has a particularly solemn character. It is further recited on the last day of Passover (see 23:15), when, according to tradition, the miracle took place. On this day, big crowds in Israel gather at the shores of the Mediterranean and the Red Sea in Eilat to read the Song at the Sea. It is not read only on special occasions, however, but has become a fixed part of the daily liturgy.

The Song of the Sea has never lost its freshness and relevance. For it not only deals with God's acts of salvation in the past but also proclaims God's power and grace for the future. When the miracle at the sea is referred to in Ps. 77, it is by a person who is seeking God's help in the present and who knows: "You are the God who works wonders; you have displayed your might among the peoples" (Ps. 77:14). The era of miracles is not past; this also applies to the day ahead. In a similar way, the prophet refers to the rescue through the sea: "Was it not you who dried up the sea, the waters of the great deep; who made the depths of the sea a way for the redeemed to cross over?" Significantly, he immediately continues: "So the ransomed of the LORD shall return, and come to Zion with singing; everlasting joy shall be upon their heads" (Isa. 51:10–11).

This intimate connection among past, present, and future is based upon both the content and the structure of the song. We notice that it does not deal only with what the Lord has already done. From 15:13 forward it opens up the future perspective. There, the issue is the continued guidance of the Lord, how he will lead his people to his "holy abode."

Soon the people will witness a miracle as great as that at the sea. The Lord will descend on Mount Sinai and take his abode among them when he has them building the tabernacle below the mountain. And, one day after the long desert walk, they will build a sanctuary on the site that the Lord has already chosen, the one called "the mountain of your own possession" (v. 17), Mount Zion in Jerusalem, the holy city.

The Song of the Sea makes it clear that the salvation through the sea is not an isolated case. The first victory is only a partial victory. New enemies are lurking. New challenges are waiting. The following chapters will immediately demonstrate what a long and difficult way lies ahead. The only hope is that God will repeat his miracles and save his people (cf.

vv. 14ff.), who are bound for freedom through God's promises and his ability to fulfill them.

Another striking feature makes the Song of the Sea, also called "the Song of Moses," the special song of future salvation (cf. Rev. 15:3). It begins with the words, "Then Moses and the Israelites sang this song to the LORD." The verb "to sing," however, is written not in the past tense but in the future, not in the perfect aspect but in the imperfect, since the liberation just experienced is not perfect. Yet.

Even though such a strict distinction between past and future tenses does not apply to ancient biblical poetry, the rabbinic tradition reads it with the hint of an underlying eschatological meaning and stresses a literal rendering of the text: "Then Moses and the Israelites will sing . . . ." The song was first sung in gratitude over the miracle on that particular occasion when the people were saved through the sea. But to the rabbis the tense of the verb also implied that there will come a day when this song will be sung again and then in a way as never before.[22]

A new song will be heard, which is new and at the same time a repetition of the first song at the shore of the "Reed Sea." The exhortation, "O sing to the LORD a new song; sing to the LORD, all the earth" (Ps. 96:1; cf. 33:3; 40:4; 98:1; 144:9; 149:1; Isa. 42:10), is not merely about renewal of the liturgy and worship in general. Ultimately, it refers to a renewal of the whole world, a new creation and a new era with a new communion, when all nations will join in the confession, "The LORD will reign forever and ever" (15:18).

The daily Jewish morning prayer contains a constant reminder of this future aspect of the exodus. With a direct reference to the "Song of the Sea," it glorifies God for the miracle in the past and immediately expresses hope for the future:

> Praise be to God the Most High, blessed be he and he is blessed. Moses and the children of Israel sang a song to you with great joy and they all said: "Who is like you, O LORD, among the gods? Who is like you, majestic in holiness, awesome in splendor, doing wonders?" With a new song the redeemed glorified your name by the shore of the sea. Together they all gave thanks and acknowledged your sovereignty and said: "The LORD will reign forever and ever." O Rock of Israel, arise to the help of Israel, and set Judah and Israel free as you have promised. O our Redeemer, the LORD of Hosts, the Holy of Israel is his name. Blessed are you, the LORD, who has redeemed Israel.[23]

Again, the past warrants final freedom. A new song of praise will be sung, amplified by the experience of miracles even more wonderful.

The oldest rabbinic commentary on 15:1 presents no fewer than ten different songs that the children of Israel sing on various occasions. In addition to the Song of the Sea, reference is made to Isa. 30:29; Num. 21:17; Deut. 32; Josh. 10:12; Judg. 5; 2 Sam. 22; Ps. 30; and 2 Chron. 20:21. After these nine references, the commentary continues, "The tenth song will be recited in the future, as it is said: 'Sing unto the Lord a new song, and His praise from the end of the earth' (Isa. 42:10). And it also says: 'Sing unto the Lord a new song, and His praise in the assembly of the saints'" (Ps. 149:1).[24]

The commentary makes an interesting observation at this point: in 15:1 a feminine form of the word for "song" is used (shirah), while the masculine form (shir) is used in the previous two references. This difference calls attention to the travail and subsequent joy of a woman after each birth. The first nine songs were followed by others, but interspersed with pain and oppression. The last song, however, will never cease, for suffering will once and forever be past. The salvation that God's people time and again have experienced throughout history is but a foretaste of what is to occur fully at the end of times.[25]

According to one midrash, the heavenly throne was located immediately over the heads of the Israelites when they first sang the Song of Moses. In the future they will once again sing this song, and then they will finally be home to sing the song in front of the divine throne. The people bound for freedom will then enjoy total freedom forever.

It is certainly this Jewish tradition that is behind the vision in Rev. 15:2ff. There the threatening waters of the sea on earth are solidified into a peaceful crystal sea in heaven, and the saved multitude sing "the song of Moses, the servant of God, and the song of the Lamb."

THE ENIGMA OF LIBERATION

The way of liberation is not easily comprehended. Only on "that day" will the mystery of liberation be finally solved. The questions surrounding this mystery are manifold: why is the road to freedom so long and hard for God's people? Why does the way to life lead through so much pain? Why do many others have to perish when God saves Israel? Why does it take such a long time before God's revelation to this tiny little nation becomes acknowledged, known, and received in the world? The questions surrounding suffering arise early in the Bible. Later, Peter wanted to escape them by suggesting a bypass around the difficult and enigmatic (Matt. 16:21ff.). In a wider sense we are dealing with ancient questions of humankind regarding the presence of evil in the world side by side with Almighty God.

These questions become urgent when we witness the rescued Israelites on the other shore surrounded by the dead corpses of the Egyptians. Was there really no other way to freedom?

The Jewish commentaries have not been able to solve this mystery, but they have not avoided wrestling with it. The rabbis realized the danger of triumphalism and self-glorification in the story of the Exodus and the final victory over the Egyptians. Jewish tradition has consistently tried to diminish the role of Moses and of the people involved in the event. Even more, we will hereafter see how the behavior of the people sets a warning to subsequent generations.

However, the fact remains that Israel is saved and a considerable part of the Egyptian people are afflicted and a number finally destroyed. That the Israelite people break into a song of victory in this situation comes exceedingly close to the danger expressed in the following warning: "Do not rejoice when your enemies fall, and do not let your heart be glad when they stumble" (Prov. 24:17; see p. 175).

Aware of this dilemma, one rabbinic commentary describes a scene in front of the heavenly throne. The angels wish to sing a song of praise when they witness what happens to the Egyptians. Before they even start, however, they are reproached and fully silenced by God himself with the words, "The work of my hands are drowned in the sea, and you want to sing songs?"[26]

This attitude of humbleness and mercy is not merely something that can be traced in one text or another. It has become such an integral part of Judaism that it has even entered the liturgy. During the three pilgrimage feasts, Passover,

Pentecost, and the Feast of Tabernacles (see 23:14–17), and during Hanukkah (the Feast of Dedication), *Hallel* is recited daily, that is the Hallelujah psalms (113–118). In this respect, Passover, however, is partly an exception. Only on the first day of Passover is the whole *Hallel* recited, while it is shortened during the remaining six days (Ps. 113–114; 117–118). According to a rabbinic explanation, this is done so that Israel should remember the destruction of the Egyptians. Because of the Egyptians' misfortune, Israel's own joy cannot be full. Neither, therefore, can the song of praise be full![27] If the enemy is destroyed that we might be saved, then salvation is only fragmentary and imperfect. Any suffering, even that of the enemy, should make us reflect upon and subdue the joy we may feel.

A similar reminder is given in a very concrete way during the Passover meal. In connection with a listing of the ten plagues in the *Passover Haggadah,* some drops of the wine in the cup are spilled out at every plague. The cup of joy cannot be full when one's own salvation is achieved while others are suffering, even if it is one's persecutors who are hit. This custom is explained during the meal and leaves an ineffaceable impression on the participants, not least on the children.

This way of wrestling with the enigma of what is difficult and mysterious in one's own history does not solve the "why?" of suffering and evil. But it does create a consciousness and a sensitivity that surpasses every effort to provide a deep theological solution.

However, such efforts are not lacking. Another way of struggling with the mystery of suffering depicts the events as a power struggle beyond what can immediately be seen and understood. We have already seen that Exodus describes the plagues as a judgment on the gods of Egypt, a judgment whose purpose is to indicate who the Lord is, or to put it in the words of the song (15:11), "Who is like you, O LORD, among the gods?"

This basic theme moves the focus away from the defeated Egyptian army and the rescued Israelites to a scene focusing on the Lord who possesses all power in heaven and earth. We could therefore use the words of the apostle as stage directions: "For our struggle is not against enemies of flesh and blood, but against the rulers, against the authorities, against the cosmic powers of this present darkness, against the spiritual forces of evil in the heavenly places" (Eph. 6:12; see also pp. 122f.).

This struggle is not finished when the Song of the Sea is heard during the first Passover. It is still rehearsed and will continue throughout the present era. After the exodus from Egypt the next stage continues: the dangerous walk through the wilderness.

8

Stumbling Steps toward Freedom

=== *Exodus 15:22–18:27* ===

A wonderful victory lies behind us. The triumphant song of
Miriam encourages the people to "sing to the LORD, for he
has triumphed gloriously" (15:21). No wonder that one almost
imagines the promised land waiting just beyond the horizon.

Then, abruptly, the scene changes. A new and difficult
lesson must be learned: there is no shortcut to freedom.
The time of quick victories and spectacular miracles is gone.
Slavery in Egypt is certainly over, but not the day-by-day tri-
als, toil, and travail. Ahead of the people lies the broad, vast,
sterile wilderness.[1] The short period of liberation is followed by a long time of wandering. Now the newborn
people will have to learn to walk. This is a long and painful
process. Freedom is not a once-and-for-all event. Freedom
has to be learned, again and again. Then freedom has to be
nourished and the boundaries of freedom defended, not
only physically but also mentally.

The desert period is a learning process for a people
bound for freedom. It is "a new school of the soul." That is
why the Israelites had to spend such a long time in the
wilderness.[2]

The compass direction is set, and the one who has
brought them to light and life will lead and support them.

BITTER WATER (15:22–27)

The song of praise has hardly died away before a totally
new reality presents itself as the people look in vain for water

for three days. Three days is not a long time, but without water it is long enough to give the people a foreboding of what they may have to endure. The very liberation had certainly entailed many frightening moments. Still, it had come upon them so suddenly and unexpectedly and been carried through in such a marvelous way that afterward they could simply burst out in thanksgiving and rejoicing. The first lesson of the wilderness has two parts: it is still a long way home, but the time of miracles is not yet over.

The song of the people ceases only to become a murmuring complaint (15:24). However, just as he has so far, the Lord knows what they need and shows Moses how to make the bitter water drinkable (15:25; cf. 2 Kgs. 2:19ff.). At the same time God reminds the people that they need their Lord even when they have quenched their thirst and satisfied all their outward needs. They need the divine word. The way home will first lead them to Mount Sinai, where the people will see that not only the water needs to be transformed, but they themselves need a healer to open their ears and liberate them from slavery in an inner sense (15:26). The desert walk inaugurates this long process of healing.

The long periods of wandering are regularly interrupted by much-needed moments of rest. After the first stage, the people catch their breath at the oasis of Elim,[3] with its twelve springs of water, one for each tribe, recalling the sufficiency of God's sources for everyone. The seventy palm trees, the number of fullness, send the same message of refuge for all under the shadow of his wings (Ps. 36:7; 57:1; 63:7).

BREAD FROM HEAVEN (16:1–36)

The intermission is not long. The people now leave the coastal area to move further east into the wilderness. For the second time after the liberation, the people begin complaining about the lack of food. More seriously, after such a short time following the miracle at the sea and with all the other wonders they have experienced, they already begin longing to return to Egypt. When they feel the pangs of hunger, the fleshpots of Egypt seem richer than ever (16:3).

It is indeed strange that memory of the past can fail so totally. In this situation the hardening of Pharaoh's heart is

inevitably brought to mind. As soon as the pain of one blow
subsides, it was as if he had never heard nor seen anything
(see pp. 58f.). Analogously, we can now observe how for Israel
each moment of stress, each miracle of delivery, seems like a
first occurrence, a truly new event. Past experiences have vanished. The people react as though they have never faced the
greatness of God's power to deliver. Perhaps it is not by
chance that the Lord has had to strike the Egyptians with ten
plagues and that he even had to say of Israel itself, they "have
tested me these ten times and have not obeyed my voice"
(Num. 14:22).

Again, we are reminded of the reality behind the old saying, "it is easier to take Israel out of Egypt than to take Egypt
out of Israel." Slavery and bondage deprive one of the ability to
carry out one's responsibility. Lack of responsibility can be
very enticing. In any case, it is the irresponsibility of slavery
that already overshadows any memory of the cruel reality they
have just left behind. It will also take a long time for the slaves
to learn the lesson that the Lord has written into their curric-
ulum, "one does not live by bread alone, but by every word
that comes from the mouth of the LORD" (Deut. 8:3).

And yet, "No bread, no Torah," as the Mishnah puts
it.[4] That is, with an empty stomach no one is able to receive
the word that proceeds out of the mouth of the Lord.
Therefore, the Lord first demonstrates care for Israel by
stilling their hunger, just as he has earlier quenched their
thirst. Verse after verse, we find repeated that the Lord hears
their murmuring (16:7, 8, 9, 11). The redeemed people are
still at the stage of a little child. God thus shows forbearance
with their lack of trust and even with their lack of faith, be-
trayed by their complaints. Only later will more be de-
manded of them (cf. Num. 11).

The Quails

"In the evening quails came up and covered the camp"
(16:13). The quail is the smallest of pheasants, hardly eight
inches long. As a migrant, it moves between northern Europe
and northern Africa in the autumn and in the spring. One
month after Passover (16:1), they are on the homeward route
back to the north. Every now and then, after the long migra-
tory flight over the Red Sea, they descend totally exhausted to

the coastal regions. They can be easily caught then.[5] They also commonly follow the winds (cf. Num. 11:31; Ps. 28:26).

Even though this miracle can bear a natural explanation, it is obvious that the hand of the Lord is behind it. God is the only one commanding the winds to blow in the right direction in order to bring the birds precisely at the moment that the people cry out for meat. The result is unequivocal, "then you shall know that I am the LORD your God" (16:12). Even more does this apply to the next miracle of nurturing.

The Manna

The ensuing biblical description leads our thoughts to a well-known phenomenon of nature in the Sinai Peninsula. The manna is described as "a fine flaky substance, as fine as frost on the ground" (16:14) and as "coriander seed, white" (16:31). These seeds are a bit smaller than peas. Particularly in rainy years the tamarisk bush, indigenous to arid areas, is invaded by a species of plant louse. The insect sucks the sap and transforms its carbohydrates into a variety of high fructose products. These are secreted through the body and fall to the ground as small drops. There they crystallize into small white pellets, which can be consumed like sugar or honey. Since they melt in the sun, they have to be gathered early in the morning, just like the biblical manna. Still today the bedouins call them in Arabic *man,* which corresponds to the Hebrew word for "manna."[6]

The taste is compared to "wafers made with honey" (16:31). The Hebrew etymon is unknown but is thought to refer to some kind of pastry baked and boiled (16:23). In Num. 11:8 the taste is compared to "cakes baked with oil." These various descriptions of manna have sparked the imagination of Jewish commentators. According to one interpretation, the manna assumed the taste that each person desired, that is, each received his or her favorite dish in the middle of the wilderness![7]

This pious tradition of course does not take into consideration the later record of the people's complaint that the manna was too monotonous (Num. 11:4ff.). It does, however, justify the miracles linked to the manna in the Bible, which defy all natural explanation. First, it fell regularly and in such quantities that it could feed the people during all the forty years in the wilderness (16:35; cf. Josh. 5:10ff.). The crystallized, sugary product under the tamarisks, on the other hand, only falls during a few weeks in June and July and in very small quantities. Moreover, its nutritive value is low, since it does not contain any protein and consequently has to be supplemented by other kinds of food. Second, the manna was distributed in such a way that everyone received an equal portion regardless of how much he or she was able to collect (16:16ff.). Here, total equality prevailed.[8] Third, nothing could be stored up for the following day (v. 19ff.). This rule was suspended once a week. On Friday, a double quantity of manna fell, since it totally ceased on the Sabbath (16:5, 22–30). The Jewish tradition to have two Sabbath loaves (Hebrew *hallah*) in connection with the *qiddush* Friday evening is a constant reminder of this miracle.

Against this background it is obvious that the manna already in biblical times was a pivotal symbol of the proclamation of God's mighty deeds, like the miracle at the sea (Neh. 9:15; Ps. 78:23ff.; 105:40). Since the miracle of the quails is only mentioned twice during the desert wandering and can easily be given a natural explanation, it never received central importance in later Jewish tradition. In the listing of the miracles in the *Dayyenu* hymn in the *Passover Haggadah* (see p. 78), it is not even mentioned.

The manna became the quintessential symbol of God's providence over the people. Therefore, a portion was later stored together with the tablets of the covenant in the Holy of Holies (16:32ff.; see 25:16; 26:34). When the ark of the covenant was hidden before the destruction of the first temple (see p. 213), the jar with the manna was concealed together with it. The ark is expected to be restored upon the arrival of the Messiah; the identical hope is equally held for the manna.[9] Even more, the manna became an integral part of a messianic hope for a renewed miracle of manna, when the Lord once again will feed his people with bread from heaven.[10] This rabbinic tradition undergirds the promise of "the hidden manna" that is to be given to those who overcome the tribulations of the last days (Rev. 2:17).

When Jesus calls himself "the living bread that came down from heaven" (John 6:51), it is this messianic tradition he expresses. He also refers to another common Jewish thought centering on the manna. The manna symbolizes the Torah—"every word that comes from the mouth of the LORD" (Deut. 8:3)—which gives nourishment and life not only for the body.[11] Paul speaks of the manna as a super-natural food (1 Cor. 10:3). John, moreover, describes Jesus as the word that became flesh (John 1:14). Even here the thought surfaces that he is the manna of the Torah, given in a renewed way.

God gives the manna not only to satisfy the physical needs but also to give life to the inner person. Like the word of God, it comes to make the people know the ways of the Lord. The deepest significance of the manna miracle is expressed in the words: "I am going to rain bread from heaven for you, and each day the people shall go out and gather enough for that day. In that way I will test them, whether they will follow my instruction or not" (16:4; cf. 15:25; Deut. 8:1–6).

The Test

Jewish commentaries discuss at length in what way God actually tests his people by giving them the manna.[12] We have seen that the manna was not given unconditionally. It could not be kept until the following day, and it was intimately linked to the Sabbath commandment. The test could, then, apply to the obedience of these precepts (cf. 16:19–20, 27ff.).

God's commandments, however, always penetrate more profoundly than outward observance only. Therefore, it was not the literal obedience of the people alone that was tested through the manna. Concurrently they were taught three lessons, respectively, dealing with (1) temperance in one's own life, (2) solidarity with one's neighbor, and above all else (3) confidence in the Lord.

Taking each lesson in turn, we should note first that already in connection with the quails, rabbinic commentaries warn against gluttony, referring to Num. 11:31–34, where the demand for meat obviously goes beyond the need of stilling hunger. The fact that only in rare cases was meat given to the people in the wilderness is in itself a warning against reveling in food (cf. also the precept regarding meat in Deut. 12:20–21). The manna is the food of temperance. It shall be "your fill of bread" (16:8), literally "bread for satiation," that is, exactly what humans need, neither more nor less. "If one ate that measure of it, he was healthy and blessed. If one ate less, it was harmful for his stomach. If one ate more, he was considered a glutton."[13]

Second, by the equal distribution of the manna to everyone (vv. 16ff.), God further demonstrates the lack of distinction between poor and rich, weak and strong. Before their Lord they have the same value and are sustained by the same care. This is set forth as a model for the people to follow. It is precisely this teaching of the manna miracle in 16:16 that Paul proclaims: "I do not mean that there should be relief for others and pressure on you, but it is a question of fair balance between your present abundance and their need, in order that there may be a fair balance. As it is written, 'The one who had much did not have too much, and the one who had little did not have too little' " (2 Cor. 8:13ff.).

Third, the most decisive test focuses on the significance of total confidence in the Lord.[14] The bread from heaven is different from the earthly bread in at least one crucial detail: though it is the Lord who grants the grain growth, we have the ability to control production of the bread. We plow, sow, harvest, grind, and store up flour, providing to some degree a guarantee for the future. We want to maintain control over our situation, to take matters into our own hands and remain independent. What we ourselves achieve may provide a degree of comfort and security, which too often makes persons selfish and arrogant. The manna, on the other hand, descended directly from the hand of God day by day. The people were totally dependent on God's promise to give them their daily bread. They could not attain any guarantees whatsoever through collecting and saving. According to several Jewish commentaries, this was the real test.

Above all, two main characteristics of the manna tested the people's trust in the Lord. It was given independently of human planning, thereby causing the people to cast all their anxieties on the Lord, trusting in his care in an ongoing daily test. Tomorrow's anxieties can bring confidence in God to naught. In descending from heaven without human effort, the manna also invited the qualitatively different danger of indulgence in overabundance. When all goes well and we receive all we need, we tend to forget God very easily. More than the previous one, this danger—the danger of wealth, convenience, and an abundance of free time—is probably of greater relevance to us in our time. In the end one easily takes the bread of heaven for granted. Prayer vanishes, thankfulness ceases, and we forget how totally dependent we remain on God, the provider of everything.[15]

Jesus expresses the lesson of the manna in the prayer "give us this day our daily bread," probably referring to the daily portion of manna. He points to the same confidence in God in his well-known words of the Sermon of the Mount: "But strive first for the kingdom of God and his righteousness, and all these things will be given to you as well. So do not worry about tomorrow, for tomorrow will bring worries of its own. Today's trouble is enough for today" (Matt. 6:33–34). Both exhortations belong together. Keeping them in mind, we can hope to escape the dangers of overabundance, anxiety, and lack of trust and faith.

WATER FROM THE ROCK (17:1–7)

The desert walk leads the people further to the east of the Sinai peninsula, on toward the next camp site, Rephidim. According to one theory, this refers to *Wadi Refayid*, about six miles northwest of the traditional Mount Sinai. It is, in any case, obvious that they are not far away from the mountain where the Lord had earlier given his call to Moses (3:1ff.), and where he would soon reveal himself to the entire people (17:6; 19:2).

For the fourth time following the exodus, the children of Israel stray into trouble and complain to Moses (cf. 14:11–12; 15:24; 16:2–3). As before, they express a wish to return to Egypt. Now, clearly a spirit of revolt is arising, since Moses expresses his fear of being stoned. The seriousness of the situation is further brought out by the two names linked to this event, *Massah* and *Meribah*. The first name means "test" or "temptation," the second one "dispute" or "quarrel" (see 17:2, 7). It is now bluntly stated that the people question whether the Lord is with them at all. They can hardly get further away from the trusting confession of 14:31 and the song of praise in chapter 15. The situation foreshadows Jer. 44:16–18 (cf. Mal. 3:14–15) and demonstrates how deeply the theology of success is rooted within the natural person.

The Lord does not condemn them, but gives them new proof of mercy and care. The same rod which had previously made the water of the Nile undrinkable (8:14–24) now serves to provide fresh water to the thirsting people.

Together with the manna, this marvelous miracle is also mentioned among God's great deeds in the redemption of his

people (Neh. 9:15; Ps. 78:15–16; 105:41). The manna in later
Jewish tradition was interpreted as a spiritual gift; the same
applies to the water of the rock. Paul has this tradition in mind
when he describes the miracle in these words: "All drank the
same spiritual drink. For they drank from the spiritual rock
that followed them, and the rock was Christ" (1 Cor. 10:4).

The rabbis recount that after Moses struck the rock, it
followed the people throughout their wandering in the desert,
just as the manna satisfied them and the cloud led them
throughout that period of time.[16] This "moving rock" is said
to have provided water so abundantly that it watered the
whole desert land as the people of Israel passed through. It
was thus a kind of movable oasis! This tradition probably goes
back to biblical times, as indicated by the exposition in Ps.
105:41: "He opened the rock, and water gushed out; it flowed
through the desert like a river" (see also Ps. 78:16).

Like the manna, the water also symbolizes the word of
God (cf. Isa. 55:1ff.),[17] and the rock stands for God (Deut.
34:4, 15, 18, 31, 37; Ps. 18:3, etc.). When opening the rock, the
Lord provides the people with much more than what the body
needs for the moment. Provided with another proof of God's
presence in every moment of their lives, they may exclaim:
"Whom have I in heaven but you? And there is nothing on
earth that I desire other than you. My flesh and my heart may
fail, but God is the strength of my heart and my portion forever" (Ps. 73:25–26).

Who possesses such a faith? Time and again the Bible
lists the miracles that the Lord performed when saving the
people out of Egypt. Just as frequently, we find listed all the
occasions when the people murmur and complain against
Moses and Aaron, and implicitly against the Lord as well. The
desert era can certainly be viewed as God's "honeymoon" with
his people (Jer. 2:2; Hos. 2:14–23). But questions of doubt and
disbelief unabatedly resound, "Is the LORD among us or not?"
(17:7; cf., for example, Deut. 9:7; Ps. 78; 95; 106; Ezek. 20).[18]

This bitter reality is revealed without embellishing re-
visions—not that we should be horrified at the disbelief of
other people, but rather that we should come to know ourselves. Only then does the biblical story achieve its objective, to serve as both a warning and a comfort for us. If we
recognize in ourselves the same lack of confidence that dog-
ged these people, we are equally entitled to accept another
basic premise: in spite of everything, God does not reject his

people. God keeps his promises (for example, Lev. 26, especially vv. 44ff.). As the good shepherd, the Lord leads them to water, restores their soul for his name's sake, prepares a table in the presence of their enemies, and defends them against all enemies.

A MORTAL ENEMY (17:8–16)

This section introduces yet another fundamental theme of the desert migration. So far we have witnessed the inner condition of the people, materially and morally. Now suddenly the first of a series of external enemies appears, the worst of all—Amalek.

The Amalekites were a nomad tribe who crisscrossed the entire area from the southern Negev down to the Sinai peninsula. Genesis 36:12 suggests their genealogy goes back to Esau. To judge from the prophecy of Balaam in Num. 24:20, it was probably a strong tribe: "First among the nations was Amalek, but its end is to perish forever." In 1 Chron. 4:42–43 the fulfillment of Balaam's prophecy is recorded.

Now they obviously felt threatened by the new people crossing their path. Rephidim is an oasis, and the lack of water among the Israelites can be explained by the Amalekites' preventing their access to the wells. In any case, the first confrontation between the two peoples leads to bitter, open, and long-enduring warfare. Again and again Amalek appears, often in alliance with other tribes, to prevent Israel from attaining the goal of their walk with God and to expel them once they do reach their home (see Num. 14:41–45; Deut. 25:17–19; 1 Sam. 15:1–9; 30).

The first battle is led by Joshua, who would later assume leadership from Moses. His name, Hebrew *Yehoshua*, means "he will save"; Jesus is the Greek transliteration of this name or its Aramaic equivalent, *Yeshu* (see Matt. 1:21).[19] He now accepts the responsibility of commanding the fight, while Moses ascends a hill together with Aaron and Hur (cf. 24:14).

The battle is another illustration of the words, "The LORD will fight for you" (14:14), symbolically expressed by the lifted hands of Moses holding "the rod of God." When Moses' power vanishes and his hands slacken, even Joshua is unable to do anything. The message is clear: the victory does not depend on Moses' strength, or on

Joshua and his army, but solely on the Lord. Israel has no banner in the battle other than the hands of Moses uplifted to the Lord, for "not by might, nor by power, but by my spirit, says the LORD of hosts" (Zech. 4:6).

The altar Moses built after the victory and named "The LORD is my banner" thus becomes a silent song of praise with the same refrain as the Song of the Sea. By this the skeptical question in 17:7 has received its clear-cut answer. The whole narration of the attack of the Amalekites actually serves the purpose of answering this question (cf. 34:9; Num. 14:41ff.; Deut. 1:41ff.).[20]

Amalek's attack was unusually cowardly and cruel. According to Deut. 25:17ff. they ambushed the people, targeting in particular the weak ones lagging behind. This attack inaugurated an animosity without parallel in Israelite history. Several times the divine command is issued to exterminate this people. Thus, Saul's failure to obey this command fully leads to his end (1 Sam. 28:17–19). It is even said that their very remembrance shall be blotted out and that the Lord will fight against them from generation to generation (17:16). In other words, we are confronting an eternal animosity.

From such sayings Jewish tradition has concluded that Amalek was not only the archenemy of Israel, but that a quasidemonic power stood behind these enemies. When they attack God's people, it amounts to a rebellion against God himself, whose plan they try to thwart. The combat against them at a deeper level represents a struggle not "against enemies of blood and flesh, but against the rulers, against the authorities, against the cosmic powers of this present darkness, against the spiritual forces of evil in the heavenly places" (Eph. 6:12; cf. pp. 110f.).

In this way Amalek comes to symbolize evil incarnate. Even if his people perish at the end, his seed is imagined to survive in a mysterious way, continuing to plot the ultimate destruction of God's people. An example of this is found in the book of Esther, where the architect of the extermination plan against the Jews is Haman, "the Agagite" (3:1). Agag was the king of the Amalekites (1 Sam. 15:8). When the book of Esther is recited at the Feast of Purim (Esth. 9:20–32), an ancient tradition admonishes the public to make so much noise that when the name of Haman is pronounced, it cannot be heard. This is a joyous way to carry out the command to "blot out the remembrance of Amalek from under heaven" (Deut. 25:19).

Throughout history, the Jewish people have been targeted for persecutions, fully reminiscent of the evil influence of Amalek's seed. In rabbinic literature the Roman empire is likewise linked to Amalek. In more recent times such applications, however, have become more cautious. Even less can one advocate the biblical guidelines for the struggle against Amalek, for who can identify his descendants? Above all, this war is God's task, not humans': "The LORD will have war with Amalek from generation to generation" (17:16).

One thing, however, remains at constant issue: the admonition to "remember!" (17:14; Deut. 25:17). It is important to recall the past in order to be ready for the present and be prepared for the future. The *Passover Haggadah* explains, "For it was not one man only who stood up against us to destroy us; in every generation they stand up against us to destroy us, and the Holy One, blessed be he, saves us from their hand."[21] The collected experience of a whole nation has formulated this historical realism.

THE VISIT OF JETHRO (18:1–27)

The people of Israel have now camped "at the mountain of God" (18:5); that is, Moses has returned to the place where he once received the calling to lead the people of God out of Egypt. When he trembled before the tremendous task (3:11), God answered: "I will be with you; and this shall be the sign for you that it is I who sent you: when you have brought the people out of Egypt, you shall worship God on this mountain" (see pp. 34f.).

This chapter looks back on the events in Moses' life between his first and second visits to "the mountain of God." At the same time, the chapter marks the intermediate stage before the great imminent miracle, when God will send the decisive sign that he is the one who has appointed Moses and will reveal his purpose in all that has happened to date.

The Family Reunited (18:1–12)

Jethro's visit is important in Jewish tradition because it introduces the weekly Torah portion including the revelation

at Sinai with the proclamation of the "ten commandments."
This portion, 18:1–20:23, is also named after Jethro (Hebrew *Parashath Yithro*), who does in fact play a role in
this chapter, with repercussions for the rest of Moses' life
and mission.

The first important task of Jethro is to see to it that the
split family will be reunited after a painful time of separation.
In 4:18–26 we were told that Moses returned to Egypt together with his wife and his sons. However, Moses apparently
sent them back while he was fulfilling his dangerous mission
(18:2). Only now does the happy reunion take place.

The rumor of what the Lord had done was obviously
widespread, and Jethro sets out together with his daughter
Zipporah and his two grandsons toward the camp of Israel.
The communion in Moses' tent can be characterized as a
four-part service with all essential elements: proclamation of
the gospel (18:8), song of praise (18:9–10),[22] creed (18:11; cf.
1 Kgs. 17:24; 2 Kgs. 5:15; Ps. 135),[23] and a sacred meal
(18:12).[24]

This intimate communion before God in thankful remembrance of great miracles, however, is soon changed into
the reality of the day's responsibilities. This also changes the
focus from the past to the future. Now it is a matter of planning for the days to come!

Judges Appointed (18:13–27)

Mount Sinai, the mountain of the Torah, stands out
against the horizon. Now the preparations begin for the great
task still ahead of Moses.[25] He will not only receive God's law
as the great teacher, but will also have to see to it that the
people understand, accept, and apply God's word in their lives.
Almost as clear-sighted as a prophet, Jethro gives Moses good
counsel, which he will now need more than ever as he con-
fronts the enormous task before him. It is simply too much for
one person to take this weighty responsibility upon himself.
The tasks will only increase with time. Already, Moses must
use all his time to guide his people and to judge all kinds of
disputes among them.

Therefore, Moses will have to learn to delegate lesser
matters to others, "able men among all the people, men who
fear God, are trustworthy, and hate dishonest gain" (18:21; cf.
23:1–9). In short, a judicial system has to be organized. The

people have to be divided into smaller units, "thousands, hundreds, fifties and tens," each one with its judge. Moses should function merely as a kind of chief justice of the supreme court. Only in this way will he have the time and the strength for all that he has been called to achieve. This should also free some quality time to spend with the family.

This organization means that Moses will delegate authority to no fewer than 78,600 people (cf. 12:37). No less than every seventh person will have a special responsibility as a leader! Instead of long lines and waiting time, no one will be more than four steps away from Moses. Jethro's contribution in organizing a functional system of national justice can hardly be overestimated.

Great persons are often reluctant to share power. Humble as he is (Num. 12:3), Moses, however, has no difficulty in listening and accepting Jethro's good advice (18:24ff.; cf. Deut. 1:9–18). With that, Israel is prepared not only to receive the Torah at Sinai, but the preconditions are also set down for a new, responsible leadership to step forward after Moses fulfills his great mission.

Herein Jethro has fulfilled his task. Moses tries to convince him to join the people of Israel (Num. 10:29–32), but obviously he is needed more among his own people and he returns to them. As a gift for them he brings a hopeful message of a God who is able to do far more than any human being is able to imagine. He brings a song of praise and a confession, which certainly will be heard among his own people.

The meeting between Jethro and Moses at the foot of Mount Sinai thus becomes a testimony of God's presence far beyond the borders of people, communities, and congregations, which all too often tend to become dividing walls. This biblical theme will continue to reverberate in the great miracle about to occur.

9

The Miracle of Pentecost

Exodus 19–20

*I*t is probably not by chance that the revelation on Mount Sinai occurs in the middle of the book of Exodus. Mount Sinai is the peak moment in the history of Israel. The book of Genesis led up to the slavery in Egypt. The book of Exodus has thus far described the miraculous liberation from Egypt. It is possible to say, though, that this liberation has all the while pointed the way to the great miracle at Mount Sinai, which the people are about to witness.

At this place Moses received his calling from God (Exod. 3). The Lord had promised Moses that he would return together with his people to "worship God on this mountain" (3:12). It is just this promise that remains to be fulfilled when the people of Israel gather before the mountain (19:2). However, this time Moses will not meet the Lord alone, but all of Israel will be present. As in Moses' case, this encounter with God will also lead to a great calling, now for all the people.

God's revelation through fire is a recurrent motif in the book of Exodus. It stands there, from the very beginning, in the revelation at the burning bush at the foot of Mount Sinai. As we will see, it is a prominent feature in the middle of the book, in the revelation at Sinai. And, to be sure, fire is also prominent in the conclusion, when the Lord descends upon the tabernacle (40:38), which can be regarded as a "portable Sinai" (see pp. 134, 264ff.), for Sinai is the focal point of God's revelation. It is thus significant that the Sinai event is given by far the greatest space in the Pentateuch: the whole section from Exod. 19 to Num. 10. Fifty-nine chapters—almost one-third of the Pentateuch—is dedicated to the narration of only one year in the history of Israel!

The liberation from slavery to freedom has actually fo-cused on Sinai the whole time. The revelation at Sinai will also put its stamp on the subsequent history of Israel, for all time. The liberation from Egypt is but the preparation for the Sinai event. Passover is the beginning of Pentecost, the feast of the giving of the Torah and the covenant at Sinai. Simultaneously, Pentecost is the conclusion of Passover, bestowing upon Pass-over its deepest significance.[1]

We can confidently state that without the miracle at Sinai, the miracles related to the liberation from Egypt would most likely have become merely part of the past. They would have been remembered as something marvelous that happened once upon a time, if they had not eventually been entirely forgotten. In any case, they would have lost their formative significance for coming generations. The liberated people would have only amounted to a group of former slaves that eventually assimilated into the surrounding peoples and vanished forever.

Without Sinai, there would have been no Israel. And without Israel, there would have been no Bible. At Mount Sinai the people of the book is born, destined to transmit the biblical revelation to the world.

As has been pointed out earlier (pp. 14f., 77), it is signifi-cant that in Hebrew the word for "slave" and "servant" is one and the same, ʿeved. What makes the difference is who the master and lord is. It is not enough to be liberated from some-thing—Pharaoh and slavery. To be really free, one has to be-come a servant, more precisely a servant of the King of kings, the Lord of heaven and earth (see pp. 76ff.).

This change of masters takes place at Mount Sinai. The revelation given there makes the full liberation of the people possible. What we have witnessed so far in the book of Exodus has been nothing but the birth pangs of the covenantal people of God, "a priestly kingdom and a holy nation" (19:6).

A HOLY PEOPLE—THE PEOPLE
OF THE COVENANT (19:3–8)

The concept of a "holy nation" is one of the most misun-derstood in the whole Bible. In order to capture the proper perspective, we should pay particular attention to verses 4–6,

framed by a repeated command to Moses: "Thus you shall say
to the house of Jacob, and tell the Israelites" (v. 3), and,
"These are the words that you shall speak to the Israelites" (v.
6). In this way the intermediate section is marked as particularly important.

In 19:4–6 Israel for the first time receives its calling to be
a holy people. In a few sentences God sums up the meaning of
the covenant with Israel. The Lord clearly sets forth the fundamental principle on which the covenant is built and the divine purpose for entering into a special relationship with this
people. Every expression is brimming with the deepest significance. The concept of the covenant is so basic for both Jews
and Christians that we must attentively hearken to what God
bids Moses to proclaim to the people. Every verse deserves
thorough attention.

Sometimes Christians believe that a basic difference
between the Old and the New Testament and between Judaism and Christianity resides in the difference between law
and grace, deeds and faith. Allegedly, in the Old Testament
and in postbiblical Judaism, human beings must gain salvation through good deeds, while in the New Testament and
in Christianity salvation is founded on God's grace, received
through faith. Such assumptions often overlook a basic
claim throughout the entire Bible, namely, that God is the
same yesterday, today, and throughout eternity. Thus, if
God is the God of grace in the New Testament, he is quite
likely the same God even in the Old Testament. If the Lord
has revealed himself as such a God to Israel, then that salvation and election even in Judaism would rest upon the same
foundation.

To be sure, the text begins by reminding Israel of what
God has done for them: "You have seen what I did to the
Egyptians, and how I bore you on eagles' wings and brought
you to myself" (v. 4). Before God makes a covenant with Israel
and before they hear what they must do, they must first recall
what God has already done. God has saved them!

The poetic imagery employed—to carry them "on eagles'
wings"—expresses the strength and the power, the intimacy
and the tenderness, through which their Lord has rescued
them and led them to the mountain. The wings spread forth
express God's presence: "How precious is your steadfast love,
O God! All people may take refuge in the shadow of your
wings" (Ps. 36:7). When the Jews wrap themselves in the

prayer shawl (cf. Num. 15:38ff.) in the morning, they recite this and the following verses of Ps. 36. These words, along with the living iconography of body language, create a daily reminder of God's word to Moses: "You have seen . . . how I bore you on eagles' wings, and brought you to myself," brought you in under the shadow of my wings.

This is the foundation of the covenant, properly not understood as a legal contract but as a loving relationship, predicated not upon what the people of Israel are to do, but upon what God himself has done unconditionally for them. So far, we have not found a single word that God lays down as a condition to save his people out of Egypt. The disobedience, ingratitude, and obstinacy of the people have not led to a change in God's mind. Without fail, God has taken care of them and given them all they need. They have experienced the Lord's grace, an overwhelming loving-kindness. Grace, from Latin *gratia,* is the etymon of our word "gratis." Indeed, this word is an accurate summation of God's unconditional salvation of Israel (see p. 259).

This state of affairs cannot, however, go on forever. Every human relationship sooner or later elicits mutuality. When the child grows older, it has to learn to stand on its own feet and take responsibility for its actions. Likewise, the oppressed who have been liberated have to grow in such a way that they cannot continue living as though still sitting helplessly in their bonds. It is tempting to remain one who is pitied and the object of others' care. Now the people bound for freedom once and for all are called to be truly free of this slave mentality.

God has a purpose for saving Israel: it is to use them for the good of humankind—not abuse them as Pharaoh did. It is to make servants of the divine out of the slaves of Pharaoh, now responsible to God alone. Therefore, we now for the first time hear the little word "if," expressive of conditions and mutuality in the relationship between God and his people: "Now therefore, *if* you obey my voice and keep my covenant, you shall be my treasured possession out of all peoples" (v. 5). This conditional "if" is but a natural consequence of what God has already done for Israel.

This verse is probably one of the most misunderstood in the Bible. The very thought that a certain people should be singled out and treated in a special way is difficult for people in general to accept, and not least for Christians. It conflicts with the ideal of equality. Thus, this verse has become a stumbling block to many Christians. Has not Paul said: "There is no longer Jew or Greek" (Gal. 3:28; cf. p. 133, n. 8)? Is then God different in the Old Testament? Or did God later change and realize the equal value of all nations?[2]

THREE PILLARS OF THE COVENANT

First, let us see what the text actually says. Many translations are misleading or even wrong in one important respect. Many take for granted that God's election of Israel occurs at the expense of other nations. For example, the King James Version—and a great number of other translations—renders the phrase "you shall be my treasured possession *out of all peoples*" by "ye shall be a peculiar treasure unto me *above all people.*" Such a translation actually reflects what many believe the text says, namely, that God has placed Israel in front of or above all others. The Hebrew preposition used *(min)* has primarily a partitive meaning and should correctly be translated "from" or "among." God separates Israel from the other peoples on earth and enters into a special relationship with them.

In order to comprehend this, we must bear in mind three things. First, this special relationship does not mean that other nations are set aside and marginalized. On the contrary, the rationale of the covenant with Israel is stated immediately: "for all the earth is mine" (v. 5b).[3] It is precisely because God cares so much for "all the earth" that he elects Israel as a special people. This people consequently are called to serve—not to dominate—other nations. Israel is elected for the sake of the world. That is why it is so important not to translate "above" the other peoples. Israel is elected to become God's servants, not the master of others. This is what God's election always means: one is elected to serve and not to be served (cf. Matt. 20:28; Mark 10:45).

Second, Israel is saved not because of a superior quality. We have seen how God saves them unconditionally. The Bible rather stresses that he elects what is small, weak, and sinful. Exodus 19:5 is rendered almost literally in Deut. 7:6, and there the text continues: "It was not because you were more numerous than any other people that the LORD set his heart on you and chose you, for you were the fewest of all peoples."

In Deut. 9 we further find a long list of Israel's sins, and other similar lists are found throughout the Bible.

Israel was born, not created. Abraham was of the same flesh and blood as Adam. Adam, and not first Abraham, was created in the image of God. Therefore, one rabbi contends that the most important summary of the Torah is Gen. 5:1: "This is the list of the descendants of Adam. When God created humankind [Hebrew *ʾAdam*], he made them in the likeness of God."[4] This reminder is indispensable to anyone who claims election by God. Another such reminder is found in the rationale of the election given in 19:5: "for all the earth is mine."

This aspect of the election is aptly expressed by Martin Buber in his comment on the eagle imagery in Exod. 19:4. He compares this to what is said of God and Jacob in Deut. 32:11–12: "As an eagle that stirs up its nest, and hovers over its young; as it spreads its wings, takes them up, and bears them aloft on its pinions, the LORD alone guided him." Buber stresses that the young birds refer to the nations, since it is written shortly before, that "when the Most High apportioned the nations, when he divided humankind, he fixed the boundaries of the peoples" (v. 8). This, however, does not prevent the eagle from taking up one young bird and treating it in a particular way: "The great eagle spreads out his wings over the nestlings; he takes up one of them, a shy or weary one, and bears it upon his pinions; until it can at length dare the flight itself and follows the father in his mounting gyrations. Here we have election, deliverance and education; all in one."[5]

The Hebrew adjective, usually rendered by "holy" *(qadosh)* originally means "separate" or "different," and the Hebrew verb for "to sanctify" *(qiddesh)* means "to separate." This essential meaning is patent in Lev. 20:26, which deals with the election of Israel: "You shall be holy to me; for I the LORD am holy, and I have separated you from the other peoples to be mine."[6] Holiness is clearly a matter of difference and not of excellence. The biblical, Hebraic concept of a holy people simply refers to a different people, separated out for a unique purpose.

Even the basic meaning of the Hebrew word for "covenant" *(berith)* is closely related to the concept of holiness. The Hebrew expression for "making a covenant" *(karath berith)* literally means to "cut" a covenant. When God makes Israel a "holy people," this in a way separates them from the other

nations. God gives them a special way of life, particular commandments and obligations, which will insure that the people
will remember and uphold their special calling. Therefore,
only "if" they listen to God's voice and keep the covenant—
the separation—will they be God's special possession among
the nations.

It is important to keep these root meanings of the words
"holy," "sanctify," and "covenant" in mind. Otherwise, we are
easily tempted to slip into the semantic trap of words like
"saints," "merits," and "privileges" when we hear these words.
The election is an act of grace and implies obligations rather
than advantages.

Third, God's election always calls his people to obedience and service with implications of a particularly great responsibility (cf. Amos 3:2). This is clearly expressed in verse 6,
where the concept of a "holy people" is paralleled with the expression "a priestly kingdom." Israel is called to be a kingdom
in the sense that God reigns as its real king. They are now liberated from Pharaoh. This means that they have left the service of him and all other earthly kings in order to serve the
Lord, the King of kings. It is now God's ways that they are
obliged to learn and to follow. They will be free from any
earthly oppressors and oppressive powers, yet they will be
bound to their liberator, who will set the boundaries for their
freedom. Only in this way will they be able to be truly free and
to preserve their freedom.

To the best of my knowledge, Israel was the only nation
in the ancient world who did not have a king or a government
who were legislators. Israel's kings—David, Solomon, and all
the others—were just as the rest of the people, subject to the
same laws that the people now receive at Sinai and during the
desert period (see Deut. 17:18ff.). As a spokesperson for God,
the prophet, in some ways, ranked higher than the king and
was obliged to expose the sins of the king (see, e.g., 2 Sam. 12
and 1 Kgs. 21). When it comes to legislation, the mandate of
the king was exclusively to see to it that God's law was known
and obeyed. Strangely enough, we do not find one single law
in the Old Testament that a king has instituted.[7] Only the
Lord is the lawmaker and the real authority in Israel, his
earthly kingdom!

This does not mean, however, that Israel should appear
as kings in the world. They are called "a kingdom of priests"
(the NRSV: "a priestly kingdom"), a kingdom of servants. Israel

is collectively called to make up a kind of priesthood in the world. This image is very accurate and fits exactly into the rationale of the preceding verse: "for all the earth is mine." As we know, the tribe of Levi was set apart among the other tribes of Israel to act as God's special servants: the Levites. Aaron and his sons were separated within the tribe of Levi to serve as priests. They received special laws to follow and special duties to fulfill.

The division within the people of Israel is used here as a model to express Israel's calling in the world at large. As a "priestly kingdom," they are to become God's special servants among the other nations. God's kingdom is much wider than Israel, but that kingdom needs Israel in the role of priests. Therefore, the covenant confers upon them a special commission, the purpose of which is that the blessing of Abraham will extend throughout the entire world: "By your descendants shall all the nations of the earth be blessed" (Gen. 22:18; cf. 12:3; 18:18; 26:4; 28:14; Acts 3:25; Gal. 3:8).[8]

PENTECOST—THE FEAST OF THE COVENANT (19:9–25; 20:18–21)

Our word "Pentecost" is derived from Greek *pentēkostē,* which means "fiftieth," namely, the fiftieth day after Passover. Pentecost to Christians commemorates the outpouring of the Holy Spirit and is sometimes called "the birthday of the church." The story about the Pentecost miracle in Acts 2 begins, however, with the words: "When the day of Pentecost had come, they were all together in one place." Pentecost was consequently celebrated long before the church was born. Those gathered for the feast were Jews. And they celebrated the Feast of Weeks *(Shavuʿoth)* seven weeks after Passover. This is the Pentecost of the Old Testament. Let us consider some of its distinguishing features.

After Seven Weeks

The Torah describes this feast as a harvest festival (see p. 180). When we see how it has actually been celebrated by the Jewish people throughout the centuries up until today, it is obvious that its primary motivation is something else.

Human beings do not live by bread alone; and precisely seven weeks after Passover, God bestowed an even greater gift than bread from the earth and manna from heaven. This Pentecost miracle is the Word descending from heaven to earth. God entrusted his Torah to Israel. Therefore, Pentecost in Jewish tradition is called *zeman mattan Torathenu,* "the time for the giving of our Torah." Since the Torah is the very seal of the covenant between God and Israel, Pentecost is also the great covenantal feast (see further pp. 184ff.).

According to 19:1–2 the wilderness of Sinai was reached "on the third new moon after the Israelites had gone out of the land of Egypt." Since the exodus took place in the middle of the month of Nisan, a time of six weeks has passed since Passover. "Then Moses went up to God" (v. 3), probably only the following day. When he ascends to the Lord a second time (v. 8), at least one other day must have passed. A literal reading of verse 9 indicates that Moses once again brings a message to Israel from the Lord, to which the people respond. We have reached a fourth day. On this and the following day the people prepare themselves for the revelation of the Lord to take place on "the third day." Here we have reached the end of the seventh week after Passover (vv. 10–15).

Now it is Pentecost. Again Israel will witness a miracle unheard of in the history of humankind. Yet, just when God is about to give them a marvelous proof of love, they are reminded of the great distance separating them from their God, just as Moses had been reminded when he received his call (cf. pp. 27, 209f.). Not only are they commanded to prepare themselves for the revelation, but they must not transgress the border separating the holiness of the mountain, into which only Moses and to a certain extent Aaron and the priests[9] are allowed to enter (vv. 21–25).

Later, the tabernacle and the temple will serve as a constant reminder of this distinctive holiness of God. Just as here at Sinai, there came to be an area to which all of Israel had access, another reserved for the priests, and finally an inner "holy of holies" into which only the high priest could enter (see pp. 211, 223, 231, 234). The model for this division is found already here, and the tabernacle becomes an important way of carrying the Sinai experience forward during the subsequent wanderings (see further chs. 25–31).

Tongues of Fire

When the people are ready, all the powers of nature, accompanied by a heavenly trumpet, play the prelude to the divine Pentecost liturgy in the tremendous open-air temple of Sinai, covered with fire and incense. The king of the universe, the God of Israel appears in his holy temple. Heaven and earth meet. The holy and the unholy, the divine and the human, unite in a way that makes all creation shake at its foundation and every human heart tremble.

The description of God's mighty revelation in 19:16–25 is interrupted by the "sermon" in 20:1–17 and resumes in 20:18–21. Let us focus on the words in 20:18 in particular: "When all the people witnessed the thunder and the lightning." In order to understand the Jewish midrash on this miracle, we have to translate the text more precisely: "And all the people saw the voices [or noises] and the flames."

But how can one "see" a voice? This justifiable question has led to an interpretation of the text in which God's voice emerged as flames, or tongues of fire, seen by all the people. This understanding is also based upon the description of the Pentecost miracle in Deut. 5. One word returns again and again: "fire" (5:4, 5, 22, 23, 24, 25, 26; see also 4:15). The mountain is burning in fire. The Lord speaks from the fire. And the poetic rendering of the miracle in Deut. 33:2 reads: "The LORD came from Sinai . . . from his right hand went a fiery law for them."[10] The connection between fire and the word of God is also expressed in Jer. 23:29: "Is not my word like fire, says the LORD, and like a hammer that breaks a rock in pieces?"

Philo opines that fire was transformed into languages, which the people could understand.[11] According to a parallel rabbinic tradition, these flames of fire are seen not only as God's speech in general; they equally imply that God's Word was divided into different tongues, comprehensible to all nations.[12] This exegesis also explains the plural form of "flames" (NRSV "lightning") in 20:18.

Such an understanding of the text has further been combined with the thought that the Gentiles in a mystical way were also offered the Torah in their different languages. They declined it, however, with certain objections to its content. Only Israel answered: "All that the LORD has spoken, we will do, and we will be obedient" (24:7; see further pp. 189f.). As a consequence of this, the nations came under a curse of the Torah, while Israel was blessed.[13] It is probably this thought that Paul expresses when he speaks about "the curse of the law": "Christ redeemed us from the curse of the law, having become a curse for us . . . that in Christ Jesus the blessing of Abraham might come upon the Gentiles" (Gal. 3:13–14; see p. 133, n. 8 and further pp. 200ff.).

This Jewish midrash constitutes the frame of reference for the Pentecost miracle described by Luke in Acts 2. Even here, "tongues of fire" emerge, which are "distributed" on each person enabling them to hear their own tongues spoken.[14]

Many scholars have claimed that the Jews began celebrating the giving of the Sinaitic revelation at Pentecost only after the destruction of the temple in 70 C.E., and that the feast before that was merely celebrated as a harvest festival. It would be strange, however, that such an important event seven weeks after Passover would not have been commemorated earlier. Moreover, this Jewish celebration of Pentecost as the feast of the giving of the Torah and the making of the covenant is documented by pre-Christian sources (see pp. 184ff.).[15]

The background of Acts 2 is consequently Exod. 19–20 and the Jewish Pentecost, and not the story of the tower of Babel, which many contend. The common interpretation that the Pentecost miracle implies that the consequences of the tower of Babel, the confusion of languages, is now reversed, not only lacks basis but is all but absurd. The multiplicity of languages certainly does continue to exist in the world even after the outpouring of the Holy Spirit. Rather, the Pentecost miracle confirms the existence of multiple languages without restoring the situation before the building of the tower. The link between Acts 2 and the covenant on Sinai, however, renders the event its deepest significance, which we will soon see in Exod. 24.

At the same time, the many languages and the understanding of the revelation in different languages announce something new as compared to the revelation at Sinai. While the consequence of the first Pentecost miracle was that only Israel received the Torah and became the covenantal people, the result of this second miracle is that the covenant is expanded to embrace other nations as well. The Pentecost in Jerusalem in Acts 2 is thus a confirmation that the particular aspect of the promise to Abraham that applies to Gentiles is now about to be fulfilled (see p. 133, n. 8).

The description of the revelation of God's own person is surprisingly sparse. It hardly gets beyond a short prelude. Rather, what takes place below the mountain is the focus of interest. Above all, while the details regarding the theophany are dealt with in a few verses, chapter after chapter will elucidate the content of what God has said. What is important is not the outer but the inner aspect of God's revelation. To hear and not to see. To obey the Lord even when not comprehending him.

Moses says to the people, "Do not be afraid!" and explains that the purpose of the revelation is "to put the fear of him [the Lord] upon you so that you do not sin" (20:20). The same Moses who precisely at this place had been filled with fear before the Most High (3:6), is now the one who comforts the people. God has not appeared to chastise but to teach. Not to lash but to lead. Not to divorce but to wed the people to God in an intimate relationship of mutual interaction.

Therefore both "Do not be afraid!" and "Let the fear of the Lord be upon you!" are needed. For the word "fear" not only has to do with dread, but also with respect, obedience, and love. To fear the Lord means to listen to God's words and follow them, just as implied by the conditional "if" in 19:5 (see also 24:7). Only then will the covenant become what God intended it to be when he called Israel to become "a priestly kingdom and a holy nation."

THE TABLETS OF THE COVENANT (20:1–17)

Few words have had greater influence in world history than what we call the "ten commandments." They have been accepted as a norm for more people than any other set of rules. When the church declared a great part of the Old Testament laws superseded, the ten commandments were kept with a few changes and reinterpretations.[16] The content is so simple that anyone can comprehend it, at least on the surface. Nevertheless, few words have received more comment than these.

Exodus 20 does not expressly mention the number of commandments. When we speak about the "two" tablets and the "ten" commandments, we base this on other texts: 24:12;

31:18; 32:15; 34:1, 28–29; Deut. 4:13; 9:9, 11, 15; 10:1, 4. There is, however, no description in the Bible of how the commandments were divided or distributed on the two tablets. Therefore, both their numbering and their arrangement are different in various Christian traditions.[17]

Neither the Bible nor later Jewish tradition speaks of the tablets of "the law" or of ten "commandments." Instead, the term "the tablets of the covenant" or "the tablets of the testimony" and "the ten words" are used (see above references). This is not an insignificant detail. It touches the innermost significance of the concept of "the law."

Herein lies a frequently misunderstood concept. Christians often view "law" as the antithesis of "grace" and "gospel." It is likewise linked with the concept of "legalism," which to many is the summing up of Judaism as a religion that tries to earn God's salvation by means of deeds. Again, a thorough study of the relationship between God's grace and human obedience to God's law as expressed in the Old Testament and in Judaism would remove such biased stereotypes. "The law" is indeed the foremost expression of grace (see further pp. 257–62). This deep connection between "law" and "grace" is spelled out already in the opening words on the tablets of the covenant in Exod. 20.

The Introduction

The often overlooked introduction of chapter 20 reads as follows: "And God spoke all these words: 'I am the LORD your God, who brought you out of the land of Egypt, out of the house of slavery.' " We notice the text reads "words," not "commandments." In Jewish tradition they are therefore called "the ten words," or the *Decalogue* (from the Greek *deka* ["ten"] and *logoi* ["words"]). What follows then is consequently the first thing written on the tablets: "I am the LORD" (see also Deut. 5:6 and Ps. 81:10–11). This declaration is counted as the first of the "ten commandments."

One may object (and rightly so) that this is not a commandment. Indeed, the first thing written on the tablet is not a commandment; it does not state what they shall do, but what the Lord has already done. He saved the Israelites long before they came to Mount Sinai and received "the law." The first statement in God's revelation is not "law" but "gospel."

We noticed the same pattern in 19:4, the verse before God commands the people to listen to his voice and keep the covenant: "You have seen what I did." Therefore, the people are now here to receive the covenantal contract, the tablets of the covenant, the Torah, as a seal of the "love affair" that was initiated by God when he saved them.

The problem with our speaking of ten "commandments" and tablets of the "law" and with the usual counting beginning with verse 3 is that it easily overlooks the "graceful" foundation of the commandments. By doing this we easily plant the false notion that God in the Old Testament above all gives commandments. We forget the very frame around the tablets: the covenantal relationship, God's endless love and free gift of grace that saves his people unconditionally. The commandments are consequently not the means of salvation but only the consequence and continuation of salvation. They are not needed to enter into the covenant, but only to remain there.[18]

I wish we might also follow the Jewish way of counting, that it might be impossible to overlook the first and most basic "word" of them all. Even though this introduction is often mentioned in catechisms (teaching books for confirmation) and commentaries, it is still marginalized in too many people's minds. What to the Jews primarily is the wedding contract and the wedding ring, is to Christians therefore often reduced to laws and statutes and hard tablets of stone that serve only to uphold law and order. Or it is seen as just a mirror in which we perceive ourselves as incapable of doing anything good. In this respect, the Jews, so often accused of legalism, can help Christians to rediscover the "gospel" in the "law," and grace as the foundation of the covenant.

The thought that God descends to us and saves us before we are able—or need—to do anything to deserve love is certainly fundamental in Christian teaching. Accordingly, the New Testament says: "In this is love, not that we have loved God but that he loved us and sent his Son to be the atoning sacrifice for our sins" (1 John 4:10). Luther also says in his explanation to the third article of faith: "I believe that I cannot by my own understanding or effort believe in Jesus Christ my Lord, or come to him. But the Holy Spirit has called me through the Gospel, enlightened me with his gifts, and sanctified and kept me in true faith."[19]

However, we often limit this unconditional love of God to the New Testament, as if God had changed character there. We need to restore the ancient biblical view of what we unfortunately call "the law." We ought to abandon this term and only use the Hebrew term "Torah." Then we would be forced to reflect on the meaning of this word and accustom ourselves to the fact that its essential import is "the word of God." It certainly also contains "law," but only law within the framework of the covenant, that is, law preceded and permeated by grace and, therefore, gospel.[20]

No wonder, then, that these words, "I am the LORD your God, who brought you out of the land of Egypt, out of the house of slavery," are the most repeated words in the Bible.[21] They can be viewed as God's signature under the "love letter" to his people. Neither is it surprising that the tablets of the covenant bearing the significant words "I am the LORD," in the beginning of the first tablet, are as common a symbol in the synagogue as is the cross in a Christian house of worship. Both symbols point to the firm foundation of the covenant and of salvation.

"I am the LORD your God, who brought you out of the land of Egypt, out of the house of slavery"—why do the tablets of the covenant not begin with a reference to creation? Why is it not written "I am the LORD, the king of the universe, who has created you"? And why is it stated "I am the LORD your (singular) God, who brought you (singular) out of the land of Egypt"? Why does God address one when he speaks about a covenant with the whole people? The answers to these questions from ancient Jewish commentaries further elucidate the depths of richness contained in the introduction to the tablets of the covenant.

The first question touches two aspects of God's relation to the world. The Lord is first of all the one who holds the whole universe. God is the lord of history and the shepherd of the nations, no matter which aspects of the divine greatness they have seen. This universal presence of the Lord is at the same time very personal, being revealed in a way that goes beyond the general revelation in creation and in the world at large. This special revelation is particular and personal: God imposes self-limitations in time and space. The eternal enters history. The Lord bows his endless glory in order to allow us access (see pp. 144, 209f., 264ff.). Above all, the Bible's example of this is the covenant with Israel. When this special relationship is introduced, it is founded on God not as the creator and sustainer of the world but as the redeemer and liberator of Israel.

This special covenant presupposes a different experience of God than the vague notion given through creation. Therefore it is possible to say, "You have seen what I did" (19:4) and "All the people witnessed" (20:18; cf. 1 John 1:1). The liberation from slavery to freedom is the collective experience of a whole nation. Nobody is abandoned to speculate on who the Lord is or what the Lord has done.

This "root experience" of God's salvation at the beginning of Israel's history has continued to live from generation to generation (see p. 96). Until this very day, the blessing is recited in synagogues all over the world both before and after the reading from the Torah: "Blessed are you, God, who gives the Torah." The verb is in the present tense. People still experience the Lord as savior in times of need and hear the living voice from Sinai. Therefore, the people of Israel still apply the words of the *Passover Haggadah* (see pp. 1, 188f.): "In every generation it is everyone's duty to look upon himself as if he came out of Egypt, as it is said: 'And you shall tell your child on that day: It is because of what the Lord did for me when I came out of Egypt' (Exod. 13:8)."

"The LORD *your* God"—just as in the following commandments, God addresses the individual. The ten words are not just a collection of rules. Instead, they are the words of the covenant, a living and personal address that expects a response. If the tablets can be compared to a marriage contract, they certainly presuppose a living and intimate relationship. Therefore, we hear this heart-to-heart language, a close "You" from an "I," who is my redeemer.

Philo shares three teachings from this personal address of God.[22] First, it is a reminder of the endless value of every single human being. Each person "is equal in worth to a whole nation, even the most populous, or rather to all nations, and if we may go still farther, even to the whole world."[23]

Further, it is a reminder of the personal responsibility of each individual. Before God one cannot hide in the multitude: "If the exhortations are received as a personal message, the hearer is more ready to obey, but if collectively with others, he is deaf to them, since he takes the multitude as a cover for disobedience."[24]

Finally, it is a pattern for our way of relating to our fellow human beings. The giving of the Torah can be compared to a royal banquet, open to everyone.

> For if the Uncreated, the Incorruptible, the Eternal, who needs nothing and is the maker of all, the Benefactor and King of kings and God of gods could not brook to despise even the humblest, but deigned to banquet him on holy oracles and statutes, as though he should be the sole guest, as though for him alone the feast was prepared to give good cheer to a soul instructed in the holy secrets and accepted for admission to the greatest mysteries, what right have I, the mortal, to bear myself proud-necked, puffed-up and loud-voiced, toward my fellows, who, though their fortunes be unequal, have equal rights of kinship?[25]

With God as my example I should instead be "affable and easy of access to the poorest, to the meanest, to the lonely who have none close at hand to help them, to orphans who have lost both parents, to wives on whom widowhood has fallen, to old men either childless from the first or bereaved by the early death of those whom they begot."[26] Philo admonishes us to demonstrate that we are human, "not only because the lot both of the prosperous and the unfortunate may change to the reverse we know not when, but also because it is right that even if good fortune remains securely established, a man should not forget what he is."[27]

This two-thousand-year-old exposition is a moving summary of what was written on the tablets of the covenant, both as regards humanity's relationship to God and one's love of one's neighbor, the dual commandment of love (Deut. 6:4–5 and Lev. 19:18, 34; see further pp. 164f., 175ff.).

No Other Gods

The introductory "I am" is followed by "You shall." God's "I" is the hook that carries all the "You shall" of the subsequent commandments. Or to use another image, first God addresses us, then we may choose to respond. It is like a Gregorian chant with the Lord as the leader and we, the congregation, singing the response.

The purpose of the commandments is not to lead the people into the covenant. The ten words are addressed to people who are already liberated. The commandments are, rather, to keep the people within the covenant (see p. 139 above). What is at stake is our response to the love of the Lord and our living worthy of the calling extended to us. Realizing the breadth and depth of the introductory words "I am the LORD," we will desire to worship no other gods.

The Hebrew of the commandment can actually be read as indicative as well as imperative, that is, as a statement ("You will have no other gods before me") as well as a commandment ("You shall have no other gods"). The former understanding would express what will be the consequence of knowing the Lord. If you know who I am and what I have done for you ("I am the LORD who . . ."), then you will not have other gods before me. Such an understanding is obviously expressed by the prophet Hosea: "I have been the LORD your God ever since the land of Egypt; you know no God but me, and besides me there is no savior" (13:4).

A literal translation of the commandment should read: "You shall have no other gods in front of me," or even "over my face." Idolatry means everything that is put in front of or over God, disguising and distorting God's true face. Images in particular are prohibited. Nothing created must ever be allowed to depict or even represent the sovereign creator. God is not part of creation and, therefore, he cannot and must not be confined by outward contours and human imaginations.[28]

Usually, however, it is things other than images that turn into those masks hiding God's face from us. In the New Testament there is a frequent warning against *Mammon,* the god of riches. The power of this idol is noticed in every layer of society today, from the palaces to the slums, causing people to break all the subsequent commandments.

It is possible to make spiritual images of God that harden into inner idols of a sort: preconceived ideas, which prevent us from opening ourselves toward the countenance that God turns toward us. It can be humanly created dogma, traditions, and authorities that are put in front of and above God's true face. Frequently, such idols are manufactured by a series of words from the Scriptures, and claim to sum up God's very character, salvation plan, and so forth. This idolatry does not allow the whole spectrum of the Bible to shine forth with all its riddles and mysteries. What is difficult to understand and to reduce to one common denominator is censored, together with everything that does not fit into one's preconceived image of God.

An image always limits and simplifies the depicted object. It shows only a few aspects of reality. Every confession and human formulation about God is precisely that kind of limitation. Yet, they are not only permitted but even necessary, since we ourselves are limited as human beings. Revelation always implies that God has limited himself in some ways for our benefit (cf. 33:19ff. and Deut. 4:15ff.).

The Bible itself limits God's word (cf. John 1:1ff.). When we forget, however, that our knowledge, denomination, confession, worship, etc., can never become more than a pale reflection of the divine glory and the heavenly truth, in that moment we have made an image that conceals God's true face. Then we easily become deaf to other peoples' experience. We deny that God has ways that we ourselves have not yet seen. We then confuse the church or our own denomination with the kingdom of God. And then the image we have made of God is easily converted into a weapon against others, obscuring the countenance that shines graciously upon us.

All other commandments are in one way or another linked to this one. Every sin emerges from the fact that God is no longer first in our lives, but is concealed by something created. Therefore, this commandment is followed by a warning and a promise (vv. 5–6). The words describing a God "punishing children for the iniquity of parents, to the third and the fourth generation" have troubled many serious readers of the Bible. What is at issue here? Does a sort of collective punishment extend for generations?

These words raised questions in biblical times, since various aspects of them are specified in other passages. In a mere juridical sense, nobody can be punished for the sins of others (Deut. 24:16). This legal rule reflects God's order (see Jer. 31:29–30 and the thorough elucidation in Ezek. 18). The indication of precisely three and four generations is probably nothing but a reference to an entire household, that is, what is generally the largest number of generations alive at one time.

We should also bear in mind that the words warning of the visitation of the fathers' iniquity only apply to "those who reject me" (v. 5). The destructive effect of evil is consequently broken by "those who love me and keep my commandments"

(v. 6). Neither let us forget that the punishment is linked to no more than four generations, while God's grace extends to "thousands" (cf. Ps. 103:17–18 and p. 260 below). (For more on this commandment, see 20:22–26; 22:18–20 [pp. 171–72]; 23:13, 24, 32–33; 32; 33:18–23; 34:12–17.)

God's Name

Expressions like "for his name's sake," "hallowed be thy name," "blessed is he who comes in the name of the Lord," and "call upon the name of the Lord" give an indication of the importance ascribed to a person's name in the Bible. The name is part of one's innermost identity. To address someone by name always expresses a relationship and often even a certain proximity to that person. In a similar way as an image expresses certain aspects of the depicted, the name is also a powerful expression of who that person is.

If it is this way in our culture today, it was even more so in the world of the Bible. Thus the authority of humankind over creation was expressed by Adam's giving names to the animals (Gen. 2:19–20). To call something by name here means to comprehend and thus master it. As we have already seen, this is the reason why human beings are not allowed to make an image of God. The Lord is our master and not vice versa. Therefore, the prohibition against images of God has the same background as the possibly equally ancient prohibition against pronouncing the name of God, *YHWH* (see pp. 31ff.). To make images of God (idols) and to take God's name in vain are consequently two aspects of one and the same sin: failure to proclaim God's total sovereignty.

The commandment is literally phrased: "You shall not lift up the name of the Lord your God for nothingness." The Hebrew word for "nothingness" or "emptiness" *(shav)* also means "falsehood" and "lie," just like the word *sheqer* in Deut. 5:11. What is forbidden is, of course, blasphemy (Lev. 24:15–16) and perjury (Lev. 19:12), but in a wider sense any use of God's name thoughtlessly or for one's own advantage. The rabbis warn against the use of God's name to appear pious and impress others, that is, hypocrisy.[29] Therefore, this commandment is relevant even in connection with worship and prayer: "Never be rash with your mouth, nor let your heart be quick to utter a word before God, for God is in

heaven, and you upon earth; therefore let your words be few"
(Eccl. 5:2; cf. Matt. 6:6ff.).

In order to go deeper into the significance of this
commandment, we should again contemplate what God has
done for us: "But now thus says the LORD, he who created
you, O Jacob, he who formed you, O Israel: 'Do not fear, for
I have redeemed you; I have called you by name, you are
mine' " (Isa 43:1). The more we become aware of the reverence and personal love with which God uses our names, the
more will God's own name be precious to us. We are en-
couraged to "call upon it in all need, pray, give thanks, and
glorify it," as Luther expresses it in his explanation of this
commandment.[30]

In Jewish tradition *hillul ha-Shem* ("profanation of the
Name") is regarded as one of the most serious of sins. It means
to live in such a way that people around us lose respect for
God's holy name (cf. Lev. 22:31ff.; Jer. 34:16ff.; Ezek. 36:20ff.;
Amos 2:7; Rom. 2:23–24). We are instead commanded to "lift
up his name" through our lives so God will be revered,
trusted, and loved by more people, whose names are so dear in
the Lord's eyes (cf. Matt. 5:16). As the psalmist says, "Blessed
be his glorious name forever; may his glory fill the whole
earth. Amen and Amen" (Ps. 72:19).

The Sabbath

The Sabbath commandment is closely related to the previous one regarding God's holy name. Israel sanctifies God's
name by imitating him in sanctifying the Sabbath. The first
thing sanctified, or "consecrated," by God in the Bible is the
Sabbath day, the culmination of the entire creation story (Gen.
2:3). As God rested on the seventh day after the six days of creating, Israel is commanded both to work and create six days a
week (20:9)[31] and to rest on the seventh day. In this way God
and his people will enter into a close partnership in working
and resting "together." God's revelation of his name to the
people is another demonstration of this intimate relationship
with them. Hence God's name is sanctified when the Sabbath
is remembered and kept holy by the people to whom he has
revealed his holy name. This deep connection between the
Sabbath commandment and the previous one is aptly expressed in the Sabbath prayers:

Our God and God of our fathers, take pleasure in our rest, hallow us
by Your commandments and grant our portion in Your Torah. Satisfy
us from Your good, gladden us with Your salvation, purify our hearts
to serve You in truth, and in Your love and favor, O *God* our God, let
Your holy Sabbath remain our inheritance, and may Yisrael, who sanctify Your Name, rest on it. Blessed be You *God*, Who hallows the
Sabbath.[32]

According to the Jewish way of arranging the ten
words on the tablets, the commandment against bearing
false witness on the second tablet is paralleled by the Sabbath commandment on the first. For God's people to dese-
crate the Sabbath is nothing short of bearing false witness
against God himself in the world (see the comment on
31:13, p. 243).

Thus it is hardly surprising that over a third of the
space on the covenant tablets is dedicated to the Sabbath
commandment, this commandment is repeated frequently,
and the violation against the Sabbath is dealt with seriously
(cf. 16:5, 22–30; 23:12; 31:12–17; 34:21; 35:2–3; Lev. 19:3,
30; 23:3; 26:2; Num. 15:32–36; Deut. 5:12–15; Isa. 56:2, 6;
58:13–14; 66:23; Jer. 17:21–27; Ezek. 20:12–24; 22:8, 26;
23:38; 44:24; Amos 8:4–6; Neh. 9:13–14; 10:31; 13:15–22).
Nor should it be surprising that one of the most extensive
tractates in the Talmud details what the observance of the
Sabbath entails.[33]

The Sabbath rest is Israel's totally unique gift to the
world, as is the radical and uncompromising monotheism
proclaimed in the previous words on the tablets of the covenant. Even though the number seven played an important
role in the surrounding cultures, there is no evidence that
they followed a seven-day week and had a regular day of
rest. The closest parallel to the biblical Sabbath would be
the Akkadian texts indicating that the seventh, fourteenth,
twenty-first, twenty-eighth, thirty-fifth, forty-second, and
forty-ninth days of a fifty-day-period were considered as ill-
fated days, therefore work performed on these days would
be considered luckless.

This parallel, however, is limited to the importance of the
number seven but is an antithesis of the biblical Sabbath,
being a day of blessing. Instead of evil spirits discouraging and
even frightening people from performing work, which would
only lead to bad luck, the good Creator invites his people to
enjoy his presence in a realm of holiness and peace on the

Sabbath. Furthermore, in ancient Mesopotamia, the ominous days were marked as days of fasting and mourning, while the Sabbath is a day of utmost joy and abundance. We also notice that the Sabbath does not follow specific dates of the month, that is, it is not linked to the cycle of the moon or to anything created. On the contrary, it is a confession of the Creator as the one above and beyond creation.[34]

The uniqueness of the Sabbath involves not just its proclamation and exaltation of the one Creator—the Sabbath being "a sabbath to the Lord" (16:23; 20:10; 35:2; Lev. 23:3; Deut. 5:14)—but also its social function. The Sabbath rest embraces the whole household, including all servants, strangers, and even animals. It demonstrates and commands the total social equality and dignity of every human being and is a visible declaration that "the earth is the LORD's and all that is in it, the world, and those who live in it" (Ps. 24:1).

In a world characterized by class divisions, most dramatically the one between masters and servants, this weekly rest from labor transmitted a radically new message—a message that ultimately every human being is bound for freedom. Philo beautifully summarizes this message: "The result of this occasional submission of the free to do the menial offices of the slave,[35] together with the immunity allowed to the slave, will be a step forward in human conduct toward the perfection of virtue, when both the seemingly distinguished and the meaner sort remember equality and repay each other the debt incumbent upon them."[36]

No wonder the Sabbath is viewed as a foretaste of the ideal world at the end of days, when God will create a new heaven and a new earth, where there will be a peaceful harmony between God and humanity, among nations, classes, and persons, between humanity and creation, and within creation itself (see, e.g., Isa. 2:2–4; 65:17–25; 66:22–23; Heb. 4:9–11; and Rev. 14:13). According to an ancient Jewish tradition,[37] the prophet Zechariah refers to this eternal Sabbath in Zech. 14:7: "And there shall be continuous day (it is known to the LORD), not day and not night, for at evening there shall be light." This verse recalls a peculiarity in the creation story. After each day it is said that "there was evening and there was morning." On the seventh day, however, this temporal indication is omitted. It is a day that transcends our temporal existence. It gives a taste of eternity.

"The Sabbath is thus both the end of the beginning and the beginning of the end, a well-spring of trust and hope for a better, perfected world."[38] This hope is expressed in the grace after the Sabbath meals. After meals throughout the week, Ps. 137 is recited, which laments the exiles' tears by the streams of Babylon. On the Sabbath, however, Ps. 126 is read, which expresses the hope that the tears will come to an end: "May those who sow in tears reap with shouts of joy. Those who go out weeping, bearing the seed for sowing, shall come home with shouts of joy, carrying their sheaves." An addition to the grace on the Sabbath reads: "May the Compassionate One let us inherit that day which shall be all Sabbath and rest for life everlasting."[39]

A Jewish prayer at the conclusion of the Sabbath sums up the deep connection between the Sabbath in this age and the eternal Sabbath: "Creator of the world, in your great mercy you have given us the holy Sabbath as a precious gift; we are unable to thank you enough for this great bounty. . . . May we be able to receive the next Sabbath in holiness, and in its time—the day of redemption that is wholly a Sabbath."[40]

For further discussion of the Sabbath, see 31:12–17 (pp. 237ff.).

Parents

The words on the first tablet deal primarily with the relationship between God and people, while the second tablet focuses on the relationships among human beings. This commandment, the fifth one according to the Jewish reckoning, marks a transition between these two aspects. Parents are not only fellow human beings. Through them God has given us life. We have also been dependent upon them as we mature and assume responsibility for our own lives. They are largely God's instruments in the service of life.

When we ask, "Who is my neighbor?" the correct answer is "Anyone who crosses my path." The commandment of love knows no boundaries. On the other hand, the rule applies that the closer my fellow human beings are to me, the greater the responsibility I have for them. Significantly, the Hebrew word for "neighbor" (reaʿ) is rendered in the Septuagint as well as in the New Testament by the Greek word for "close" (plesion). This translation reflects an important principle regarding the commandment of love: the closer, the warmer.

Our parents come closest. That is the reason why one particular commandment, followed by a great promise, is dedicated to parents (see Eph. 6:1ff.). At the same time, violation of this commandment is linked to severe warnings and punishments (see 21:15, 17, pp. 160f., and further Deut. 27:16; Prov. 19:26; 28:24; 30:17). These references make it clear that this commandment primarily addresses adult children and commands them to take care of their parents when age makes them weak and dependent on others.

Life

According to the Jewish reckoning of the commandments, this one comes first on the second tablet; that is, it corresponds to the "I am the LORD, your God" at the top of the first tablet. These two "headlines" of the tablets thus become a concrete reminder of the double commandment of love, where the commandment regarding the neighbor is "like" the one regarding the love of God (Matt. 22:39).

To extinguish a human life is equivalent to attacking the image of God. As one midrash puts it:

> A king of flesh and blood entered a province and the people set up portraits of him, made images of him, and struck coins in his honor. Later on they upset his portraits, broke his images, and defaced his coins,[41] thus diminishing the likenesses of the king. So also if one sheds blood it is accounted to him as though he had diminished the divine image. For it is said: "Whoso sheddeth man's blood . . . for in the image of God made He man" (Gen. 9:6).[42]

That one's fellow human being is a reflection of God is also expressed in 1 John 4:20: "Those who say, 'I love God,' and hate their brothers and sisters, are liars; for those who do not love a brother or sister whom they have seen, cannot love God whom they have not seen." While the plants and the animals were created in great multitude, "man was created alone, to teach you that whoever destroys a single human soul, is charged by Scripture as though he had destroyed a whole world, and whoever rescues a single human soul, is credited by Scripture as though he had rescued a whole world."[43]

The commandment says: "You shall not murder." There are several ethical problems linked to this commandment. It is not always easy to define the boundaries between murder and permissible killing. For instance, to kill in self-defense is permissible according to a broad consensus in both the Jewish and Christian tradition. The reverence for the sanctity of life, even one's own, supersedes all other commandments.[44] Only God rules over life and death. To assume the right to terminate life means nothing less than usurping God's throne (cf. pp. 14f.).

The subsequent commandments on this second tablet can be regarded as commentaries on the "headline." To violate the sanctity of the marriage of one's neighbors, steal their property, destroy their name, and covet what they may have depreciates their life and hence in equal measure the creator and giver of life in whose image one's neighbor is created. The intimate link between these commandments is even more clearly expressed in their parallel (Deut. 5), where they are all connected by an "and," which translations usually disregard. A Jewish midrash explains this "and" by stressing that "this teaches us that all the commandments belong together. If anyone breaks one, they will violate them all."[45] See further 21:12–13, 18–21 (pp. 160ff.).

Marriage

Together with idolatry and murder, adultery is one of the three gravest sins; humans are obliged to give their lives rather than commit these (see n. 44). This sin is frequently linked with idolatry, and the covenant between God and Israel is often compared to a marriage (see pp. 91, 131, n. 6). To worship other gods is equivalent to infidelity toward God, analogous to adultery (see, e.g., Jer. 3:1–11; 5:7–11; Ezek. 16:22; Hos. 2–3; Mal. 2:10–16).

On the other hand, adultery is proof of such a contempt for God's ways that it can be compared to idolatry. One rabbinic tradition counts no fewer than fourteen commandments that an adulterer directly or indirectly violates.[46] It is therefore not surprising that the rabbis discern a deeper meaning behind the fact that idolatry and adultery both occur second on their respective tablets.[47]

The covenant between God and Israel is sealed and signed in the collective wedding act at Sinai, where the "law," the wedding contract containing God's promises and commandments, spells out the marriage conditions. No wonder, therefore, that deviation from any of the commandments is labeled as "prostituting" or "whoring" in Num. 15:39, literally translated: "and you shall remember all the commandments of the LORD and do them, and not go about after your heart and eyes, after which you are whoring."[48] In other words, law and love, commandments and covenant, are inseparable (see also Deut. 7:6–8; 10:12–15; 30:15–20 and further pp. 127ff., 139f., 142f., 189–96, 242).[49]

Since polygamy was practiced in ancient Israel, this prohibition first of all applies to sexual intercourse between a betrothed or married woman and another man, whereas a betrothed or married man was allowed to take another wife as long as she was not betrothed, married, or had received a bill of divorce, according to Deut. 24:1–4. In reality, though not in principle, monogamy became the prevailing rule in Judaism. There are clear indications of this in the Qumran texts and within the strictest part of the Pharisaic movement, the school of Shammai (who practiced significantly stricter rules for divorce than the more liberal school of Hillel). The former view was shared by Jesus, and therefore Christianity from the very beginning practiced monogamy (for example, Matt. 5:31–32; 19:1ff.; Luke 16:18). See also below 22:16–17, 19 (p. 171).

Property

According to the Jewish reckoning, this commandment is number three on the second tablet, occurring parallel to the commandment regarding God's name on the first tablet, "because the one who steals will end up swearing falsely."[50] This rabbinic tradition also refers to Jer. 7:9 and Hos. 4:2, where theft appears together with murder, adultery, and false oaths.

More important than the arrangement of the commandments on the tablets is the insight that there is a deep connection among them, and that one sin generates another. There is, for instance, hardly any doubt that many murders originate in violation of this and the previous commandment. The stories of David and Uriah (2 Sam. 11–12) and of Naboth's vineyard (1 Kgs. 21) certainly indicate a basic theme in the history of human sin and degradation. See further 21:16 (p. 161) and 22:1–17 (pp. 170f.).

The Tongue

For the same reasons mentioned above, this next commandment is particularly linked to its "neighbor" on the first tablet, the Sabbath commandment. The Sabbath is Israel's witness to the world that God is the Creator and Savior— "You are my witnesses" (Isa. 43:10). To violate the sanctity of the Sabbath is equivalent to bearing false witness against God, just as this commandment forbids false witness against one's neighbor.[51]

The commandment deals first and foremost with false witness in a court (see also 23:1–3, p. 175). The fact that theft often generates false testimony may explain the placement of the commandment on the tablet (see Lev. 19:11–12). Since witnesses at court hold the destiny of a fellow human being in their hands, and a community governed by law is built upon the integrity of its courts, false testimony is judged by the same criterion as the crime to be adjudicated before the court (see Deut. 19:15–21).

However, this commandment deals with any testimony that a person advances against his neighbor. In Jewish tradition, an entire literature has arisen regarding *leshon hara*, "the evil tongue." The fact that we so often underestimate the sins of the tongue probably explains the strong warnings against these sins: "There are four companies of men who will not behold the presence of God: the company of scorners . . . , the company of hypocrites . . . , the company of slanderers . . . , and the company of liars. . . ."[52] The devastating consequences of slander is drastically, yet aptly, expressed as follows: "It kills three: the one who speaks it, the one who listens to it, and the one about whom it is spoken."[53]

Violation of this commandment involves, however, not only slander and untruth, as illustrated by the following statement:

> Three the Holy One, blessed be He, hates: he who speaks one thing with his mouth and another thing in his heart; and he who possesses [good] evidence concerning his neighbor and does not testify for him; and he who alone sees something indecent in his neighbor and testifies against him.[54]

In the last case, it is a matter of putting one's neighbor to shame publicly and making him or her lose face. It is consequently not enough that what we say may be true. We must also ask to what good will my telling it lead?

Are there cases when a lie is justified? According to what was said relative to the sanctity of life above, one is obliged to lie if this may save the life of a human being (see 1:19ff., p. 12).

Rabbinic ethics mention another case: if the "white lie" can make peace between people, it may be defended as well. It is, however, not easy to define exactly when this is the case. At any rate, this rule expresses the spirit of this commandment. When the letter of James 3 deals with the use of the tongue, it similarly concludes by speaking about those who make peace.

In Num. 12 Miriam became leprous after she spoke evil against Moses. Based on this text, the thought has emerged in Jewish tradition that the sins of the tongue defile persons, just as leprosy does in the Bible. Therefore, these sins were regarded as more serious than most other sins. They were sometimes even mentioned together with the three mortal sins: idolatry, adultery, and murder.[55]

What the tongue elicits from one's innermost being can defile. On the other hand, it is never said that one who violates the dietary laws is defiled. This thought is expressed in Jesus' words: "It is not what goes into the mouth that defiles a person, but it is what comes out of the mouth that defiles." He continues: "For out of the heart come evil intentions, murder, adultery, fornication, theft, false witness, and slander. These are what defile a person, but to eat with unwashed hands does not defile" (Matt 15:10–20). In a typical rabbinic way, Jesus here points to the inner coherence and the greater weight of sin with respect to its origin. In doing so, he also puts the last commandment in the center, which sums up all the other commandments.

The Conclusion: The Heart

Since the introduction of the "ten words" is fundamental for understanding the commandments, special importance should be attached to the conclusion, that is, the tenth word, "You shall not covet." This commandment can indeed be regarded as a summary of the previous ones, just as the first "word" affects all the following ones.

In many confessions of sin, there is a formulation about sinning in "thoughts, words, and deeds." In each respect, one can commit sins against every commandment. Yet, the preceding commandment primarily deals with the sins of the tongue, and the previous ones with concrete actions where other parts of the body are involved. The last commandment, on the other hand, deals exclusively with the sins of the heart: lust, egoism, jealousy, etc. The concrete act of sin begins in the heart, where the very source of murder, adultery, theft, slander, etc. is to be found.

In the Sermon on the Mount (Matt. 5:21ff.), Jesus' emphasis on the violence of the commandments in the very heart of human beings is consequently part of an ancient biblical and Jewish understanding of the commandments.[56] Obedience to the last commandment (as well as of all the others) presupposes a clean and undivided heart. Since no human can attain that in this world, one of the promises regarding the coming age is the bestowal of a new heart (Jer. 31:33; Ezek. 36:26–27).

Another observation further stresses the last commandment as a kind of summary of "the ten words." While they are introduced by "I am the LORD," they are concluded by the words "your neighbor." We consequently find the double commandment of love as two pillars and as the foundation of everything written in between. It is significant that these two commandments particularly stress the condition of the heart: "You shall love the LORD your God with all your heart" (Deut. 6:5), with the love of one's neighbor immediately preceded by the words, "You shall not hate in your heart" (Lev. 19:17).

This conclusion of the "ten words" is essential for Christians to keep in mind, since a frequent prejudice against Judaism—and sometimes even against the Old Testament—is that the commandments and their obedience only concern external manifestations according to the letter, while the New Testament and Christianity emphasize the inner significance of the law, the spirit, and the heart. This latter aspect is already stressed on the tablets of the covenant, given by the same God whose commandments embrace the whole human being, even the most secret thought: "for the LORD does not see as mortals see; they look on the outward appearance, but the LORD looks on the heart" (1 Sam. 16:7).

The tablets of the covenant provide the most basic rules for the relationship between God and Israel. They largely coincide with the general principles that every human society follows in order to survive. No society, however, can rely solely on such general principles. A court must have detailed rules regulating crime and punishment. The same applies to Israel. Therefore, God further provides his people with more detailed rules than those found on the tablets of the covenant. Some of these are given in the chapters immediately following.

10

The Book of the Covenant

*C*hapters 21–23 are usually called "the book of the covenant." This name is taken from chapter 24, where we read (v. 7) that Moses "took the book of the covenant, and read it in the hearing of the people." Its content is also indicated: "Moses came and told the people all the words of the LORD and all the ordinances" (v. 3). "All the words of the LORD" refer to "the ten words" in chapter 20 with its introduction, "Then God spoke all these words, saying . . ." In a similar way, we also find an introduction to the three following chapters: "These are the ordinances that you shall set before them" (21:1).

The "words" and "ordinances" that Moses is to read to the people in connection with the sealing of the covenant, "the book of the covenant," consist mainly of the laws and statutes about to be examined. From the outset, it is important to recognize that these rather detailed ordinances are presented as equally divine and just as important for the people as the basic principles in the "ten words." The whole book of the covenant, and not only the tablets of the covenant, constitutes the foundation of the covenant. This is the reason why even the laws in chapters 21–23 are presented before the covenant can be sealed in chapter 24. We could perhaps say: first comes the confirmation book and then the confirmation itself. The section can be divided into three main parts.

(1) 21:1–22:17. Ordinances dealing with various themes related to day-to-day life. Their common denominator is that they first describe a situation or a crime, usually in a very de-

tailed manner, and then the appropriate law or penalty. These kinds of laws are usually labeled "casuistic laws," since they deal with particular *cases*. Therefore, they have a totally different judicial style than the "ten words," which describe neither single cases of crimes nor the exact penalty. On the other hand, the laws in the book of the covenant also do not form a code of laws in a judicial sense. They are not systematically arranged, and important areas of legislation are not considered at all.

Rabbinic tradition therefore stresses that God's law consists of a written and an oral part. It is obvious that the people of Israel needed far more laws than those we find within the covers of the Bible.[1] When we read the ordinances in these chapters, we realize that other laws and traditions are already presumed to be known. The fact that the revelation transmitted during the intimate communion between the Lord and Moses (and Israel) could not be contained in writing is certainly no more surprising than the conclusion of the Gospel of John: "But there are also many other things that Jesus did; if every one of them were written down, I suppose that the world itself could not contain the books that would be written" (John 21:25).

Neither can we forget that the Israelites had laws and traditions which they to a certain extent shared with other nations. Parts of the legislation in these chapters, therefore, demonstrate numerous striking parallels in both style and subject matter to collections of laws among the surrounding peoples. As we will see, the differences are no less striking, often reflecting a different social and religious value system.[2]

(2) 22:18–23:19. Laws differing from the previous ones in both style and content. They consist of general rules for the worship of God and relationships with one's neighbor in a way paralleling the "ten words." Except for the first three verses no specific punishment is meted out for violation of these laws. This does not, however, mean that they have less importance. While the casuistic laws are cases for the civil court, these laws are a matter for everyone's conscience. It is certainly understood that one is directly responsible to the divine legislator, who is superior to any human court. Instead of subjection to human penalties, the transgressor is subject to God's curse. Such laws are absolute and unconditional. Therefore they are sometimes called "apodictic laws," after the

Greek *apodeiknynai* ("to point out," "to proclaim"). These laws are thus above human deliberation.

(3) 23:20–33. Concluding promises and warnings.

SLAVES (21:1–11)

Just as the tablets of the covenant are introduced by a reference to Israel's salvation out of Egypt, the land of slavery, and continue with an ordinance regarding Sabbath rest even for the slave, these laws begin with rules regarding the conditions of the slaves. Even later the concern for slaves is demonstrated (see 21:20, 26–27).

The memory of Israel's own slavery is to be reflected in a particular sensitivity toward the slavery of others, just as the remembrance of the estrangement in Egypt should be a driving force to live according to the commandment of love, which relates to the stranger in particular (23:9; Lev. 19:33–34). In this respect, Israel's laws were unique in the world of that time.[3]

Nevertheless slavery was a reality. A Hebrew person could become a slave by being sold (21:2). This could happen if anyone were sold by poor parents or forced to sell oneself because of poverty (Lev. 25:39; cf. 2 Kings 4:1; Neh. 5:1–13). A thief who could not restore the stolen goods could also be sold as a slave (22:2).

The statute to free the slave after six years limits slavery at a decisive point. The Hebrew word for "go out" in 21:2 is the same as the one used for the liberation of Israel from Egypt, *yatsaʾ*. And when the slave was freed, he should not leave empty-handed:

> Provide liberally out of your flock, your threshing floor, and your wine press, thus giving to him some of the bounty with which the LORD your God has blessed you. Remember that you were a slave in the land of Egypt, and the LORD your God redeemed you; for this reason I lay this command upon you today." (Deut. 15:13ff.)

It is obvious that the laws regarding slaves are built on Israel's own experience when they went forth out of Egypt (3:21–22; 12:35–36, pp. 93ff.).[4]

Normally there was no lifelong slavery. The seriousness of this commandment is clearly expressed in Jer. 34:8–22. At his own request, however, a male slave could serve his master throughout his whole life. As an irrevocable sign of this choice, the ear of the slave was pierced in a kind of covenantal act (21:6). It is not clear what lies behind this rule. One rabbinic interpretation is particularly interesting, since it reflects the opposition against slavery:

> How is the ear different from the limbs so as to be pierced? Because it heard [the words] from Mount Sinai, "For to me the people of Israel are servants; they are my servants" (Lev. 25:55);[5] yet it cast off the yoke of the kingdom of Heaven and took upon itself the yoke of flesh and blood. Therefore, the scripture says that it shall be pierced since it did not obey what it had heard."[6]

The thought that the people of Israel are slaves of the Lord as contrasted to all human slavery is often expressed (cf. pp. 14f., 75, 77, 127). In the midrash to Ps. 113:1 ("Praise the LORD! Praise, O servants of the LORD; praise the name of the LORD"), we read, "We were Pharaoh's slaves, but you redeemed us and made us your slaves. Therefore it is said, 'Praise, O servants of the Lord,' and not 'Praise, O servants of Pharaoh.' " Paul presents a similar teaching: "For whoever was called in the Lord as a slave is a freed person belonging to the Lord, just as whoever was free when called is a slave of Christ. You were bought with a price; do not become slaves of human masters" (1 Cor. 7:22–23).

Many in biblical times probably regarded slavery as a questionable institution. We do not find one single verse defending slavery, while there are numerous laws protecting the rights of slaves. Early Jewish commentaries show a clear tendency to humanize this unfortunate social practice. The phrase "since he is well off with you" in Deut. 15:16 is thus taken to mean that the slave has to be equal to his master:

> "Since he is well off with you" (means that) he must be with you in food and drink. You shall not eat white bread and he dark. You shall not drink old wine and he new. You shall not sleep on a feather bed and he on straw. Hence it was said that whoever buys a Hebrew slave is like buying a master for himself.[7]

If we did not know that it is a slave who is being referred to, we might think of an ancient version of the regulations of a trade union! When viewing slavery in a context like this, one may even question whether "slave" is a proper rendering of the word ʿeved. Would not "servant" be more appropriate (see pp. 14f.)?

It is even possible that behind the rule in Deut. 23:15–16 not to give up to his master a slave who has escaped, there is a hidden desire that slavery should be totally abolished. In all other contemporary law codes, it is ruled that such a slave should be returned to his master. Some laws even imposed the death sentence upon one who disregarded that law.[8]

Special rules applied to female slaves. They usually became concubines, but with the same status as a married woman. If her master did not want to keep her any longer, he had to see to it that she was redeemed by her own relatives. If she belonged to the son, she should enjoy the same rights as a daughter. Further, if her master took yet another wife, this could not infringe upon the slave's status as a wife.

SHEDDING BLOOD, HUMILIATING PARENTS, KIDNAPPING (21:12–17)

These laws give further details concerning three of the commandments on the tablets of the covenant. Not surprisingly, the death sentence is meted out for murder. For involuntary manslaughter, a possibility is opened for the perpetrator to flee to certain cities (Num. 35:6, 9–34; Deut. 4:41–43; 19:1–13) or to the altar (right of asylum). For voluntary manslaughter no such protection was provided, not even in the sanctuary (1 Kgs. 1:50ff.; 2:28ff.; cf. Luke 1:69). Holiness of place can never supersede holiness of life (cf. pp. 237f.).

The purpose of this institution was to protect the life of a person who by accident had caused the death of another. As long as blood revenge was still practiced, the perpetrator was in danger. Through a strong centralized judicial system, this kind of revenge could later be stopped. The right of asylum also lost its importance then.

To insult and outrage one's parents was judged as severely as shedding blood and blasphemy (Lev. 24:16). What is at stake in 21:15 is not the slaying of one's parents but striking them as an expression of insult or wrath. The fact that manslaughter has already been dealt with in the previous verses makes this clear.

Further, cursing one's parents is enough to sentence one to death (21:17). The verb translated "curse" expresses the very opposite of the verb "honor" in the commandment on the tablets of the covenant (20:12). It expresses humiliation and spitefulness in general. Even one who "dishonors" his or her father or his mother is labeled as "cursed" (Deut. 27:16).

The great seriousness in which the relationship between child and parent was held is further demonstrated by how God's relationship to Israel is often compared to that between parents and children. Israel is God's firstborn son, to whom God is "father" and "mother" (4:22; Deut. 32:16; Ps. 89:27; 103:13; Isa. 49:15; cf. Num. 11:11ff.).

Kidnapping is the third serious crime dealt with in this section. The death sentence is imposed on the perpetrator even in this case, which is certainly the most serious violation against the commandment, "You shall not steal" (see p. 152). In addition, kidnapping endangers human life. A concrete example is provided by the Joseph narrative (Gen. 37:12ff.; see also Deut. 24:7). Since a person's belongings—material goods, work, reputation, etc.—are integral parts of that person's identity, theft of whatever kind and any act destroying another's life can be regarded as a subdivision of this sin.

As regards the death sentence, which is so frequently expressed in this text and the Bible, one should be aware that both the death sentence as such and its implementation were in reality extremely rare, at least in postexilic times. Based on the principle that at least two witnesses were required for imposition of the death sentence (Deut. 17:6), the burden of proof was made so onerous that it became virtually impossible to prove the case. If the testimonies of the witnesses were too similar, they could be suspected of conspiracy, and if they were too divergent, they would certainly also not be considered as trustworthy.

The courts followed the principle of giving the accused every possible benefit of the doubt. Should a death sentence be required, the court had to wait with the definite sentencing until the following day. The members of the court were obliged to fast and were allowed to change their opinion, albeit only in one direction, toward acquittal. One who had once pronounced himself in favor of acquittal could consequently never vote for conviction later.[9]

The following incisive statement probably does justice to the humanity which, in spite of the severe biblical laws, characterized the judicial system in Judaism: "A court which executes one person in seven years is termed tyrannical. Rabbi Eleazar ben Azariah says: One person in seventy years. Rabbi Tarphon and Rabbi Aqiba say: If we had been in the court,

nobody would ever have been executed."[10] By their statement
the latter rabbis claim that they would have found possibilities
in the Torah of demolishing every line of proof leading to a
guilty verdict. Rabban Simon ben Gamaliel adds, however,
that their attitude would have caused more bloodshed in Israel. The modern debate over the death sentence probably
finds here its earliest precursor in history.

"EYE FOR EYE, TOOTH FOR TOOTH"—
THE LAW OF DAMAGES (21:18–27)

First, a case of bodily injury resulting from a fight is dealt
with: the perpetrator is liable for payment of damages for lost
wages and health care. The following law, which particularly
addresses a slain slave, demonstrates both that slaves were ju-
dicially discriminated against and that their human dignity remained a concern. The life of a slave is inviolable, and
therefore the killer "shall be punished" (21:20). However, the
Hebrew text is clearer and strongly states that the slave "shall
certainly be revenged," that is, the perpetrator himself shall receive the death penalty.[11]

The following verse shows that the life of a slave was not
entirely equal to that of a free person. If death occurred after a
day or more, the perpetrator was obviously regarded as having
caused the death only indirectly. The motivation for freeing
the killer in this case is that "the slave is his money." This motivation probably intends to prove that the owner was concerned about his own property and therefore could have
caused the death of his slave involuntarily. This verse has
often been taken out of context and distorted by slave owners
as a biblical motivation for slavery and as a pretext for treating
slaves as property without human dignity. Nothing could be
further from the text's original intention.

The next case is about a pregnant woman who has given
birth to her child prematurely as the result of trauma. She is
adjudged damages even if both she and the child escaped lasting injuries. In the case that she and/or the child are injured or
even die, the consequences are not quite clear. We have to assume that the law concerns a case of accidental injury or
death. Otherwise, the rule in 21:12 applies.

This case is dealt with also in laws of the surrounding cultures. The punishment could vary from monetary damages to the death sentence. We also find examples in which the children of the perpetrator could be killed as punishment. Another striking characteristic is that they usually differentiate the severity of punishments based upon class-distinction between the perpetrator and the victim.[12] However, such punishment of a third party, in the case of capital crimes, is totally alien to the biblical laws.

The next principle of penalty is the most well-known, discussed, and misunderstood in the whole Bible. It is sometimes called "the law of revenge," or, in judicial terms, *ius* (or *lex*) *talionis,* from the Latin word for "law" plus *talio,* which means retaliation. "Eye for eye, tooth for tooth" is to many the epitome of the so-called Old Testament God and one of the reasons for characterizing the Old Testament and Jewish ethics as harsh, brutal, and inhuman. It has sparked endless anti-Jewish outbursts from pulpits and in theological literature. It is also the basis of Shakespeare's Shylock in "The Merchant of Venice," a vicious portrayal, that has imprinted upon the masses for centuries an image of the mythological greedy Jew and his allegedly rigid and cruel sense of justice.

Since the principle appears in several classical law books of the ancient Near East, we will first make a brief comparison with these. Then we will look at the biblical legislation in its original context and in Jewish tradition. Finally we will examine how the law was interpreted in later times, and how Jesus' exposition of it in the Sermon on the Mount is to be understood in the light of contemporary Jewish interpretation.

(a) *"Eye for eye, tooth for tooth" in ancient Near Eastern texts.* The rule "eye for eye, tooth for tooth" is first known from the law of the Babylonian king, Hammurabi (eighteenth century B.C.E.):

> If a seignior has destroyed the eye of a member of the aristocracy, they shall destroy his eye. If he has broken a(nother) seignior's bone, they shall break his bone. . . . If a seignior has knocked out a tooth of a seignior of his own rank, they shall knock out his tooth.[13]

If the victim comes from a lower class, however, this rule no longer applies. Only compensation in monetary terms is meted out: "If he [namely, a seignior] has destroyed the eye of a commoner or broken the bone of a commoner, he shall pay one mina of silver. If he has destroyed the eye of a seignior's slave or broken the bone of a seignior's slave, he shall pay one-half his value. . . .[14] If he has knocked out a commoner's tooth, he shall pay one-third mina of silver."[15]

Experts on ancient Near Eastern law have stressed the innovative and revolutionary approach of Hammurabi's law and even observed its positive juridical effects,[16] whereby the infliction of bodily injuries was transferred from civil to criminal law. Earlier, such injuries were regarded as a private matter between those involved. Only under the best of circumstances could an amicable settlement be reached, usually payment of damages to obviate a violent chain reaction.

Hammurabi's law was a first step toward making violence a concern of the entire society. Violence between private persons became a public crime, to be punished by the state. In other words, it became a societal responsibility to safeguard the security of citizens and to prevent private acts of retaliation, with the objective of achieving absolute fairness through the principle of tit for tat.

This judicial revolution significantly improved individual legal rights, above all for society's weak and marginalized classes. As in other nonbiblical collections of laws, however, it was still marked by a class consciousness which partially eliminated the intended equality and fairness. The principle was consequently applied only within one class. Moreover, punishment of a third party was acceptable, which could mean that children of a perpetrator were maimed or killed.

In this respect, the following example may suffice to illustrate the fundamental difference from the biblical laws:

> If a builder constructed a house for a seignior, but did not make his work strong, with the result that the house which he built collapsed and so has caused the death of the owner of the house, that builder shall be put to death. If he caused the death of the a son of the owner of the house, they shall put the son of that builder to death. If he has caused the death of a slave of the owner of the house, he shall give slave for slave to the owner of the house.[17]

(b) *"Eye for eye, tooth for tooth" in the Bible and in Jewish tradition.* In spite of the principle "eye for eye, tooth for tooth," mutilation is a totally unknown punishment in the Bible.[18] Only at one place is such a punishment mentioned: Deut. 25:11–12. In this case, however, it is obviously not applying the rule "eye for eye, tooth for tooth."[19] The sole known application of the so-called law of retaliation in 21:23–25 with its

two parallels in Lev. 24:17–21 and Deut. 19:18–21 is restricted to "life for life," according to the principles discussed
above. This in no way excludes the possibility that the law
may have once been applied even in cognate cases, for example, when only limbs were injured. One thing remains
clear, however: such use of the law disappeared entirely in
later legislation, with the sole exception of "life for life" in
connection with premeditated murder. In Jewish tradition
"eye for eye, tooth for tooth" exclusively dealt with monetary
compensation and nothing else.

There are several reasons why this interpretation replaced the principle of retaliation (if it was ever applied). Rabbinic commentaries provide biblical as well as humanitarian
arguments to prove the literal application of this law to be
unbiblical, unjust, absurd, and impossible.

As regards language, the Hebrew preposition translated by "for" in "eye for eye" *(tahath)* can also mean "instead of" and "as compensation for" (see, for example, Gen.
4:25). The same applies to the Greek preposition *anti,* used
in the Septuagint.[20]

The rule also appears in a wider context, which deals
with damages and not retaliation (see 21:18–22, 26–36). In
21:26–27 it is obvious that the loss of the eye and the tooth
leads to compensation, that is, the slave has to be freed. One
may therefore justifiably generalize this principle of compensation and apply it even to the previous verses.[21] There
may be a hint of this also in the formulation, "if any
harm follows, then *you shall give* life for life, eye for eye"
(21:23–24). In 21:22 the same verb, *nathan* ("to give"),
has precisely the meaning of paying compensation: "When
people who are fighting injure a pregnant woman so that
there is a miscarriage, and yet no further harm follows, the
one responsible shall be fined what the woman's husband
demands, paying [literally 'he shall give'] as much as the
judges determine." According to rabbinic interpretation,
this verb has the same meaning even in the following verse.
In other words: you shall give a compensation that corresponds to the damage inflicted.[22]

Even in Lev. 24:17–21 a connection is discerned between
the law ("eye for eye, tooth for tooth") and compensation for
damages. In verse 18 the phrase "life for life" is used to express
the principle that one must compensate another for an animal
that has been killed. In verse 21 it is further stressed that the

rule of compensation only applies to a slain animal, not a human being. Human life is above any material value that one can compensate. In the same manner, Num. 35:31 rules that there is no ransom "for the life of a murderer." From this it can be inferred that the Bible leaves open the possibility of paying compensation in all other cases, that is, when only bodily injury is involved.

The rabbis also emphasize that it would be unjust and impossible to apply "eye for eye, tooth for tooth" literally. It would be unjust, since the eye and every other part of the body is of individual importance for different people. For example, the punishment would be unfair it it were applied to a person already blind in one eye, and it would be overly severe for a disabled person to lose a leg or a hand. The damage caused by various injuries further depends upon a person's profession. The hand naturally means more to a craftsman than to a teacher. In other words, the exact justice of the commandment would be violated by a literal implementation. Another decisive argument against this literal application is that it endangers the life of the perpetrator. Since the protection of life is the highest principle in the Torah, the conclusion can thus be drawn that this principle is exclusively limited to paying damages for injury of any kind with the single exception of murder.[23]

Exactly how various parts of the body should be valued was a question to be decided in each single case according to certain principles. The damages should be proportional to such aspects as loss of income and pain and suffering. These rules remind one of modern insurance regulations designed to cover numerous cases in a satisfactory manner. As regards the slave who is to be freed (21:26–27) as compensation for an injury, rabbinic law specifies which parts of the body apply for such a compensation in addition to the eye and the tooth.[24]

In the time of Jesus, the application of the law was still under discussion. We know that the Sadducees favored a literal implementation. Even other groups probably did so, such as "the strictest party" among the Pharisees, the school of Shammai, with Rabbi Eliezer as its foremost representative (beginning of the second century C.E.).[25]

However, these voices soon became silent. Even though the ambiguous formulation of the law allows both for retaliation against the perpetrator and for compensation of the victim, the latter possibility eventually took precedence.

This marks a further step toward the humanization of societal judicial systems.

Just as in Matt. 7:2 (= Mark 4:24; Luke 6:38) and Matt. 25, retaliation more and more became something related to God's justice alone, mostly in connection with the judgment at the end of time. In human courts, on the other hand, the law of compensation became the only legitimate guideline for the implementation of "eye for eye, tooth for tooth."

When Maimonides gives examples of interpretations not immediately and unambiguously supported by the Torah, yet generally accepted in Jewish tradition, he emphasizes the law of compensation underlying "eye for eye, tooth for tooth":

> The following principle should be understood properly, namely, that the explanations received from Moses are without controversy whatsoever because until now we have never found a difference in opinion amongst the Sages any time from the days of Moses until Rav Ashi,[26] such that one Sage would say, "He who blinds the eye of his friend shall have his eye removed as it is written *An eye for en eye,*" and the other would say, "He is only obligated to pay indemnity (for the blind eye)."[27]

Thus, in the twelfth century Maimonides, the great master of Jewish tradition, contended that without exception all rabbinical authorities agreed to the latter understanding of the law. Since then, the picture has remained constant.

It should finally be emphasized that "eye for eye, tooth for tooth" could never be used to justify private revenge. This is deduced from the simple but basic principle of interpreting Scripture with Scripture. The commandment of love in Lev. 19:18 is introduced by the prohibition, "You shall not take vengeance or bear a grudge."[28] It is thus clear that "eye for eye, tooth for tooth" does not address the one who has suffered an injury but the one who has inflicted it. We could even say that this biblical command is the foundation of the golden rule: "In everything do to others as you would have them do to you; for this is the law and the prophets" (Matt. 7:12).

(c) *"Eye for eye, tooth for tooth" in the Sermon on the Mount.* Notwithstanding this, in later times "eye for eye, tooth for tooth" in the minds of many Christians became the quintessence of Jewish law and ethics, regarded as a justification for retaliation and revenge. The main reason is no doubt the way in which it is quoted in the Sermon on the Mount: "You have heard that it was said, 'An eye for an eye and a tooth for a tooth.' But I say to you, Do not resist an evildoer" (Matt. 5:38–39).

According to the common Christian interpretation, Jesus cancels the law of revenge and replaces it with the law of love. Such an understanding contradicts Jesus' own words about "the law" twenty verses before (Matt. 5:17–18), which have been accurately characterized by a Jewish scholar in the following significant way: "In all Rabbinic literature I know of no more unequivocal, fiery acknowledgment of Israel's holy scripture than this opening to the Instruction on the Mount."[29]

Moreover, even a superficial comparison with the other commandments that Jesus quotes makes it obvious that he does not cancel them but rather focuses on their deepest significance. In Matt. 5:21 and 27, for example, he stresses that sin against the commandments begins in the heart, exactly in accordance with the "ten words" and their traditional Jewish understanding.[30] Since Jesus does not cancel the commandments in the previous cases but rather confirms their validity, it is safe to assume that this is the case even in Matt. 5:38–39.

The Greek text does not really state a "but" between Jesus' biblical quote ("You have heard that it was said . . .") and his exposition of the quote ("But I say to you . . ."). A more adequate translation, which does justice to the Greek syntax, should rather say, "*And* I even say to you."[31] In this respect virtually all translations are misleading, probably reflecting the common prejudice that Jesus speaks against "the law."

If this is not the case, then, what does he mean in Matt. 5:38–39? First of all, it is clear that he opposes a vulgar, literal understanding of Exod. 21:24. However, nothing could be more off the track than to contrast Jesus' teaching with Jewish tradition or even to claim that Jesus contradicts the commandment as such. According to him, there is nothing amiss in the commandment: how could it possibly be, in the light of his words in Matt. 5:17–18! What he addresses are human interpretations and implementations of the commandments. In this case he obviously had groups and individuals in mind, such as those mentioned above, who abused the commandment as a pretext for personal revenge. As we have seen, such an interpretation of "eye for eye, tooth for tooth" never became normative in Judaism.

Second, we have to differentiate between the outward, judicial aspect of a law and its inner, ethical implications (see pp. 154f., 190ff., 239ff.). There is certainly a difference between a law code and a sermon, between the most minimal aspect of a law in strict legal terms and its maximal consequences for people who want to love the Lord with all their hearts and their neighbor as themselves. In the Sermon on the Mount, Jesus focuses on this latter aspect, just as there are similar rabbinic expositions of "the law" as it touches the innermost chambers of our hearts.[32] To abstain from insisting upon one's right and to ignore insult is considered one of the greatest virtues.[33]

A comparison has to be fair. Comparing one's own ethical and spiritual interpretation of a commandment with its strict legal aspect in order to set up "antitheses" between the Old and the New Testament, and between Judaism and Christianity, is nothing short of bearing false witness against one's neighbor.

It is indeed sad that so many Bible interpreters have used Jesus' words to ascribe to the Jewish people a view that Judaism itself consistently opposes. All too often Matt. 5:21–48 is labeled "the antitheses." This heading is misleading and altogether false when it is misused to signify both the alleged antitheses between Jesus and "the law" and those between Jesus and Judaism. The "antitheses" in this section on the Sermon of the Mount are nothing but "supertheses."[34] The only "antitheses" present are the ones between the good teaching of "the law" and human abuse of God's revelation for selfish purposes. In this respect, Christians and Jews still share the same concern as did Jesus and the rabbis two thousand years ago.

NEGLIGENCE (21:28–36)

In this section, damages are dealt with which are inflicted only indirectly, chiefly through negligence. Thus the owner of a rogue ox is held responsible only if the ox has a previous record of goring. In this case, he ought to have taken precautionary measures. Whether or not he has done so, if the ox kills somebody, the ox must be killed. This is based on the principle laid down in Gen. 9:5–6, according to which human blood must be accounted for: "from every animal I will require it and from human beings, each one for the blood of another, I will require a reckoning for human life." If negligence can be proven, the owner is also to be killed. In such a case, however, he can redeem himself by paying a ransom, since negligence is at issue and not voluntary manslaughter. If the victim is a slave, payment is awarded to the owner of the slave. But since the life of the slave remains inviolable, the ox in all cases must die. The examples of the goring ox as well as the uncovered pit have close parallels in ancient nonbiblical law collections.[35]

VIOLENCE AGAINST PROPERTY (22:1–17)

The first four verses focus on theft. As regards compensation for the stolen goods, an interesting difference is made here between one who has slaughtered and then sold an animal and one with whom an animal is found alive. In the first case, a four- or fivefold restitution is to be paid (cf. Zacchaeus in Luke 19:8), in the second, only double the value. The underlying reasoning is in the first case that the owner has lost the animal, while in the second case it can still be restored, and that the malicious intention of the thief is more evident in the first case.

These cases all have a number of parallels in the law of Hammurabi and in other ancient Near Eastern legal collections. In these, however, theft is judged much more severely than in the biblical laws. Thus we find both the death penalty and a tenfold restitution as punishment.[36] A general feature of these laws is that any humanitarian consideration is totally overshadowed by a materialistic one. Property has to be protected and compensated for at any price. Therefore we find no parallels to, for example, 22:26–27, where the human dignity of the slave is at stake. Neither is there a principle similar to the view of the Bible regarding the inviolability of human life, expressed in yet another distinction made in our text.

Exodus 22:2–3 distinguishes between a thief slain in the night and a thief slain after sunrise. Only in the latter case has the killer brought upon himself blood guilt. This distinction in judging the shedding of blood demonstrates how highly a human life is valued. The starting point is that no blood must be shed, not even that of a common thief. He is created in the image of God. He is a human being for whom society has responsibility. The basic principle, safeguarding life, is therefore overshadowed by only one other principle, namely, that one's own life takes precedence in the case of self-defense: "If anyone comes to kill you, rise early and kill him first."[37]

In the darkness of night it may be difficult to know whether an intruder poses a danger to life. It is then less easily avoidable to use more violence than necessary or to kill somebody involuntarily. One can also assume that a thief may be more inclined to kill in order to escape being recognized under cover of night. If he or she is killed in daylight on the other hand, one can presume that the killer could have seen that the thief was intending to steal and not to kill. It would therefore have been enough to apprehend or chase him or her away. Clearly, this basic principle does not exclude killing in self-defense during the day, nor unnecessary violence even at night. In that case, however, an investigation by the court is necessary.

In 22:5–6 restitution is to be made for a destroyed crop, in one case caused by cattle, in the second by fire. Verses 7–15 deal with restitution of property that someone has either borrowed or assumed responsibility for, but which has been destroyed, stolen, or lost. In the latter two cases the keeper must submit proof or swear an oath to support his or her innocence.

It is certainly not in accord with modern standards to classify 22:16–17 under the legal category of "damages." Underlining these rules is the thought that a virgin through sexual intercourse[38] has been transferred from the ownership of the father to that of the seducer.[39] If the father consented to marriage, there was no remaining problem other than payment of the stipulated dowry to the father (Deut. 22:28–29).[40] If the father withheld consent, he was still entitled to the dowry, since the man had failed first to request the father's consent, and the daughter was no longer a virgin.[41]

THREE MORTAL SINS (22:18–20)

These verses introduce the second large section of laws in the book of the covenant (see pp. 156ff.). These laws deal with three sins related to idolatry and are especially grave, since they impinge upon the very foundation of the covenant between God and Israel: "I am the LORD."

(a) Verse 18. The word translated "sorcerer" refers to one who is involved in any kind of religious magic. Confidence in one God, creator of heaven and earth and therefore supreme administrator of all existence, excludes not only "black magic" with malicious intent but any effort at mastering life in a supernatural way. The struggle against this sin is ongoing (see further Lev. 19:26, 31; 20:6, 27; Num. 23:23; Deut. 18:9–14; 1 Sam. 28; 2 Kgs. 9:22; 17:17–18; 21:6; 23:24–25; Isa. 3:1–3; 44:24–25; 47:9–15; Jer. 27:9–10; Micah 5:12; Nah. 3:4; Mal. 3:5; Gal. 5:19–20; Rev. 9:21; 18:22–23; 21:8; 22:15).

(b) Verse 19. This sin is probably mentioned in the context of idolatry because it may connect fornication and idolatry (see pp. 151f.) and because cohabitation with animals is such a well-known theme in pagan mythology,[42] where gods often appear as a mixed breed of human and animal, such as the Egyptian sphinx and the Greek centaur (see further Lev. 18:23; 20:15–16; Deut. 27:21).

(c) Verse 20. To be "devoted to destruction" as punishment not only implies the death sentence (Lev. 27:28–29) but also the destruction of property belonging to the one sentenced.[43] (See pp. 142ff. and further Deut. 13:12–18; 17:2–7.)

CARE OF THE WEAK (22:21–27)

Violation of the regulations in this section is often regarded as the most flagrant example of rebellion against God (see particularly Ezek. 18; Neh. 5; James 2). Four categories of people are listed as objects of God's particular care: strangers or immigrants, widows, orphans, and the poor (cf. Deut. 10:17–19; 27:19; James 1:27).

Previous laws have so far been presented in a rather strict juridical form. Now the style becomes more personal and intimate in that God ("I") speaks directly to his people ("you"). With great seriousness of mind, the Lord admonishes that violating these commandments will result in terrible punishments. "I will surely heed their cry," the text says, and next uses words reflecting God's previous concern regarding the oppression of Israel in Egypt (2:24; 3:7, 16).

The message is crystal clear: You have been strangers yourselves, so you know what it means (see 23:9). If you insult and oppress the stranger in the same way that Pharaoh did, you will also be punished! Those bereft of human defenders, I myself will watch over (see further Ps. 94:6–7; 109:31; 140:13; 146:9; Prov. 22:22–23; 23:10–11; Jer. 22:16).

In a most touching and intimate way, God pleads for mercy, describing the situation of the poor in the commandment that a garment taken in pledge shall be returned to the owner every evening, "for it may be your neighbor's only clothing to use as cover; in what else shall that person sleep?" (22:27). The lord and king of the universe cares even about the pajamas of a single poor human being! Is there any more moving appeal to us to be merciful? (See also Deut. 24:6, 10–13, 17–18.)

The prohibition against taking interest in 22:25 needs special explanation. According to Deut. 23:20–21, it is permitted to take interest from a stranger. The Hebrew word used here for "stranger" (nokhri) refers to a person who only occasionally stays in the country; such a person could thus be suspected of leaving the country with unpaid debts. In this case, too, interest was not taken from a poor, vulnerable human being.

In medieval Europe, the church adopted this prohibition against taking interest and applied it to Christians.[44] At the same time, society had become dependent on the practice of moneylending. Therefore, the profession was given to Jews. Even though Jews performed a task regarded as necessary by society, they were despised as usurers. The Old Testament prohibition certainly gives no space for such double standards. In ancient Israelite society, no interest at all was permitted. The visiting stranger was obliged to pay interest, but he certainly could not be used to execute a task otherwise forbidden and even despised.[45]

With modern banking, people depend even less on private loans, and thus this commandment loses some of the relevance it once had. What is indeed eternally valid, however, is the view of God, humanity, and the world at the foundation of these commandments. This fact must be emphatically proclaimed in every generation. The example and source of inspiration for human generosity and mercy is God, who owns all and freely provides everything, solely by grace:

> Those who exact usury say to God: "Why dost Thou not take payment from the world in which Thy creatures are? Payment for the earth to which Thou givest drink; for the flowers which Thou makest to grow; for the lights which Thou makest to shine; for the soul which Thou guardest?" God says to them: "See how much I have lent, yet have I not

taken interest, and how much the earth hath lent and hath not taken interest; but I take the capital only which I have lent (i.e., the soul), and she (i.e., the earth) takes hers (i.e., the body), as it says, *And the dust returneth to the earth as it was, and the spirit returneth unto God who gave it* (Eccl. 12:7)."[46]

The eradication of yet another false stereotype is long overdue. The Old Testament and Judaism have often been accused of narrow nationalism. In commentaries on the commandment of love in Lev. 19:18, we find it frequently claimed that the word "neighbor" would only include one's own people. Yet, in the same chapter, the stranger is assigned a particular commandment of love of his own with the same wording, "you shall love him as yourself" (19:33–34). This commandment is then additionally repeated with slight variations about forty times in the Old Testament!

THE REAL OWNER (22:28–31)

The laws in this section differ considerably from the previous ones. Yet, there is a clear connection between the two paragraphs. To revile God and curse authorities is probably a temptation especially for the poor and oppressed (Isa. 8:21). To regard our property as something of which we can dispose as we please is a temptation for all, but especially for the rich. The rightful owner is God, who lent us all that we have. God takes no interest, and only asks us to administer it responsibly. This means above all following the guidelines set forth in the previous verses. Now laws are given that constantly remind us that God owns both what we regard as ours and our very beings as well.

As we have seen in 13:11ff. (pp. 91f.), the consecration of the firstling symbolizes that everything else is consecrated as well. The offering of the firstfruit of the crop (see 23:19; Lev. 23:9–14; Deut. 26:1–11) proclaimed the Lord as the rightful owner,[47] the one from whose hands we receive "our daily bread." The same applies to food from cattle. Each time a firstborn is presented to the Lord and redeemed, the words in 22:31 (cf. 19:5) are proclaimed: "You shall be people consecrated to me."

This deeply spiritual statement is surprisingly followed by a very concrete prohibition, to abstain from meat not slaughtered according to prescribed regulations.[48] We note with interest that the same connection between dietary laws and Israel's election is found in Lev. 20:25–26: "You shall therefore make a distinction between the clean animal and the unclean. . . . You shall be holy to me; for I the LORD am holy, and I have separated you from the other peoples to be mine."

In this way, the dietary laws become a sign of the covenant. The Bible permits no separation between the external and the internal, the worldly and the spiritual, the ritual and the moral. All God's commandments have but one validity and immutable authority. The deepest secret behind Jewish survival throughout the ages is certainly to be found as much in the kitchen as in the temple and the synagogue!

LOVE YOUR ENEMIES! (23:1–9)

This section reiterates and inculcates what has previously been outlined. A holy people regard equally what enters through the mouth and what comes out of it (see pp. 152ff.). In this way the first verses of this chapter centering on the sins of the tongue and the violation of "the ninth word" on the tablets of the covenant are thematically linked to the final verse of chapter 22 proscribing certain food.

Hereafter, we encounter a commandment presented for the first time in the book of the covenant. Manifestly related to the ordinances concerning the stranger, concluding this section, it deals with a subject much more challenging: the enemy, the foe (23:4–5). These verses are immediately preceded and followed by prohibitions against perversion of justice (false testimony, partiality, and bribes), and this is probably so because personal animosity easily leads to such transgressions.

The commandment in 23:4–5 addresses, however, a more personal and immediate problem. In chapter 15 we mentioned the prohibition against rejoicing at the fall of one's enemy (Prov. 24:17; see p. 109). Here it is more than a mere prohibition. The example of the ox and the donkey implies a positive commandment to act beneficially toward one's enemy, just as epitomized in the book of Proverbs: "If your enemies are hungry, give them bread to eat; and if they are thirsty, give them water to drink" (Prov. 25:21–22; Rom. 12:20). Thus to refrain from returning evil for good or evil for evil is simply insufficient; one must actively return good for evil.[49]

The case addressed in 23:4–5 is vividly discussed in the rabbinic commentaries. One discussion wrestles with the question of how one is to act in choosing between helping to unload the donkey of one's friend and loading that of one's enemy. Not surprisingly, the latter case takes precedence. The care of the animal might mean that one should rather unload the friend's donkey. The relation friend/foe, however, is what governs the struggle between the evil and the good inclination. Therefore, the enemy must be helped first. The struggle against the natural, evil inclination is more important than anything else.[50]

Two answers are given to the question, "Who is strong?" They are: "He who overcomes his [evil] inclination," and "He who makes of his foe a friend."[51] According to Jesus, love of one's enemies should be something "typically Jewish," which stands out from pagan morality (Matt. 5:47).[52]

In the final analysis, whether a difference exists between Jesus' command to "love" one's enemies and the commandment in 23:4–5 with its rabbinic commentaries is no more than a question of how the word "love" is to be defined. In both the Old and the New Testament, love is demonstrated through action. In the commandment to love in Lev. 19:18 ("You shall love your neighbor as yourself"), the word "love" is followed by the preposition *le,* which means "to" or "for." A more precise translation should therefore be, "You shall prove your love to your neighbor."

This means to act in a selfless, giving way, quite independently from what the emotions may dictate. The very fact that we use words such as "enemy" and "foe" certainly implies that the feelings toward these people are different from those toward the "friend," but love must be manifested as something active and concrete, above personal emotions. Love is active, and its expression is manifest toward those who get in my way, those for whom I can and should do something beneficial. Thus, Jesus' teaching the commandment of love in the parable of the good Samaritan sets neighborly love in its right perspective when he poses the concluding question, "Which of these three, do you think, was a neighbor to the man who fell among the robbers?" The lawyer with whom Jesus discusses the issue answers quite correctly, "The one who showed him mercy" (Luke 10:36–37).

Considering the concrete treatment of the enemy in this section and elsewhere, little qualitative difference between the commandments in the first and the second parts of our Bible is discoverable. Moreover, if we look at how these ordinances have been applied in reality by both Jews and Christians, it is certainly impossible to post an antithesis to one's own advantage.

"FOR THE WORLD AND ALL THAT IS IN IT IS MINE" (23:10–13)

These words from Ps. 50:12 may serve as a summary of the underlying motif behind the laws in this section. They differ from those preceding in that they deal with religious obligations at given times and places. At the same time, they further deepen what has been developed earlier by focusing on God as the sole owner of all and the special protector of the poor.

In 23:10–12 we find commandments regarding the sabbatical year and the Sabbath itself. In both cases there is first a positive commandment, then a prohibition, followed by an explanation. The commandment is to sow, harvest, and cultivate the soil and generally to work six days a week. This is a service of God that demands obedience as much as the prohibition against working by letting the land "rest and lie fallow" during the seventh year and by giving oneself rest on the seventh day. The rationale is similar in both cases: in one case it is care for the poor and the wild beasts; in the other it is concern for the servant, the stranger, and domestic animals.

The sabbatical year is also discussed in Lev. 25:1–7, 18–22, and Deut. 15:1–11, where we find an additional rule to remit all debts. The laws regarding both the sabbatical year and the Sabbath (see further 31:12–17, pp. 237ff.) are founded on the essential principle laid down in Lev. 25:23: "The land is mine; with me you are but aliens and tenants."

Every seventh day and every seventh year what actually occurs is nothing short of a public proclamation of this quintessential truth. Both land and creation are, so to speak, returned to God, from whom a new beginning comes. He is truly a good and beneficent landlord. Therefore, one can confidently abstain from creating and producing without worrying about

losing control over one's needs. Lev. 26:34ff. is a strong testimony to the seriousness of this commandment.

In reality the sabbatical year implied that the land re-
verted to all Israel's ownership—rich and poor, citizens and
foreigners, human beings and animals. One could say that the
"very border" of the field, which should always be left for the
poor (Lev. 19:9–10; 23:22), was extended to embrace the entire land throughout the sabbatical year.[53]

Despite the many practical difficulties in applying this
commandment (since agriculture was the very lifeblood of
society), it was observed during the Second Temple period.
Nehemiah's restoration program in the fifth century B.C.E. included it (Neh. 10:31), and during the Hasmonean war in the
second century B.C.E. people were starving because of their
obedience to this commandment (1 Maccabees 6:49, 53–54).
According to Josephus both the Greek conqueror Alexander
the Great and the Roman emperor Julius Caesar granted tax
releases to the Jews during the sabbatical year.[54] Rabbinic tradition reports that it was observed at least until 135 C.E., when
the Romans destroyed Jerusalem again and expelled the Jews
from Judea. This time the Roman emperor Hadrian was mer-
ciless and not only imposed a heavy tax on the population but
also forbid the practice of Judaism. In this situation it became
virtually impossible to survive without compromising this
commandment by cultivating the land every year.[55]

Since the commandment applies exclusively to the land
of Israel, it remained of merely theoretical significance to the
Jews in the Diaspora. It gained a renewed importance in the
mid-nineteenth century, when Jewish immigration to the land
of Israel began to increase and agriculture became essential
for Israel's economic development. When the state of Israel
was founded, the problem of practicing the sabbatical year was
further debated. It is difficult for a modern country to follow
such a commandment. Yet, there will always be observant
groups who defend its literal and eternal validity. At the market in the most orthodox neighborhoods (for example, Meah
Shearim in Jerusalem), conspicuous signs assure clientele
during the sabbatical year (most recently in 1993–94) that the
products do not come from the land of Israel. A stamp from
the rabbinate on canned fruits and vegetables guarantees that
the contents have not been produced in Israel during the sabbatical year.

Even though this commandment only applies to Jews in Israel, it certainly holds an eternal message, relevant for everyone. In a world relentlessly plundered of its resources, where animals are brutally hunted to extinction, rich countries seize raw materials from already impoverished nations for sham prices, poor inexorably increase and the already indebted sink deeper into financial catastrophe, and humanity endeavors to usurp the throne of the sovereign Lord of creation, this ancient commandment of the sabbatical year imperatively stands forth as never before. The timeless message of this divine precept from the king of the universe is unequivocal: "For the world and all that is in it is mine" (Ps. 50:12). How do we proceed actively to proclaim this message today?

"OFFER TO GOD A SACRIFICE OF THANKSGIVING" (23:14–19)

Our heading is taken from Psalm 50:14. We may also read these words as summing up this section of chapter 23. Gratitude toward the Lord of creation and of the land is above all actively demonstrated through the hands and feet, as pointed out in the previous verses. It must, however, also be expressed through the lips and the heart, through songs of praise and gifts of thanksgiving. Therefore, ordinances concerning the three great pilgrimage feasts are now set before us.

The expression "hold a festival for me" in 23:14, as well as "appear before the Lord GOD" in 23:17, expressly concerns worship at a particular place. The Hebrew verb translated "hold a festival" (hagag) originally meant to go around something in a procession, and the word for "festival" (hag) expresses that it is to be celebrated through a pilgrimage to the sanctuary. The corresponding Semitic root appears also in the Arabic words for "make a pilgrimage" (haja) and "pilgrim" (haj), which have patently retained the original, concrete meaning.

Even in the expression "three times" (23:14), pilgrimage is indicated in that the word for "time" (regel) also means "foot." Thus, "pilgrimage" is called ʿaliyah leregel in rabbinic literature, literally "ascent on foot." After the building of the temple, pilgrimage meant, of course, ascent to Jerusalem.[56]

Today Jews try to visit Jerusalem during these three biblical feasts. This visit is then called ʿaliyah leregel. The word
ʿaliyah is otherwise well-known as the technical term for Jewish immigration to Israel (cf. p. 7). The thought, however, remains unchanged: those who immigrate to Israel always retain
the holy city of Jerusalem as the ultimate goal of their journey.

Three pilgrimage feasts are mentioned here. Obviously,
the recurrent theme of the "sacrifice of thanksgiving" is gratitude for the harvest. This is, perhaps, the reason why this section is preceded by a warning against idolatry (23:13). In
Canaanite cult ritual similar feasts played an important role
(cf. Judg. 9:27). There, however, the borderline between the
creator and the creation was blurred. The worship of Baal was
linked to worship of "Nature," whose fertility rites were an important component of the ritual. Anything of such a practice
is incompatible with the view that the earth belongs to the
Lord, "Maker of Heaven and Earth," who is the provider of all
good gifts. To him—and not the earth—belong the glory, the
honor, and the thanksgiving!

In Israel, though, the revealed God could not be set apart
from the God of creation in the celebration of the feasts. God's
redemptive intervention in the history of Israel eventually became the most important aspect of these three feasts, even
though this motif never entirely replaced the ancient harvest
motif. Just as the liberation from Egypt was celebrated at Passover, so were the firstfruits of the barley brought before the
Lord (cf. Lev. 23:9–14). When the giving of the Torah at Sinai
was celebrated at Pentecost (see pp. 133ff.), the firstfruits of
the wheat were offered (34:22; Lev. 23:15–21). Therefore, this
feast is also called "the Feast of Harvest" or "the day of the
firstfruits" (Num. 28:26). The third feast, "the Feast of In-
gathering," celebrated the harvest of the olives, grapes, and
other fruits "at the end of the year," that is, in the fall (Lev.
23:39; Deut. 16:13). It is better known as "the Feast of
Tabernacles" or Sukkoth (Lev. 23:34; Deut. 16:13–16). Even
though the building of booths is reminiscent of Israel's dwelling in such booths during the harvest, it is also linked to their
exodus from Egypt and to their wandering in the wilderness
(Lev. 23:42–43).

According to 23:17 the commandment of pilgrimage applied only to males. However, it should be kept in mind that
this expresses its minimal aspect alone. Women and children
would certainly not have the obligation to leave their homes

three times a year, but all those able to do so probably did participate (cf. Deut. 16:11; Luke 2:41ff.).

Finally, a prohibition is mentioned having nothing to do with the feasts directly: "You shall not boil a kid in its mother's milk" (23:19). It could have been inserted here in reaction to a particular rite in the Canaanite cult, previously warned against in general (23:13). While no extrabiblical evidence confirms the rite's existence,[57] it is possible if we also infer that the prohibition against sacrifices offered with leavened bread (23:18) concerns a Canaanite practice. Leavened bread was never to be offered. Moreover, Lev. 2:11 also mentions honey as a proscribed offering, and we do know that honey was indeed a common offering among Canaanites and Egyptians. The prohibition against boiling a kid in its mother's milk is subsequently repeated two more times, in 34:26 and Deut. 14:21. In the latter verse it is preceded by the explanation, "for you are a people holy to the LORD your God," which may indicate that this practice was prevalent among the surrounding nations, from whom Israel is called to be separate.

Another plausible explanation would see kindness to animals as the background of the commandment, parallel to the prohibition against slaughtering an animal during the first seven days after its birth so that it can be with its mother (22:30; Lev. 22:27), slaughtering an animal on the same day as its young (Lev. 22:28; cf. Deut. 22:6–7), plowing with an ox and a donkey yoked together (Deut. 22:10), and muzzling an ox while it is treading out the grain (Deut. 25:4).[58]

Philo offers the most profound understanding of the commandment: "For he [namely, God] held that it was grossly improper that the substance which fed the living animal should be used to season and flavor the same after its death."[59] The basic motif would thus reflect respect for life. What sustains life must not be used in connection with anything pertaining to death, in this case boiling. The same notion lies behind the prohibition against consuming blood (Gen. 9:3–4). Even the prohibitions in Lev. 22:27–28 and Deut. 22:6 are evidently based on a similar thought, namely, that the life-giving process must be sharply distinguished from anything occasioning death.[60]

According to rabbinic interpretation, there are no "empty words" in the Scriptures; neither are there redundancies (cf. pp. 260ff.). This implies that a commandment, each time it recurs, proffers new insight. Based on this view, the prohibition against boiling a kid in its mother's milk is rabbinically expanded to include not only a kid but all kinds of meat, not only a mother's milk but all milk, and precludes not only boiling meat and milk together but the consumption of anything containing a mixture of milk and meat.[61]

This practice is certainly justified by the profound thought behind the commandment: separating the principle of life (the milk which sustains the newborn animals) from the process of death (the slaughter which is a necessary process to make meat fit for consumption).

"I WILL DELIVER YOU" (23:20–33)

Again, we borrow the heading from Ps. 50 (v. 15), which expresses a conditional promise. Along this line, the book of the covenant concludes with exhortations, warnings, and promises of help and blessings before the ongoing trek through the wilderness and the subsequent arrival in the promised land. The section shares several similarities with Deut. 6–7.

We limit ourselves to the most problematic themes dealt with: the conquest of the land and the destruction of its inhabitants, indeed both a promise and a precept. This theme is not of historical interest alone, for it unquestionably brings out many complex issues regarding how we view the "difficult" texts in the Bible. These questions have been raised in both chapters 15 and 17 above (pp. 108ff., 121ff.), and even here no more than a hint at a solution can be provided.

The peoples listed (see 3:8; 13:5) have their geographical areas indicated within the borders in 23:31, namely, from the Red Sea at today's Eilat in the south to the Mediterranean in the west,[62] and from the Negev desert to the Euphrates in the northeast (in today's Syria and Iraq). In reality, Israel would never have had these borders. We also notice that the borders are considerably narrowed in Num. 34:1–12. They most likely go back to the territory ruled by Egypt at the time of the exodus, when the Egyptians probably did not distinguish between Canaan and southern Syria.[63]

Jewish interpretations agree that the commandment to destroy the inhabitants is something as unparalleled as the exodus itself. It was thought to be unique to a particularly critical situation in Israel's history, and absolutely not applicable in subsequent generations. The text justifies the harsh treatment of the inhabitants as a safeguard against the danger of idolatry (23:24–25, 32–33). The newly liberated people are an utterly fragile vessel to receive God's revelation. We will soon see (ch. 32) that they have not yet left Sinai when they violate the most basic commandment on the tablets of the covenant (20:2ff.), a commandment to be repeated again and again (20:23; 22:20; 23:13). This injunction even concludes the entire book of the covenant (23:32–33).

As we have previously seen in connection with the struggle against Amalek, this "holy war" can be taken to represent the combat between the one, true God and his mortal enemies (pp. 121ff.). At stake is not only the survival of a people in general. Israel has witnessed God's presence. As bearers of that divine revelation, they have been entrusted with a particular message to the world. Consequently, their survival and that of their faith is crucial in order that the knowledge of the true God be transmitted to others, also bound for freedom. The Lord will eventually reach all these also through the weak and vulnerable Israel whom he has elected for this purpose.

The question why God chooses such a narrow, dark, and painful path is one of the deep mysteries to be understood on "that day," when the people of God will finally be exalted from the dark valleys of this existence after having fulfilled its task. Until then we must rest content with the answers provided in Deut. 29:29 and Isa. 55:8–9.[64]

11

The Confirmation

*W*e have seen that Pentecost in the Bible and in post-biblical Judaism is the great celebration of the covenant and the Torah, upon which the covenant is founded (Chapter Nine). For Christians, the New Testament miracle of Pentecost equally lays down the foundation of the covenant, which God has made with us through Jesus Christ. The outpouring of the Holy Spirit is the confirmation of the meaning of Jesus' life, suffering, death, and resurrection. The Holy Spirit again confirms something that God has already done.

However, what God confirms to his people also has to be confirmed by his people. The covenant has two partners. It is founded exclusively on what God has done, but it cannot be fulfilled without the people's confirmation that they indeed desire to be God's people and to live faithfully according to the divine will (see pp. 129f.). The giving of the Torah must be followed by the reception of the Torah. It is this mutuality that the covenantal relationship is about.

The miracle of Pentecost, inaugurated in Exodus 19–20 and continued with the "book of the covenant" in chapters 21–23, is now completed in this chapter, where the covenant is confirmed and sealed by both God and the people.

PENTECOST—THE FEAST OF CONFIRMATION

It is well-known that the liberation from Egypt is celebrated year after year at Passover. We also know fairly well how this feast has been celebrated throughout the ages.

How Pentecost has been celebrated is less known. Neither the Old nor the New Testament offers any direct description of this celebration. While the two other pilgrimage feasts, Passover and the Feast of Tabernacles, are assigned a detailed tractate of their own in the Mishnah,[1] there is only sparse information in the rabbinic literature about Pentecost, *Shavuᶜoth*. It would be peculiar, however, for such a decisive event in Israel's history as the giving of the Torah and the establishing of the covenant at Sinai to have played an insignificant and marginal role in the religious life of the people.

Bearing in mind that Pentecost is the feast of the covenant, we will find more texts testifying to the importance of this feast than immediately meet the eye.[2] Both biblical and postbiblical sources contain descriptions of covenantal acts between God and his people, which took place precisely at Pentecost. In 2 Chron. 15:10–15 we read how the people in the time of King Asa (908–867 B.C.E.) return to the Lord after a period of apostasy:

> They were gathered at Jerusalem in the third month of the fifteenth year of the reign of Asa. They sacrificed to the LORD on that day. . . . They entered into a covenant to seek the LORD, the God of their ancestors, with all their heart and with all their soul. . . . They took an oath to the LORD with a loud voice, and with shouting, and with trumpets, and with horns. All Judah rejoiced over the oath; for they had sworn with all their heart, and had sought him with their whole desire, and he was found by them, and the LORD gave them rest all around.

Several details in this description are reminiscent of the revelation at Mount Sinai. The event takes place in the third month (cf. 19:1). To be sure, the Aramaic targum is even more detailed and states, "during *Shavuᶜoth*." Sacrifices were also offered at Sinai (24:5–6) and trumpets blown (19:16, 19; 20:18). Further, the words "oath" *(shevuᶜah)* and "swear" *(nishbaᶜ)* are conspicuous. They are derived from the same Semitic root. "Oaths" in the plural is *shevuᶜoth;* one need not know Hebrew to detect the phonetic similarity with the word *shavuᶜoth,* which means "weeks" but is also the name of "the Feast of Weeks," Pentecost. Since no vowels are written in the text, the consonants can be read either as "oaths" or "(the feast of) weeks." Considering how central the swearing of an oath is when entering a covenant, as we see at Mount Sinai (24:3, 7; see further below), it is hardly surprising that later Jewish tradition discerns a deeper connection between these two readings of the same consonants.

Jubilees 6:21 thus states that the Feast of Weeks "is two-fold and of two natures," which probably regards it as both a harvest feast and a covenant feast. This passage may also focus on the double meaning of the consonants in the name of the feast, *shavuʿoth* and *shevuʿoth,* respectively, since the oaths in connection with the covenant are stressed in the book of *Jubilees.*[3] *Jubilees* 6 records the covenant with Noah (cf. Gen 8–9), which it says took place in the third month (v. 1). In *Jubilees* 6:10 Noah and his sons promise under oath to keep what the Lord commands: "And he made a covenant before the LORD God forever in all of the generations of the earth in that month." With direct reference to the Sinaitic covenant, the text then continues: "Therefore, he spoke to you so that you also might make a covenant with the children of Israel with an oath in this month upon the mountain" (6:11). This covenant is thereafter to be celebrated year by year: "Therefore, it is ordained and written in the heavenly tablets that they should observe the feast of Shebuot[4] in this month, once per year, in order to renew the covenant in all (respects), year by year" (*Jubilees* 6:17; see also vv. 20–22).

A Yearly Renewal of the Covenant

This tradition may be unhistorical and anachronistic. One thing, however, remains certain: it could not have arisen had Pentecost never really, at some point, been celebrated as a yearly renewal of the covenant. The book of *Jubilees* actually reflects a living practice and tries to carry it as far back as possible in biblical history. Therefore, the covenant with Abraham is also said to have been made at the same time of the year—both the covenant in Gen. 15 (*Jubilees* 14) and the covenant of circumcision in Gen. 17 (*Jubilees* 15). Even in these cases it is claimed that a renewal of the event afterward took place annually (*Jubilees* 14:20). This feast was therefore also celebrated by Isaac, Jacob, and Ishmael according to the same interpretive tradition (*Jubilees* 6:18–19; 22:1). Moreover, during the Feast of Weeks, Jacob and Laban enter a covenant with one another (*Jubilees* 29:5–8), and during the same feast Jacob later receives the calling and the promises (Gen. 46; *Jubilees* 44). Later, the community at Qumran also celebrated a yearly renewal of the covenant. New members sought acceptance, and veteran members confirmed their promises.[5]

Against this background it is probable that at least two psalms functioned as "Pentecost psalms," or "confirmation psalms." In other words, they originated in the Pentecost service in the Jerusalem temple. In Ps. 50:5 we read: "Gather to me my faithful ones, who made a covenant with me by sacrifice!" The description of God's appearance in verses 2–3 reminds us of the revelation at Sinai. In verse 7 there is an allusion to "the first word" on the tablets of the covenant: "I am God, your God," and in verses 18–20 three of "the ten words" are dealt with.

Even in Ps. 81 the echo from Sinai is clearly heard. In verse 10 we find quoted the beginning of the tablets of the covenant, and in verse 9 the second "word" is referred to. Before that (vv. 5–7) events in connection with the exodus are related. The exhortations, warnings, and promises given in both these psalms harmonize well with the Jewish liturgy for *Shavuᶜoth,* where a particular section in the Sephardic rite is called *ᶜazharoth,* which means warnings. This part of the liturgy possibly finds its earliest predecessor in these psalms, the content of which is appropriate in connection with the renewal of the covenant with all its conditions.[6]

In the light of these texts it is probable that the pilgrimage to Jerusalem at Pentecost implied a yearly renewal of the promises to remain faithful to the covenant, which we find in this chapter (24:3, 7). That this was an important part of the celebration is indicated by another name of the feast, which became common in postbiblical times, *ᶜatsereth.* It means "congregation" or "assembly" and probably goes back to an expression in Deut. 9:10; 10:4; 18:16, *yom haqahal* ("the day of the assembly"), which refers to the miracle of Pentecost at Sinai.[7] On that occasion, all of Israel gathered together (see 19:16; 20:18; 24:3, 7–8, 17). This unique situation in the history of Israel, when all the people were united around the Torah in one unified body, may explain why *ᶜatsereth* came to have such importance as an alternative name of the feast.

However, names often emerge in specific situations. Since *ᶜatsereth* does not appear in the Bible as a synonym of *Shavuᶜoth,* we can postulate that it was adopted by later generations, when Pentecost was celebrated as a reminder and

confirmation of the Sinai covenant. The celebration of Pentecost and the pilgrimage to Jerusalem acknowledged the desire
to be an integral part of the "assembly" at Sinai. This certainly
even applies to the crowd that experienced the Pentecost miracle in Acts 2: "When the day of Pentecost had come, they
were all together in one place." They were together to remember and renew the covenant.[8]

Every Generation at Sinai

The generation who had gathered together at Sinai was
followed by another, who had experienced neither the miracle
of Passover nor that of Pentecost. These two miracles, however, must never be allowed to slip into the realm of historical
memory. "In every generation it is everyone's duty to look
upon himself as if he came out of Egypt," the *Passover Haggadah* admonishes (see pp. 1, 141). As we have seen, Pentecost is
no less a part of God's miracle of liberation than is Passover.
Therefore, it is crucial that every generation places itself at
Mount Sinai, listens to the same heavenly voice, and utters the
same confession as their forefathers: "The words of the Torah
should be new to you as though they were given this very
day."[9]

The desert period is approaching its end, and the Sinai
experience is now in the past. Moses therefore emphasizes:
"The LORD our God made a covenant with us in Horeb. Not
with our ancestors did the LORD make this covenant, but with
us, who are all of us here alive today" (Deut 5:2–3). Further, in
Moses' speech addressing the renewed covenant to be made
before entering the promised land, he includes even future
generations in the covenant (Deut. 29:10–15):

> You stand assembled today, all of you, before the LORD your God . . . to
> enter into the covenant of the LORD your God, sworn by an oath,
> which the LORD your God is making with you today; in order that he
> may establish you today as his people, and that he may be your God, as
> he promised you and as he swore to your ancestors, to Abraham, to
> Isaac, and to Jacob. I am making this covenant, sworn by an oath, not
> only with you who stand here with us today before the LORD our God,
> but also with those who are not here with us today.

Later, King Josiah and his generation certainly united
themselves with the Sinai generation when they echoed the
words of 24:7, "All that the LORD has spoken we will do, and
we will be obedient," as we read in 2 Kgs. 23:1–3:

> Then the king directed that all the elders of Judah and Jerusalem should be gathered to him. The king went up to the house of the LORD, and with him went all the people of Judah, all the inhabitants of Jerusalem, the priests, the prophets, and all the people, both small and great; he read in their hearing all the words of the book of the covenant that had been found in the house of the LORD. The king stood by the pillar and made a covenant before the LORD, to follow the LORD, keeping his commandments, his decrees, and his statutes, with all his heart and all his soul, to perform the words of this covenant that were written in this book. All the people joined the covenant.

Generations later, similar words of commitment to the commandments given at Sinai are heard in the time of Nehemiah (Neh. 10:28–29):

> The rest of the people, the priests, the Levites, the gatekeepers, the singers, the temple servants, and all who have separated themselves from the peoples of the lands to adhere to the law of God, their wives, their sons, their daughters, all who have knowledge and understanding, join with their kin, their nobles, and enter into a curse and an oath to walk in God's law, which was given by Moses the servant of God, and to observe and do all the commandments of the LORD our Lord and his ordinances and his statutes.

In line with such sayings, all Israel were regarded by Jewish tradition as having been present at Sinai, including all future generations. Whenever they listen to and accept the Torah, they are there. This basic view of the covenant unites every generation with Sinai and makes this chapter eternally relevant and alive. To receive the Torah means nothing less than becoming one with ancient Israel and joining in their confession and confirmation of the covenant: "All that the LORD has spoken we will do, and we will be obedient" (24:7).

OBEDIENCE AND LEGALISM

The people had already made a promise similar to the one in 24:7 at the beginning of the Pentecost miracle: "All that the LORD has spoken we will do" (19:8). Only now, however, when Moses has proclaimed "all the words of the LORD and all the ordinances" (24:3), do they begin to realize what this promise implies: "All that the LORD has spoken we will do, and we will be obedient." The last two verbs ("do" and "be obedient") in Hebrew are *na⁽aseh ve-nishma⁽*, which literally mean "do and hear."

The formulation of the promise in 24:7 differs from the earlier ones (19:8 and 24:3) in the addition of the phrase "and hear." It is as though God is dissatisfied until both verbs are contained in the confession: "do *and* hear." Not only "do," and not only "hear," but both together, just as in God's formulation of his covenantal promise: "Now therefore, if you will *obey* [Hebrew 'hear'] my voice and keep my covenant" (19:5). Only in 24:7 does God receive a response corresponding to the condition he has laid down for the consummation of the covenant, namely, "hear" and "do." In this way, chapters 19 through 24 are fused into a unity, expressing the conditions, content, and mutuality of the covenant.

To hear and do (19:5) and to do and hear (24:7) thus concretely introduces what faithfulness to the covenantal relationship implies. It is how all the commandments and ordinances given in the tablets of the covenant and the book of the covenant are to be received and realized in daily life.

From one point of view, hearing certainly comes first. Without hearing, it is impossible to know what to do. But the reverse order also has much to teach us. There is always a temptation to stress knowledge at the expense of daily application in real life. The commandments easily tend to become a kind of mirror, revealing our own imperfection in fulfilling them.

As a healthy balance to "hear and do," the order is reversed in the answer of the people. This answer expresses one's willingness immediately to begin doing what God has commanded. What you can do today, that do, then hear! Do what you can, but do it with open ears! Then you will become aware of new dimensions and depths in the word of God. More and more will then be revealed of God's will. Not for nothing does Israel's "credo" begin with the word *Shema*ᶜ, "Hear!"—"Hear, O Israel: The LORD our God is one LORD" (Deut. 6:4). The daily recital of the *Shema*ᶜ is a reverberating echo and an ongoing confirmation throughout the generations of the promise God gave to the forefathers at Sinai.

Halakhah and Haggadah

To do and to hear: these two key words elucidate other aspects of God's revelation. The rabbis term them halakhah and haggadah, which literally mean "guidance"[10] and "narrative," respectively. The first includes everything possible to do in a concrete way. It is visible and can be measured. This category consequently includes commandments such as eating unleavened bread during Passover, keeping the dietary laws, refraining from specific kinds of work on the Sabbath, fasting on the Day of Atonement, building a *sukkah* (booth) on the Feast of Tabernacles, binding *tefillin* (see pp. 90f.), etc. Halakhah provides answers to questions such as "what," "when," and "how."

To the second category belongs everything else, for example, stories, proverbs, hymns, ethics, explanations, and motivations of the commandments. When it comes to commandments, haggadah provides the answer to the question "why." Even commandments, the extension of which cannot be measured, belong here, such as the commandment of love. Often one and the same commandment has one halakhic and one haggadic aspect. "An eye for an eye" primarily deals with the payment of damages (halakhah). In another context, however, it may be applied just as the golden rule even to the point of refraining from claiming one's right, from resisting evil, of going the second mile, etc. (haggadah). The dietary laws apply to particular foods (halakhah) but are also signs of the covenant, a reminder of the exodus, the giving of the Torah at Sinai, and the calling to be a holy people (haggadah).

We can also say that these two terms distinguish between an external and an internal aspect of the word of God. As has been pointed out before (pp. 154f., 169; see also pp. 239ff.), a commandment often has both a legal, minimal aspect (halakhah) and an ethical, maximal aspect that cannot be measured (haggadah). Sometimes we use other terms for this distinction, like deeds and faith, letter and spirit.

Which aspect is most important? Those thinking the answer is simple, ought again to ponder the phrases "hear and do" and "do and hear." What comes first is not immediately clear. As a matter of fact, we confront a constant interaction between the two aspects. One rabbi used to say that we might as well ask what is most important in the human body, the bones or the muscles, the blood vessels or the blood itself. Without one, the other cannot function. A human being is a living creature with heart, brain, and limbs. The whole body belongs to God. Therefore, Scripture addresses the whole human being and seeks to make use of all its various aspects—knowledge and understanding, desires and feelings, voice and tongue, hands and feet. God's word is received through ears and eyes, is registered in the brain, appeals to the heart, and is applied through the concrete actions of the body.

Yet another qualification in slightly different terms may shed light on the meaning of the commandments and the response of the people. It is the distinction among the material and the spiritual, the social and the sacred, the judicial, ritual, and moral aspects of the commandments. What is most important? Again, those with an immediate answer should review the chapters just examined.

Bible scholars have analyzed and systematized the content of these chapters into various categories of laws, each with its own origins and characteristics. The Bible, however, makes no division according to degrees of importance or validity. It deals both with God and humanity, heaven and earth, worship and human rights, sanctuary and home. The sum of God's will on the tablets of the covenant has hardly faded at the glorious heights of Sinai when Moses has to descend into the deep valley of reality, where laws concerning slavery, oppression, sexual offenses, damages, and punishments are necessary. At the same time there is an appeal to loving-kindness far beyond the realms of juridical courts. And in the midst of all this, altars, sacrifices, and feasts are intermingled. All of a sudden there is an ordinance regarding the menu. The most human and seemingly superficial never loses contact with the spiritual and divine.

No Distinction

However important and helpful our distinctions regarding the content of the word of God may be, they are totally challenged by the tablets of the covenant and the book of the covenant. Moses does not censor the content. He does not grade it into important and marginal, divine and human. He does not even distinguish between the "ten words" and all the other ordinances of the book of the covenant: "Moses came and told the people all the words of the LORD and all the ordinances" (24:3).

The only tenable answer to the question, what is most important, is therefore the one given by the people of Israel: "*All* that the LORD has spoken we will hear and do." All! Halakhah and haggadah, external and internal, secular and spiritual, social and sacred! It is enough that God has spoken it in order that it should be an integral part of the conditions of the covenant now to be sealed.

Is this, then, not legalistic? The question is partially answered in the commentary on the introduction to the tablets of the covenant (pp. 138ff.). However, since the concept of "legalism" to so many Christians has almost been made synonymous with the Old Testament and Judaism, another distinction is important and appropriate in this context, that between obedience and legalism.

Christians often associate legalism with the external, formal observance of the commandments (halakhah). Since this aspect is so obvious in Judaism, Christians have constantly accused the Jewish people of practicing a religion of law, as well as of being legalistic. Such a connection between legalism and the external observance of the commandments is unfortunate and nonscriptural, while the distinction between legalism and obedience is indeed helpful and clarifying.

By "legalism," I mean a formalistic approach to the commandments, keeping them merely in order to gain favor before God, prompting forgiveness, righteousness, eternal life, or other personal benefits. Hypocrisy is a subdivision of legalism. In this case, one would seek to obtain public approval by keeping the commandments. In both cases, legalism replaces what ought to be the real force behind what we do or refrain from doing: obedience to the will of God.

The rabbis use an expression to describe the significance of obedience. They say that a commandment should be kept "for its own sake" (Hebrew *li-shmah,* literally "for its name"). This means that the sole motivation for keeping a commandment should be that God has commanded it and that our fellow human being needs it, in other words, again the practice of the double commandment of love.

"Be not like servants who serve the master in order to receive a gift, but be like servants who serve the master without the intention of receiving a gift, and let the fear of Heaven be upon you."[11] Whether it is a matter of external or internal obedience to the commandments is indeed of no consequence. It is possible to be as legalistic when it comes to inner and invisible things as when it comes to the outward and visible, and our obedience to the word of God is certainly, as we have seen demonstrated when discussing the book of the covenant, both down-to-earth and supremely "spiritual."

It is always a temptation to play off one category of commandments against another. The Bible addresses the danger of being rigorous when it comes to sacrifices and the celebration of feasts while overlooking the demands for mercy and love, the innermost aspect of the commandments.

In this context Amos 5:21–24 even says that God wants no sacrifices and songs of praise:

> I hate, I despise your festivals, and I take no delight in your solemn assemblies. Even though you offer me burnt offerings and grain offerings, I will not accept them; and offerings of well-being of your fatted animals I will not look upon. Take away from me the noise of your songs; I will not listen to the melody of your harps I will not listen. But let justice roll down like waters, and righteousness like an everflowing stream.

The same theology surfaces in Ps. 51, ascribed to King David after the sin with Bathsheba. In that situation there was no room for any sacrifices: "For you have no delight in sacrifice; if I were to give a burnt offering, you would not be pleased" (Ps. 51:16). Why? Certainly, sacrifices in general had not been canceled, since these were indeed ordained by God. One thing, however, we may never forget: there were no sin offerings for willful sins. We know this from the sacrificial laws in the book of Leviticus, where the word for "sin" in connection with the sin offerings consistently refers to unintentional sins. "When anyone sins unwittingly . . . , he shall offer for the sin"—this phrase is reiterated again and again (see esp. Lev. 4).

So what should they do, those who had sinned willfully? They must offer the sacrifice of the heart through repentance. There existed no sacrificial replacement for repentance. Before offering sacrifices, the relationship with God had to be restored. This is what the psalmist knows when writing: "The sacrifice acceptable to God is a broken spirit; a broken and contrite heart, O God, you will not despise" (Ps. 51:17).[12] Only after the inner sacrifice of the heart were outward sacrifices acceptable: "then you will delight in right sacrifices, in burnt offerings and whole burnt offerings; then bulls will be offered on your altar" (Ps. 51:19). The precondition was to restore the unity between the internal and external obedience (see also Isa. 66:2–4).

Jesus addresses the same problem in the New Testament: "Woe to you, scribes and Pharisees, hypocrites! For you tithe mint, dill, and cummin (namely, things which were not even directly commanded), and have neglected the weightier matters of the law: justice and mercy and faith" (Matt. 23:23). The continuation makes it clear, however, that not even here is it a matter of one aspect stressed at the expense of the other: "these you ought to have practiced without neglecting the others" (see also Matt. 5:23–24 and James 1:26–27).

Obedience of the commandments must never lead anyone to become like a mindless robot, insensitive to the realities of life. The commandment of love stands above all else. Still, it does not cancel any of the other commandments; otherwise the book of the covenant would have been superfluous.

In certain situations it may be necessary to stress some aspects more than others. The fact that Paul focuses on faith, while James emphasizes deeds (see, for example, Rom. 4:1ff. and James 2:14ff.) does not necessarily mean that they contradict one another. Both struggle to avoid pitting one against the other, lest the fullness of God's word be obscured. At stake is the application of God's word, which requires recognizing any aspect in danger of neglect. This is the prophetic task of any teacher of God's law.

At Sinai the people of Israel professed their willingness to obey the word of God unconditionally and with no reservations. To this day, the pious Jew does this every morning by putting on a prayer shawl with the fringes, the symbol of "all the commandments of the LORD" (Num. 15:39), and wearing the covenantal sign of the *tefillin* (see pp. 90f.). Next comes a prayer, which intimately binds together the literal as well as the innermost aspects of the Torah, touching thought and deed, heart and life. This exemplary prayer also expresses awareness of the distance in real life between "hearing" and "doing," principle and practice, and therefore the constant need for a righteousness that is not our own. After blessings and praise, the prayer concludes: "May it be your will, the Lord our God and the God of our fathers, that this commandment may be regarded as if I had fulfilled it with all its details and particulars and intentions together with all the 613 commandments which are linked with it."

The two words, "details and particulars," emphasize primarily the halakhic aspects of the law, while "intentions" puts the finger on the pulse of the commandment and its endless haggadic dimensions. No wonder this prayer contains the significant conjunction "as if" (Hebrew *keʾillu*), giving expression to the impossibility of totally fulfilling God's word.

Righteousness is possible only when God in his mercy "regards" it "as if" we had fulfilled his commandments. Luther expressed the same thing through the term *iusticia imputativa,* which refers to the righteousness that God "puts in"—what humans possess without having acquired it themselves. This is the sole hope for righteousness according to good Jewish and Christian teaching.

It is incumbent to stress this repeatedly in the shadow of the common Christian prejudice against the Jewish people as being legalistic and self-righteous. How many Christians begin every day by committing themselves to obedience to God's commandments and simultaneously petition God's righteousness? This Jewish act of obedience—not legalism— exemplified in the daily morning prayer is nothing short of a dynamic dramatization and reiteration of ancient Israel's commitment and promise at Sinai: "All that the LORD has spoken we will do and we will hear."

These words summarize the response to the three questions of obedience: the *what* of obedience—everything; the *why* of obedience—the Lord has spoken; the *how* of obedience—putting God's words into concrete action in real life, while being keenly attentive to expanded instructions.

THE SINAITIC COVENANT AND THE NEW COVENANT

It is hard to busy oneself with the book of the covenant and its cognate laws without also wondering what they mean to us today. To what extent are they still binding upon us? A Christian may further ask: what is the relationship between the covenant at Sinai and the new covenant?

As we read about Moses sprinkling the blood of the covenant against the altar and upon the people, proclaiming, "See the blood of the covenant that the LORD has made with you in accordance with all these words" (24:6, 8), we naturally think of Jesus' words in connection with the institution of the Holy Communion, "This is my blood of the covenant, which is poured out for many" (Mark 14:24).[13] What does this covenant mean, and what consequences does it have for the covenant at Sinai?

Since the covenant at Sinai is inconceivable without the revelation of all God's laws as a condition, the basic question centers on these laws. In this regard, Judaism and Christianity

have diametrically opposite starting points. Both certainly discuss the continuous validity of various laws and how to apply
them in real life. However, to the Jewish people the point of
departure is that in principle they are still in force. The question is then, why a specific law might no longer be applicable.
It may be a matter of ordinances, which could only be fulfilled
when the temple was standing, such as sacrifices, tithes, etc. In
classical Christianity the starting point is at the opposite pole,
that the Old Testament laws no longer have any applicability,
since Christ has "fulfilled the law." A frequent proof text for
such a view is Rom. 10:4 (see further below). The question is
then, why some laws indeed might still be valid, for example,
the so-called ten commandments. In this case, one is obliged
to rationalize why certain commandments should be followed
at all. In Judaism, on the contrary, one must clarify why certain laws in specific cases may no longer be followed.

This fundamental difference is in itself not surprising. As
heirs and bearers of the Torah throughout the turbulent vicis-
situdes of history, the Jewish people are the only ones to cling
persistently to the eternal validity of the Sinaitic covenant and
its binding obligations.

This basic view indubitably does justice to the claims of
the Old Testament itself. The covenant and its conditions are
consistently presented as something irrevocable (see 31:13,
16–17; pp. 242ff.). Not even the new covenant cancels the law,
for quite the contrary, it is confirmed and established by this
everlasting, original covenant (Jer. 31:33–34).

The same view also prevails in the New Testament. The
conflicts between Jesus and other Jewish teachers concern
only the interpretation of the laws, the validity of all of which
is taken for granted (see pp. 167ff.). Jesus' question, "Is it lawful
to do good or to do harm on the sabbath?" (Mark 3:4), presupposes, of course, that he regards the Sabbath commandment as binding. He wears the fringes, which symbolize "all
the commandments" (Matt. 9:20; 14:36), participates in the
worship of the temple and the synagogue, and celebrates the
Jewish festivals, even the postbiblical feast of Hanukkah (John
10:22–23). Throughout his life, he remains faithful to his declaration in Matt. 5:17–19.

Not even the first congregation of believers in Jerusalem
questions the ongoing validity of the Torah: "they are all zeal-
ous for the law" (Acts 21:20). When a rumor arises that Paul
has taught Jews to forsake Moses (Acts 21:21), he goes up to

the temple in order to demonstrate actively that the rumor is false by making the vow of a Nazarite, which even includes offering sacrifices (Acts 21:22ff.; Num. 6).

Equally clear is the fact that Paul, writing to Gentile believers, does contrast Christ and circumcision, law and grace (Gal. 5:1–6), and that his Gentile congregations consequently did not live according to the law of Moses. In time, the church at large eventually came to regard the law as canceled for Jew and Gentile alike: "for Christ is the end of the law" (Rom. 10:4; cf. Gal. 3:28).

Since the covenant at Sinai in point of fact stands or falls with the Torah, just as the survival of the Jewish people is inseparably linked to the laws of the covenant, not only the law was held to be canceled, but also the covenant between God and Israel. From this perspective, there was no longer a place for the people of Israel in Christian theology. The church consequently dogmatized itself as the "new Israel" and the "true Israel" (Latin *Verus Israel*), which had superseded and replaced the "old Israel" (Latin *Vetus Israel*). This teaching is reflected in the unfortunate terminology, "Old Testament" versus "New Testament," perhaps better to be rendered the "Earlier Covenant" and the "Latter Covenant."

THEOLOGY OF REPLACEMENT

Considering that such supersessionist and replacement theology stands in sharp conflict with the scriptural view, both of the Old and of the New Testament, it is perplexing that it could develop so overwhelmingly as to dominate church teaching and remain for all practical purposes unchallenged for almost two thousand years.

Why do we Gentile Christians not keep the law of Moses? Quite obviously not because Christ might have canceled the law, but owing to a quite different motive. Few have seen this as clearly as Martin Luther. In a sermon on the theme, "How Christians Should Regard Moses,"[14] he emphasizes that the law of Moses does not belong to us, since we are not Jews. He comments on the introduction to the tablets of the covenant in the following way:

That Moses does not bind the Gentiles can be proved from Exodus 20, where God himself speaks, "I am the Lord your God, who brought you out of the land of Egypt, out of the house of bondage." This text makes it clear that even the Ten Commandments do not pertain to us. For God never led us out of Egypt, but only the Jews. . . . Therefore it is clear enough that Moses is the lawgiver of the Jews and not of the Gentiles. He has given the Jews a sign whereby they should lay hold of God, when they call upon him as the God who brought them out of Egypt. The Christians have a different sign, whereby they conceive of God as the One who gave his Son.[15]

It is true that God commanded this of Moses and spoke thus to the people; but we are not this people. . . . It is all God's word. But let God's word be what it may, I must pay attention and know to whom God's word is addressed. You are still a long way from being the people with whom God spoke.[16]

We are not this people! The church is not Israel! We are still not the addressees when God speaks at Mount Sinai. This is why we as Gentile Christians do not follow these commandments—not because they have been canceled!

The main reason why there is so much confusion concerning observance of "the law" within Christian teaching is without doubt that Christians easily and unconsciously imagine that they once received the law, since it is the word of God. When they then have to explain why they do not keep it, they fall into the false explanation that Christ canceled the law. Usually a more subtle terminology is used: Christ has "fulfilled" the law. Who has not heard statements such as, "Christ has fulfilled the law, and therefore we do not need to keep the Sabbath"? Whatever it means that Christ has fulfilled the law, it can in no case mean that he has canceled it; in Matt. 5:17 the word "cancel" is used as the very opposite of "fulfill"!

However, as non-Jews we need no justification for not keeping the Sabbath or any of the other commandments, given by God exclusively to the people of Israel. As Luther stresses, we are not that people. We were not at Sinai. The covenant with all its conditions was not given to the nations, but as a special covenantal sign to the Jewish people.

The numerous commandments, often labeled "ceremonial" or "ritual," are not practiced by Christians, not because they have been rendered "old" (as if God would revoke his calling; see Rom. 11:29), but simply because they are not our commandments. They belong to the people of Israel. This does not exclude the possibility, however, that there is often also a generally human aspect of the commandments, which are equally relevant and valid for all human beings. Not to steal and kill and oppress the poor is, of course, not behavior that should characterize only one specific people. It is equally clear that any human being can learn much about God's character by reading about the encounter with Israel.

At this point, Luther is crystal clear. It is therefore incomprehensible how in the same sermon he slips into the same old anti-Jewish replacement theology, which has characterized Christian teaching ever since the church fathers. Since he so obviously contradicts himself, there is no other explanation than that he does so unconsciously and out of tradition. After having stated that the law was only given to the Jews at Sinai, he thus continues: "Here the law of Moses has its place. It is no longer binding on us because it was given only to the people of Israel."[17] How can the law have ceased to be binding on us, if we have never received it? The expression "no longer binding" reasonably has to imply that it was once valid but is now superseded!

This is the cornerstone of all supersessionism and replacement theology; the law is superseded and replaced, as is the Jewish people. In spite of his biblical onset, the Reformer thus fails to remove this nonscriptural and anti-Jewish stumbling block. Not surprisingly, even he eventually stumbles into the same pitfall to which replacement teaching inevitably leads.

Again, if we posit that the law is superseded, then the covenant between God and his people Israel is annulled as well. Consequently, Judaism should no longer exist—nor should Jews. This and little else is the logical conclusion of all supersessionist and replacement thought. Luther's hate-filled book, *About the Jews and Their Lies,*[18] written near the end of his life (1542–1543), stands forever as a monument of shame in the history of Christianity and antisemitism.

THEOLOGY OF CONFIRMATION

Our view of the relationship between Christ and God's law is critical for how we understand the covenant at Sinai and the new covenant, as well as the question of Christian nonobservance of the Mosaic law. Again, let us consider two possibilities.

(a) Christ has canceled the law, and then necessarily also the covenant at Sinai. For reasons we have already dealt with, this view not only contradicts the basic view of the Old Testament but also of Jesus and the early church as described in the New Testament.

(b) As non-Jews, we have never received the law and therefore do not even need to justify our not keeping it.

Which of these two starting points one chooses is no matter of minor detail. It is a difference as vast as east and west, day and night, and even life and death. In the first case, the faithfulness of God to the covenant is thrown into question, which implicitly threatens the very foundation of the new covenant as well. If precepts and promises, which the Old Testament certifies to be eternal, are no longer valid, then what assurance is there that God's mind may not change again? Perhaps the church is now replaced by another covenantal people which has produced better fruits than we?

If our faith is indeed built upon God's mercy and trustworthiness, we have no other basis for our hope than that God keeps promises in both in the Old and the New Testament, "for the gifts and the calling of God are irrevocable" (Rom. 11:29).

Therefore, our point of departure is not that Christ has canceled the law, but that he has fulfilled it. This means above all that things that previously were promised have now become reality. Paul mentions in this context the promise of Abraham (Gal. 3:8ff.), more precisely its second part (see p. 133, n. 8), a blessing to the Gentiles—the uncircumcised who were not present at the liberation from Egypt and did not participate in the covenant at Sinai. Nevertheless, they were not forgotten.

When God calls Israel and makes a covenant with them, he does so for the sake of "all the earth" (19:5; see p. 130). The gospel teaches that through the life, death, and resurrection of Jesus Christ the promises to the Gentiles have been realized. Paul therefore says that "now, apart from law, a righteousness of God has been disclosed, and is attested by the law and the prophets" (Rom. 3:21). Most translations are inaccurate, stating that "the righteousness of God has been manifested." This gives the false impression that God's righteousness has not been revealed before. What Paul states, however, is that "a righteousness" has been revealed, namely, one dimension of God's righteousness that was previously only promised, a righteousness "apart from the law," apart from Sinai.[19] This refers to the blessing previously promised to Abraham for the Gentiles who had not received the law at Sinai.

The fact that Paul thus has his Gentile Christian congregations in mind, becomes obvious when he continues: "For we hold that a person is justified by faith apart from works of the law. Or is God the God of Jews only? Is he not the God of Gentiles also? Yes, of Gentiles also, since God is one" (Rom. 3:28ff.).

The expression "works of the law" does not imply observing the commandments as such but refers to specific deeds that Gentiles voluntarily took upon themselves after they had abandoned paganism and began worshiping the God of Israel.[20] In the New Testament they are called "God-fearers" (see Acts 10:2 and 13:16). Eventually they or their children usually became proselytes; through circumcision and baptism they entered the Sinaitic covenant, determined to live according to the Torah.

At this point, the apostle to the Gentiles calls a halt. God's promises to the Gentiles—the uncircumcised—are now realized through Jesus. They no longer need to walk the way of Sinai to enter into God's covenant. Through Jesus Christ, God has fulfilled what he promised through Moses and the prophets. He has "opened a door of faith for the Gentiles," a door "apart from law" (Acts 14:27; Rom. 3:21).

Hence, at the apostolic council in Jerusalem the elders decided that Gentile believers in Jesus need not become proselytes to Judaism but should remain as they were, uncircumcised (Acts 15; cf. 1 Cor. 7:17ff.). The whole discussion at the apostolic council is, of course, senseless, unless it is understood that the Jews should continue to keep the commandments of the Torah. The only item on the agenda of the meeting concerned whether the Gentiles should also begin to do so.

Against this background, we see how vitally important it is to Paul that his Gentile congregations not adhere to the Sinaitic covenant, as though Christ had brought about no change regarding the Gentiles through Christ. This explains his contrast between circumcision and Christ in Gal. 5:2. Were the Christians there to try to adhere to the Sinaitic covenant, to keep only certain "deeds of the law" would prove insufficient, for, indeed, they would be "bound to keep the whole law" (Gal. 5:3). Were they to chose to walk the way of Sinai, then they would actually demonstrate that they rejected Christ as the fulfillment of God's promises to the Gentiles through Abraham (Gal. 5:4). Moreover, they would question God's truthfulness as well, since their conversion to Judaism would imply that the covenant at Sinai and the giving of "the law" would have annulled the earlier promise to Abraham (Gal. 3:15–18).

End, Goal, Confirmation

Christ is consequently not the "end" of the law (Rom. 10:4), a centuries-old misunderstanding of Paul's use of the Greek word *telos* to describe Christ. While this word can occasionally mean "end," the most common usage is "aim," "goal" (see 1 Tim. 1:5). What Paul maintains is consequently that Christ is the fulfillment of the law, that is, of the Torah.

Contrary to common interpretation, the commandments of "the law" are not the issue, but the promises. In order to grasp the intent of this crucial verse, we must bear in mind that when Paul uses the Greek word *nomos,* "law," he is referring not to particular laws and ordinances, but rather to the entirety of the first part of the Scriptures—the Torah, the five Books of Moses—just as he explicitly does in Rom. 3:21 when he speaks about "the law and the prophets." If only this essential meaning of the word "law" had been considered (see pp. 139f.), it would, of course, have been impossible to argue that Christ is the "end" of the law. It would be as absurd as saying that Christ is the "end" of the word of God; he can only be its goal and fulfillment. Again, Paul is referring here to the promises in the Torah, in particular to God's promise to Abraham (cf. Rom. 4), rather than to particular commandments.

As we have emphasized above, saying that Christ is the fulfillment of God's promises in no way suggests that he has canceled the law or that the ongoing validity of the covenant at Sinai is put at risk. Importantly, we note that when Paul in Rom. 15:8–9 explains what Christ means for a Jew and a Gentile, respectively, he makes no reference to liberation from the law.[21] He uses instead another key term—confirmation: "For I tell you that Christ [on the one hand] became a servant to the circumcised to show God's truthfulness, in order to confirm the promises given to the patriarchs, and in order that the Gentiles [on the other hand] might glorify God for his mercy."[22]

That the latter are his primary concern becomes indisputable from the following quotations, all of which deal with promises relevant to Gentiles. Since they had neither received the patriarchs nor Moses, Christ could simply not serve as confirmation to them. They could only be included "apart from the law," through the mercy of God, and his faithfulness to his promises regarding them.[23]

In conclusion, let us briefly reflect on why Moses and the Old Testament remain of such enduring importance to us even though they were not given to us directly as Gentiles. Luther proposes three solutions.

(1) The commandments serve as good examples of wise conduct: "If I were emperor, I would take from Moses a model for [my] statutes; not that Moses should be binding on me, but that I should be free to follow him in ruling as he ruled," he says.[24] At the same time Luther emphasizes that these are Israel's laws specifically and therefore need not necessarily be copied by others.

Luther applies this axiom even to the "ten commandments," inasmuch as the Sabbath commandment is given to Israel exclusively (see 31:12ff. and pp. 242ff. below). On the other hand, these commandments coincide to a great extent with the natural law that God has inscribed in the hearts of every human being (Rom. 2:14–15).

> Therefore it is natural to honor God, not steal, not commit adultery, not bear false witness, not murder; and what Moses commands is nothing new. For what God has given the Jews from heaven, he has also written in the hearts of all men. Thus I keep the commandments which Moses has given, not because Moses gave the commandment, but because they have been implanted in me by nature, and Moses agrees exactly with nature, etc. But the other commandments of Moses, which are not [implanted in all men] by nature, the Gentiles do not hold. Nor do these pertain to the Gentiles, such as tithe and others equally fine which I wish we had too.[25]

> Thus we read Moses not because he applies to us, that we must obey him, but because he agrees with the natural law and is conceived better than the Gentiles would ever have been able to do. Thus the Ten Commandments are a mirror of our life, in which we can see wherein we are lacking.[26]

(2) In the law of Moses we can find promises about Christ. He writes,

> In the second place I find something in Moses that I do not have from nature: the promises and pledges of God about Christ. . . . And it is the most important thing in Moses which pertains to us. The first thing, namely, the commandments, does not pertain to us. I read Moses because such excellent and comforting promises are there recorded, by which I can find strength for my weak faith.[27]

Luther refers specifically to Gen. 3:15; 22:18 and Deut. 18:15 and concludes: "Summing up this second part, we read Moses for the sake of the promises about Christ, who belongs not only to the Jews but also to the Gentiles; for through Christ all the Gentiles should have the blessing, as was promised to Abraham."[28]

(3) In the history of Israel, we find important examples of faith and love, as well as exemplary admonitions against unbelief and sin with their attendant consequences: "Examples like these are necessary. For although I am not Cain, yet if I should act like Cain, I will receive the same punishment as Cain. Nowhere else do we find such fine examples of both faith and unfaith."[29]

In addition to Luther's considerations, I would like to bring up a fourth point. The Bible certainly has much to teach, even when it does not directly address us. When it describes how God with no conditions whatsoever elects and saves Israel, I recognize the same God who then is revealed through Jesus Christ. In the book of the covenant, I come to know how precious life is in God's eyes and to understand the divine care of the poor and defenseless—God's passion for justice and righteousness.

I find here paradigms of God's actions that deserve to be imitated in daily life. I find models of what God expects from everyone. Obedience means precisely this, *imitatio Dei,* the imitation of God. God remains immutably the same generation after generation, as does basically his creation, humankind. Even though the Lord adopts one people in particular, which he separates through special laws, I recognize the Father of Jesus Christ in the way God deals with this people. I also recognize myself in the way Israel receives—or rejects—the divine love.

In the chapters to follow, we will come to know more profoundly an aspect of God which we have already encountered:

holiness, which mortal humans can neither grasp nor endure. The prescriptions for the tabernacle entail both a lesson of the endless distance between God and humankind and of the intimacy and communion with his people, which is God's innermost desire.

12

The Sanctuary of Freedom

This section of Exodus differs greatly from the previous one in both form and content. In chapters 19–24 diverse laws and ordinances are intertwined with narratives about Moses and the people confronting the divine revelation at Mount Sinai. Chapters 25–31, on the other hand, consist of one long set of instructions that Moses receives from the Lord during his forty days on the mountain (see 24:18; 25:9, 40; 26:30; 27:8). In its content, the focus moves away from the social to the sacred, from the moral to the ritual. The previous chapters primarily emphasized righteousness, mercy, and love in relationships with one's fellow human beings as the foundation of the covenant. Here the stress is exclusively laid on the direct relationship between God and Israel.

We have already seen that one aspect cannot be played off against the other. The ordinances regulating the tabernacle are not a marginal addition to the moral laws. This becomes obvious not least through the space given over to the details of these ordinances in the book of Exodus. The section occupies no fewer than seven chapters. As if this were not enough, the entire portion is repeated almost literally in chapters 35–40 (cf. also Num. 7–8);[1] in total, almost one-third of the whole book of Exodus deals with the tabernacle!

Despite the differences, they are nevertheless harmoniously woven together. The instructions regulating the construction of the tabernacle continue the revelation at Sinai. We could even affirm that it is only with the building of the tabernacle that the covenant is sealed and its confirmation finally fulfilled, for it is clear that God's intention to "dwell among them" (Exod. 25:8) will now be demonstrated to the people.

Now the obedience of the people is to be tested, for they must also confirm the fact of their promise: "All that the LORD has spoken we will do and we will hear" (24:7; pp. 189f.; cf. 25:9, 40; Num. 8:4; Heb. 8:5; 9:23). There are still multiple obstacles to be overcome until the Lord moves the cloud of glory, now covering the mountain, into the sanctuary as a compelling sign that the miracle of Pentecost has achieved its purpose. Only then will the people be ready to continue their walk toward the promised land, confident in the assurance of the Lord's indwelling presence among them (40:34–38).

The instructions begin with an inventory of the contents of the tabernacle (ch. 25), continue with the tabernacle itself (ch. 26), and proceed outward to the forecourt with its appurtenances and enclosure (ch. 27). Then the priests and their vestments, consecration, and sacrifices are dealt with (chs. 28–29). After supplementary ordinances (ch. 30), the master builder and his assistants are presented, just as is usually the case in any building project (31:1–11). Finally, we see a different kind of tabernacle, ready and prepared even before the Lord shows one single detail of the construction soon to be described (31:12–17).

INTRODUCTION (25:1–9; 35:1–9)

The introduction to chapter 25 makes clear that this construction concerns the entire people, just as did the revelation at Sinai with all its commandments. Each person will be invited to contribute materials needed for the sanctuary (25:2ff.). The response from the people is so overwhelming that Moses will eventually have to ask them to stop (36:3ff.).

Even if Moses alone receives the blueprint and leads the work overseeing a few selected craftsmen, he does so by order of God and on behalf of the people, just as the same will later apply to the service of the priests in the sanctuary. We thus read about the whole people: "Have them make me a sanctuary, so that I may dwell among them" (25:8).

The Lord will dwell "among them," not in the sanctuary itself, but among the people. This minute detail betrays a deeper problem applicable to any place blessed with the presence of God and to any building built to God's glory. The one who "stretches out the heavens like a curtain, and spreads them like a tent to live in" (Isa. 40:22) needs no human structure, or as the prophet expresses it: "Heaven is my throne and the earth is my footstool; what is the house that you would build for me, and what is my resting place?" (Isa. 66:1) In a deeper sense, all our sanctuaries are erected not for God's sake but for our own sake. They are the visible means by which we in our human limitations may hope to experience the presence of the eternal, almighty God, whom no mind can fully grasp or comprehend.

The divine presence has two aspects, expressed by the words in 25:8–9: "sanctuary" and "tabernacle."

(1) The first word, in Hebrew *miqdash,* means a "holy site." The temple in Jerusalem was likewise called *beth ha-miqdash,* "the house of holiness." God is revealed as the holy one, majestically exalted and supreme, in whose presence no human being stands worthy (see pp. 27, 134). The children of Israel have just encountered him as a "devouring fire" (24:17). The very structure of the sanctuary now becomes a constant visible sermon on God's holiness and humankind's unholy status in the presence of the divine.

The sanctuary is divided into three zones of holiness, discreetly separated from one another: the innermost sanctum, "the holy of holies," ten cubits square; the outer sanctum, "the holy place," twenty cubits long and separated from the former by a magnificent curtain; and the forecourt surrounding the tabernacle itself (see further below).

This graded holiness is also expressed through the various materials used in the different zones, from gold to silver to copper (25:3), and through the various colors of the textiles, from "blue" to "purple" to "crimson" to undyed "goats' hair" (25:4). Even within the textiles themselves there is a gradation in the workmanship, from *ma'aseh hoshev,* translated "skillfully worked" (26:1, 31; 28:6, 15), to *ma'aseh roqem,* translated "needlework" (26:36; 27:16; 28:39), to *ma'aseh 'oreg,* translated "woven" (28:32; 39:22, 27). The difference between these three kinds of workmanship is probably that the first is multicolored and contains figures, like cherubim, while the second is only multicolored, and the last monochromatic.[2]

The people also are divided according to these three zones of increasing sanctity. Only Moses has constant access to the holy of holies, Aaron under certain circumstances (Lev. 16), while the priests, the Levites, and the rest of the people are assigned areas according to decreasing grades of holiness.

(2) The second word, in Hebrew *mishkan,* often refers to a tent, the simplest of human dwellings. Another synonym for "tent," *ʾohel,* is also used for the tabernacle (see 28:43 ["the tent of meeting"], Num. 9:15 [literally "the tent of the testimony"; cf. 38:21], and 39:32, where both names are combined). The verb translated "to dwell" in 25:8 *(shakan)* can also be rendered "to live in a tent." The tabernacle is thus a constant visible proclamation of a God who, in spite of heavenly exaltation and holiness, descends to people, dwells with them, and shares their desert conditions here on earth.

It is surely to this gospel that John alludes when he states: "The Word became flesh and lived [Greek *eskēnōsen,* literally, 'pitched his tent,' or 'tabernacled'] among us" (John 1:14). It is as if the evangelist makes this statement with a smile of recognition and thinks of the words in 25:8, "I will dwell [in a tent] in their midst," and exclaims: now it has happened again! On this occasion, however, the "tent" is a small child (cf. p. 254, n. 8).

The tent sanctuary thus becomes the focal point of the double aspect of God's character, summed up by the prophet in the following incisive declaration: "For thus says the high and lofty one who inhabits eternity, whose name is holy: I dwell in the high and holy place, and also with those who are contrite and humble in spirit" (Isa. 57:15).

The experience of this character of God, so obvious and tangible in ancient Israel, was expressed in later Jewish tradition by the term *Shekinah,* referring to God's presence. This word is etymologically connected both with the noun *mishkan* and the verb *shakan.* God was present when dwelling in a tent here on earth. In this way, the encounter of the intimate nearness of the Lord by Israel through the tabernacle put its stamp on their experience of God for all future time.

These aspects of God—transcendence and immanence, exaltation and closeness, distance and proximity—are further expressed in the first and most holy of the tabernacle's furniture, now to be described.

THE ARK OF THE COVENANT
AND THE MERCY SEAT (25:10–22; 37:1–9)

In the description of the tabernacle and its utensils, the measure of length is the "cubit" (Hebrew ʾammah; 25:10), the length of the forearm from the fingers to the elbow,[3] about 17 to 20 inches or almost half a meter. Hence, the ark had rather modest measures, hardly four feet (1.2 meters) long with a height and breadth of about 29 inches (75 centimeters). Since the tablets of the covenant were deposited here, these dimensions also indicate their approximate size.

The holiness of the ark is expressed by its golden overlay[4] and by the poles that were never to be removed (25:11ff.; cf. 1 Kgs. 8:7–8). In this respect it was different from the table of the showbread (25:23ff.), as well as the altar of incense (30:1ff.). It is true that they were manufactured in a way similar to the ark, but the poles with which these latter two objects were carried could be removed. This probably reflects the unique holiness of the ark, an object that everyone was forbidden to touch directly (cf. Num. 4:15).

The gold-overlaid chest was also equipped with a cover (Hebrew kapporeth). In the NRSV and a number of other translations the cover is called the "mercy seat." This translation is based on the important role played by this object in the sprinkling of blood on the Day of Atonement (Lev. 16:12ff.). In this context, the word kapporeth and the verb for "to atone for" (Hebrew kipper) appear side by side, with both an etymological and a substantive connection between the two (see further pp. 231, 234).

Even in the time of the Greek translation of the Hebrew Bible, the Septuagint (ca. 200 B.C.E.), the word is obviously understood in this way, since it is translated hilastērion, which means a place or means of atonement.[5] In the New Testament, this word is used in Heb. 9:5 and in Rom. 3:25, where Paul applies it to Christ.

Great significance was ascribed to this cover, as demonstrated by the name of the "holy of holies" in 1 Chron. 28:11, "the room of the mercy seat" (Hebrew beth hakapporeth),[6] while, for example, the name "the room of the ark" is never used.

Moreover, its workmanship emphasizes another special function. On each short side, two cherubim were cast in one piece with the cover (25:17ff.). The only thing we know about these figures is that they had faces, probably human, turned toward each other, as well as reverently down toward the cover and the ark itself (25:20). Additionally, they had wings spread over the ark. This description probably reflects a mixture of human and beast found in various places in the ancient Near East.[7]

Since details of their appearance are scarce and varied (cf. Isa. 6; Ezek. 1; 10; 41:17ff.), it is not easy to gain a clear impression of what they looked like. Their description is perhaps purposefully vague, expressing the awareness that they were little more than symbolic figures to which the prohibition against images (20:4) did not apply.[8]

More important than their appearance is their function. In Gen. 3:24 they seem to be guards. The way in which their wings spread over the ark would indicate a similar function here as well, that is, as guards of the holy ark. Even in Solomon's temple, the cherubim spread their wings protectively over the ark (1 Kgs. 8:7; 1 Chron. 28:18). In this case, however, we have before us other cherubim functioning differently. About fifteen feet (five meters) high, they turned toward the veil (1 Kgs. 6:23–28; 8:1–12). They probably served symbolically to support the invisible throne of God. A like notion may lie behind the position of the cherubim even here, given that they turned their faces down toward the ark as if they dared not look at what was above them.

Winged figures carrying or guarding the throne of a king are a common motif in the decorative arts of the ancient Near East. These depictions illustrate the expression that the Lord of hosts is "enthroned on the cherubim" (1 Sam. 4:4; 2 Sam. 6:2; 2 Kgs. 19:5; 1 Chron. 13:6; Ps. 80:1; 99:1; Isa. 37:16). Within this tradition, the ark is evidently regarded as God's footstool (1 Chron. 28:2; Ps. 99:5; 132:7).[9] The sanctuary then represents a kind of miniature universe, wherein God who has heaven as a throne and earth as a footstool self-effacingly dwells among the people in a man-made sanctuary (see further pp. 239f.).

As the intersection between heaven and earth, the holy of holies, the place "between the two cherubim" (25:22), becomes the foremost locus of divine revelation (30:6; Num. 7:89).[10] Hence, it is natural that the tablets of the covenant were kept in the ark.[11]

Again, we find striking parallels in treaties between rulers in the ancient Near East. When Rameses II and the Hittite king concluded a pact with one another (ca. 1280 B.C.E.), they deposited a copy of the text with the conditions "beneath the feet" of each one's gods, that is, at the most central place in their temples.[12] Hence, the tabernacle with the Torah becomes the seal of the covenant and a visible testimony of its validity.

The ark of the covenant disappeared with the destruction of the first temple in 586 B.C.E. and was never replaced by a new one (2 Maccabees 2:4–8; cf. Jer. 3:16ff.); in Herod's temple the holy of holies was consequently empty. According to Jewish legend, the ark was not destroyed but concealed; only at the end of time will it again come to light. According to 2 Maccabees 2:4–8 it was brought to Mount Nebo by the prophet Jeremiah:

> And Jeremiah came and found a cave dwelling, and he took the tent and the ark and the incense altar into it, and he blocked up the door. And some of those who followed him came up to mark the road, and they could not find it. But when Jeremiah found it out, he blamed them and said, "The place shall be unknown until God gathers the congregation of his people together and shows his mercy. Then the Lord will show where they are, and the glory of the Lord will appear, as they were shown in the days of Moses."

The Syriac *Apocalypse of Baruch* 6:4–10 claims that it was devoured by the earth, where it will remain until Jerusalem "shall be restored again for ever."[13]

THE TABLE FOR THE BREAD OF THE PRESENCE (25:23–30; 37:10–15)

A table was to be placed along the northern wall in front of the veil (26:33, 35). "The bread of the Presence" (25:30) is a translation attempt to render the Hebrew expression, *lehem panim,* where *lehem* means "bread" and *panim* means "face" as well as "surface" and "front." The phrase is also frequently translated "showbread." According to Lev. 24:5–9 twelve loaves of bread were to be placed on this table. Like the pillars in 24:4, the onyx stones on the ephod in 28:9–12, and the precious stones on the breastpiece in 28:21, the bread represented the twelve tribes of Israel. They were to be consumed by the priests and replenished each Sabbath day.

Rabbinic temple traditions have preserved information about how the bread should be baked, as well as their form and arrangement on the table.[14] According to Lev. 24:6, they should be placed "in two rows, six in a row." The Hebrew word translated as "row" *(ma'arekheth)* means "order,"

"arrangement" in general and not necessarily a row lengthwise. According to tradition the loaves of bread were placed
one upon another in two stacks. Given that the surface of the
table measured about 40 by 20 inches (100 by 50 centimeters)
and that the size of each loaf was approximately 20 by 10
inches (50 by 25 centimeters), they could not possibly have
been laid out in a row. The only remaining possibility was
thus to stack them on top of each other.

The pieces of bread were bent upward into a u-shape
and their corners were further formed in a way reminiscent of
the horns of the altar. Through this form air could move, preventing the bread from molding. They were also supported by
a rack of thin bars in five layers; the first layer of bread was
placed directly on the table.[15]

The purpose of the objects mentioned in 25:29 remains
obscure. According to rabbinic tradition, the first two ("plates
and dishes") refer to the twelve containers, in which the loaves
were kept on the table, and to two bowls, in which the incense as
prescribed in Lev. 24:7 was arranged. This incense was lit on the
altar of burnt offerings (27:1–8) when the bread on the Sabbath
was renewed. The words translated "flagons and bowls" are
problematic as regards both meaning and function. According to
rabbinic tradition, the first word describes the vertical struts on
the long side of the table that supported the bars with the bread
containers, while the second word refers to the bars themselves.
These were pipes slit lengthwise, forming a groove.[16]

In surrounding cultures, it was common to display food
and drink of various kinds on a table for the gods, but in Israel
this practice was rejected because of the misconception of
God underlying such pagan customs (cf. Isa. 65:11). Hence,
the table of the showbread was not placed in the holy of holies
together with the ark of the covenant. Furthermore, sacrifices
and offerings were totally consumed either by fire or by the
priests, which was the case with the showbread.

"One does not live by bread alone" (Deut. 8:3). The ark
of the covenant with its precious contents testifies to this fundamental truth. The table of the showbread conveys an important testimony to the fact that we live by bread and that, in
order to receive the bread of life in our hearts through God's
word, we also need something for the tongue and stomach.
Word and sacrament are thus united from the very beginning
of humanity's relationship with the Almighty: "O taste and see
that the LORD is good!" (Ps. 34:8).

The seeing of the eye, not only the hearing of the ear, is evoked when the Lord reveals his goodness. Such is the message conveyed by the next object.

THE MENORAH (25:31–40; 37:17–24)

No other object is described in such detail as the menorah, the seven-branched lampstand. It was placed at the south side, opposite the table of showbread (26:35). Of all the furniture in the tabernacle, it is only the menorah that has become a religious and national symbol. For at least two thousand years, Jews all over the world have depicted it on coins, mosaics, tombstones, lamps, jewelry, etc.[17]

When the newly founded state of Israel sought to design its official emblem, the choice was not hard to make. No other Jewish symbol had such deep roots in the history and consciousness of the Jewish people as the menorah.[18] As a "tree of life" with its pattern in heaven (25:40; Num. 8:4) it is a worthy and deeply meaningful symbol of the exodus people after its homecoming. Combined with two olive branches, the emblem also directly alludes to the golden menorah flanked by the two olive trees described in Zech. 4:2–3. When the question is asked, "What are these, my lord?" (Zech. 4:4), the answer is given, "Not by might, nor by power, but by my spirit, says the LORD of hosts" (Zech. 4:6). When we contemplate the humanly inexplicable and existentially awesome survival of the Jewish people, together with the historical background of modern Israel, we come face-to-face with perhaps the most profound answer to the many questions this miracle solicits.

Despite the detailed description of the menorah, many things remain unclear. For example, its dimension is not mentioned. According to rabbinic tradition it was eighteen handbreadths high, approximately three cubits.[19] Numerous ancient depictions help us to visualize the biblical account. Israel's national symbol reflects the bas-relief of the menorah at the Arch of Titus in Rome, where a number of temple objects looted during the destruction of Jerusalem in 70 C.E. are represented.[20] The resemblance to other early depictions, like those in the synagogues of Beth Alpha and Dura Europus (third century C.E.),[21] supports the authenticity of this representation.

The menorah from the Second Temple was most probably manufactured according to the biblical record and historic memory transmitted from generation to generation since pre-exilic times. A striking feature in the biblical description is the botanical terminology. The menorah is described as a tree or plant with stem, branches, flowers, calyxes, petals, and cups. In Egyptian art and architecture botanical motifs frequently appear, and it is noteworthy that the design of the menorah is typical of the art from the Late Bronze Age, namely, the time of exodus.[22]

A particular plant may very well have served as the model of the menorah. It is a type of sage (salvia) common in the Middle East, of which the coupled branches and symmetrical leaves reveal striking similarities with the menorah.[23] Equally likely is a stylized tree as a prototype for this sacred object; the tree frequently recurs as a symbol in many religions.[24] Trees also play a prominent role in the Bible. The tree of life in the garden of Eden may be significant for our understanding of the symbolism behind the menorah, since the number seven symbolizes completion and fullness in the creation story.

A kindled candlestick in the sanctuary also invokes the motif of light, central to the creation story and throughout the Bible. It symbolizes both life itself and the giver of life, "for with you is the fountain of life; in your light we see light" (Ps. 36:9). It further stands for "the way and the truth," God's revelation and presence, linked to the sanctuary: "O send out your light and your truth; let them lead me, let them bring me to your holy hill and to your dwelling [mishkan]. Then I will go to the altar of God, to God my exceeding joy" (Ps. 43:3–4). The psalmist gratefully acknowledges: "Your word is a lamp to my feet and a light to my path" (Ps. 119:105).

It is also possible that the almond tree (Exod. 25:33–34), which blooms on a bare twig in early spring, is symbolically represented by the menorah as a reminder of returning life. As in Jer. 1:11–12, it may likewise express the watchfulness and protection of the Lord, since the verb "watch" (shaqad) is derivative from the same Hebrew root as "almond" (shaqed).[25]

See further 27:20–21 and 30:7–8.

THE TABERNACLE (26:1–37; 36:1–38)

After the inventory of the tabernacle furniture, the tent itself is dealt with. First, four different layers of materials are described. These served to cover the tabernacle, thirty cubits in length and ten cubits in breadth and height.[26]

(a) 26:1–6. The innermost tapestry was predictably the most beautiful, composed of blue, purple and scarlet, and was to be "skillfully worked," decorated with cherubim.

(b) 26:7–13. The first protective layer consisted of a goats' hair fabric, probably not unlike the black bedouin tents of today. The clasps were simple copper, rather than gold.

(c) 26:14. Another two layers of skins assured the protection of the tabernacle with its costly inventory, lending to the sanctuary a most worthy and dignified appearance.

After the description of the wooden frames and bars in 26:15–30,[27] the magnificent curtain, designed to separate the outer sanctum from the inner sanctum—the holy of holies—is set forth (26:31ff.). "Skillfully worked," like the inner tapestry, it was embroidered with cherubim and composed of the three precious colors. The veil was suspended from golden hooks over golden pillars with silver bases, standing ten cubits from the western wall. Hence, the holy of holies was cubic, while the holy precinct adjoining it was twice as long as wide.

In front of the entrance to the tabernacle hung yet another curtain (26:36), made from the same material as the inner veil but of simpler workmanship, "needlework" instead of the "skillful work" of the former (see pp. 209f.). The difference remains obscure, except that less fine artistry did mark the descending grade of holiness proportional to the distance from the holy of holies.

The entire edifice had to be movable without great effort (see Num. 4 and 10) and, consequently, had to be easily disassembled and reassembled again.[28]

The terms "sanctuary" and "tabernacle," like the later term "temple," may refer to the tent structure as well as to the whole sacred precinct, including the forecourt and its inventory. In the next chapter, we move out to the vicinity immediately surrounding the tent.

THE ALTAR OF BURNT OFFERING
AND THE COURT (27:1–21; 38:1–31)

The altar now to be described was situated in the forecourt outside the tent. In 30:28 it is called "the altar of burnt offering" to distinguish it from "the altar of incense" inside the tent (30:1–10, 27). Because of their locations, the rabbis later termed them "the outer altar" and "the inner altar," respectively. In reference to their different materials, they were also called "the bronze altar" and "the golden altar" (39:38–39). Since most of the worship occurred outside the tent, into which the people had no access, the service was centered on the outer altar.

Measuring a height of only three cubits, hardly five feet (1.5 meters), it was relatively small compared to the altar of burnt offering in Solomon's temple (10 by 20 cubits; 2 Chron. 4:1) and that in Herod's temple (15 cubits high and 50 cubits square—almost as tall as a two-story building).[29] The Israelite stone altar found in Arad has the same modest dimensions as described here.[30] It also has "horns," which play an important role in the sacrifices (see 29:12). It served as well as a place of refuge for people who had inadvertently killed someone (cf. p. 160).

The altar of burnt offering was a portable wooden box overlaid with bronze. According to 27:8, it was hollow, which means it was open at the top and filled with earth, sand, and unhewn stones according to 20:24–25. This prevented the wood from being damaged by the altar fire.

The purpose of the "grating" (27:4) and of the "ledge" (27:5) is left unexplained. Archaeologists have found altars bearing ledges on their upper half. According to rabbinic tradition, when blood was sprinkled against the wall of the altar (cf. 29:16), it was aimed against the walls above a line midway up the altar if it was a sin offering, and below the line in all other cases. The blood was therefore labeled "upper" and "lower" blood, respectively.[31]

The location of the altar in the large court, which measured 100 by 50 cubits, is not specified. We know, however, that it must have been placed somewhere east of the entrance to the tabernacle and the laver (30:18). It is likely that the tabernacle itself was located equidistant from the southern, western, and northern walls of the court, leaving twenty cubits between the walls of the tabernacle and the enclosure of the court. The entrance to the tabernacle was located in the middle of the court. The ark in the middle of the holy of holies (twenty-five cubits from the entrance) would then have been located at the center of the western half of the court. The altar of burnt offering was probably placed at the center of the eastern half of the court, that is, on the central axis, midway between the entrance to the court and the entrance to the tabernacle.[32]

THE PRIESTLY VESTMENTS (28:1–43; 39:1–43)

All Israel was sanctified to be a "priestly kingdom and a holy nation" in the world (19:5–6; pp. 129–33). All Israel received the Torah with all its commandments as a sign of its calling, as a kind of priestly "insignia." This general priesthood, however, did not exclude a special priesthood within the holy people. The priesthood received specific signs of their unique vocation within Israel. Upon the separation of all Israel from the other nations, Aaron and his sons (and later the whole tribe of Levi) were set apart from the rest of Israel through special commandments and ordinances. Among these instructions, those for making vestments figure prominently.

The Ephod (28:6–14; 39:2–7)

The etymology and exact meaning of the term "ephod" are still unknown. However, it is related to other Semitic words designating a garment and probably indicates a precious robe in general, which later was refashioned into a particular design as part of the ceremonial robes of the high priest.[33] Its pattern seems to have resembled an apron with suspenders, outfitted with an ornate belt. According to Josephus, it had sleeves. If this were the case, the term "shoulder pieces" (28:7) would refer to shoulder straps rather than suspenders.[34] Of the materials listed, gold is mentioned first, indicating it was the main ingredient. It was probably also very sturdy and heavy because of the gold, "hammered out and cut into threads to work into the blue, purple, and crimson yarns" (39:3).

The function of the garment is more explicitly described than its design. On the shoulder pieces Aaron was to wear two onyx stones with the names of Israel's twelve tribes inscribed in the order of their birth (28:9ff.): Reuben, Simeon, Levi, Judah, Dan, and Naphtali on one and Gad, Asher, Issachar, Zebulun, Joseph, and Benjamin on the other. Rashi notes that, with this order, each inscription had the same number of letters, twenty-five.[35]

The arrangement described in 28:13–14 leads to the next portion of the robe, which may also be regarded as part of the ephod.

The Breastpiece (28:15–30; 39:8–21)

The "breastpiece of judgment" was a square case about half a cubit square (28:16). With the identical masterful workmanship as the ephod, it was worn at the front center of the ephod like an ornament, attached to its shoulder pieces and ornate belt with chains of pure gold (28:22–28).

The etymology of the Hebrew word *hoshen* is uncertain.[36] Two functions are mentioned. Just as the stones on the shoulder pieces, the breastpiece represented symbolically the twelve tribes of Israel with twelve precious stones. The list of stones reminds one of both the precious stones in the garden of Eden (Ezek. 28:13) and the foundation stones in the city wall of the new Jerusalem (Rev. 21:19–20). Only some of the stones can be identified.[37]

The ephod and the breastpiece symbolized Aaron's bearing of the children of Israel upon his shoulders as well as "on his heart" as a constant remembrance before the Lord (28:12, 29). He stood as the representative of the people before God and performed his service on their behalf. He shouldered responsibility for the well-being of his people and took upon himself their burdens both openly and in private. His people were to be inscribed on his heart in such a way that their needs became his needs.

To bear the people on one's shoulders is a sign for all servants of God who take their task seriously. It is told of a famous hasidic rabbi that he was once asked how he could remember all the people who came before him asking him to bring their burdens to the Lord.

> I do not need to enumerate them. When somebody comes to me and tells me about his troubles, I feel so deeply with that person that his ordeal gives me a wound in my heart. When later I stand before God in prayer, I only have to open my heart and cry out to our Father in heaven, "See!" And when he looks into my heart he can read every little detail about the people who have shared their sorrows and burdens with me.

The breastplate had a second function, for it is described as a "breastpiece of judgment" (28:15). It was "doubled," probably designed as a pouch, the content of which was "the Urim and the Thummim" (28:30). These two words are not explained; they were obviously already so well-known that no explanation was considered necessary. Now, however, their exact meanings are lost. Linguistically, they are usually derived from the two Hebrew words for "light" (ʾor) and "perfect," "pure," "innocent" (tam). The derivation of the latter word is probably correct. Since it was a matter of an instrument through which a positive or negative verdict could be rendered, however, the former word ought to have a negative connotation. Therefore, it should probably be linked to a word signifying "cursed" (ʾarur).[38]

The Urim and the Thummim functioned presumably as a kind of lots that revealed the will of God (Num. 27:18–23; 1 Sam. 14:36–46; 23:1–13; 28:6; 30:6–8; Ezra 2:61ff.; Neh. 7:63ff.). These references clearly indicate that only the leaders of the people were entitled to use them. Not evident, however, is whether the response was simply affirmative or negative. If the expression, "inquire of the LORD" (shaʾal be-YHWH), refers to the use of the Urim and the Thummim, it is apparent from several contexts that a more detailed answer could be expected (see Judg. 1:1–2; 20:18; 1 Sam. 10:22; 2 Sam. 2:1; 5:23–24).

One hypothesis therefore assumes that the Urim and the Thummim were inscribed with the letters of the alphabet. An indication in this direction is the fact that the word "Urim" begins with the first letter, ʾaleph, and "Thummim" with the last, taw (cf. p. 31). If so, words or phrases could be obtained when these lots were cast. Should the letters that surfaced prove impossible to read, this might have been interpreted as if the Lord were silent.[39]

It seems that their usage eventually became more rare. There is actually no biblical evidence that they were used after the time of King David. According to both Josephus and rabbinic tradition, they had ceased to function during the latter part of the Second Temple period.[40]

The Robe (28:31–35; 39:22–26)

This garment was woven in one piece, and, like a chasuble, had an opening for the head. Its blue color (also used in the tabernacle's inner tapestry, veil, and curtain at the entrance) was extracted from a sea snail. Under influence from light and certain chemicals, it could shift from dark blue to reddish purple. While the blue variant above all was the high priestly color, the red was the royal (cf. Mark 15:17–18; John 19:2).

It has been estimated that twelve thousand specimens were needed to extract 0.05 ounces (1.4 grams) of the dye.[41] Surprisingly, the blue cord on the fringes (Num. 15:38) that every Israelite should wear on a four-cornered garment, was also dyed with this very expensive substance, otherwise reserved exclusively for the rich and the noble (Judg. 8:26; Esth. 1:6; 8:15; Ezek. 23:6; Dan. 5:7; Luke 16:9). This implies a remarkable symbolical democratization of both the priestly and royal dignity to embrace all Israel as a kingdom of priests and a holy nation (19:6; see also p. 223, n. 43).

This magnificent robe, worn under the ephod and over a linen tunic (28:39), was decorated with little golden bells and pomegranates attached to the lower hem. (Pomegranates also decorated the capitals of the pillars at the entrance of the temple, according to 1 Kgs. 7:18–20, 42.) The bells certainly had a purpose beyond that of a decoration. The constant sound surrounding the high priest was a reminder of the holiness of the Lord, whom he represented. The people who could not see the high priest inside the sanctuary could still hear him and were thus aware of what was transpiring within. To the high priest himself, the bells were a reminder of the one he approached.

The Turban and the Diadem (28:36–38; 39:30–31)

The turban was royal attire, as was the crown (cf. Ezek. 21:26). Josephus, himself a priest and thus an eyewitness of the service in the temple, calls it a "tiara."[42] He describes it as a headgear like that worn by ordinary priests (see 28:39–40), but adds that an ornate blue embroidery overlaid the turban of the high priests.

Additionally, the high priest wore an object reminiscent of a royal crown, the golden plate attached to the front of the turban with a cord of bluish purple. The word used (tsits) appears in other texts as a parallel to both "bud" (or "flower," Hebrew perah; Num. 17:8 [Hebrew 17:23]) and "garland" (or "crown," Hebrew ʿatereth; Isa. 28:1);[43] in 29:6 and 39:30 the word *netser* is used, which in other places describes a royal crown (2 Sam. 1:10; 2 Kgs. 11:12; Ps. 132:18). Josephus claims that it was indeed a golden crown,[44] while the biblical description refers rather to an ornament, a diadem. According to rabbinic tradition it was "two fingers broad" and went from ear to ear.[45]

The ornate costliness of the high priest's vestments served to recall both God's holiness and Israel's vocation to be a holy people. The inscription on the diadem was *Qodesh la-YHWH*, which literally means "Holiness to the LORD." The expression focuses on the call of the high priest to be sanctified to the Lord and to see to it, as representative of the people, that the holiness of the covenantal relationship should be sought and maintained. Jeremiah 2:3 applies this expression to all the people of Israel. Therefore, the priest sought to remove all unholiness from Israel, for unholiness obstructs the relationship between the Lord and his people (see particularly Lev. 16 and below, pp. 231, 234).

These four parts of Aaron's ceremonial robe have partially survived in some church traditions: the white alb, the siculum, the chasuble, and the miter/tiara. In the synagogue, similarly, the Torah scrolls are "robed" in a manner suggestive of the robes of the high priest. In the Ashkenazi (Central and East European) tradition they are kept in an embroidered cover over which a decorated shield is hung. This shield is called the *hoshen*, the same name used for the breastpiece of the high priest. On the scrolls, crowns are fitted, often embellished with pomegranates and bells.

One needs no imagination to feel the deep emotions of the people as their eyes followed the high priest in the splendor of his robes, expressed in the following testimony now over two thousand years old:

> Their appearance makes one awestruck and dumbfounded: a man would think he had come out of this world into another one. I emphatically assert that every man who comes near the spectacle of what I have described will experience astonishment and amazement beyond words, his very being transformed by the hallowed arrangement of every single detail.[46]

The description of the high priestly garments has not drawn to its end. Another four items remain, which both Aaron and his sons (the ordinary priests) were to wear.

The Tunic (28:39–40; 39:27)

This white linen garment with long sleeves was woven, according to a special technique, into a checkered or braided pattern. The garment of the ordinary priests was essentially the same, only more simply made. Like the tunic generally worn by people in the ancient Near East, it consisted of two pieces sewn together at the shoulders, but, unlike the common dress, it reached down to the ankles.

The Turban of the High Priest and the Priestly Headdresses (28:39–40; 39:28)

Different words are used for the headgear of the high priest and of the ordinary priests, *mitsnefeth* ("turban") and *migba'oth* ("headdresses"). The latter obviously exhibited a simpler workmanship. Josephus describes the turban of the high priest as consisting of the headgear of the ordinary priests. This headgear he describes in every detail, as only someone who has worn it himself could:

> Upon his head he wears a cap without a peak, not covering the whole head but extending slightly beyond the middle of it . . . fashioned so as to resemble a coronet, consisting of a band of woven linen thickly compressed; for it is wound round and round and stitched repeatedly. This is then enveloped by a muslin veil descending from above to the forehead, thus concealing the stitches of the headband with their unsightly appearance and presenting to the skull a completely even surface. This headgear is adjusted with care so as not to slip off while the priest is busy with his sacred ministry."[47]

The Sash (28:39–40; 39:29)

The sash was woven in the same colors as the ephod (39:29). According to Josephus, it had a pattern like the skin of a snake. It was four fingers broad and so long that it had to be wrapped around twice. Josephus also points out that it was not wrapped around the waist as we usually think, but around the chest "up to the armpits." Still, it reached down to his feet. Therefore the priests threw it over their left shoulder when they ministered.[48]

The only difference between the ornate belt of the high priest and that of the ordinary priests was the gold interwoven into the former. According to 39:29, the linen sash had "blue, purple, and crimson yarns" woven into it, the identical colors of the veil before the holy of holies. All the colored textiles were wool, which was more easily dyed. Usually, people's clothing was also woven from wool, which was less expensive, while the priestly vestments were linen, and even contained an otherwise forbidden mixture of linen and wool (Lev. 19:19; Deut. 22:11).[49] The priestly vestments were holy, distinct, and thus exempted from the general rule, as were the fabrics in the sanctuary (see also p. 223, n. 43).

In a solemn ceremony, Aaron and his sons will be arrayed in these holy garments when they are consecrated as priests. Exodus 28:41 consequently looks forward to the following chapter.

One item of the priestly vestments remains to be considered. Of a lesser degree of sanctity, however, it finds no mention in the narrative of the priestly consecration.

The Breeches (28:42–43; 39:28)

Breeches were rare in the ancient Near East. Their function and the seriousness of the instructions relating to them are to be understood against the background of cultic nakedness, common in surrounding cultures. In Egyptian hieroglyphic murals, priests are frequently seen clad only in a minimal loincloth (see also 20:26).

The White Linen Clothes

The Day of Atonemnt stands out from all other days of the year. On this holiest day, the high priest had to divest himself of his ornate apparel and don the simplest of robes, namely, the four previously mentioned items of clothing, now, however, manufactured from ordinary white linen (Lev. 16:4). On this occasion, the high priest on principle wore the same garments as ordinary priests.[50]

Even though he administered the Yom Kippur service as the representative of the people, at the same time he took their place as an ordinary priest and an ordinary Israelite. Therefore, he also confessed his own sins and brought his own sin offering (Lev. 16:6, 11). His simple linen robes became in fact the holiest of all garments, used only on the holiest day, when the high priest came closest to the Lord and closest to the people.

It is surely this stripping of the high priest's own dignity to which the letter to the Hebrews refers when it states that

Christ as the great high priest "had to become like his brethren in every respect, so that he might be a merciful and faithful high priest in the service of God, to make a sacrifice of atonement for the sins of the people" (Heb. 2:17).[51] Significantly, the heavenly host are robed in linen (Ezek. 9:2–3; Dan. 10:5; 12:5ff.; Rev. 15:6; 19:14), as are the saints (Rev. 19:8).

THE CONSECRATION OF THE PRIESTS (29:1–46)

This chapter contains the first detailed description of a sacrificial service in the Bible. The ritual for the consecration of the priests laid out in this chapter is later performed in Lev. 8, virtually a literal repetition of this chapter.

After the presentation of the various parts of the service (29:1–3), the ritual is set out in the following steps.

The Dressing (Investiture) (29:4–9)

Moses receives not only the instructions regarding the tabernacle, priests, and service, but he also accepts the task of performing the first ordination of priests. The Lord has appointed and consecrated him to this task. Later, Moses will also ordain the successor of Aaron (Num. 20:22–29).

After having been washed (cf. 30:17–21; Heb. 10:22), first Aaron and then his sons are robed in the holy garments as a sign of their sacred ministry. "You shall then ordain Aaron and his sons" (29:9). A literal rendering of the Hebrew text, however, would be, "And you shall fill the hands of Aaron and the hands of his sons." This indicates reception of a formal "mandate" for their priesthood. Interestingly, the English word "mandate" is based on the Latin noun *manus* ("hand") and the verb *dare* ("give"). The word "mandate" thus probably goes back to an ancient ritual, at which those who were installed into an office received a symbol of their new post. Donning the priestly garments symbolizes accepting the new dignity. We will soon see parts of the consecration sacrifices put into the hands of Aaron and his sons (29:22ff.).

The Anointing (29:7)

Even though only Aaron's anointing is mentioned (28:41; 40:13–15), the description of the oil in 30:22–33 makes it clear that his sons were also anointed in like fashion (see also Lev. 2:2–3; 4:3ff.; 6:20ff.; 8:30; Num. 3:3). Moreover, the entire sanctuary and its appurtenances were to be consecrated with this oil (29:36; 40:9ff.; Lev. 8:10ff.). The anointing of the priests thus endows them with the same holiness as the tabernacle, which enables them to approach and even touch the holy objects.

Israelite kings were also so anointed (1 Sam. 10:1; 16:12–13; 1 Kgs. 1:39), as were some prophets. Accordingly, Elijah anoints his successor, Elisha (1 Kgs. 19:16). See also pp. 236f.

The Hebrew verb "anoint" is *mashah,* and "the one anointed" is called *mashiah,* which through the Greek transliteration, *messias,*[52] made its way into English as "messiah." Although the anointed king, "the son of David," serves as the primary paradigm for the future redeemer, the idea of the messianic figure in Jewish literature has borrowed features from the anointed prophet and priest as well.

According to one view, the future redeemer will be a prophet like Moses (Deut. 18:15–18). The exodus from Egypt under the leadership of Moses formed the pattern for all future acts of salvation. These would even surpass the greatness of the first exodus (cf. Isa. 52:12; Jer. 16:14–15; 23:7–8). It is consequently to be expected that God's special servant in this salvific event would be compared to Moses, the prophet above all prophets.[53]

The Samaritans, who accept only the five books of Moses as canonical Scriptures, base their messianic hope exclusively on the promise of a new Moses in Deut. 18. Thus their messiah is called *Taheb,* which means "the restorer" or "the returner," that is, Moses restored and returned. The prophetic messiah is a prominent figure also in the Qumran literature. In the *Rule of the Community* (1QS) 9:11 he is actually mentioned first among three messiahs, namely, a prophet (like Moses), a high priest (like Aaron), and a king (like David): "They shall . . . be ruled by the primitive precepts in which the men of the community were first instructed, until there shall come the prophet and the messiahs of Aaron and Israel."[54]

However, a priestly messianic figure appears together with a royal one probably already in Zech. 4, where the two olive trees on the right and the left of the lampstand (Zech. 4:3, 11) are interpreted as "the two anointed ones who stand by the Lord of the whole earth" (Zech. 4:14). They most likely refer to the high priest Joshua (cf. Zech. 3; 6:9–15) and the ruler of David's seed, Zerubbabel (cf. Zech. 4; 1 Chron. 3:1, 19). In the New Testament, the letter to the Hebrews depicts Christ entirely as the great high priest.

The Sin Offering (29:10–14)

Sin offerings were sacrificed only for sins committed unintentionally. For willful sins atonement was achieved through the sin offerings on the Day of Atonement, provided that the sinner had repented (cf. pp. 194f.). Sin offerings were further required only for particular, concrete sins linked to specific punishments. Consequently, sin offerings were not sacrificed as an expression of guilt in general. For sins among human beings, forgiveness and ritual purification were conditional upon restitution and reconciliation (cf. Matt. 5:23–24).

The Bible makes a distinction between collective and individual sin offerings. In the latter case, the sacrificial animal had to be female. The blood was daubed against the horns of the altar of burnt offering and poured out at the base of the altar. The fat around the entrails was burnt on the altar, and the meat was consumed by the priests (Lev. 4:27–5:13; 6:24–30; 10:16–19).

The collective sin offerings were sacrificed on behalf of the whole people or on behalf of those representing the people, namely, the priest and the king. In this case, the sacrificial animal had to be a bull or a male goat. The blood was sprinkled on the veil before the holy of holies and daubed on the horns of the altar of incense (30:1–10); then it was poured out at the base of the altar of burnt offering. While the rabbis called the former sacrifices "outer sin offerings," these are called "inner sin offerings." As in the former case, the fat was burned on the altar, while the rest of the animal was burned "outside the camp" (Lev. 4:1–26; 6:30). The sacrifices on the Day of Atonement were of this kind, since they were offered for the high priest, the priests, and the people (Lev. 16; cf. Heb. 13:10ff.).

The sin offering sacrificed for Aaron and his sons in connection with their consecration was burned "outside the camp" (29:14). Nevertheless, this sin offering is different from the inner sin offerings mentioned above, since the blood only was to be put on the horns of the altar of burnt offering and not to be brought into the sanctuary (29:12). This sin offering is consequently unique and can be explained by the fact that the priests were purified through this sin offering before they were finally consecrated to represent the people. Hence their offering is categorically not a collective sin offering at all. Moreover, they could not eat of their own sin offering, which is why it had to be burned outside the camp.[55]

Through the laying of hands upon the sacrificial animal (29:10), the priest consecrated it for its designated purpose. On the Day of Atonement, the laying on of hands was linked to the confession of sins. In this case, the act also symbolized that the sin was transferred over to the animal.

The Burnt Offering (29:15–18)

Burnt offerings were the most common of all sacrifices. They were offered during most services and were also frequent as voluntary, individual offerings of various kinds. In the sacrifice of a burnt offering, reverence for God was expressed through the aroma ascending from the altar. As the name makes clear, the burnt offering was entirely consumed on the altar after the priest carefully cut it up according to detailed rules and after aspersing its blood on the lower half of the altar (see p. 218 and further Lev. 1 and 6:8–13).

The Consecration Offering (29:19–37)

The second ram was a special offering for the consecration act itself. It was formally an "offering of well-being," more commonly translated "peace offering," which was partly burned on the altar and partly consumed by the person who brought it (Lev. 3 and 7:11–36).[56]

The act of putting blood on the ear, right thumb, and right big toe (29:20) only occurs in one other case, that of the purification of lepers (Lev. 14:14; cf. p. 36, n. 18). These parts of the body were specified presumably to reflect a cultural correspondence to our expression "from head to toe"; the entire person was cleansed and received a new status through this ritual. Philo offers an interpretation recalling the profound connection between "hearing and doing" (see pp. 189f.), since there must be a correspondence between word and action in the life of the priest: "The fully consecrated must be pure in words and actions and in his life; for words are judged by the hearing, the hand is a symbol of action, and the foot of the pilgrimage of life."[57]

The remaining blood was splashed against the altar of burnt offering (29:20). A mixture of blood and the anointing oil was further sprinkled on the priests and their clothes (v. 21). Through these acts, the priests were brought into a special covenant with the Lord similar to the aspersion of the sacrificial blood on both the people and the altar when Israel was consecrated to be a "priestly kingdom and a holy nation" (19:6; 24:6–8). The priests were thus made "holy." The tabernacle and its inventory were consecrated in the same way (40:9ff.; Lev. 8:10ff.).

Aaron and his sons should further "raise as an elevation before the LORD" those portions listed in 29:22ff. The verb used, *henif,* means that the sacrificial gifts should be elevated like many church traditions continue to do with the elements of the holy communion. The word *tenufah,* most frequently rendered "wave offering," should more correctly be rendered "elevation": "You shall elevate it in an elevation before the LORD" (29:26). There was no special offering called a "wave offering" or even an "elevation offering" (as in NRSV). There was, however, a particular ceremony in which sacrificial gifts of various kinds were elevated before the Lord, symbolizing dedication of the gifts to the Lord. It marked the transfer from the profane realm to the holy, from human ownership to divine. Only then could they be brought to the altar (cf. 29:24–25).[58]

Moses in his priestly office was to offer this sacrifice on behalf of the priests, just as the priests would later offer sacrifices on behalf of the people. Just as Moses was to put the gifts into the hands of the priests and to elevate them before the Lord, so too would the priests later elevate those parts of the people's "offerings of well-being" that were brought to the altar (the fat) and given to the priests (the breast; Lev. 7:28–36).[59]

The breast from the people's "offerings of well-being," which would later be consumed by the priests (29:27–28), was then to be consumed by Moses (v. 26), officiating as a priest of the priests. Verses 27–30 are a parenthetical addition dealing with instructions applicable to all future priests. The ensuing part of the consecration ritual continues in verses 31–34, setting out the instructions regulating the "holy communion" meal that finally seals the consecration service.

According to the ordinances detailing the "offerings of well-being," the one bringing the sacrifice consumed the meat

(Lev. 7:15–21). In this case, the priests participated in this meal, which would consist of the rest of the sacrificial animal and the remaining bread in the basket. The covenantal act in chapter 24, sealed by the sprinkling of blood, was followed by a sacred meal (24:11). Even here, the special relationship into which the Lord has entered with Aaron and his sons is confirmed by a holy communion, barred to all outsiders (29:33).

The ritual was repeated for seven days (vv. 35–37). By this act, atonement was brought not only for the priests themselves but also for the altar (vv. 36–37; cf. v. 12). The thought appears further in connection with the Day of Atonement, when Aaron is summoned to "make atonement" for the "sanctuary," the "tent of meeting," and the "altar" (Lev. 16:16–18, 33). It is thus obvious that the translation "make atonement" for the Hebrew verb *kipper* is inappropriate. At stake is rather that these objects are "purified." Commonly, this verb is erroneously understood as meaning "to cover." Sin and impurity, however, cannot be covered; they have to be removed. Hence, "to purify" and "to cleanse" more adequately express the proper meaning of the verb *kipper,* and *Yom Kippur* can very well be translated the "Day of Purification."[60]

The sanctuary and the altar have to be purified in response to a profound biblical idea. When the children of Israel commit sins, the sanctuary and its appurtenances become defiled. This is equally so of any transgression against God's commandments, whether ritual or moral, willful or unintentional. From this we comprehend why sin offerings had to be brought for unintentional sins. Like a giant magnet, the sanctuary attracts to itself all the impurity consequent to sin. If this impurity is not removed, the Lord can no longer be present there. Therefore, a great "Day of Purification" once a year was necessary in addition to the daily cleansing of the unintentional sins and the repentance for willful transgressions (see p. 234).

The purification days in connection with the consecration of the priests were a powerful reminder of the seriousness of sin and of its constant threat to obstruct one's relationship with the Lord. The promise in 29:45 is conditional: "I will dwell among the Israelites, and I will be their God." Through sin, we are actually able to drive away God, upon whose presence we are totally dependent: this is the serious message of ancient Israel's sacrificial cult.

The Daily Offering (29:38–42)

The offering described here is not part of the ritual for the consecration of the priests. It is, however, dealt with in this context, probably because of its association with the holiness of the altar discussed in the previous verses. The daily offering was by far the most frequent sacrifice. Every day—Sabbath, feast, workday—this sacrifice was to be brought to the altar morning and evening as long as the tabernacle, and later the temple, existed.

The description of this sacrifice in the context of the consecration of the priests may indicate that tradition held that this sacrifice was actually instituted on that occasion. In the parallel passage of Num. 28:3–8 it is called "a continual burnt offering, which was ordained at Mount Sinai," perhaps in reference to this event. In rabbinic tradition the abbreviated name *tamid,* which means "constant," "uninterrupted," or "regular," was chosen for the daily offering. The mishnaic tractate by this name describes in detail the sacrificial service as it was performed at the time of the Second Temple.

Together with the lambs, a cereal offering consisting of wheat flour, olive oil, and a libation of wine was also brought.[61] The amount of flour is specified as "one-tenth of a measure" (Hebrew *ʿissaron* = *ʿomer,* equals 2.2 quarts or 2 liters), and the amount of oil and wine as "one-fourth of a hin" (1 *hin* equals about 3.6 liters or almost a gallon). Another aspect of this service was the cleaning and lighting of the menorah (27:20–21) and the kindling of the incense on the inner altar, soon to be discussed (30:1–10).

"I Am the LORD" (29:43–46)

Again and again the command "you shall" is repeated throughout the chapters we have studied. It applies to materials and measures, colors and constructions, ceremonies and sacrifices. However, even here, let us bear in mind what we stressed regarding the tablets of the covenant: "you shall" was neither the first nor the most fundamental thing written on these tablets, but "I am the LORD your God," with all the promises it entails (20:1ff.; pp. 138ff.).

In an analogous way, God began all the ordinances regarding the tabernacle with a promise: "And they shall make me a sanctuary, and then I will dwell among them" (or "in order that I may dwell among them"; 25:8). This comforting promise is the preamble and rationale for all the subsequent uses of "you shall." Almost verbatim, God now repeats the words at the beginning of the tablets of the covenant and at the beginning of the tabernacle ordinances: "And they shall know that I am the LORD their God, who brought them out of the land of Egypt that I might dwell among them; I am the LORD their God" (29:46).

God has just commanded Moses to consecrate the altar (v. 36), and now says: "I will consecrate the tent of meeting and the altar" (29:44). Whatever Moses did in obedience to the Lord's "you shall," in the deepest sense was still neither initiated nor carried through to completion by him. It is true that Moses consecrated Aaron and the priests, but now the Lord himself states: "Aaron also and his sons I will consecrate" (v. 44).

In every ceremony and service, this is the Alpha and Omega; the Lord himself affirms his "I am" and fills our sanctuaries, acts, words, prayers, and songs with his divine presence. Whatever we do, say, and think in obedience to his "you shall" will then ultimately transform into a wonderful response to his assurance, "I am the LORD your God."

Hence, all the ordinances regulating the first "church building" and the first ordination in the Bible ultimately bear the authoritative seal of the Lord: "I will reveal myself . . . I will speak . . . I will sanctify . . . I will consecrate . . . I will dwell . . . I am the LORD!" To be sure, when all the ordinances are later implemented, this will be the resounding final chord of the entire book of Exodus (see 40:34–38).

ADDITIONAL INSTRUCTIONS
(30:1–38; 37:25–29; 38:8, 24–26)

A few items and ordinances still remain for the proper functioning of the tabernacle. For several reasons they are presented only now.[62]

The Altar of Incense (30:1–10; 37:25–28)

The little altar of incense was of the same craftsmanship as the ark and the table of showbread. Its place was in the holy area before the curtain between the menorah and the table of showbread. In connection with the daily offering morning and evening, the kindling of incense (see 30:34–38) was prescribed. According to rabbinic tradition, this was the holiest service a priest could ever perform.[63]

The smoke rising from the incense symbolized the presence of the Lord, just as did the incense in the holy of holies on the Day of Atonement (cf. 30:36; Lev. 16:2, 12–13). In a wider sense, God's presence was symbolized by a cloud hovering over the people and later over the tabernacle (13:21–22; 40:34–38; cf. 1 Kgs. 8:10–13). We may surmise that this is the reason that the altar of incense is mentioned only now, after the Lord has promised to be present in the sanctuary and through the sacrifices prescribed above.

Another reason this altar is not dealt with together with the other objects in the outer sanctum may lie in the fact that through its function it was linked to the less holy altar of burnt offering in the court. In connection with the "inner sin offerings" (see p. 228), the altar of incense received blood from the altar of burnt offering. In the description of the appurtenances according to a declining degree of holiness, the golden altar would thus not be fit to be listed together with the menorah and the table of the showbread.[64]

While the outer altar was constantly purified through sin offerings, the inner altar was purified only once a year. The reason is that the unintentional sins of the people communicated pollution only to the outer altar (see pp. 217ff., 231). On the Day of Atonement, however, purification was brought for the entire collective sin of the people, including sins committed willfully (provided that the sinner had repented). The impurity of such sins penetrated into the tabernacle even as far as the holy of holies and the ark of the covenant. Consequently, on this day blood was to be sprinkled on the ark, the veil, and, of course, on the polluted altar of incense (30:10; Lev. 16:14–19).

The Census and the Shekel Tax (30:11–16; 38:24–26)

Here we find discussed a tax as part of a census of all males at least twenty years old, namely, all those able to bear arms (Num. 1:3). Every male was required to pay the same amount. In this way the amount of silver revealed the number of Israelite males: 603,550 (38:26; cf. 12:37; Num. 1:45–46). This collection of funds must be distinguished from that mentioned in 25:2, which regulates the freewill offering (see also 35:5, 22, 29).

Even though it was God who ordered Moses to count the people (30:11; Num. 1:1ff.), the census was nevertheless regarded as something dangerous, perhaps even sinful (see also 2 Sam. 24). A plague might occur (30:12). Further, the payment is called "ransom" (Hebrew *kofer;* v. 12) and "atonement money" (Hebrew *kesef ha-kippurim;* v. 16). The latter term is used in 21:30 to denote the ransom paid by one who has indirectly caused another person's death (see also Num. 35:31–33) and is better translated "ransom money."[65] The divinely commissioned census thus paradoxically triggered the requirement of expiation.

According to 38:25–28, the silver was used for making some of the items in the tabernacle. The *shekel* was first a weight (see 30:23ff.); money came into use only hundreds of years later, probably not before the sixth century B.C.E. At archaeological excavations both *shekel* and *gerah* weights have been found. The shekel weighs about 0.4 ounce (11 grams). This ancient shekel measure, which later became a monetary unit, was again taken up as the official coinage of the modern state of Israel.

Even though this census is not necessarily portrayed as a recurrent procedure, it later developed into a fixed institution. During the last month of the year, the spring month of Adar, the "temple tax" was annually collected, both in Israel and in the Diaspora. The mishnaic tractate *Sheqalim* gives detailed rules (cf. Matt. 17:24ff.).

The Bronze Basin (30:17–21; 38:8)

The following instructions touch on the specific preparations for the service, which explains why they have not been mentioned earlier. The size and shape of the laver is not described. The word, *kiyyor,* indicates that it was round. The metal used in the court was copper-bronze. However, it was not made from the metal of the peoples' offering but from the women's mirrors, indicating a lesser degree of holiness (38:8, 29ff.). The reason is probably that the basin was not directly used in the service, but only in the preparation for it. In the temple, this basin had impressive dimensions and an intricate artistic design (1 Kgs. 7:23–39).

The ablutions of the priests before the service have survived in Judaism in the practice of having Levites wash the hands of those of priestly descent *(kohanim)* before the synagogal recital of the Aaronite blessing (Num. 6:23ff.). This ancient tradition also lives on in Islam, where hands and feet (and also eyes, ears, nose, and mouth) are washed before prayer.

The Sacred Oil and the Incense (30:22–38; 37:29)

Together with gold and precious stones, spices, perfume, and incense were regarded as the most precious of treasures (cf. 1 Kgs. 19:2; Matt. 2:11). The various ingredients of the anointing oil and the incense had to be imported from abroad. In addition, a great amount of raw material and complicated techniques were required to extract the concentrated end product. We thus find listed large quantities of spices requisite for producing the oil. When the priests and the tabernacle with its paraphernalia were anointed, it was probably merely a symbolic daubing or sprinkling. According to rabbinic tradition, it was performed by making the Greek letter X on what was to be consecrated.[66]

Not surprisingly, the messianic association with the sacred oil (see pp. 226ff.) generated a Jewish tradition according to which the messianic king would be anointed with the same oil, miraculously preserved for use at the end of time. The expression "throughout your generations" (30:31) certainly might have seemed to support this pious expectation.[67]

In the case of both the oil and the incense, we find their holiness strongly emphasized. The general rule applied that objects, offerings, ingredients, and gifts that pertained to the tabernacle (and to the temple) were never to be copied for use outside the sacred precinct. Therefore, the exact recipes for the oil and the incense were kept secret.[68] In the Second Temple period, only two families were entrusted with the baking of the showbread and the preparation of the incense. When they once went on strike for higher salaries—one of the first such recorded in history— no one could replace them, so their demands were met.[69]

The punishment for replicating the oil or the incense for profane use outside the temple was severe: "he shall be cut off from the people" (30:33, 38).[70] This punishment and its implementation, however, was not a capital crime answerable to a human court. The rabbis speak about "death through the hand of God," which was understood to mean dying childless before the age of fifty or losing eternal life.[71] The forbidden replication of the oil or the incense parallels the prohibition against copying the menorah (see p. 215, n. 17).

THE CRAFTSMEN (31:1–11; 35:30–36:1)

The Spirit of God imparts the skill and artistry required to implement the blueprint of the tabernacle. In 31:6 God literally says: "I have given wisdom in the heart of all wise of heart." It is thus not just a matter of having skillful hands but of being close to God.

The name Bezalel literally means "in the shadow of God" and Oholiab "my tent (tabernacle) is the Father." These names allude to the very precondition for humans to build anything to the glory of God. We have to place ourselves so totally at God's disposal that we walk in his shadow. Only then are we able to construct anything pointing to our heavenly Father, drawing people closer to God, not to us, and enunciating God's praise, not ours (cf. Matt. 5:16). *Soli Deo Gloria*—Glory be to God and only to him! "Unless the LORD builds the house, those who build it labor in vain" (Ps. 127:1). This is the unceasingly pertinent message in the description of the tabernacle.

One dimension of the sanctuary remains to be considered. There is a tabernacle not built of earthly materials according to outward measures. At the same time, it is neither ethereal nor something that belongs only to the future. It stands present here and now, yet is not built in the dimension of space but in the dimension of time.

A SANCTUARY IN TIME (31:12–17)

This heading is inspired by Jewish rabbi and philosopher Abraham Joshua Heschel's description of the seventh day as "a palace in time with a kingdom for all."[72] The biblical account certainly expresses the thought that it is possible to build something in time when it inserts the Sabbath commandment here as the conclusion and climax of the ordinances regulating the building of the tabernacle. Moreover, the Sabbath commandment is repeated at the beginning of the description of how these ordinances were carried out (35:1ff.). The same link between Sabbath and sanctuary also appears in Lev. 19:30 and 26:2. Hence, the Sabbath apparently parallels the tabernacle as a "tabernacle in time," the holiness of which surpasses that of the physical place.

Holiness in Time

The concept of holiness can be compared to an object with three sides: time, space, and person. The first thing the Bible designates as holy is a period of time. At the conclusion of creation, God sanctifies the seventh day (Gen. 2:3). Later, other days are set apart as feasts for Israel. Both Jacob (Gen. 28:17) and Moses (3:5) experienced holiness in space. As we have seen, the whole tabernacle is a visible proclamation of holiness in space. Finally, the people of Israel are a demonstration of holiness in person. They are separated from the other nations (19:5–6). Even *within* Israel the firstborn (13:2), as well as Aaron and his sons and later the whole tribe of Levi, are sanctified in a special way.

Israel is sanctified through the commandments and ordinances in the book of the covenant and the instructions for the tabernacle just discussed. The covenant and its conditions are the instruments through which the God of Israel separates out people. The commandments are thus signs of the covenant and a means of sanctification.[73]

In this section one such sign is dealt with in detail: holiness in time is an expression of God's covenant similar to the way the tabernacle is a sign of the Lord's wish to dwell among the people of Israel (25:8; 29:45–46). When the tabernacle in time is built every seventh day, the construction of the earthly tabernacle recedes in honor of that Sabbath and relinquishes its requirements before it. In other words: holiness in time takes precedence over holiness in space.[74]

Like the tabernacle in the wilderness, even the sanctuary in time can be divided into different spheres. Perhaps we find creation and the world at large in the forecourt, while the tabernacle itself is the sphere of God's intervention in history through the liberation of Israel from Egypt and the establishment of the covenant at Sinai.

Creation and the Sabbath

All of creation is God's dwelling, of which heaven is the throne and earth the footstool (Isa. 66:1). In a similar way the tabernacle was a microcosmic reflection where God's self-limited glory dwelt and was perceived (see pp. 209ff.).

Above all, Philo, but also the later sages of Israel, saw in the description of the different materials of the tabernacle a symbol of the world, the universe, and its various elements—the sun, moon, and stars, etc. This allegorization stems from a deep sensitivity to the correspondence between the biblical description of creation, in which the creation act is followed by God sanctifying the Sabbath and the fall of Adam and Eve (Gen. 1–3), and the building of the tabernacle: its creation (Exod. 25–31), the Sabbath commandment (31:12ff.), and the fall (Exod. 32ff.). As the Sabbath is mentioned for the first time at the end of the creation act, the ordinances regarding the tabernacle's construction immediately lead into the Sabbath commandment, proclaiming God as master of time and space.[75]

In this respect, the Sabbath stands unique among the sacred days of the year. The other holy days all fall on particular dates, linking them to the solar and lunar cycles. Since the biblical months follow the moon and the seasons, they begin when the moon is new.[76] The Sabbath, however, pulses from the very beginning with divine constancy. It is above and beyond creation and proclaims God as the Lord of creation (see pp. 146ff.).

In creation humankind is called to be God's coworker: "Six days shall work be done" (31:15; cf. 20:9; 34:21). To keep the Sabbath every seventh day means, as it were, to return creation into God's hands, thereby actively proclaiming him as the One holding the whole world in his hand, totally independent of our own efforts and responsibilities: "For all the world and all that is in it is mine" (Ps. 50:12).

There are principally two ways of building the tabernacle in time. The first is to cease from all creativity. Time shall be divided into six days of work and one day of rest—rest from the urge to create, cessation from all creation. The

Bible contains only a few concrete commandments that
clarify the forbidden activities, above all the prohibition
against kindling a fire (35:3), cultivating the soil (34:21; cf.
Num. 15:32ff.), carrying burdens (Jer. 17:21ff.), trading
(Amos 8:5; Neh. 10:31; 13:15ff.), and indirectly also baking
and cooking (16:5). Because of the scriptural connection
between the instructions for the tabernacle and the Sabbath
commandment, Jewish tradition has inferred that the various kinds of work necessary for the construction of the
tabernacle are forbidden as well, since all work on the tabernacle ceased in honor of the Sabbath. Altogether there are
thirty-nine main categories of labor involved.[77]

The second way of building the tabernacle in time involves activity. It means to build something spiritually. The
construction of the tabernacle required activity. The same
applies also to the building of the tabernacle in time. In
31:16 two verbs express how to go about sanctifying the
Sabbath. One, *shamar,* is translated "to keep," which covers
all forbidden creativity. The second, *ᶜasah,* is translated "to
observe." Literally, it means "to do, make." The Sabbath is
to be "made" in a similar way as the tabernacle (25:8). This
means something positive: to enjoy, rejoice, praise God, listen to his word, listen in order to be able to do more of his
will (see pp. 189f.). In short, it means to rest before the presence of the Lord. The Sabbath is above all a gift. "The
Sabbath is given to you but you are not surrendered to the
Sabbath."[78] Jesus expressed the same idea: "The sabbath
was made for humankind, and not humankind for the
sabbath" (Mark 2:27).

A similar distinction between the negative and positive
aspect of the Sabbath is expressed in the variant formulations of the Sabbath commandment on the tablets of the
covenant in 20:8 and Deut. 5:12. In the first version the verb
"remember" is used; in the second "keep." The "keep" of the
outward prohibitions serves as a kind of fence around the
forecourt of the tabernacle in time. The worship within this
tabernacle, however, involves the total human being with all
his or her senses. It demands the direction not only of
the hands and the feet but also of the mind and the heart.
Again we note how the commandment is endowed with an
outer and an inner—a negative and a positive—aspect (see
pp. 154f., 169, 190ff.). Isaiah 58:13–14 expresses the same
duality:

> If you refrain from trampling the sabbath,
> from pursuing your own interests on my holy day;
> if you call the sabbath a delight and the holy day of the LORD honorable;
> if you honor it, not going your own ways, serving your own interests, or
> pursuing your own affairs [literally "speaking words"];
> then you shall take delight in the LORD.

Rabbinic tradition beautifully endeavors to respond to these two aspects of the Sabbath, poetically terming it both the "queen" and the "bride," that is, the one to honor and respect, as well as the one to love and desire. Both aspects of the Sabbath are important and ultimately inseparable: to keep and to remember, to refrain from out of respect and to delight in out of love, to humbly bow down and to joyfully embrace—to be bound and free at the same time. The same duality is aptly expressed by Luther when he introduces his explanations to each of the ten commandments: "We should fear and love God, and so we should do not ... [followed by negative prohibitions], but should ... [followed by positive injunctions]."[79]

The Sabbath commandment is without comparison in world history. Even though the Jewish people alone keep the Sabbath in its original, biblical sense, it has become the supernal gift of God to all humanity. Far beyond the domains of Jewish civilization one day of rest per week has become the common order.

We who stand outside the Sinaitic covenant need not comply with the commandment given by God as a covenantal sign to Israel (see pp. 242ff.). Its spiritual meaning, however, is of universal application. Whoever we may be, we also need designated places where we can encounter God in a particular way. To the same extent we too need a sanctuary in time, where the very antithesis of creativity can take place—recreation in the literal sense of the word, a new creation. To rest from creation and creating in order to find our rest in God is to this day the great divine gift of the Sabbath to humankind.

In order to receive this blessing, we must, however, learn from the Jewish people. We must build a fence around the tabernacle in time, which excludes creating once a week. Like Israel, we will then discover that it is not we who keep the Sabbath but the Sabbath that keeps us.[80] Such a day of rest is of fundamental significance for an ongoing, living relationship with the Lord.

As the holy of holies contained the ark with the tablets of the covenant, the Sabbath is comparable to a precious ark of the covenant within the holy of holies of Israel.

The Covenant and the Sabbath

Exodus 20:8–11 emphasizes the universal character of the Sabbath and its link to all of creation. However, Deut. 5:12–15 focuses upon the liberation from slavery in Egypt and God's intervention in the history of Israel. In our text both aspects are united, creation (v. 17) and covenant (vv. 13, 16–17). This is also the case in the Sabbath liturgy. Thus, the Sabbath is received by the following prayer at the *qiddush* ceremony Friday evening:

> Blessed be You God, our God, King of the Universe, Who has sanctified us by His commandments and taken pleasure in us, and, in love and favor, has given us His holy Sabbath as an inheritance, the memorial of the work of the world's beginning. For it is this day which is the first among all the days of holy convocation, a remembrance of the Exodus from Mitzrayim [i.e., Egypt].[81]

Nonetheless, it is evident that the emphasis is on the Sabbath as the particular gift to the people of Israel. First, the Sabbath is "a sign between me and you" (31:13), namely, between God and Israel. Second, its objective is that the Lord might sanctify Israel among the nations (v. 13). Third, it is characterized as a "perpetual covenant" (v. 16) and, again, as a "sign forever" (v. 17).

Most of the commandments can be characterized as signs of the covenant (see pp. 90f., 175, 190f., 195, 238). This becomes clear when we examine commandments in which the observance is immediately visible. God, as it were, puts a sign on the body (circumcision; see also Lev. 19:27–28), clothes *(tsitsith, tefillin),* homes *(mezuzah),* food *(kosher* rules), etc. The promised land in itself is surely one of the most important covenantal signs; God separates a piece of land carrying the signature of the covenant. It is in this context that we view the Sabbath as a sign of the covenant in time. God separates a piece of time with which he marks his people, "for this is a sign between me and you throughout your generations, given in order that you may know that I, the LORD, sanctify you" (v. 13).

Hence, to take upon oneself these signs is to commit oneself to faithfulness toward the covenant. The commandment becomes in fact a confession of God; it is a creed put into practice. Those who fail to see this intimate connection between commandment and covenant will misunderstand obedience and faithfulness as "legalism" (see pp. 127ff., 139f., 142f., 189–96, 238).

Throughout the ages, the sanctuary of the Sabbath has expressed the covenant between God and Israel in a very tangible way, both as a reminder of the covenant within the people and as a sign of their covenant to the world. These two aspects of this covenantal sign are included in the ambiguous formulation of its purpose in 31:13, of which a literal translation would be: "You shall keep my sabbaths, for this is a sign between me and you throughout your generations, in order to know that I, the LORD, sanctify you." The text does not clearly specify who will know this.

In the first place, we do think of the people of Israel. The Sabbath is a perpetual reminder of the covenant at Sinai to the Jewish people themselves. However, the text opens the possibility for yet another subject, an indefinite "one," referring to the surrounding peoples. The point would then be that the world will recognize that God has set Israel apart in a special way when they notice how they observe the Sabbath. Hence, the Sabbath would be a confession to the world (cf. p. 147).

Rabbinic commentaries do justice to both of these important possibilities of understanding the text. Indubitably, the Sabbath has become one of the most potent reminders to the Jewish people of their special calling, as well as a creed expressed in action before the whole world, that distinguishes them wherever they have lived. Both aspects certainly suggest one of the most profound explanations of the miraculous survival of the Jewish people throughout the centuries as a dispersed minority.

It is significant that Exodus concludes the exposition of the Sabbath commandment with the delivery of the prime covenantal document, the tablets of the covenant (31:18). These would all too soon be smashed. The tabernacle would be replaced by the temple, which, in turn, would also be destroyed. But the sanctuary in time has withstood all assaults throughout the ages. It has proven itself to be precisely what God calls it.

An Eternal Sign

The eternal character of the Sabbath is stressed no fewer than four times in this section alone. Twice it is said that it is a sign "throughout your generations," that is, as long as there are Jews, as long as heaven and earth remain (Jer. 31:35–36; 33:24ff.). Further, it is a "perpetual covenant" and a "sign forever."

Like the tabernacle, the Sabbath was portable. Unlike the tabernacle, it was indestructible and irreplaceable. The attempts of supersessionist theology to argue that the seventh day Sabbath had been replaced by a first day Sunday failed to convince Jews who understood what the Scriptures indeed unequivocally declare.

To this day, the Jewish people continue to build their tabernacle in time every seventh day to recall and confess their covenant with God and to demonstrate their firm hope of final freedom. In this sanctuary they have found rest and refreshment for body and soul, strength and security even in the most turbulent times, solidarity and unity in times of discord. Here they have dwelt in the presence of the Lord, who put a sign upon them by entering into an eternal covenant with them. Hence, the Sabbath will forever stand as a sign of both God's and Israel's faithfulness.

Since the God of Abraham, Isaac, and Jacob is also our God, we can turn our day of rest into a sign, through which we bear witness in the world. It can become even for us a life-giving source of strength, a shelter from the raging winds of this world, and an island in the ocean of time. Looking back to the place and time where the Sabbath commandment was first given, it also can become an oasis in the wilderness of our existence, as we ourselves walk forward toward the promised land in joyful anticipation of the heavenly tabernacle and the eternal Sabbath.

13

The Fall and the New Covenant

=== *Exodus 32–40* ===

𝒯he next part of the book of Exodus will take us to the
darkest depths of apostasy and humiliation as well as to
the brightest summits of forgiveness and reconciliation. We
will face wanton looseness and devotion before an idol, the
threat of destruction and the promise of restoration, and grief
and repentance before the one true God who is able to heal
that which human beings have broken. In short, we encounter
life and death, condemnation and salvation.

There are several reasons why these chapters in Jewish
tradition are regarded as one of the most crucial milestones in
the history of Israel. To help us understand, I have chosen
two fundamental Christian concepts in the chapter heading
above: the fall and the new covenant. These terms are justified
both as regards the crucial drama described in this portion of
the Bible and its unmistakable reverberation in the rest of the
Bible and the later Jewish tradition. This will be obvious when
we join the crowds at Sinai and witness what takes place both
at the foot and at the top of the mountain.

THE FALL (32:1–33:11)

There are four primary reasons why the Bible and Jewish
tradition deal more with the sin of the golden calf in Exod. 32
than with the fall in Gen. 3. First, according to ancient Jewish
wisdom, one should not occupy oneself too much with the
beginning or the end. What is described in the very first chapters of our Bible is, like the events at the end of times, partly

hidden behind a veil. What God did in the morning of creation, as well as what he is going to do in the last days of this
era, are things which we do not need to understand fully.
Therefore, we are admonished to accept humbly that there are
mysteries that are not clearly revealed (cf. Deut. 29:29). The
exact meaning of the fall in Gen. 3 can be interpreted in various ways, while what happens in Exod. 32 is totally clear and
unambiguous.

Second, in the Bible, God's interaction with humankind is primarily focused on one people. The first eleven
chapters of the book of Genesis offer a condensed and
sparse presentation of creation and the first stages of human
history. After that, everything is focused on God's election
of Israel and the people's response to this calling. The sin of
the golden calf in Exod. 32 consequently comes much
closer to us both in time and in detail than the sin of Adam
and Eve at the beginning of humankind. This is not to say
that the fall of the first humans is disregarded in Jewish
tradition. However, Israel is admonished to remember the
fall in the wilderness, while there are no similar admonitions regarding the fall in the Garden of Eden (see Deut.
9:7–10:11; Neh. 9:16–19; Ps. 106:19–23).

Third, the sin in Exod. 32 seems to be more serious
than the fall in Gen. 3. First of all, the worship of the
golden calf is idolatry of the worst kind. But the most serious is that it takes place *after* the Lord has demonstrated so
much love toward the people. God has saved them from
slavery and oppression through unprecedented miracles.
The children of Israel have come closer to God than any
other people. And they have not only accepted the first of all
his commandments, "You shall have no other gods before
me," but also have promised to do all that the Lord has
commanded (24:7). Obviously they know what they are
doing.

In short, we witness the fall of the saved people. All of a
sudden, it is as though God has done nothing for them. The
marriage has not been consummated. Moses has just received
the "wedding contract" (Exod. 31:18) but has not yet delivered
it, when the infidelity of the bride becomes obvious. A slight
delay (32:1) is enough for the people to betray both God and
Moses, their leader.[1] Now they have revised history and have
proclaimed a molten calf to be the god who led them out of
Egypt (32:4). In the light of all that happened earlier in the his-

tory of Israel, this verse is doubtlessly one of the most distressing ones in the whole Bible!

Nevertheless, we should not look at their precipitous fall in a judgmental or smug way. The dance around the golden calf has become a well-known symbol of idolatry in general. Applying the text to ourselves, perhaps we ought to consider that the people of Israel were on that occasion ready to give up their gold to make a god. How many people today willingly give up God to make money and achieve earthly success?

Finally, the depth of the fall is further stressed by the terrible punishment that God proclaims for this sin: God does not want to accept Israel as his people any longer! In 32:7 the Lord therefore addresses Moses using the expression, "your people." The consequence of this "divorce" is death. When the wrath of God burns against them, they will all perish (32:10). It thus seems that God will abandon these people who have survived Pharaoh's oppression and murderous plans. Through their own sin, they have signed their death sentence. PParallel to Gen. 22, where the survival of Isaac, the very son of the promise, is endangered, the survival of the people and, therefore, the fulfillment of God's promises are now at stake. The history that began with the calling of Abraham in Gen. 12 has reached its abrupt and tragic end. Or has it?

May Thy Will Not Be Done! (32:11–14, 30–34)

We recognize similar scenarios from other parts of the Bible: people have fallen in sin, and God threatens to destroy them. At the same time God shares his plans with a human servant.

(a) *Noah.* The evil of mankind has assumed such dimensions that God, having decided to start all over again, says to Noah: "Everything that is on the earth shall die. But I will establish my covenant with you; and you shall come into the ark, you, your sons, your wife, and your sons' wives with you" (Gen. 6:17–18). The drama continues: "Noah did this; he did all that God commanded him" (Gen. 6:22; 7:5). Undeniably this sounds pious and upright. Moreover, in the letter to the Hebrews, Noah is listed among the examples of faith: "By faith Noah, warned by God about events as yet unseen, respected the warning [the King James Version has more accurately 'moved with fear'] and built an ark to save his household" (Heb. 11:7).

Jewish interpretive tradition, however, questions some aspects of Noah's behavior. Above all, he seems indifferent to the destruction of the world. We do not hear one word of objection or protest from his side. He silently obeys God in order to "save his household." A literal reading of the text may therefore lead to the conclusion that Noah was concerned only that he and his family be saved.[2] The "fear" mentioned in the letter to the Hebrews is not necessarily something wholly good. Superior to *fearing* God is, without doubt, loving God. It is perhaps love with all its ramifications that Noah is lacking.

Even if we side with Noah—and there are of course also reasons for that—it is clear that he is only relatively good[3] as compared to the next figure, who experiences a similar challenge.

(b) *Abraham.* What does Abraham ask when God has decided to destroy Sodom and Gomorrah (Gen. 18:16ff.)? We read, "Then Abraham came near and said, 'Will you indeed sweep away the righteous with the wicked? Suppose there are fifty righteous within the city; will you then sweep away the place and not forgive it for the fifty righteous who are in it? Far be it from you to do such a thing.' " And so Abraham continues to plead that the wicked be spared. He argues and bargains and pleads with God to change his plans. Abraham cares for the people of Sodom and Gomorrah. He does his utmost to avert a catastrophe that will destroy them all.

The rabbis have noticed an interesting linguistic difference in the descriptions of Noah and Abraham. On the one hand, it is written that "Noah walked with God" (Gen. 6:9), while Abraham receives the calling, "Walk before me" (Gen. 17:1; cf. 18:22). To walk with God and to walk before him— what is the difference? Maybe it is the difference between being passive and being active. Abraham is called to walk before the Lord, to be an active partner, not a submissive robot.

Abraham indeed lives up to his calling. Unlike Noah, he gives proof of his responsibility and his ability to respond to God, sometimes in the negative. Encountering God may occasionally evoke the prayer, "May Thy will not be done!" This is the essence of Abraham's intercession. In this respect Abraham's petition on behalf of Sodom and Gomorrah is a good example of human responsibility, care, and love. Nevertheless, as compared to the next servant of God, even Abraham's example is surpassed.

(c) *Moses*. There are at least three main differences between Abraham and Moses. First of all, who are the objects of their solicitation? Abraham intercedes only for the righteous, but Moses for the sinners. Abraham is concerned about the faithful, Moses about the fallen. All have in one way or another participated in the manufacture of and devotion to the molten calf. There is no one righteous! This does not, however, prevent Moses from approaching God on behalf of the people. A major difference between Abraham and Moses is that Abraham appeals to God's righteousness, while Moses appeals to his mercy. There is no other alternative for Moses, and he does not give up that hope.

This leads to a second difference. Abraham stops at ten, while Moses is obviously ready to bargain down to zero. At any rate, Moses intercedes for his people without any restrictions whatsoever. The story of Sodom and Gomorrah ends with destruction; the story of the golden calf comes to a totally different conclusion. The question then presents itself, what might have happened if Abraham had continued to intercede for fewer than ten righteous people and to persevere in the seemingly hopeless situation of no righteous people at all? The question might be speculative, but in light of Moses' prayer in connection with the sin of the golden calf, it is a legitimate question that indeed throws light upon the greatness of Moses.

Third, Moses not only bargains down to no righteous people at all, but he actually takes a great step further, which makes him unique among all the prophets of Israel (cf. Deut. 18:18; 34:10). He is ready to include even himself among the sinners and to unite his own destiny with theirs: "So Moses returned to the LORD and said, 'Alas, this people has sinned a great sin; they have made for themselves gods of gold. But now, if you will only forgive their sin—but if not, blot me out of the book that you have written' " (32:31–32; cf. further Ps. 69:28; Isa. 4:3; Dan. 7:10; 12:1; Phil. 4:3; Rev. 3:5; 13:8; 17:8; 20:12, 15; 21:27).

No Replacement Theology

Moses cannot accept being spared while his people perish. He refuses to accept God's proposal: "Now let me alone, so that my wrath may burn hot against them and I may consume them; and of you I will make a great nation" (32:10).

Moses does not want to become the progenitor of a "new Israel" that replaces the old apostate Israel, nor does he try to cover up or diminish the sin of the people. Yet, he knows that there are reasons why the people have to be spared. He mentions two main reasons, both of which have to do with God's own credibility and glory.

First, he appeals to all that God has already done for his people, when he brought them out of Egypt. If he should now destroy Israel, the Egyptians would interpret this as if God did so solely in order to inflict harm upon them (32:11–12). According to Deut. 9:28 (cf. Ezek. 20:14), the Egyptians would also say that God hated them and was not able to bring them into the promised land.

Second, Moses refers to God's own words. By reminding God of the patriarchs and the promises given to them, Moses draws attention to something that is above and beyond the present distressing situation. God has sworn to multiply the descendants of Abraham, Isaac, and Israel, as the stars of heaven and to give them the promised land forever (32:13). This oath specifically applies not to Moses, but to "Abraham, Isaac, and Israel." Therefore, Moses cannot take their place.

We should notice that Moses does not use the customary listing of "Abraham, Isaac, and Jacob." It is probably not by chance that he uses the name *Israel,* which is so deeply linked to the promise of God (see Gen. 32:22–29). We should also observe how Moses draws attention away from himself to God. While God had used the expression "your people" (32:7), Moses now returns the same words to God stressing that the people notwithstanding their shortcomings are his people, and that he is the one who has liberated them from Egypt (32:11–12). As a matter of fact, Moses claims that the apostasy of the people cannot abolish the promises of the Lord. The covenant is stronger than human sin!

A prayer of Solomon Ibn Gabirol echoes Moses' struggle with God and expresses in a moving way the same attitude of total reliance on God's mercy as a way out of total despair:

> Lord, if my sin is great—too great to bear—
> How wilt Thou shield thine own yet greater name
> From obloquy? And if I may not dare
> Hope for thy mercies, on whom have I claim
> For pity, save on Thee? Nay, then, I say,
> E'en though Thou shouldst me slay

Nathless my hope on Thee should still abide;
And if my sin Thou searchest, then away
From Thee I flee—to Thee, myself to hide
In thy shade from thy broiling wrath, and cling
Fast to thine apron-string
Of mercy, till Thou bidst thy mercy hold
Me firm, nor will I let Thee go, unless
Like Jacob's angel Thou dost deign to bless.[4]

As we learn from 32:14, God approves of Moses' argument: "And the LORD repented of the evil which he thought to do to his people" (RSV). At first glance it may seem absurd and offensive that God repents and gives in under the pressure of a human being. Is then Moses more merciful than God? From this we can learn two things about the character of the Bible and the nature of God. The rabbis stress that "God speaks the language of man." This means that God meets us at our own level, under our own human conditions, in a way adapted to our own limitations. God encounters us almost as one of us. How else could there be any relationship between a finite human being and the infinite one who possesses the entire universe and each creature? Therefore, God approaches us in a human way in order to demonstrate his great confidence in us and the weighty responsibilities with which we are entrusted.

This is what the Lord's elected servant, Moses, now experiences. God listens to him and accepts his arguments, even when they are a protest. One almost gets the impression that this is precisely what God wants to hear. There are rabbis who assume that God is testing Moses here, for had the decision been definite, why then would God have said, "Let me alone, that my wrath may burn hot against them" (32:10)? Can we not see in these words an invitation to Moses indeed not to leave God alone with his wrath?

In any case, this is the chance Moses takes in his endless love for his people. He is not able to leave God alone and to abandon Israel to destruction. As never before, Moses proves what it means to be a true servant of the Lord. Behind Moses' intercession, we indeed hear the voice of the good shepherd, who is ready to give his life for his flock (see pp. 33f.). "What we learn from this section is not only God's forgiving nature but something significant about Moshe: faced with a dictator's dream—the cloning of an entire nation from himself—he opts for staunchly defending the very people who have already

caused him grief through their rebelling, and who will contin-
ually do so in the ensuing wanderings."[5]

Noah, Abraham, and Moses should serve as a mirror.
Are we similar to Noah, caring only for our closest relatives
and friends? Or are we more like Abraham, primarily praying
for those who share our faith? Or are we even ready to be a
Moses to our neighbors, whoever they are, particularly to
those who are far away from God?

Another reflection is also accurate. Moses was put to a
test and passed it when he refused to accept a "replacement
theology," according to which Israel would be written off because of its sin. It is sad to notice that Christianity at large did
not pass the same test. At an early stage, the church began to
proclaim itself "the new Israel" or even "the true Israel," which
had replaced the "old" Israel. Christians searched for—and
found—passages in the Bible to support this arrogant and
triumphalist attitude.

Imagine for a moment a different scenario. Imagine
Christians searching the Scriptures to find support for God's
faithfulness to the children of Israel through the eternal covenant with them. Imagine Christians showing love for them
commensurate to the love Moses had for his people, that very
people who transmitted God's revelation to us—our elder sib-
lings in faith! This would, indeed, have befitted our Christianity that claimed to be "the religion of love."

It would certainly not have been difficult to find support
for such love in the New Testament. Did not the Lord, who
gave his life for sinners, intercede: "Father, forgive them, for
they know not what they do" (Luke 23:34; cf. Acts 3:17; 13:27;
1 Cor. 2:8)? And did not the apostle Paul act in the spirit of
Moses when he wrote, "For I could wish that I myself were ac-
cursed and cut off from Christ for the sake of my brethren, my
kinsmen by race" (Rom. 9:3)? Further, did he not remind the
congregation in Rome that "the gifts and the call of God are
irrevocable" (Rom. 11:29)?

In the name of Moses, Jesus, and Paul, the Christian
church ought, therefore, to have relied on the faithfulness of
God toward the covenantal people and expressed an attitude
of love toward them, praying:

> Lord, you cannot break what you have promised Abraham, Isaac, and
> Israel! Remember your eternal covenant with them! And should you
> reject your people, then reject even us, for we have not deserved any-
> thing better than they deserved! If you have forgiven us our sins, then

forgive also them! We do not want to be a new Israel at their expense! Have mercy upon them and upon us!

Such a biblical attitude of faith and love would have made any kind of supersessionism and replacement theology impossible. See further below, pp. 262ff.

Sin, Punishment, Repentance (32:15–33:11)

The fall of the people is grave. We find Moses struggling with God in prayer, both before he descends from the mountain (32:11–14), and after he has witnessed what his people have done (vv. 30–32). We learn from Deut. 9:25 that he spent no fewer than forty days and nights before the Lord. This indeed indicates the depth of the fall and the seriousness of the sin.

Therefore, it is not sufficient that Moses has been promised that the people will not be destroyed. As a prophet and mediator between God and the people, he also has to take the people in hand. What avail is it if the gate of repentance has been opened, and the people choose to stay outside? When Moses descends from the mountain with the tablets of the covenant (32:15ff.), the purpose is to lead his people through that gate. But when he views the extent of their sin, he realizes that there is a long and painful way to go before reaching that goal.

In the deepest sense, it is not only a matter of one concrete sin, but of a much more profound degradation of the spirit of the people; the root cause of their problem is to be found in the heart (cf. pp. 154f.). In Acts 7:39 we read: "In their hearts they turned to Egypt." Once again we notice that the liberation does not only imply merely taking Israel out of Egypt, but also taking Egypt out of Israel. The forty-year period of wandering in the desert is a necessity. And therefore the liberation also implies a painful *via dolorosa* from darkness to light. We can see four stations on this way.

(1) *Broken tablets* (32:19). When Moses casts away "the marriage contract" between God and Israel, this is a proclamation that Israel has broken the covenant![6]

But how could Moses shatter the words engraved by God's own finger (31:18; 32:16)? The Bible does not provide any direct answers. The rabbinic commentaries list several possible motivations. Maybe Moses shattered the tablets not out of uncontrolled anger but rather in order to spare the people. Maybe he could be compared to the messenger of a king in a parable:

> The messenger comes to the prospective bride to deliver the marriage contract. When he arrives, he learns that she has been unfaithful, so he decides to destroy the contract in order that she may not be accused of having broken a contract she has not seen. In a similar way Moses hoped that the people of Israel might be punished less severely since they had not yet received the tablets of the covenant.[7]

Still another commentary sees mercy and love behind Moses' act. When he realized how easily the people had fallen into idolatry, that is, how easily what is visible and limited could take the place of the invisible and eternal God (cf. pp. 142ff.), he feared that the tablets of the covenant might become their next idol. God's handwritten word might be worshiped as if it were God! Since God, of course, is greater than the Torah, Moses crushes the tablets in order to remove this temptation from the people.[8]

These various rabbinic explanations contain a great deal of wisdom, deeply rooted in the Bible. However, it appears that it is "holy wrath" that motivates Moses' breaking of the covenantal tablets. The sin of the golden calf has bitter consequences and the people need to go through the painful fire of purification. First, the idol itself must once and for all be removed.

(2) *A broken idol* (32:20). The idol of the golden calf is smashed. Even this description provokes questions. Why should the people drink the water of the pulverized idol? It is possible that this act is simply an active, visual proclamation that the idol has been totally annihilated.[9] The rabbinic references to Num. 5:11–31, however, are worth considering. We find there a complicated ritual for the treatment of a woman suspected of adultery. Dust from the floor of the tabernacle is mixed with water, which the woman must drink.

We have already pointed out that God's covenant with Israel can be compared to a marriage (see pp. 91, 131, n. 6, 151f.), so idolatry could be compared with adultery.[10] The breaking of the tablets of the covenant, like the act of drinking the powder of the destroyed idol, may serve as a visible proclamation that Israel has broken the marriage vows.

(3) *Punished sinners* (32:25–29). This text is no doubt among the most difficult in the Bible. How could this terrible massacre be carried out in God's name? What crimes had these three thousand committed that mandated their execution? And why should the executioners specifically kill their "brothers," "companions," and "neighbors"? (32:27) Another very disturbing question is, why was Aaron spared? As we see in 32:2–4, 25, 35 his participation is undeniable. His statement of defense in 32:22–24 does not place him in a positive light either. Showing no trace of Moses' love for the people, Aaron refers to their evil. Further, he does not tell the whole truth and does not repent of his own participation. How, then, could he escape being punished?

The Bible does not answer these questions, thereby opening up for the pious imagination of the commentaries. For instance, it is said that the Levites should kill their closest relatives and friends, in order that their sole motivation was the zeal for God and the hatred of sin and not personal animosity against someone. One explanation of the sparing of Aaron opines that he did not intend to make an idol but something comparable to the cherubim in the tabernacle, a kind of throne for God. Does he not say that they want to make "a festival to the LORD" (32:5)?

None of these explanations, however, do justice to what is stated in the text.[11] Maybe another reflection is appropriate: since Aaron was to become the high priest, is it not remarkable that the record of his shameful deed was retained in the Scriptures at all? Nothing would have been more natural than putting him in a more positive light. In a wider sense we should ask why this whole humiliating story of the fall of Israel, as well as numerous similar ones, was not totally censored.

When reflecting along these lines we soon realize that this unvarnished description of Israel's history prevents it from disappearing into an idealized sphere above and beyond our human reality. In fact, stories like these testify to the divine nature of the Bible. If people had written their history according to their own ambitions it would have looked very different, as we can see in several of the glorious and self-serving chronicles from the surrounding countries. The description of the grim history of Israel with all its shortcomings and apostasy is unique in world literature.

Thus, the disturbing questions raised should rather fill us with admiration and awe. We do not need heroic stories. God does not elect angels and saints to be the chosen people here on earth, but rather weak human beings of flesh and blood. Therefore, we can learn much even when we follow Israel through its darkest hours. Here we can recognize ourselves and our own situations and identify with the fallen people.

Then we can also follow this people with hope and joy when they are raised again out of the dark valley to the recognition of the one true God, often incomprehensibly great, but always the same God—a hot fire of holiness but in the deepest sense a warming light of mercy and love. Israel will soon realize this truth, but not immediately.

(4) *A distant God* (33:1–11). This is perhaps the hardest punishment for the people: God withdraws and will no longer be in their midst during the subsequent journey toward the promised land. Through their evil the children of Israel have repudiated God and made his presence impossible. His presence could even be disastrous to the people in their present situation (33:3, 5). Not even Moses can encounter God among the people any longer. The meeting place has to be outside of the camp, where the tabernacle is set up (33:7).[12]

A new situation has arisen as a consequence of the fall. It is obvious that God's absence is deeply felt by the people. As a sign of their grief and repentance they remove their jewelry and ornaments (33:4–6). Fall and punishment, guilt and grief—these comprise the content of this tragic chapter of Israel's history. However, the chapter is not yet concluded.

THE NEW COVENANT (33:12–40:38)

Even though Moses has succeeded in averting the immediate wrath of God, he has won only a partial victory. The people are not to be condemned or destroyed. At the same time they hold the broken pieces of what once was a whole relationship. God is not present among them as before, and in front of them is the vast, dangerous desert that separates them from the promised land. In this situation, Moses cannot abandon his people and be satisfied with the close communion he himself enjoys with God (33:11). What would then be the destiny of the people? The struggle with God must therefore continue. What Moses asks from God can be summarized in five particular prayers.

Five Prayers (33:12–23)

"Show me your ways" (33:13). A prayer that the revelation at Sinai may not signal the end of Israel's relationship with God and that the shattered tablets may not represent God's final communication with Israel.

"Consider too that this nation is your people" (33:13). A prayer that God may again regard Israel as a firstborn son—or beloved bride—and that Israel may find grace in his sight (vv. 13, 16). In these two verses Moses uses the expression "your people" three times in an effort to reverse the words of God to Moses in verse 1, which express such a distance in the relationship: "You and the people whom you have brought up out of the land of Egypt."

"Let your presence go with us" (33:14–15). A prayer that God may alter his decision to withdraw from the people. Substantially repeating the bold blackmail Moses used in his argument with God in 32:12, he now hints that they will remain there in the wilderness, unless God will be present among them as before.

"Mark us out among the nations" (33:16). A prayer that the people of Israel will be the kingdom of priests and the holy nation that God once called them to be (19:5–6). Moses asks that they will receive the covenantal signs that will sanctify (separate) them from the nations.[13]

"Show me your glory" (33:18). An enigmatic prayer in many ways. Moses is only granted to see God's back, "for no one shall see me and live" (v. 20), and, "my face shall not be seen" (v. 23). At the same time the text has previously stated that "the LORD used to speak to Moses face to face" (v. 11; cf. Num. 12:8; Deut. 34:10). Here it is obvious that Moses asks for something that cannot be granted. It is equally clear that this prayer is the only one of the five that God does not grant. All the others are granted without any restrictions whatsoever. How do we know? God says so directly (v. 17) and above all, translates words into action. This is what we witness in the following chapter.

The Law as Gospel (34:1–28)

When commanding Moses to hew two new tablets of stone (v. 1), the Lord has in a deeper sense already collected the shattered pieces of the broken covenant, renewed it, and made it whole. God allows Israel to start all over again. Moses is going to receive the proof of this love of God.

When healing what is broken, God does so completely. Therefore, the renewed covenant with Israel does not mean that the "old covenant" is replaced by anything new or different. In this and the following chapters we see that nothing of the "old covenant" is actually changed or canceled. The new tablets contain the same words as the original tablets (vv. 1, 4). In verses 10–27 we find numerous parallels to ordinances previously given. In the whole section until the end of the book of Exodus, there are very few verses that deal with new content.

The new covenantal act recorded in this chapter contains the same major events that we witnessed in connection with the making of the covenant at the beginning of the revelation at Sinai: God's descent upon the mountain (ch. 19); the ten words (ch. 20); special laws, the book of the covenant (21:1–23:19); promises (23:20–33); the covenantal act and the revelation of God's glory (ch. 24); the ordinances for the tabernacle (25:1–31:11); and the Sabbath (31:12–17). With only slight differences, the same main elements are now repeated: God's revelation to Moses and the receiving of the new tablets (34:1–9); promises and special laws (34:10–26); the covenantal act and the revelation of God's glory (34:27–35); the Sabbath (35:1–4); the making of the tabernacle (35:4–40:33); and God's dwelling among the people and joining them during their subsequent journey toward the promised land (40:34–38).

The sins of the people have not caused God to change commandments and promises for the people. The "old covenant" is restored. It is the confirmation of this "gospel" that Moses receives when the Lord gives "the law" a second time. Therefore, it is accurate to speak about "the law as gospel." Against the background of the fall, it is more obvious than ever what a marvelous proof of grace "the law" is. The giving of the Torah is to be seen as a great demonstration of God's forgiveness, mercy, love, and grace, or even, as we will see, "grace upon grace."

God's "Measures" (34:6–7)

These verses are so central to Jewish tradition that they could almost be compared to certain summaries of the gospel among Christians, such as John 3:16. They are quoted and alluded to in the Bible no fewer than forty times and are cited frequently in postbiblical Jewish literature. They are written on arks that house the Torah scrolls in synagogues and on the curtains covering the arks (see p. 212, n. 11). In short, they are a focal point in God's revelation.

This is not surprising. It is precisely when Moses has ascended to the mountain to receive the confirmation that the covenant has been renewed that God proclaims:

> The LORD, the LORD, a God merciful and gracious, slow to anger, and abounding in steadfast love and faithfulness, keeping steadfast love for thousands, forgiving iniquity and transgression and sin, yet by no means clearing the guilty, but visiting the iniquity of the parents upon the children and the children's children, to the third and the fourth generation.

To Jews these words have become a kind of confession that expresses God's character. Based on this text, the rabbis speak about "the thirteen attributes [Hebrew *middoth*, literally, 'measures'] of God."[14] We notice that they deal with mercy and forgiveness as well as punishment. Therefore, they are divided into two main categories: the measure of mercy and the measure of judgment.

A similar thought is expressed in the Bible when God is characterized as both gracious and righteous. The Hebrew word for "grace" *(hesed)* has a very concrete basic meaning. It is that part of an overfull and crammed measure that is on the top of the measure itself, which is the portion in a bargain that one receives free. One can consequently not pay for *hesed;* the moment one pays for it, it ceases to be *hesed* and is immediately part of the measure itself. The word "gratis" (from Latin *gratia*) is of course related to the word "grace," which comes close to the basic meaning of its Hebrew counterpart. In contrast, the Hebrew word for "righteousness" has the basic meaning of the exact, leveled measure.[15]

These concrete meanings indeed help us to understand how these terms expressed a spiritual reality. God's grace can never be earned or bought by human beings. Because of divine grace, "my cup overflows" (Ps. 23:5). Therefore, we are admonished, "Give, and it will be given to you. A good measure, pressed down, shaken together, running over, will be put in your lap. For the measure you give will be the measure you get back" (Luke 6:38).

God the righteous judge uses, however, also the measure of righteousness. We are always tempted to stress one aspect at the expense of the other. In that case God is either portrayed as only forgiving and gracious (the difficult passages about judgment and punishment being overlooked) or is depicted primarily as only severe and strict, under whose close surveillance we are constantly scrutinized and judged. In various periods of church history and in different ecclesiastical traditions, there have been difficulties in doing justice to both aspects of God's character, expressing the full spectrum of the biblical revelation.

Two common names of God in Jewish tradition can here serve as an example: "our Father," and "our King"—the merciful Father, full of love, who receives the prodigal son, and the mighty king who has the whole world in his hand and who has the right to call us to account.

How can these two aspects of God be reconciled? If the exact measure is used, it applies not only to us but also to God. That means that the Lord fills his own measure to the brim and faithfully keeps promises. All the promises of mercy, forgiveness, and grace, as stated in 34:6–7, are equally contained in this divine measure. To be sure, he punishes, even to the third and the fourth generation (see pp. 144f.). Yet, we see that most of the characters can be ranked within the measure of grace, and that this grace is not only kept for three or four, but even "for thousands." Even when forgiving sins, God remains righteous, fulfilling his measure of promises. This means no less than "grace upon grace."

Grace upon Grace

Let us closely examine the end of verse 6 and the beginning of verse 7. A literal translation reads, "full of grace and truth, keeping grace for thousands." The word "grace" appears twice. According to an ancient rabbinic rule of interpretation, there are no redundant words in the Bible. Such an assumption invites a thorough interpretation of each detail in the text. Each word has a deep meaning. If the same word is repeated, then it does not have exactly the same meaning in both places. A new aspect of the word "grace" is thus added when it appears the second time.

In this context, one such difference is obvious. God gives grace to Israel by renewing the covenant and gives them a new set of tablets; it is a matter of grace manifested to Israel at Mount Sinai. In the phrase, "keeping grace for thousands," it is a matter of a grace that is "kept" for the future, more precisely, "for thousands." It is, in other words, a promised grace. The word translated by "keeping" also means to "store" something, and "thousands" can refer to coming generations or to a great multitude in general. The latter possibility would consider the nations rather than Israel, the minority nation in the world (cf. Deut. 7:7). Therefore, we can conclude that God, when giving the Torah to Israel, at the same time promises grace for future generations and for many nations.

The same pattern appeared when God called Abraham and promised to bless both him and all the nations of the earth (Gen. 12:3; cf. p. 133, n. 8). The covenant made with Israel in 19:5–6 rested upon the following motivation: "For all the earth is mine" (see p. 130). There is thus no contradiction between God's making a covenant with one special people and caring for all nations. Instead, God's love for Israel is motivated by love for the whole world. Furthermore, there is no contradiction among "law," "gospel," and "grace." On the contrary, it is precisely God's renewal of the tablets of the covenant and the ordinances formerly given that proves the divine desire to dwell among the people and grant them the grace for which Moses asks in his intercessions. The giving of "the law" is nothing less than "grace upon grace."

This biblical understanding of the law as gospel throws light upon a central New Testament text that is usually misinterpreted: "For the law was given through Moses; grace and truth came through Jesus Christ" (John 1:17). Most commentaries understand this verse as expressing a contrast between "the law" and "grace and truth." Such an understanding quite obviously has caused the King James Version and many other translations to insert a "but" between these two concepts. This insertion is not found in the original Greek text. Placement of the word "but" between these two concepts obscures the line of thought expressed by the evangelist.

John 1:14 quotes 34:6 when it says that the Son is "full of grace and truth." Through him the time of fulfillment has come. This means that he also fulfills what so far was only promised for the future. Therefore, John 1:16 claims that we have received a "fullness," which means "grace upon grace" or a double measure of "grace." Being well versed in the Jewish scriptural interpretation, he refers to the twofold reiteration of the word "grace" in 34:6–7.

In John 1:17, introduced by the explanatory "for," the evangelist further spells out in what way we have received a double measure of "grace": (a) "The law was given through Moses," and now also (b) "grace and truth have come through Jesus Christ."[16]

The fulfillment has thus come, which means that those aspects of the Torah that until now were only promised have also been realized. Therefore, there is not a shade of a contrast between what God has done through Moses and what has occurred through Jesus Christ. There is only a continuity of grace, "grace upon grace." Again, the Torah ("the law") is gospel!

THE STORY OF THE GOLDEN CALF
IN CHRISTIAN ANTI-JEWISH TRADITION

In glaring contrast to this biblical perspective stands the role that the story of the golden calf has played in later Christian polemics against Judaism. Perhaps no other Old Testament text has been so frequently and so viciously used against the Jewish people as this. It has been made to prove that the people of Israel, because of their apostasy, have been rejected by God and replaced by the Christian church as his new elected people and that the old covenant is forever broken and replaced by the new (cf. pp. 249ff.). Therefore, the history of interpretation of the golden calf deserves a place in the hall of shame of anti-Jewish theology.

This tendency of turning the message of this text to its very opposite began early in church history. The *Epistle of Barnabas,* from the first decades of the second century C.E., contains the following complaint against the people of Israel:

> They had already lost it [i.e., the covenant] as Moses received it. Scripture says, "And Moses fasted on the mountain forty days and forty nights and received from the Lord the covenant, the tablets of stone, written by the finger of the hand of the Lord" [cf. 31:18; 34:28]. But because they had turned to the idol they lost it. The Lord says, "Moses, Moses, go down at once! Your people, whom you brought out of the land of Egypt, have acted perversely" [32:7]. Moses understood and threw away the two tablets he held in his hands. And their covenant

was broken, until the covenant with the beloved Jesus was sealed in our hearts in the hope of faith in him.[17]

We notice that nothing is said here about what happened when Moses came down, nothing about his successful intercession, nothing about God's renewal of the covenant.[18] The author actually has a less blatant precursor in the New Testament itself, where Stephen, barely short of contending outright that the covenant never was renewed, describes the event in Acts 7:39–43:

> Our ancestors were unwilling to obey him; instead, they pushed him aside, and in their hearts they turned back to Egypt, saying to Aaron, "Make gods for us who will lead the way for us; as for this Moses who led us out from the land of Egypt, we do not know what has happened to him." At that time they made a calf, offered a sacrifice to the idol, and reveled in the works of their hands. But God turned away from them and handed them over to worship the host of heaven, as it is written in the book of the prophets: "Did you offer to me slain victims and sacrifices forty years in the wilderness, O house of Israel? No; you took along the tent of Moloch, and the star of your god Rephan, the images that you made to worship; so I will remove you beyond Babylon."

The story of this first apostasy of Israel became the standard Old Testament text to underpin the classical Christian claim of being the new and true Israel that had taken the place of the old, rejected people of God. If at all mentioned, the renewed tablets of stone and the subsequent laws were depicted as inferior—if not given as an outright punishment to the Israelites, then at least as given to keep the apostate and obstinate people under control. The food rules, for instance, could be interpreted as restrictions necessary to curb the alleged carnal character of the people, restricting their desires to indulge in satisfying their bodily urges. Needless to say, the new superior people of God did not need them. In this way, the story of the golden calf could be used to support the view that "the law" had been abrogated through Christ and with it the whole covenant (if it had ever been valid).

As a matter of fact, the law was frequently seen as a suitable burden for a people whose minds were more directed toward Egypt and slavery than toward the freedom to which God had called them. This thought was used to explain their resistance to Jesus as a parallel and continuation of their rejection of Moses in the wilderness, most obviously expressed through the sin of the golden calf: "The king was derided in the desert and similarly the son of the king in Jerusalem. The father was exchanged for the calf and various idols, and the son for a bloodstained robber."[19]

Through distortions like these, the church fathers during the first centuries of Christianity set the agenda for a continuous degrading of the Jewish people, which found its vocal advocates throughout history. A complete list of quotations related to the story of the golden calf would fill books. Justin, Irenaeus, Tertullian, Origen, Cyprian, Ephraem, Jerome, Basil, Gregory of Nyssa, John Chrysostom, Augustine, Cyril of Alexandria, etc.—all give their tragic contributions to the abuse of a text which, as we have seen, is indeed one of the most "graceful" in the whole Bible.[20]

The accusations seldom reached the low of John Chrysostom, whose vitriolic outbursts ominously anticipate what later in history would become more than ugly rhetoric:

> So, the Jewish people out of intoxication and obesity fell into the worst of sins, rebelled, did not want to receive the yoke of Christ, nor draw the plough of discipline. . . . But these brute animals unsuitable for work, become suitable for the slaughterhouse. Christ said: "My enemies, who did not want to reign over them, bring them here and kill them."[21]

It is urgent to let texts which have been distorted into a weapon in anti-Jewish polemics reveal their true biblical message. Then the story of the golden calf will help us transform unnecessary stumbling blocks into bridges of respect and understanding between Christians and Jews.

THE GLORY OF GOD ON EARTH (34:29–40:38)

The total restoration that Israel experiences after the fall should not be taken for granted. It has been preceded by a long crisis and a hard struggle. But finally one of the greatest days in the history of Israel has come. After forty days of close communion with the Lord (v. 28), Moses can descend from the mountain with a new covenantal contract (v. 29). According to Jewish tradition, it happened on 10 Tishri, that is, on the day that later would be the Day of Atonement (Lev. 16; 23:27). However, on whatever day it occurred, it was indeed a Day of Atonement that would throw light upon all the coming Days of Atonement, even over the whole future of Israel.[22]

Until this very day, forty days of repentance precede the Day of Atonement, reminiscent of the time that Moses and the people waited with tension for the final confirmation that the sin was forgiven. With the renewed tablets of the covenant as a visible sign of the atonement, Israel could now continue toward an unknown future.

In order to remember the magnitude of their sin and the greatness of God's grace, the children of Israel, according to an old Jewish tradition, brought not only the new tablets with them but also the pieces of the old ones as a healthy reminder of their past.[23] In this way, the content of the ark of the covenant held its constant sermon on sin and grace, fall and restoration—indeed a marvelous treasure to accompany Israel on their journey toward the promised land.

A precious treasure, however, is not to be stored haphazardly. Before the people depart, they are commanded to prepare the proper "package" for the most precious of treasures, the tabernacle with the ark of the covenant. The Lord will dwell in their midst through this sanctuary, just as promised (25:8). God's glory will accompany them step by step. In this way the tabernacle becomes a kind of Sinai in miniature, a portable Sinai (see pp. 126, 134), where the Lord will continue to commune with the people who are bound for freedom.

It is remarkable that the instructions for the building of the tabernacle in 25:1–31:11 are repeated almost word by word in 35:4–39:43, the difference being that the latter section describes how the people actually carry out what God had previously commanded. Not surprisingly, the order of the objects mentioned is different, now following the natural order of construction (beginning with the curtains, frames, and bars) rather than the sanctity of the objects (beginning with the ark and the mercy seat), as was the case in chapters 25–31.

One may ask why all this has to be repeated in five long chapters. Could it not simply have been stated that the people fulfilled what God had instructed them to do? Certainly. However, when reading this reiteration we should remember what has taken place between the two descriptions of the tabernacle: the fall!

With this in mind, we can view the repetition as stressing two important truths that are hard to believe for those who have fallen in sin. (1) God has not in any way revoked the promise to be fully present among the people. The tabernacle was precisely the sign of this divine presence. (2) God has not in any way revoked the calling and mission given to the people before the fall. Now they understand that God has indeed reinstated them in every respect and mended all that was broken. To sum up, then, these chapters are a living illustration of the words, "The gifts and calling of God are irrevocable" (Rom. 11:29).

Therefore, God moves back into the camp. The tabernacle in the midst of the people is the visible proof of his presence. Centuries later, the gospel testified about God's word, that it "dwelt among us" (John 1:14). The word used for "dwelt" can best be translated as "camped" or more precisely "tabernacled." Needless to say, the evangelist has in mind how God dwelt gloriously in the tabernacle among his people in the wilderness (see p. 210).

"But will God indeed dwell on the earth? Even heaven and the highest heaven cannot contain you, much less this house that I have built!" These are the words Solomon preaches at the inauguration of the Temple (1 Kgs. 8:27). The answer is a clear "Yes!" owing to God's self-abasement for our sake. The Lord adjusts to our limitations, in order that we should in some way be able to perceive the divine glory. In this way God can dwell on earth.

Therefore, we can still say, "The LORD is in his holy temple," even though God's "throne is in heaven" (Ps. 11:4). "For though the LORD is high, he regards the lowly" (Ps. 138:6). This is the experience that Moses and the people are now granted. God fulfills what was promised before the fall, "Let them make me a sanctuary, that I may dwell in their midst" (25:8; cf. 29:45).

Already when Moses descends from the mountain, he reflects the glory of the Lord (34:29–35).[24] When the tabernacle is ready (40:33), a cloud descends over it and it is filled with the glory of the Lord (v. 34). Now there can be no more doubt that Moses' prayer is heard and that the Lord is in the midst of the people to lead them home.

This wonderful final vision is at the same time the prelude to the next book of the Torah, the book of Leviticus, which deals above all with how the people approach their God. For, however close to his people on earth, God always remains the exalted and holy one. Therefore, the last verses of the book of Exodus give an important reminder: not even Moses, who had mediated the atonement for the sin of the people and whose face reflects the glory of God (34:29ff.), is able to enter the sanctuary when it is filled with God's glory (40:35).

Against this background, the book of Leviticus, with all its regulations on sacrifices and purity, becomes a necessary reminder of God as both the one who "dwells on high" and the one who inhabits those with "a contrite and humble spirit" (Isa. 57:15). Only at the final arrival into the promised land and the heavenly Jerusalem will the glory of God shine in its full splendor. Not even the sun will then be needed, because in the new tabernacle of God, darkness belongs to the past.

Then Moses' prayer will receive its final answer. Then the liberation will reach its ultimate goal. Then, finally, the redeemed people of God will see God face-to-face and will dwell in a temple that is not made by humans for God, but made by God for humans (Rev. 21:1–4, 22; 22:1–5). Only then will the biblical fugue reach its jubilant final chord, which at the same time will continue with something that "no eye has seen, nor ear heard, nor the heart of man conceived—what God has prepared for those who love him" (Isa. 64:4; 1 Cor. 2:9).

Notes

INTRODUCTION (pages 1–3)

[1] The form of the word LORD in capital letters is a conventional way for translations (e.g., the NRSV) to represent the Hebrew personal name for God (i.e., *YHWH*). This is also true for GOD: for example, "Lord GOD" represents the Hebrew phrase *ᵓadonay YHWH*.

[2] *The Passover Haggadah, with English Translation, Introduction and Commentary* (ed. N. N. Glatzer; New York: Schocken Books, 1969), 48f.; cf. *m. Pesahim* 10:5.

[3] *m. Pirqe Avot (Sayings of the Fathers)* 3:5 and 6:2.

CHAPTER 1 (pages 5–15)

[1] The NRSV and many other translations do not render the Hebrew text adequately, probably because we usually do not begin a text with the word "and." Even this little word, however, in Hebrew only one letter *(vav)*, contains a message that should not be overlooked.

[2] On this paranoia and the alleged Jewish world conspiracy, see my *Fact or Fraud: The Protocols of the Elders of Zion* (Jerusalem: Jerusalem Center for Biblical Studies and Research, 1994).

[3] If one were to take literally the figures given in 12:40–41, 15:13, and 1 Kgs. 6:1, an earlier date for the exodus would be more accurate; but see Sarna, *Exploring Exodus,* 7ff.

[4] In this passage, the name is used anachronistically under the influence of later use.

[5] See further P. Montet, *Egypt and the Bible* (trans. L. R. Keylock; Philadelphia: Fortress, 1968), 16ff.

[6] *ANET,* 470.

[7] Ibid.

[8] Diodorus Siculus—Diodorus from Sicily—was active during the latter part of the second century B.C.E. For an extensive and very

readable biography, see K. A. Kitchen, *Pharaoh Triumphant: The Life and Times of Ramesses II, King of Egypt* (Warminster: Aris and Phillips, 1982); or P. Montet, *Everyday Life in Egypt in the Days of Ramesses the Great* (London: E. Arnold, 1962).

[9] W. F. Edgerton and J. A. Wilson, *Historical Records of Ramses III: The Texts in* Medinet Habu (Chicago: University of Chicago Press, 1936), Plate 42f. For the illustrations, see *Earlier Historical Records of Ramses III* (University of Chicago Oriental Publications 8; Chicago: University of Chicago Press, 1930), Plate 42f.

[10] Pharaoh develops a plan that implies shrewdness: "Come, let us deal shrewdly with them. . . . Therefore they set taskmasters over them" (vv. 10–11). This sequence of events may indicate that the slavery was gradually introduced. The *Book of the Righteous* (*Sefer Hayashar;* thirteenth century C.E.), suggests that Pharaoh first employed both Hebrews and Egyptians to build the cities Pithom and Rameses. Gradually, he diminished the Egyptian work force and cut the salaries of the Hebrews. Eventually the salaries were withdrawn entirely, while the workload increased drastically. Then it was too late to revolt (*Sefer Hayashar—The Book of the Generations of Adam* [New York: Ktav, 1993], 171–72).

[11] *Song of Songs Rabbah* 1:12.

[12] M. Lichtheim, *Ancient Egyptian Literature* (3 vols.; Berkeley: University of California Press, 1971–1980), 2:170–71; cf. Kitchen, *Pharaoh Triumphant,* 183.

[13] *Jewish Antiquities* 2.205–206; b. *Sotah* 12b; *Exodus Rabbah* 1:22.

[14] The meaning of the names Puah and Shiphrah cannot be established with certainty, but much speaks in favor of a derivation from the Hebrew roots *yafaᶜ* and *shafar,* respectively, both designating "beauty" and "splendor." The latter name has been identified on a list of Egyptian names, which further indicates that the midwives were Egyptians; see W. F. Albright, "Northwest-Semitic Names in a List of Egyptian Slaves from the Eighteenth Century BC," *JAOS* 74 (1954): 229.

[15] E. Wiesel, *A Jew Today* (New York: Random House, 1978), 183.

[16] The Hebrew text is obscure. The Hebrew expression *ki hayoth hennah* is translated "for they (i.e., the Hebrew women) are vigorous." The word *hayoth,* which appears only here in the entire Old Testament, is derived from the Hebrew root *hay* (pronounced *khai*), which means "life," and can also be understood as "being in labor," i.e., being in the process of giving life. An alternative translation of the verse would then be: "Because the Hebrew women are not like the Egyptian women; when they are in labor, they give birth before the midwife comes to them." See G. F. Davies, *Israel in Egypt: Reading Exodus 1–2* (JSOTSup 135; Sheffield: Sheffield Academic Press, 1992), 66–67.

[17] Josephus, *Jewish Antiquities* 2.206. The Septuagint reads *tais malais tōn Ebraiōn,* and the Vulgate *Dixit autem rex Aegypti obstetricibus Hebraeorum.* See also D. Luzzatto, *Commentary to the Pentateuch* (ed. P. Schlesinger; Tel Aviv: Devir, 1965), 213–14, referring to Jer. 31:29; Fox, *Now These Are the Names,* 13; and Greenberg, *Understanding Exodus,* 266.

[18] The fear of God does not exclude the midwives from being Egyptians, since this reverence is not limited to the people of Israel (cf. Gen. 20:11; Deut. 25:18). The statement that the midwives feared God seems rather to indicate that they were not Israelites. As pointed out by Luzzatto (op cit., 214), if they were Hebrew midwives, no particular motivation for their action would be necessary, since it is natural to love one's own people (cf. Matt. 5:46–47).

[19] Therefore, God often introduces his address to humans with the words, "Do not be afraid," even before it is mentioned that some are afraid (see, e.g., Gen. 15:1; 26:4; cf. Exod. 9:30; 20:20; see further G. F. Davies, *Israel in Egypt,* 76ff.). In the New Testament, statements from angels of God and Jesus often begin with these words (see, e.g., Matt. 14:27; 17:7; 28:5, 10; Mark 6:50; Luke 1:13, 30; 2:10; 5:10; 8:50; 12:27; John 6:20; 12:15; 14:27; Acts 27:24).

[20] The Hebrew term for "idolatry" is thus ʿavodah zarah ("foreign worship"), and there are numerous Jewish prayer books with titles like ʿAvodat Yisraʾel ("Israel's worship").

CHAPTER 2 (pages 16–25)

[1] The difference between the rescue of the world through Noah and the liberation of Israel through Moses, however, is also obvious. The oppression of Israel, for instance, is certainly not to be regarded as a punishment for the evil that characterized the world at large in the time of Noah. Since the destiny of humankind is linked to the destiny of Israel, the comparison remains adequate.

[2] The universal aspect of the covenant is central (see 19:5; pp. 130, 133, n. 8.)

[3] J. Siebert-Hommes, "But If She Be a Daughter . . . She May Live! 'Daughters' and 'Sons' in Exodus 1–2," in *A Feminist Companion to Exodus to Deuteronomy* (ed. Athalya Brenner; Sheffield: Sheffield Academic Press, 1994), 62–74, esp. 71.

[4] The Nile is, of course, the source of life in Egypt. Later it will be changed into blood (7:14ff.), which signifies life in the Bible, yet becomes a source of death, since it cannot replace water. Water further will play a decisive role in the rescue of the Israelites and the killing of the Egyptians (chs. 14–15). It will also miraculously keep the Israelites alive in the wilderness (17:1ff.).

[5] See A. H. Gardiner, "The Egyptian Origin of Some English Personal Names," *JAOS* 51 (1936): 192–94; J. G. Griffiths, "The Egyptian Derivation of the Name Moses," *JNES* 12 (1953): 225–31.

[6] J. C. Exum, "Second Thoughts about Secondary Characters: Women in Exodus 1.8–2.10," *A Feminist Companion to Exodus to Deuteronomy* (ed. Athalya Brenner; Sheffield: Sheffield Academic Press, 1994), 75–87, esp. 78, with reference to Siebert-Hommes (see above n. 3).

[7] A. Erman, *Life in Ancient Egypt* (London: Macmillan, 1894), 76.

[8] In fact, the murder of the Hebrew sons foreshadows the final plague, which will be the direct cause of the exodus.

⁹According to this tradition, he was forty years old when he left the court, eighty years old when he received his calling (ch. 3), and 120 years old when he died (see Deut. 34:7 and Acts 7:23, 30).

¹⁰*On the Life of Moses* 1.18–24.

¹¹The tutors of the princes were among the highest court officials (Erman, *Life in Ancient Egypt,* 77).

¹²The god of creation.

¹³The scribe of the gods.

¹⁴A. Erman, *The Literature of the Ancient Egyptians, Poems, Narratives, and Manuals of Instruction, from the Third and Second Millennia B.C.* (London: Methuen, 1927), 187.

¹⁵A. Erman, *The Literature of the Ancient Egyptians,* 188–242, esp. 190. For a good overview of "the wisdom of the Egyptians" (e.g., astronomy, biology, hieroglyphic writing, magic, mathematics, medicine, theology), see the chapter "Learning" in Erman, *Life in Ancient Egypt,* 328–68.

¹⁶Erman, *Life in Ancient Egypt,* 328.

¹⁷Ibid., 550.

¹⁸Lichtheim, *Ancient Egyptian Literature* (3 vols.; Berkeley: University of California Press, 1971–1980), 2:169–70; cf. Sarna, *Exploring Exodus,* 21–22.

¹⁹Erman, *Life in Ancient Egypt,* 68–69; see also Lichtheim, *Ancient Egyptian Literature,* 2:171; and Sarna, *Exploring Exodus,* 21–22.

²⁰ʾ*Otsar Ha-midrashim* II (New York: J. D. Eisenstein, 1915), 363.

²¹*Exodus Rabbah* 1:28.

²²*Leviticus Rabbah* 32:4; cf. U. Cassuto, *A Commentary on the Book of Exodus* (Jerusalem: Magnes, 1967), 22; N. Leibowitz, *Studies in Shemot (Exodus)* (2 vols.; 6th ed.; Jerusalem: World Zionist Organization, 1986), 1:44.

²³That is, his covenantal promise to Abraham, Isaac, and Jacob (Gen. 15:13ff.; 50:24).

²⁴Both verbs, *zakar* and *raʾah* ("to remember" and "to see") have a much deeper meaning than anything intellectual and cognitive. They have a juridical connotation implying interference in order to create justice, as well as an emotional connotation, expressing sympathy and care; see Davies, *Israel in Egypt,* 170ff.

²⁵The Hebrew verb *yadaʿ,* which we commonly translate by "to know," is not primarily linked to the intellect either, but rather to the senses and to activities. "To know" primarily means to commit oneself to those persons one "knows," a relationship implying contact and mutuality. In the deepest sense, this verb expresses the intimate relation of love between man and woman (see, e.g., Gen. 4:1).

CHAPTER 3 (pages 26–39)

¹See further J. D. Levenson, *Sinai and Zion,* 16ff.

²See particularly the marvelous ʾ*Avinu-Malkenu* prayer in *The Hirsch Siddur: The Order of Prayers for the Whole Year* (trans. and ed. S. R. Hirsch; New York: Feldheim Publishers, 1997), 622–28.

[3] *Exodus Rabbah* 2:5.

[4] *Mekhilta d'Rabbi Shimᶜon b. Jochai, Shemot* 3 (Epstein ed., 2).

[5] The role of this motif in Islam is dealt with by K. Prenner, "Der brennende Dornbusch nach koranischer Darstellung," in *Meqor Hajjim, Festschrift G. Molin* (ed. I. Seybold; Graz: Akademische Druck- und Verlagsanstalt, 1983), 279–89.

[6] The rabbis were not without scriptural support for such thoughts; see the list of references in *Mekhilta Piskha* 14 (Lauterbach ed., 1:114ff.). The words in Ps. 91:15, "I will be with them in trouble," suggest that God takes part in the affliction of the people as well as in the pain of each individual. In Jer. 13:17 it is said, "But if you will not listen, my soul will weep in secret for your pride; my eyes will weep bitterly and run down with tears, because the LORD's flock has been taken captive" (cf. Jer. 14:17). A key verse is Isa. 63:9, possibly translated "In all their affliction, he was afflicted." This understanding of the enigmatic Hebrew text is not the only possible one (see various translations), but it has a strong following in the rabbinic sources.

[7] The Hebrew word for "honey" *(devash)* does not only mean honey from bees but in a wider sense sweet juices, above all, the sweetness of dates. When the booth *(sukkah)* at the Feast of Tabernacles is decorated with the seven fruits of the good land according to Deut. 8:8, "honey" is therefore usually represented by dates. Honey here appears in a context where grains and fruits are mentioned, which are regarded as the main agricultural products of the land.

[8] *y. Sanhedrin* 1:1 (18a).

[9] It was only pronounced in the temple, which is founded in the words in 20:24: "in every place where I cause my name to be remembered" (the Hebrew word translated by "remember" can also mean "mention"). In the temple there were only two cases when the name could be pronounced: (a) by the high priest on the Day of Atonement (in a loud voice), and (b) by the priest at the reading of the Aaronite blessing (Num. 6:24ff.). Then it was barely audible, blurred by the song of the Levites (see *m. Yoma* 6:2; *m. Tamid* 3:8; 7:2; *m. Sota* 7:6; *b. Sota* 38a; *b. Qiddushin* 71a). The name *ʾAdonay* replaces *YHWH* when it is read from the Bible or the prayer book. Otherwise God is referred to as "The Name" (Hebrew *Hashem*), "Heaven" (see Luke 15:18), and the "Power" (see Mark 14:62), etc. It is also common to allude to God as the subject by putting the verb in the passive (see John 1:17).

[10] The Hebrew words translated by "God" *(ʾEl* or *ʾElohim)* are not a name but a qualifying word like "god," "human being," etc. (The same word in Arabic is *ʾAllah.)* It appears in many Hebrew names, for example, Israʾel, Daniʾel, ʾElijah, and ʾEliezer.

[11] *Targum Pseudo-Jonathan* on v. 14. For an extensive survey of the scholarly debate, see *TDOT* 5:500–521, esp. 512–13.

[12] The translation, "I will be with you" instead of "I am with you," somewhat obscures the fact that it is the same "I AM" in vv. 12–13 as in v. 14. The same applies to 4:12, 15.

[13] *Exodus Rabbah* 2:2–3.

[14] There may be a conscious allusion between the Hebrew word for "bush" *(seneh)* and the name of the mountain, Sinai.

[15] A. Erman, *Life in Ancient Egypt* (London: Macmillan, 1894), 353ff.

[16] Sobek and Hapy were two gods associated with the Nile.

[17] Technically, the Pharaoh became one with the god Osiris only at death. During life, he could be said to be like the gods or the son of a deity. Whether he was regarded as fully divine is now subject to some doubt. See the discussion in Ronald J. Leprohon, "Royal Ideology and State Administration in Pharaonic Egypt," in *Civilizations of the Ancient Near East* (ed. Jack Sasson; 4 vols.; New York: Scribners, 1995), 1:274–75.

[18] Saadya Gaon (882–942 C.E.), quoted by Ibn Ezra (1093–1167 C.E.). Since the skin does not become white from leprosy, another disease is probably meant, for example, psoriasis. See further E. V. Hulse, "The Nature of Biblical 'Leprosy' and the Use of Alternative Medical Terms in Modern Translations of the Bible," *PEQ* 107 (1975): 87–105. I am indebted to my student, Rev. Jesper Svartvik, Lund, Sweden, for the reference to this article.

[19] A. S. Yahuda, *The Accuracy of the Bible* (London: Heinemann, 1934), 95ff.

CHAPTER 4 (pages 40–52)

[1] The name "Moses" is added in the translation of 4:25 in the NRSV and in many other translations. This addition must be based on the assumption that the word "bridegroom" can refer only to the bridegroom Zipporah had, namely, Moses. Since Moses is not mentioned in this story, it is more natural to refer the expression to the only other males who appear in the story, that is, the son or the Lord (cf. n. 6).

[2] See M. Fishbane, *Text and Texture: Close Readings of Selected Biblical Texts* (New York: Schocken, 1979), 121ff.; Y. Zakovitch, *"And You Shall Tell Your Son . . .": The Concept of Exodus in the Bible* (Jerusalem: Magnes, 1991), 60–67, 121–25.

[3] Zakovitch, *"And You Shall Tell,"* 64.

[4] For an extensive review of the religious and cultural background, see H. Kosmala, "The 'Bloody Husband,' " *VT* 12 (1962): 14–28; Brevard Childs, *The Book of Exodus,* 95ff.; M. Greenberg, *Understanding Exodus,* 110ff. See also F. Lindström, *God and the Origin of Evil* (Coniectanea Biblica, OT Series 21; Lund: Gleerup, 1983), 41–55.

[5] The Hebrew word translated by "bridegroom" *(hathan)* has several connections with the circumcision. The word *muloth* in v. 26 is a plural and is therefore best translated by "the circumcised" rather than by "circumcision."

[6] A problem, however, is that unless we assume a change of objects between the one she is touching and the one she is addressing, Zipporah would have to touch the Lord's feet with the foreskin, an incongruous idea. In a challenging interpretation, Lindström (*God and the Origin of Evil,* 47), however, understands the Hebrew construction, *naga^c* in Hiphil + the preposition *le* to express a movement,

as is commonly the case. Thus Zipporah would not have touched the Lord but only have fallen down at his feet as a gesture of veneration.

[7] *Pirqe de Rabbi Eliezer* (Friedlander ed., 210); *Mekhilta Piskha* 5 (Lauterbach ed., 1:33–34).

[8] *Targums Onqelos, Jonathan,* and *Neofiti;* cf. also *Exodus Rabbah* 5:8.

[9] R. A. Caminos, *Late-Egyptian Miscellanies* (Brown Egyptological Studies 1; London: Oxford University Press, 1954), 188–89.

[10] K. A. Kitchen, "From the Brick-fields of Egypt," *Tyndale Bulletin* 27 (1976): 137–47; cf. Caminos, *Late-Egyptian Miscellanies,* 106.

[11] J. Cerny and A. H. Gardiner, *Hieratic Ostraca I* (Oxford: Printed for the Griffith Institute at the University Press by Charles Batey, 1957), 22–23, plates 83–84.

[12] P. H. Peli, *Torah Today: A Renewed Encounter with Scripture* (Jerusalem: B'nai B'rith Books, 1987), 60.

[13] *b. Sanhedrin* 111a.

[14] Nachmanides (*Commentary on the Torah,* 60ff.) rightly stresses that the point of Moses' complaint is that God has not saved his people—not in the worsened situation. It should further be noticed that the Hebrew formulation of Moses' words (paronomasia) sharpens his words: "You have really not saved your people!"

[15] *Exodus Rabbah* 5:22.

[16] The verb for "to know" is passive (Niphal). Rashi stresses the difference between "being known" *(noda͑ti)* and "proclaim" *(hoda͑ti)*. See also Cassuto, *Exodus,* 78–79, and Childs, *Exodus,* 113.

[17] Again, the word for "to know" is passive (Niphal).

[18] See Leibowitz, *Studies in Shemot,* 1:132–40, with further references.

[19] In Hebrew the words for "slavery," "service" and "worship" are the same; see pp. 14f., 77, 127. Decisive for the meaning is who owns us and in whose service we stand.

[20] Leibowitz, *Studies in Shemot,* 1:122.

[21] There are rabbis who stress that the subjective consciousness of what God has done is the most important aspect of the liberation. Rabbi Aqiva states in *m. Pirqe Avot* 3:18: "Beloved is man, for he is created in the image [of God]. But greater yet is the love that it has been made known to him that he is created in the image [of God]." The point of the statement is, of course, that it is only when people become mindful of their likeness to God and aware of human dignity that their lives are affected (see Leibowitz, *Studies in Shemot,* 1:125–26).

CHAPTER 5 (pages 53–79)

[1] H. Kees, *Götterglaube,* 14ff., 17ff., 434ff.,

[2] Ibid., 52ff., 55–56, 237, 247–48.

[3] The verb not only means "to be strong" but also "to be courageous" (see, e.g., Ps. 27:14). The negative aspect of a "strong" heart is obviously obstinacy (see, e.g., Ezek. 2:4). In both examples it is

connected with the heart. In Exod. 7:3 the verb *qashah* ("to be hard") in the Hiphil is used, which obviously also expresses stubbornness. See further R. R. Wilson, "The Hardening of Pharaoh's Heart," *CBQ* 41 (1979): 18–36, esp. 22ff. Both verbs related to the heart have parallels in the ancient Egyptian language (ibid., 24, n. 22).

[4] The literal meaning is not expressed in the translations.

[5] S. Ben Reuben, *"Wayyikhbad lev Phar'oh," Beth Mikra* 99 (1984): 112–13; Montet, *Everyday Life in Egypt in the Days of Ramesses the Great* (London: E. Arnold, 1962), 302ff. and Plate 14; E. A. Wallis Budge, *The Book of the Dead* (New York: E. P. Dutton, 1923), 22–34. For magnificent illustrations, see *The Ancient Egyptian Book of the Dead* (trans. R. O. Faulkner, ed. C. Andrews; London: The Trustees of the British Museum, 1985), 14, 30–31, 34–35.

[6] Maimonides, *Hilkhoth Teshuvah (Mishne Torah* I). Chapter 4 deals with sins that make repentance particularly difficult and chapter 5 with the problem of the free will and predestination. Chapter 6, finally, focuses on the hardening, that is, the punishment that makes repentance impossible.

[7] *Midrash Sekhel Tov* to 8:6 (Buber ed., 45); cf. *Midrash Leqah Tov* to 8:6 (Buber ed., 37).

[8] This expression, ʿ*eser makkoth,* found, for example, in the *Passover Haggadah,* is based on the fact that the Hebrew verb *hikkah* ("to hit, strike") is used as a technical term in connection with the plagues in the book of Exodus (3:20; 7:17, 25; 8:12–13; 9:15, 25; 12:12–13, 29; 17:5–6). See also Ps. 78:20, 51, 66; 105:33–34.

[9] See Fox, *Now These Are the Names,* 45.

[10] As was the case when the Hebrew baby boys were thrown into it (ch. 1). Like water, even blood is the prime substance of life. In this first plague, however, it paradoxically brings death.

[11] *Exodus Rabbah* 20:1.

[12] *Mekhilta Beshallah* 7 (Lauterbach ed., 3:243–44).

[13] It remains to be explained, however, how Pharaoh's magicians could imitate the miracle if all the waters were already turned into blood. Jewish commentaries assume either that they performed their act later, after the blood had been turned back into water or that they dug and found subterranean water, which was not affected by the miracle; see E. L. Greenstein, "The Firstborn Plague and the Reading Process," in *Pomegranates and Golden Bells: Studies in Biblical, Jewish, and Near Eastern Ritual, Law, and Literature in Honor of Jacob Milgrom* (ed. D. P. Wright, D. N. Freedman, A. Hurvitz; Winona Lake, Ind.: Eisenbrauns, 1995), 555–68.

[14] *ANET,* 441. The text is from about 1300–1100 B.C.E. but relates to events that occurred in a time of chaos a thousand years before.

[15] "Hymn to the Nile" from the time of the exodus, in *ANET,* 372–73.

[16] The mythological significance of the frog is dealt with in Kees, *Götterglaube,* 61ff., 144, 307.

[17] *Midrash Hagadol* (Margulies ed., 121).

[18] Even in this case, a rabbinic tradition tries to explain why Aaron and not Moses has to carry out the command: "God said to Moses: 'It is not proper that thou shouldst smite the

earth which protected thee when thou didst kill the Egyptian' " (*Exodus Rabbah* 10:7). This refers to Moses' burying the Egyptian in the sand.

[19] Kees, *Götterglaube,* 237ff., 241ff.; Yahuda, *Accuracy of the Bible* (London: Heinemann, 1934), 86–87.

[20] Rashi; Maimonides; Cassuto, *Exodus.*

[21] The Hebrew word *yad* ("hand") is here frequently translated "work."

[22] *Exodus Rabbah* 11:2–3; 15:27.

[23] *Jubilees* 48:5; Philo, *On the Life of Moses,* 1.130.

[24] Plutarch, *On Isis and Osiris* 72 (in *Moralia* V, trans. F. C. Babbitt; LCL, Cambridge: Harvard University Press, 1962), 168–69.

[25] That is, an ass. Both Jews and Christians were accused of worshiping this animal.

[26] This god was depicted with a ram's horns.

[27] Tacitus, *Histories* 5.4.1 (trans. Moore, LCL).

[28] The NRSV: "deadly pestilence."

[29] See further my *The Jews! Your Majesty* (Jerusalem: AMI— Jerusalem Center for Biblical Studies and Research, 1996), 37.

[30] The NRSV translates freely, "upon you yourself."

[31] A genizah is a storeroom for sacred texts that have become worn out or else have been rendered unfit for further use.

[32] It is certainly ironic that Pharaoh now wants to keep the children whom his predecessor had once tried to kill. The importance of bringing the children is, in fact, indicated in the very beginning of the description of this plague: "that you may tell your children and grandchildren how I have made fools of the Egyptians and what signs I have done among them—so that you may know that I am the LORD" (10:2). Not only the Egyptians have to know who is the Lord but also the people of Israel. The way to this knowledge is still ahead.

[33] Cassuto, *Exodus,* 126. See also S. Rosenblatt, "A Reference to the Egyptian God Re in the Rabbinic Commentaries of the Old Testament," *JBL* 60 (1941): 183–85.

[34] Cassuto (*Exodus,* 127) refers to Job 15:2 and Hos. 12:1.

[35] *Exodus Rabbah* 14:1; Nachmanides, *Commentory on the Torah,* 108; see also Josephus, *Jewish Antiquities* 2.308.

[36] "The Prophecy of Neferti" (2040–1650 B.C.E.), in *ANET,* 445.

[37] See the extensive listing of references to Re^c in the index of *ANET.*

[38] See Greenstein, "Firstborn Plague," 557–58.

[39] See "The Divine Attributes of Pharaoh," in *ANET,* 431.

[40] *Papyrus Anastasi II,* 5.7–6.4; see R. A. Caminos, *Late-Egyptian Miscellanies* (Brown Egyptological Studies 1; London: Oxford University Press, 1954), 49; cf. also p. 17 about Rameses II.

[41] The reference to Pharaoh as the sustainer of the green land, even surpassing the Nile itself, is remarkable in the light of the past strikes against both the Nile (the first plague) and the land (the seventh and eighth plagues). Now the light itself is to be removed from him. The hymn is taken from a stela glorifying Pharaoh Ni-maat-Re, namely, Amen-em-het III (ca. 1840–1790 B.C.E.), in *ANET,* 431.

[42] See the mnemonic of Rabbi Judah in groups of three in *The Passover Haggadah* (Glatzer ed., 40–41); Abrabanel; Rashbam. See further Childs, *Exodus,* 149ff.; Fox, *Now These Are the Names,* 8.

[43] G. Hort, "The Plagues of Egypt," *ZAW* 69 (1957): 84–103; 70 (1958): 48–59. Hort's article sheds light upon the outward appearances of the various plagues but does not do justice to the claim of the text itself to describe a unique miracle.

[44] The second, third, and fourth plagues may also be linked to creation in that "the frogs are associated with *water,* the lice with *earth,* and the flies with *air*" (Z. Zevit, "Three Ways to Look at the Ten Plagues," *BR* 6 (1990): 16–23, 42–43, esp. 22; see also Z. Zevit, "The Priestly Redaction and Interpretation of the Plague Narrative in Exodus," *JQR* 66 (1976): 193–211.

[45] Zevit, "Three Ways to Look at the Ten Plagues," 22.

[46] A positive answer is given by Zevit (ibid., 23), who also wants to see the fact that Ps. 78 and 105 list seven plagues as "clearly evoking the seven days of creation."

[47] "Had He executed judgment on them [that is, on the Egyptians], but not on their gods, we should have been content!" The hymn records the various miracles in connection with the exodus and the walk through the wilderness as a gradual intensification (*The Passover Haggadah* [Glatzer ed., 42ff.]).

CHAPTER 6 (pages 80–95)

[1] In Exod. 13:4, 23:15, 34:18, and Deut. 16:1 the month is called *ʾAviv.* The word means "young ears" but would also stand for "spring" in general. In later times, the name was changed to Nisan due to Babylonian influence (see Neh. 2:1 and Esth. 3:7). Also the month of Tishri in the fall (September-October) is counted as the first month of the year. The Jewish New Year, *Rosh Hashanah,* is celebrated then (cf. the expression "at the end of the year" in 23:16 and 34:22). In Judaism the two traditions are explained by distinguishing between the religious year, beginning in spring, and the civil year, beginning in fall. The church has taken over the Jewish way of calculating the time for Passover/Easter. Since the biblical months always begin with the new moon, it is always the full moon on 15 Nisan. Among Catholics and Protestants, Easter falls on the first Sunday after the first full moon after the vernal equinox. Therefore, it is usually celebrated around the same time as the Jewish Passover *(Pesah).* In the Orthodox traditions, however, Easter has to be celebrated after the Jewish Passover, viewed as foreshadowing the Christian feast; this is why it is usually celebrated at least a week later.

[2] *Exodus Rabbah* 19:5.

[3] *Exodus Rabbah* 19:5.

[4] *b. Bava Metsia* 86b.

[5] The meaning of the Hebrew verb *pasah,* usually translated by "to pass over," is unclear. In Isa. 31:5 it obviously means to protect. In connection with the blood sign this meaning is more likely than "pass over"; see *Mekhilta Piskha* 7 and 11 (Lauterbach ed., 1:56, 87).

The noun *pesah* stands both for the lamb (12:21) and for the feast (Deut. 16:1).

[6] *Mekhilta Piskha* 7 and 11 (Lauterbach ed., 1:57, 88).

[7] *b. Pesahim* 64b.

[8] *m. Hallah* 1:1; *m. Pesahim* 2:5; 3:1. Consequently, a lot of food products contain *hamets* in one form or another. It is important to recognize and remove these during the week of Passover. In addition to the general *kosher* rules, there are therefore a set of special *kosher* rules for Passover. All products which could possibly contain any *hamets* are inspected and, if proved to be clean, labeled *kosher le-Pesah*.

[9] *b. Pesahim* 46a.

[10] The leaven cakes in Lev. 7:13 and 23:17 were an exception to this rule. They were, however, never brought to the altar (see further Levine, *Leviticus*, 42–43).

[11] I have used "leaven" where the NRSV reads "yeast," which is not quite accurate. It is true that old leaven was used as yeast for the new bread, but leaven is a much wider concept than yeast.

[12] See also Matt. 16:6; Mark 8:15; Luke 12:1; Gal. 5:9. In the rabbinic literature the same thought is expressed in *b. Berakhoth* 17a; *Genesis Rabbah* 34:10; *Tanhuma* (Buber) *Noach* 2:4.

[13] The words *pesah* and *matsah* are not explained in the Bible; they are obviously presumed to be well known. It is possible that the lamb and the unleavened bread were parts of a pre-biblical cult that aimed at furthering fertility among the animals and at producing a good crop. These traditions, then, have been demythologized in the Bible to become a proclamation of God as the sovereign Lord of both creation and history (Sarna, *Exploring Exodus*, 85ff., and further J. B. Segal, *The Hebrew Passover from the Earliest Times to C.E. 70* [London and New York: Oxford University Press, 1963]).

[14] "The hymn" mentioned in Matt. 26:30 refers to the *Hallel*, that is, Psalms 113–118. The first two Psalms are read before the meal and the others after. These are the ones more precisely meant in the gospel.

[15] For an extensive and richly illustrated survey of the history of the *Passover Haggadah*, see Y. H. Yerushalmi, *Haggadah and History: A Panorama in Facsimile of Five Centuries of the Printed Haggadah from the Collections of Harvard University and the Jewish Theological Seminary of America* (Philadelphia: JPS, 1975). The main content of the *Haggadah* is indicated already in the Mishnah, in the tractate of *Pesahim* 10, but only in the tenth century is there a fixed version of the *Haggadah* with only minor differences from the present one.

[16] This offering is dealt with in the mishnaic tractate *Hagigah*, which belongs to the second order, *Moed*.

[17] The NRSV translates somewhat freely, "a reminder on your forehead, so that the teaching of the LORD may be on your lips."

[18] According to the *Letter of Aristeas* 159, such a concrete application of the commandment is taken for granted. So does also Josephus, *Jewish Antiquities* 4.213. At the Dead Sea, capsules *(tefillin)* have been found that are at least two thousand years old. They are only marginally different from the ones manufactured today.

[19] The word translated "hand" can also designate the whole arm.

[20] According to the Jewish halakhah, the arm capsule should be put on the weak arm, which means that a left-handed person should wear them on the right arm.

[21] The donkey should be killed by breaking its neck in order to avoid any resemblance to a sacrifice.

[22] From the beginning, the firstborn served as priests (cf. 1 Sam. 1:22). When the tribe of Levi and the priests were later sanctified for this service, they took over the priestly function (Num. 3:11ff., 40ff.).

[23] The ceremony is called *pidyon ha-ben,* "redemption of the son." The laws are dealt with in the mishnaic tractate *Bekhorot,* included in the fifth order, *Qodashim.* Since this act is not linked to any sacrifices, it can be performed even today. The ritual can be found in any Jewish prayer book. After the destruction of the temple, this is the only priestly function left besides the reading of the Aaronite blessing (Num. 6:22–27) in the synagogue service.

[24] Cf. Greenstein, "Firstborn Plague," 566–67.

[25] Cf. Gen. 12:3. In Deut. 15:18 one who is generous to a freed servant is promised a special blessing from the Lord. According to one rabbinic tradition, Pharaoh's asking for a blessing reflected his own fear of death, since he was a firstborn himself; *Mekhilta Piskha* 13 (Lauterbach ed., 1:97–98) and Rashi on Exod. 12:32.

[26] This is the meaning of the verb in the Hiphil form. Verbs in Piel and Hiphil often have a similar meaning.

[27] See Y. T. Radday, "The Spoils of Egypt," *ASTI* 12 (1983): 127–47, 143ff.

[28] For the biblical laws regarding slaves in the light of this text, see Daube, *Exodus Pattern,* 47–61.

CHAPTER 7 (pages 96–111)

[1] *Mekhilta Shirata* 3 (Lauterback ed., 2:24).

[2] Emil Fackenheim, *God's Presence in History: Jewish Affirmations and Philosophical Reflections* (New York: New York University Press, 1970), 8ff.

[3] It is therefore no wonder that Paul can speak about the miracle at the sea as a "baptism," a transfer from death to life. The people are born here and begin a new life (1 Cor. 10:1–2; cf. Rom. 6:4; Col. 2:12).

[4] On the expression "the land of the Philistines," see p. 294, n. 62.

[5] The translation of the name *Yam Suf* by "the Sea of Reeds" is not unproblematic. Papyrus does not grow in the salty area we are talking about. Another possibility would be to read the word *suf* as *sof,* "end," or even "termination." The name would then express that these waters marked the border to the unknown, or chaos; see B. F. Batto, "Red Sea or Reed Sea? How the Mistake Was Made and What Yam Sup Really Means," *BAR* 10/4 (July–August, 1984): 57–63.

[6] The word *Ba'al* refers to the same Canaanite god who is mentioned at other places in the Bible; see, e.g., 1 Kgs. 18. The cult of *Ba'al* had its center in today's Syria but was widely spread along the

whole Mediterranean coast down to Egypt. Since *Ba'al* was worshiped as the special patron of sailors, the cult was particularly widespread in coastal areas.

[7] At least nine different suggestions have been presented and thirteen theories as to where Mount Sinai was located; Sarna, *Understanding Exodus,* 108, referring to M. Har-El, *The Sinai Journeys: The Route of the Exodus in the Light of the Historical Geography of the Sinai Peninsula* (Los Angeles: Ridgefield, 1983).

[8] See the extensive account in O. Eissfeldt, *Baal Zephon, Zeus Kasios und der Durchzug der Israeliten durchs Meer* (Halle: Niemeyer, 1932), 59–65.

[9] The land of Israel, the city of Jerusalem and the Temple Mount are ascribed an intrinsic holiness only because, according to the Bible, God expressly has chosen these places forever.

[10] *Mekhilta Beshallah* 4 (Lauterbach ed., 1:216).

[11] See *Exodus Rabbah* 21:3–4. In his history, Josephus (*Jewish Antiquities* 2.335–337) imagines how Moses' prayer may have sounded:

> Thou thyself knowest full well that escape from our present plight passes alike the might and the wit of man; nay, if there be any means of salvation at all for this host which at thy will has left Egypt, thine it is to provide it. For our part, despairing of other hope or resource, we fling ourselves upon thy protection alone, and expectantly, if aught be forthcoming from thy providence of might to snatch us from the wrath of the Egyptians, we look at thee. May it come quickly, this aid that shall manifest to us thy power; raise the hearts of this people, whom hopelessness has sunk into the depths of woe, to serenity and confidence of salvation. Nor are these straits in which we find ourselves without thy domain; nay, thine is the sea, thine the mountain that encompasseth us: this then can open at thy command, or the deep become dry land, or we might e'en find escape through the air, should it please thine almighty power that after this manner we should be saved.

[12] The inscription is dated from the reign of Pharaoh Amen-em-het III (ca. 1840–1790 B.C.E.), in *ANET,* 431.

[13] Even though the text mentions Pharaoh together with the Egyptians, and states that "not so much as one of them remained," one cannot necessarily draw the conclusion that Pharaoh personally perished. "Pharaoh" can very well stand for the governing authority, that is, Pharaoh gives the order that the Israelites shall be brought back without participating in the campaign himself.

[14] Hebrew *ruah,* as well as Greek *pneuma,* means both "spirit" and "wind" (cf. John 3:8).

[15] Faith in the Lord is certainly different from faith in Moses, but faith in the Lord has the consequence that the people now realize that Moses has acted on behalf of the Lord and has received his authority to lead them. The rabbinic commentary thus states: "This is to teach you that having faith in the shepherd of Israel is the same as having faith in Him who spoke and the world came into being. In like manner you must interpret: 'And the people spoke against God and against Moses' (Num. 21:5). This comes to teach you that speaking against the shepherd of Israel is like speaking against Him who spoke and the world came into being" (*Mekhilta Beshallah* 7 [Lauterbach ed., 1:252]). Cf. 2 Chron. 20:20; John 12:44–45; 20:21.

[16] *Mekhilta Shirata* 9 (Lauterbach ed., 2:69). The Hebrew word translated "steadfast love" and "mercies" is *hesed* (see p. 259).

[17] A complete commented translation is rendered by Lichtheim, *Ancient Egyptian Literature* (3 vols.; Berkeley: University of California Press, 1971–1980), 2:57–72. The song of his son, Merneptah, is very similar; see ibid., 73–78; *ANET,* 376ff.

[18] Lichtheim, *Ancient Egyptian Literature,* 2:71.

[19] For a thorough analysis of the miracle at the sea as a biblical theme, see S. Norin, *Er spaltete das Meer: Die Auszugsüberlieferung in Psalmen und Kult des alten Israels* (Coniectanea Biblica, OT Series 9; Lund: C.W.K. Gleerup, 1977).

[20] *The Passover Haggadah* (Glatzer ed.), 37.

[21] In the ancient commentary on Exodus, the *Mekhilta,* no other text receives even close to as extensive commentary as "the Song of the Sea." The ten chapters dedicated to these twenty-one verses hardly leave any detail in the text without attention. For a thorough analysis, see J. Goldin, *The Song of the Sea: Being a Commentary on a Commentary in Two Parts* (New Haven: Yale University Press, 1971).

[22] Cf. *Mekhilta Shirata* 1 (Lauterbach ed. 2:1ff.); Goldin, *The Song of the Sea,* 65ff., 205f.

[23] The prayer ʿ*Ezrath* ʾ*Avothenu* ʾ*Attah* between the *Shema*ʿ and the *Shmoneh* ʾ*Esreh;* see *The Hirsch Siddur: The Order of Prayers for the Whole Years* (trans. and ed. S. R. Hirsch; Jerusalem: Feldheim Publishers, 1997), 124ff.

[24] *Mekhilta Shirata* 1 (Lauterbach ed., 2:2–5).

[25] This interpretation is certainly problematic in view of the fact that the masculine form, *shir,* also appears in some of the references to the first nine songs (Isa. 30:29; Judg. 5:12; Ps. 30:1). J. Goldin has convincingly showed, however, that this list of references is a later addition to the commentary; see his essay, "This Song," in *Salo Wittmayer Baron Jubilee Volume on the Occasion of His Eightieth Birthday* (ed. S. Lieberman and A. Hyman; 3 vols.; Jerusalem: American Academy for Jewish Research, 1974), 2:539–54 (in Hebrew).

[26] *b. Megilla* 10b; *b. Sanhedrin* 39b.

[27] *Pesiqta de-Rav Kahana,* supplement 2:8 (Braude and Kapstein ed., 472).

CHAPTER 8 (pages 112–125)

[1] It is called the wilderness of Shur. The Hebrew word *shur* means among others "wall." It is known that the Egyptians built huge fortification walls in the eastern part of the Nile delta in order to prevent an invasion from the east. The area referred to is then the northwestern part of the Sinai peninsula (see Sarna, *Exodus,* for further references).

[2] Walzer, *Exodus and Revolution,* 53–54.

[3] This place is usually identified with *Wadi Gharandel,* which runs out at the eastern shore of the Red Sea, about fifty miles south

of Suez. There is still a lush oasis, which fits the biblical description very well.

[4] Literally, "without flour, no Torah" *(m. Pirqe Avot [Sayings of the Fathers]), 3:21.*

[5] According to Josephus *(Jewish Antiquities 3.25),* the arrival of the quails in this way is a recurrent phenomenon, which has also been confirmed by modern travel records. Even in this century, the quails made up an important part of the food in the autumn for the people living along the coast south of Gaza. Since they arrived in huge numbers, they were also an important source of income in this area. In recent years the stock has drastically diminished. The meat is regarded as a delicacy. The bird has become known to a wide audience through one of the main dishes in the exquisite repast described in the famous movie "Babette's Feast," based on a story by Karen Blixen.

[6] The word is explained according to popular etymology as "What is it?" in 16:15, in Hebrew *man huʾ*.

[7] Wisdom of Solomon 16:20; *Mekhilta Vayassa* 5 (Lauterbach ed., 2:118); *Exodus Rabbah* 25:3; *b. Yoma* 75a.

[8] One *omer* is about 2 liters or 2.2 quarts (cf. v. 36).

[9] *Mekhilta Vayassa* 6 (Lauterbach ed., 2:125–26).

[10] *Mekhilta Vayassa* 5 (Lauterbach ed., 2:119); *2 Baruch* 29:8; *Sibylline Oracles* 3:746.

[11] According to *Mekhilta Beshallah* 1 (Lauterbach ed., 1:171), the Torah was absorbed by those who ate from the manna and drank from the rock (17:1–7). *Exodus Rabbah* 25:7 combines the words about the manna in Exod. 16:4 with Prov. 9:5: "Come, eat of my bread and drink of the wine I have mixed." From the context it is clear that it is God's wisdom that is revealed in the Torah. In a similar way Philo identifies the manna with God's wisdom *(On the Change of Names,* 259–260). For an extensive analysis of John 6 in the light of the manna traditions, see P. Borgen, *Bread from Heaven: An Exegetical Study of the Concept of Manna in the Gospel of John and the Writings of Philo* (NovTSup 10; Leiden: Brill, 1965).

[12] A good survey is given by Leibowitz, *Studies in Shemot.*

[13] *Mekhilta Vayassa* 5 (Lauterbach ed., 2:115).

[14] The Sabbath expresses the same trust in God (see pp. 239ff.). Therefore, it is not accidental that the Sabbath commandment plays an important role in this context.

[15] A similar lesson can certainly be learned from the rain, the water from heaven, as pointed out in Deut. 11:10–17. There, a comparison is made between Egypt and the promised land. In Egypt one could water the field with one's feet, "like a garden of vegetables." For that, the Egyptians made a god out of the Nile (cf. pp. 36, 54f., 60f.). "But the land which you are going over to possess is a land of hills and valleys, which drinks its water by the rain from heaven." There God is in control, and the trust in him and the obedience of his commandments are vital for well-being in the land. Again, the people will be tested by being dependent on what God sends from heaven.

[16] *b. Taanith* 9a; *Numbers Rabbah* 1:2; 19:25–26; *t. Sukkah* 3:11; *Targum Jonathan* to Num. 21:17.

[17] See note 11 and further *Mekhilta Bahodesh* 5 (Lauterbach ed., 2:237); *Numbers Rabbah* 1:7; cf. *m. Pirqe Avot (Sayings of the Fathers)* 1:4.

[18] These two opposite aspects of the desert period are extensively analyzed by S. Talmon, "The 'Desert Motif' in the Bible and in Qumran Literature," *Biblical Motifs, Origins and Transformations* (ed. A. Altmann; Cambridge: Harvard University Press, 1966), 31–63.

[19] The Greek alphabet does not have a letter for the sound *sh* but renders it as *s*. In the name Jesus, *yeshua,* like in other Hebrew names (Barabbas, Zacchaeus, etc.), the masculine nominal ending *-s* is added.

[20] This conclusion can be drawn also from Deut. 25:17–18. Most translations hardly do justice to the Hebrew text when they refer the expression "did not fear God" to Amalek. The end of v. 18 should literally be translated as "and you were tired and weary and did not fear God." When following the proper word order of the text in the translation, it becomes obvious how strange it is to change subject and insert Amalek as the subject of "did not fear God." Instead this expression makes a direct reference to the situation of the Israelites at Massah and Meribah, when they asked, "Is the LORD among us or not?" The only correct translation and interpretation of this passage I have found appears in Zakovitch, *"And You Shall Tell Your Son,"* 121.

[21] *The Passover Haggadah* (Glatzer ed.), 31.

[22] The introduction of the song, "Blessed be the LORD," is in Hebrew *barukh YHWH,* or (as said when the name of God is not pronounced) *barukh ha-Shem,* "blessed be the Name." This formula is very common in today's modern Hebrew among orthodox Jews. We recognize it in Zechariah's song of praise (Luke 1:68). It was thus uttered for the first time by one who did not belong to the people of Israel but who became convinced of the greatness of the Lord when he heard about what God had done for the children of Israel.

[23] The exact formulation of the creed is uncertain because of the condensed style of the Hebrew. A literal translation would be: "Now I know that the Lord is greater than all gods concerning that in which they were arrogant with them." The word "arrogant" then does not necessarily refer to the Egyptians, but can also have "all gods" as the subject. If this is the case, we would have a variation of the theme, "on all the gods of Egypt I will execute judgments" (12:12).

[24] The burnt offering was totally consumed by fire, while the meat from other sacrifices was consumed by those present. The offering to the Lord, the burnt offering, was always sacrificed first, while the communion meal was consumed only afterward (see further pp. 228f.).

[25] The commentaries usually take their point of departure from the context in which this section is inserted. Several facts, however, indicate that Jethro's visit originally took place in a situation after the revelation at Sinai. We see, for instance, that the people are already encamped at the mountain when Jethro arrives (18:5), while, according to the following chapter (19:1–2), they arrive only later. Numbers

10:11–12, 29–31 and Deut. 1:9–18 further indicate that the event took place only later. Moreover, the whole situation of judging described here fits better into one in which the laws have already been revealed. As a contrast to Amalek's animosity, however, Jethro's friendly visit fits well into this context. The event also brings a welcome relief after all the agonies the people have gone through and before the great revelation still awaiting them (see further Sarna, *Exploring Exodus,* 127ff.).

CHAPTER 9 (pages 126–155)

[1] In Jewish tradition, the Feast of *Shavuᶜoth* (Pentecost) is also called *ᶜAtsereth Pesah,* which means the "conclusion of Passover" (see further pp. 187f., particularly n. 7).

[2] Such thoughts are occasionally expressed in the discussions regarding the validity and value of the Old Testament for Christians. Only one hundred years after Christ, Marcion wrote his infamous *Antitheses,* in which he depicted the Jews, their God, and their Bible as the absolute contrast with the Christians and the gospel of Christ. In spite of declaring him a heretic, the church never totally succeeded in ridding itself of his legacy. Still today Christians speak about the "Old Testament God" as if this were another God than that of Jesus and of us all (see also p. 287, n. 20).

[3] The translation of the NRSV, "Indeed, the whole world is mine," is inaccurate, since it does not properly indicate that this sentence, introduced by the Hebrew conjunction *ki* ("for"), is the rationale of the previous statement.

[4] Ben Azzai in *Sifra* 89b; *Genesis Rabbah* 24:7. The Hebrew word translated by "man" is *ʾAdam,* which is not only the name of the first person but also the general Hebrew word for a human being. It is probably not by accident that the word used for "holy people" in 19:6 is *goy,* which usually stands for all nations. Israel is not in itself holy but is made holy, when God separates this people from the others. In the same way the word *goy* is used also in Gen. 12:2, where Abraham is promised to become "a great nation"—another healthy reminder that the election is not a matter of quality and superiority.

[5] Buber, *Moses,* 121–22.

[6] Against this background it is not surprising that the covenant between God and Israel is compared with a marriage (see pp. 91, 151). To this very day, the groom says to the bride in the Jewish wedding ritual: "Behold, you are sanctified ('separated') to me through this ring." Furthermore, the mishnaic tractate that deals with the marital laws is called *Qiddushin,* which means "sanctification" or "separation."

[7] One exception might be 1 Sam. 30:23–25. David's decision, however, could also be an application of Num. 31:25–27; the problem is dealt with by Zakovitch, *And You Shall Tell Your Son,* 112–13. It is consequently not surprising that the very thought of a human king is very controversial (see Judg. 8:22–23 and 1 Sam. 8:7).

[8] The promise has two parts: (a) Abraham and his seed, that is, Israel; and (b) all nations. It is therefore natural that this promise so well fits the purpose of Paul when he argues against Gentiles becoming Jews upon receiving the Christ (see Rom. 4 and Gal. 3). Since Christ is the fulfillment of the Torah ("the law"), now the second part of the promise has also been realized: the blessing of Abraham has come upon the Gentiles (Gal. 3:14). When Paul then states that "there is no longer Jew nor Greek" (Gal. 3:28), he does not contend that the special calling of God to the Jewish people has been canceled and that Jews should now become like Gentiles. This would be as absurd as arguing that all differences between men and women were eliminated after Christ. The point of his statement is rather that something new has been realized that so far had only been promised: now both Jews and Gentiles can be blessed. Therefore, Gentiles shall remain what they are and need not convert to Judaism (see also 1 Cor. 7:17–18). See further pp. 196–206.

[9] According to Jewish tradition, "the priests" here, as in 24:5, refer to the firstborn, who were sanctified to the Lord (13:11ff.; 23:29). The Aaronite priesthood was sanctified only later (ch. 28).

[10] The word translated "fiery law" (ʾeshdath) is problematic since it appears only here in the entire Bible. The translation is based on the assumption that it is composed of the Hebrew words ʾesh ("fire") and dath ("law"). For an extensive discussion on the Jewish interpretation of Deut. 33:2ff., see Steven D. Fraade, *From Tradition to Commentary: Torah and Its Interpretation in the Midrash Sifre to Deuteronomy* (Albany: State University of New York Press, 1991), 25–68.

[11] Philo, *On the Decalogue* 33ff., 46; cf. Philo, *On the Migration of Abraham* 47. Philo uses the Greek word *dialektos*. The targums *Pseudo-Jonathan* and *Neofiti* in a similar way understand the word of God as tongues of fire.

[12] According to this tradition, God first revealed the Torah in seventy languages, since seventy is the number of all the nations in the world (cf. Gen. 10); *b. Sanhedrin* 88b; *Exodus Rabbah* 5:9; 28:6; *Midrash on Psalms* 92:3. The number of languages is not specified in *Mekhilta Bahodesh* 9 (Lauterbach ed., 2:266ff.); *Pesiqta de-Rav Kahana* 12:25.

[13] *Mekhilta Bahodesh* 5 (Lauterbach ed., 2:234ff.); *b. Shabbath* 88a–b; *Exodus Rabbah* 5:9; 28:6; *Midrash on Psalms* 92:3; *Tanhuma Shemoth* (Buber ed.) 1:22; *Numbers Rabbah* 11:7.

[14] Both the Hebrew *lashon* and the Greek *glōssa* have the same ambiguity as the English "tongue." Thus they can stand for languages as well as "tongues" of fire.

[15] See further M. Weinfeld, "Pentecost as a Festival of the Giving of the Law," *Immanuel* 8 (1978): 7–18, and pp. 184ff. below.

[16] The Sabbath was moved to Sunday. The prohibition against making images lost its original meaning. The Greek Orthodox and Reformed Church traditions kept it as a separate commandment, but in the former, images were not only permitted but even assigned a particular religious function (icons).

[17] Catholics and Lutherans count verses 3–6 about idolatry as one commandment and the commandment concerning God's name

as number two. To obtain the number ten the last commandment about coveting (v. 17) is artificially split in two (house—wife, etc.). Since the Orthodox, Anglican (Episcopal), and Reformed traditions count the prohibition against images separately and not as a specification of verse 3, for them the commandment on God's name is number three. Verse 17 can then be kept as one commandment. The Jewish reckoning, beginning with 20:1–2, counts vv. 3–6 as one commandment as well as v. 17 (see further below). The Christian traditions want to distinguish between commandments regarding God on the one hand and commandments regarding the neighbor on the other. Therefore, they usually put "Honor your father and your mother" as the first commandment on the second tablet. Stressing the love of one's neighbor as an expression of the love of God, Jewish tradition does not make such a distinction but puts five on each tablet. For a thorough exposition of various aspects, see B. Reicke, *Die zehn Worte in Geschichte und Gegenwart, Zählung und Bedeutung der Gebote in den verschiedenen Konfessionen* (Tübingen: Mohr, 1973); and B.-Z. Segal and G. Levi, eds., *The Ten Commandments in History and Tradition* (Jerusalem: Magnes Press, 1990). In the latter volume, D. Flusser deals with the status of the commandments in the New Testament ("The Ten Commandments and the New Testament," 219–46).

[18] In numerous articles and books, the prominent New Testament scholar E. P. Sanders has aptly coined the term "covenantal nomism" to express the proper context of "the law"; see, e.g., his *Jesus and Judaism* (Philadelphia: Fortress, 1985), 335ff.; also *Paul and Palestinian Judaism* (Philadelphia: Fortress, 1977), 422ff.; and *Paul, the Law, and the Jewish People* (Philadelphia: Fortress, 1983).

[19] See Martin Luther's *Small Catechism* (1529), Third Article of the Creed.

[20] Our concept of "the law" has reached us via Greek and not directly from the Hebrew word *Torah,* which has led to a misunderstanding of the concept of *Torah* as exclusively commandments, regulations, and decrees—"law." See *Torah* in the Glossary, p. 326.

[21] Just as in Exod. 20, they are constantly referred to as the reasons behind various commandments (see, e.g., Num. 15:40–41 and further Lev. 17–26). Since these words are so central and can be assumed to be known by the readers, they are often not even fully quoted; "I am the LORD" is frequently the short form of the reference to Exod. 20:1.

[22] Philo, *On the Decalogue* 36–42.

[23] *On the Decalogue* 37. One rabbinic tradition draws a similar conclusion from the fact that only one human was created, while the other species were created in multitudes. See the quote in the comment on "You shall not kill" below.

[24] *On the Decalogue* 39.

[25] *On the Decalogue* 41.

[26] *On the Decalogue* 42.

[27] *On the Decalogue* 43.

[28] The prohibition against making an image of "anything that is in heaven above, or that is in the earth beneath, or that is in the water

under the earth" reflects the common use of images in contemporary cults. Thus the sun and most animals represented some god (see pp. 17, 36, 54f., 61, 64f., 71f.). The fish was a symbol of life and represented occasionally Osiris (Kees, *Götterglaube,* 66). Even the Philistine agricultural god Dagon (*dagan* = "grain") was depicted as a fish, perhaps inspired as a pun on the southern Canaanite word *dag* ("fish").

[29]Hypocrisy and false piety are certainly a danger in every religion. Like Jesus, the rabbis were very aware of this evil. Their warnings against, e.g., false Pharisees can compete even with the harshest words of Jesus. They are called "tainted" Pharisees, hyenas, chameleons, and even "destroyers of the world" (*m. Sota* 3:4). It is sad that our way of reading the New Testament texts have made us believe that the Pharisees were invariably hypocrites, when, as a matter of fact, the typical Pharisees strongly condemned that kind of false piety.

[30]See Luther's commentary on the Ten Commandments in the *Small Catechism.*

[31]Jewish tradition treats this verse as a positive commandment, highlighting the positive value of the work as a divine task (*Mekhilta d'Rabbi Shimᶜon Bar Yochai* on Exodus 20:9).

[32]The *Amidah (Shmoneh ᶜEsreh,* Eighteen Benedictions) for the Sabbath; Samson Raphael Hirsch, *The Hirsch Siddur: The Order of Prayer for the Whole Year* (Jerusalem: Feldheim Publishers, 1978), 272–73, 328–29, 364ff.

[33]The tractate *Shabbat* in the second order, *Moed.* Even the next tractate, *Eruvin,* deals with the Sabbath.

[34]See Sarna, *Exploring Exodus,* 147, and the extensive exploration of the matter by Hildegard Lewy and Julius Lewy, "The Origin of the Week and the Oldest West Asiatic Calendar," *HUCA* 17 (1942): 1–152, particularly 50–51 and 105ff.

[35]That is, the masters will not be served by their servants on the Sabbath as on the other days.

[36]Philo, *On the Special Laws* 2.68.

[37]*Pirqe de Rabbi Eliezer* 18.

[38]Pinchas Hacohen Peli, *Shabbat Shalom: A Renewed Encounter with the Sabbath* (Tel Aviv: World Wizo Department of Education, 1984), 17.

[39]*The Hirsch Siddur,* 706–7.

[40]Nahum N. Glatzer, ed., *Language of Faith: A Selection from the Most Expressive Jewish Prayers* (New York: Schocken Books, 1967), 260.

[41]By destroying the image of the king on the coins.

[42]*Mekhilta Bahodesh* 8 (Lauterbach ed., 2:262).

[43]*m. Sanhedrin* 4:5.

[44]According to a generally accepted tradition, there are three exceptions when one is obliged to give up one's life rather than break God's commandments: (a) if one is forced to commit murder, (b) if one is forced to abandon the God of Israel (convert to another religion); or (c) if one is forced to commit adultery. In all other cases, a Jew is obliged to avoid martyrdom, since the commandments are given in order that man "shall live" (Lev. 18:5), not die, by them.

[45] *Mekhilta d'Rabbi Shimʾon ben Yochai* to Exod. 20:14, *Yithro* 20 (Epstein ed., 154). A similar thought is expressed in James 2:10–11: "For whoever keeps the whole law but fails in one point has become guilty of all of it. For he who said, 'Do not commit adultery,' said also, 'Do not kill.' If you do not commit adultery but do kill, you have become a transgressor of the law." Flusser ("The Ten Commandments and the New Testament," 226) has noticed that it is actually said "and do not kill," which makes it probable that James follows the same Jewish tradition that gives weight to this "and." The commandment regarding adultery is mentioned first owing to the fact that James follows a textual tradition on which the Greek translation of the Septuagint is based.

[46] Deut. 6:5; Exod. 20:7,14; Deut. 5:18; Lev. 19:13, 18; Deut. 22:9, 10; 24:4; and Num. 15:39; Lev. 18:7–17, 19; *Sifre Zuta* to Num. 15:39 (Horowitz ed., 289). Some of these references may seem irrelevant unless they are understood according to a certain rabbinic method of interpretation. They give, however, a sufficient indication of the great importance attached to this commandment.

[47] *Mekhilta Bahodesh* 8 (Lauterbach ed., 2:262–63).

[48] Num. 15:37–41 is recited immediately after the *Shemaᶜ* text (Deut. 6:4–9) and is considered part of the creed, the acceptance of the "yoke of heaven," or, in other words, the renewal of the marriage promises.

[49] On the covenant as marriage, see also Levenson, *Sinai and Zion*, 75–86.

[50] *Mekhilta Bahodesh* 8 (Lauterbach ed., 2:263).

[51] *Mekhilta Bahodesh* 8 (Lauterbach ed., 2:262–63).

[52] *Midrash* on Psalms 101:7.

[53] *Numbers Rabbah* 19:2; cf. Prov. 6:19.

[54] *b. Pesahim* 113b.

[55] *Deuteronomy Rabbah* 6:8ff.; *b. Arakhin* 15b.

[56] On these so-called antitheses in the Sermon of the Mount, see pp. 162–69, 175ff. below.

CHAPTER 10 (pages 156–183)

[1] In addition to the laws and applications spread throughout Exodus–Deuteronomy and in other parts of the Bible, there are two major collections of laws similar to the one with which we are now dealing: Lev. 17–26 ("the law of holiness") and Deut. 12–28.

[2] Childs (*Exodus*, 462–63) presents a survey of the parallels to "the book of the covenant" in the laws of Hammurabi and Sumerian, Hittite, and Assyrian legislation. For an extensive evaluation of similarities and differences, see Sarna (*Exploring Exodus*, 158–89), with further references.

[3] Sarna, *Exploring Exodus*, 180ff.; see also 21:20–21, 26–27.

[4] *b. Qiddushin* 17a–b provides detailed rules regarding how a slave should be outfitted when freed.

[5] The Hebrew word for "servant" and "slave" is the same (see pp. 14f., 77, 127).

[6] *t. Bava Qamma* 7:5; similarly, *b. Qiddushin* 22b and *y. Qiddushin* 1:2 (59d). The tradition is ascribed to Yohanan ben Zakkai who lived at the time of the destruction of Jerusalem in the year 70 C.E.

[7] *b. Qiddushin* 22a.

[8] Sarna, *Exploring Exodus,* 181.

[9] *m. Sanhedrin* 4:1; 5:2–5.

[10] *m. Makkoth* 1:10.

[11] Sarna, *Exodus;* Cassuto, *Exodus;* and others. Childs *(Exodus),* referring to the following verse, considers it more probable that the life of a slave was worth less and that the punishment could therefore be milder than the basic rule in 21:12.

[12] For a survey of these laws, see *ANET,* 175; and Cassuto, *Exodus.*

[13] *ANET,* 175.

[14] That is, to the owner of the slave. As contrasted with biblical law, the slave has no value of his own (cf. above).

[15] *ANET,* 175; cf. Cassuto, *Exodus;* Sarna, *Exodus.*

[16] Sarna, *Exploring Exodus,* 182ff. and n. 77.

[17] *ANET,* 176. Again we notice that the slave has no human value of his own (see above).

[18] Again, mutilation is a common punishment in ancient Near Eastern law, such as castration for sexual violations and cutting off various body parts for medical maltreatment and other offenses (see *ANET,* 175–76; and Sarna, *Exploring Exodus,* 177).

[19] Sarna, *Exploring Exodus,* 197. It is worth noting that rabbinic law even in this case levies fines instead of imposing mutilation (*b. Bava Qamma* 25a).

[20] In Deut. 19:21, where it is a matter of punishing a false witness, and where therefore compensation cannot come into question, the preposition *be-* is used. This may indicate that the preposition *tahath* in other cases is used precisely because it is ambiguous, thus enabling the principle of compensation.

[21] The reason for mentioning the slave's compensation in particular is, of course, to cover all cases; if even a slave is to be compensated, it goes without saying that free people also are entitled to the same. Later, this was to become the first of the seven exegetical principles of Hillel the Elder, called *qal va-homer,* literally "light and heavy," that is, an inference which permits deductions from a minor to a major case.

[22] *b. Sanhedrin* 79a–b.

[23] *Mekhilta Mishpatim* 8–9 (Lauterbach ed., 3:67, 85–88); *m. Bava Qamma* 2:6; 8:1–2; and *b. Bava Qamma* 83b–84a. According to Josephus, *Jewish Antiquities* 4.280, the victim could choose between retaliation and damages. Rabbinic tradition, however, opposes such a choice (*b. Bava Qamma* 83b).

[24] In *b. Qiddushin* 25a, 24 different parts are listed. For the discussion on damages in general and the principles for compensation, see the previous note.

[25] *b. Qiddushin* 84a. In this talmudic section, the rabbis (amoraim, fourth century C.E.) discuss the view of Rabbi Eliezer. It is interesting to note how difficult it is for them to believe that Rabbi Eliezer really could have advocated a literal implementation

of the commandment. Therefore, they try to explain away his words. The whole discussion demonstrates in the clearest way possible how unthinkable a law of retaliation was to the rabbinical mind. Philo seems to favor retaliation in *On the Special Laws* 3.181ff. Since his main interest, however, is the allegorical meaning of the law (see particularly 3.184), no definite conclusions can be drawn from his exposition.

[26] The most influential Babylonian sage in his day (ca. 335–428 C.E.).

[27] *Maimonides' Introduction to His Commentary on the Mishnah* (trans. and ed. F. Rosner; Northvale, N.J.: Aronson, 1995), 39. See also *b. Sota* 9b; *b. Sanhedrin* 100a.

[28] The second half of this verse is without doubt among the most well-known in the whole Bible. It is tragic, however, that fifty percent of the verse is not only often overlooked but that its very opposite—themes of vengeance—have become among the most well-known negative stereotypes against Judaism! The beginning of Lev. 19:18 is dealt with as an important part of the commandment of love in the rabbinic literature. The following comment is typical:

> What is "revenge" and what is "bearing a grudge"? If one said to his fellow, "Lend me your sickle," and he replied "No," and on the morrow the second comes [to the first] and says, "Lend me your axe," and he replies, "I will not lend it to you, just as you would not lend me your sickle," that is revenge. And what is bearing grudge? If one says to his fellow, "Lend me your axe," he replies "No," and on the morrow the second asks, "Lend me your garment," and he answers, "Here it is. I am not like you who would not lend me [what I asked for], that is bearing grudge" (*b. Yoma* 23a).

[29] Pinchas Lapide, *The Sermon on the Mount: Utopia or Program for Action?* (Maryknoll, New York: Orbis Books, 1986), 14.

[30] See pp. 154f. (cf. pp. 190ff.).

[31] The usual Greek word for "but" is the adversative *alla*. The two sentences are, however, united by the particles *men . . . de*, which unite sentences standing in an adversative or parallel relationship. The translation "but" is, therefore, not necessarily wrong. Since, however, the quote and its interpretation express an intensification and not a contrast, the harmony between Scripture and exposition should be expressed in the translation. Therefore we prefer to say, "You have heard that it was said . . . , and I even say to you . . ." This translation also does justice to the most probable Hebrew expression behind it: *va'ani 'omer lakhem*. See also Lapide, *The Sermon on the Mount*, 43–44.

[32] See pp. 154f. on the conclusion of the tablets of the covenant.

[33] See, e.g., *b. Yoma* 23a: "He who passes over his retaliation has all his transgressions passed over."

[34] The term is chosen by Lapide, *The Sermon on the Mount*, 45–46. Jesper Svartvik (p. 274, n. 18) suggests the term "hypertheses."

[35] *ANET*, 175; Cassuto, *Exodus*; Childs, *Exodus*; Sarna, *Exploring Exodus*, 176ff.

[36] See Cassuto, *Exodus*; Childs, *Exodus*; Sarna, *Exodus*.

[37] The principle is derived from 22:2–3, which indicates that it is legitimate to kill somebody who is prepared to commit murder *(b. Berakhoth* 58a; 62b; *b. Sanhedrin* 72a; see Sarna, *Exodus).*

[38] "Seduce" means that the woman consents. Regarding rape, see Deut. 22:25ff.

[39] If anyone had sexual intercourse with a betrothed or married woman, the stricter laws in Deut. 22:22ff. applied. Otherwise, the considerably milder law in Exod. 22:16–17 applied. The betrothal (Hebrew *qiddushin* or *ʾerusin*) signified that the couple in reality were regarded as married. They remained, however, with their parents till the wedding (Hebrew *nissuʾin*), usually about a year later. Only then did their married life together begin. According to the Gospel of Matthew, Joseph and Mary were seemingly in this interim period when Mary became pregnant (Matt. 1:18). When Joseph discreetly tried to divorce Mary, he consequently did so out of concern to spare her (Matt. 1:19).

[40] The custom of paying a marriage gift is well-known all over the ancient Near East. Even though it was paid to the father of the bride, it was regarded as the property of the bride. The lament of Leah and Rachel in Gen. 31:15 is thus justified (see Sarna, *Exodus).*

[41] Cf. Lev. 21:10–15; Deut. 22:13–21.

[42] Cassuto, *Exodus;* Sarna, *Exodus.*

[43] Sarna, *Exodus,* refers to *Targum Jonathan,* which probably expresses a very ancient tradition.

[44] The decision was officially made at the Third Lateran Council in 1179.

[45] See *m. Bava Metsia* 5:6 and the discussions in *b. Bava Metsia* 61b, 70b–71a. It is obvious here that a Jew should avoid lending money against interest even to non-Jews. If they do so, however, they are only allowed to take interest sufficient for "the necessities of life." In the medieval Talmud commentary *Tosafot to b. Bava Metsia* 70b, the commentator explains why it is so common that Jews are involved with this contemptuous occupation: "It is because the king and the ministers lay burdens upon us. What we take is only what we need for our living." And further: "As long as we live among the nations, we cannot earn our living in another way . . . therefore, it is permitted." This explanation reflects the restrictions imposed upon Jews and the methods of discrimination that often forced them into these activities.

[46] *Exodus Rabbah* 31:15.

[47] As is obvious from Deut. 26, these sacrifices could later only be offered in the temple. After the destruction of the temple in the year 70 C.E., this commandment could therefore no longer be performed. The ordinances regarding the firstling are treated in the mishnaic tractate *Bikkurim,* which belongs to the first order, *Zeraim.* This first section of the Mishnah focuses on laws that, above all, are related to the land and its yield. According to Jewish tradition, however, the law about firstfruits applies only to the seven fruits mentioned in Deut. 8:8.

[48] Exactly how an animal is to be slaughtered is not revealed in the Bible itself. From Deut. 12:21 it is clear, however, that there is such a commandment, though only orally transmitted. The Hebrew

word for the procedure is *shehitah;* it is dealt with in the mishnaic tractate *Hullin,* which belongs to the fifth order, *Qodashim.*

[49] See the rabbinic discussion on Prov. 17:13 in *Genesis Rabbah* 38:3.

[50] *t. Bava Metsia* 2:26; *b. Bava Metsia* 32b.

[51] *m. Pirqe Avot (Sayings of the Fathers)* 4:1, referring to Prov. 16:32; and *Avot of Rabbi Nathan* 23, referring to Prov. 21:22.

[52] The commandment Jesus previously quotes, "You shall love your neighbor and hate your enemy," does not appear in the Bible. Therefore Jesus probably refers to a principle which was accepted in certain circles. A saying in the Qumran literature may reflect this principle: "Love all the children of light and hate all the children of darkness" (*The Rule of the Community* [1QS] 1:9). The word "neighbor" often, but not always, stands for a friend. A narrow understanding of this word combined with the expression "as yourself" in the commandment of love (Lev. 19:18) could lead to the false conclusion that we only need to love our friends and that we are entitled to treat others as they treat us. Such an understanding would come very close to Jesus' words above and to a literal explanation of "eye for eye, tooth for tooth." However, such an understanding was not accepted in mainstream Judaism.

[53] A whole tractate in the Mishnah is dedicated to the sabbatical year—*Sheviit.* It is found in the first order, as is also the tractate dealing with the application of the commandment regarding the "very border" of the field—*Peah.*

[54] Josephus, *Jewish Antiquities* 11.338 and 14.202.

[55] References to these difficulties are found, for example, in *m. Sanhedrin* 3:3 and *b. Sanhedrin* 26a.

[56] For an extensive investigation of the development of the pilgrimage feasts, see M. Haran, *Temples and Temple-Service in Ancient Israel* (Oxford: Clarendon Press, 1978; repr. Winona Lake, Ind.: Eisenbrauns, 1985), 289–316.

[57] The tablet from Ugarit (Ras Shamra) in today's Syria, the fourth section of CTA 23, which at one time was commonly referred to as archaeological evidence that the Canaanite cult included sacrifices of kids boiled in milk, is, however, ambiguous (see M. Haran, "Seething a Kid in Its Mother's Milk," *JJS* 30 [1979]: 23–35; and J. Milgrom, "An Archaeological Myth Destroyed, 'You Shall Not Boil a Kid in Its Mother's Milk,' " *BR* 1 [1985]: 48–55; also Childs, *Exodus,* 485–86).

[58] Ibn Ezra and Rashbam make this connection; cf. Haran, *Temples and Temple-Service,* 29–30; Sarna, *Exodus.*

[59] *On the Virtues* 143.

[60] Milgrom, *Numbers,* 54–55. See further Jacob Milgrom, "The Biblical Dietary Laws as an Ethical System," in his *Studies in Cultic Theology and Terminology* (Leiden: Brill, 1983), 104–18.

[61] For various interpretations of the threefold reiteration of the commandment, see *Mekhilta Kaspa* 5 (Lauterbach ed., 3:187–96); and *b. Hullin* 115a–116a. This strict separation of meat and diary products probably existed at a very early stage and only afterward found its scriptural motivation in the recurrence of the commandment three times.

⁶²This is called the "sea of the Philistines," because the Philistines possessed the area along the coast, with the cities of Gaza, Ashkelon, and Ashdod (plus Ekron and Gath further inland) as their main centers.

⁶³Sarna, *Exodus,* referring to J. M. Weinstein, "The Egyptian Empire in Palestine: A Reassessment," *BASOR* 241 (1981): 1–28.

⁶⁴This section, consequently, cannot be used to exonerate similar actions in later times, e.g., in today's Middle East conflict. There it is Israel's security, and not the danger of idolatry, which is the decisive question. In that context only the principle of killing in self-defense applies.

CHAPTER 11 (pages 184–206)

¹*Pesahim* and *Sukkah* in the second order, *Seder Moed,* which deals with the sacredness of time.

²The following largely builds on M. Weinfeld, "Pentecost as a Festival of the Giving of the Law," *Immanuel* 8 (1978): 7–18, with further references.

³Ibid., 11, n. 17. Another double aspect of the feast, also mentioned in the book of *Jubilees,* is the promise (or "oath") of the Lord to the fathers, and the promise of Israel to the Lord in connection with entering into the covenant. The translations that follow are from O. S. Wintermute, "*Jubilees* (Second Century B.C.E.): A New Translation and Introduction," in *The Old Testament Pseudepigrapha* (ed. James H. Charlesworth; 2 vols.; Garden City, New York: Doubleday, 1985), 2:67.

⁴Wintermute renders the word "Shebuot" in an effort to retain the ambiguity of "oaths" and "weeks"; the latter word appears as *shevuᶜoth* in the construct state.

⁵*The Rule of the Community* (1QS) 1:16–2:18 describes the reception of new members, which implies the sealing of a covenant, and 2:19–24 prescribes a yearly renewal of this covenant. According to J. Milik (*Ten Years of Discovery in the Wilderness of Judea* [London: SCM Press, 1959], 116–17), this renewal took place during Pentecost; see also Weinfeld, "Pentecost as a Festival of the Giving of the Law," 12.

⁶See further Weinfeld, "Pentecost as a Festival of the Giving of the Law," 9–10 and Levenson, *Sinai and Zion,* 80, 206–7 with further references.

⁷Weinfeld, "Pentecost as a Festival of the Giving of the Law," 12. Josephus has left the name untranslated in *Jewish Antiquities* 3.252, which demonstrates how common it was in this time. In the Bible it designates the last day of Passover (Deut. 16:8) and of the Feast of Tabernacles (Lev. 23:36; Num. 29:35; Neh. 8:18). It is therefore probable that the name was originally used for Pentecost as the conclusion and culmination of Passover, i.e., *ᶜatsereth shel pesah* (cf. p. 127). When the name *ᶜatsereth* is later used solely for Pentecost, it most likely refers to a solemn assembly in general, as in 2 Kgs. 10:20; 2 Chron. 7:9; Isa. 1:13; Joel 1:14; 2:15.

[8] Josephus's description of the huge crowds gathered in Jerusalem at Pentecost from various provinces in the Diaspora strongly reminds us of Acts 2 (*Jewish Antiquities* 14.337; 17.254; *Jewish War* 1.253; 2.43).

[9] Rashi on Exod. 19:1.

[10] From the Hebrew verb *halak* ("to walk") in a form (Hiphil) which expresses a causative sense: to make someone else walk, i.e., "lead," "guide"; cf. the expression "the Way" in the New Testament for the Christian movement (Acts 19:9, 23; 22:4; 24:14, 22).

[11] *m. Pirqe Avot (Sayings of the Fathers)* 1:3.

[12] The only sin offerings for intentional sins were brought on the Day of Atonement. In order for the rite to be efficacious, however, the sinners first had to repent and become reconciled with their neighbors.

[13] In Matt. 26:28 the words "for the forgiveness of sins" are added. They probably allude to Jer. 31:34: "for I will forgive their iniquity, and I will remember their sin no more." As we know, this chapter deals with the new covenant. Luke 22:20 and 1 Cor. 11:25 mention the "new" covenant in connection with the wine. For the significance of the blood, see pp. 42f., 82f.

[14] "Eyn Unterrichtung wie sich die Christen ynn Mosen sollen schicken," which is part of a series of sermons on the book of Exodus, given in 1524–27 (Weimarausgabe 16, 363–93; English translation: *Luther's Works* (ed. E. T. Bachmann, H. T. Lehmann; 55 vols.; Philadelphia: Fortress, 1960), 35:157–74. The quotes are taken from this edition.

[15] Ibid., 165.

[16] Ibid., 170.

[17] Ibid., 164.

[18] *Von den Juden und ihren Lügen.*

[19] The translation "apart from law" instead of "apart from the law" in the NRSV is unfortunate, since it blurs the fact that it is the Torah, and not just any collection of commandments, that is referred to.

[20] M. Barth, *Ephesians: Introduction, Translation, and Commentary on Chapters 1–3* (AB 34; Garden City, N.Y.: Doubleday, 1974), 244–48; L. Gaston, *Paul and the Torah* (Vancouver: University of British Colombia Press, 1987), 24ff.

[21] Cf. pp. 136f., n. 8.

[22] Translation according to the RSV.

[23] We will not deal with the difficult question regarding the situation of the Jews outside of Christ. We will just refer to Paul's twofold statement in Rom. 11:28–29: "As regards the gospel they are enemies for your sake; but as regards election they are beloved for the sake of the fathers. For the gifts and the call of God are irrevocable." The addition "enemies of God" in many translations does not appear in the Greek text and should be omitted. What exactly this statement means remains a mystery. Every theological statement that removes this mystery is unacceptable. In the light of history, I claim, however, that we as Gentile Christians should rather stress the second part of Paul's statement, both in order to avoid the boasting against which Paul warns (Rom. 11:18), and in order to apply the

word properly, i.e., to ourselves. And whenever we mention the first part, we must consider the enigmatic motivation, "for your sake," which includes what has happened under God's merciful plan. Finally, let us not forget that Paul, when he has dealt with this deep mystery, immediately bursts out in a joyful song of praise (Rom. 11:33ff.). This bright final chord is probably the best hint as to how the previous statement shall be understood.

[24] Luther, "Eyn Unterrichtung," 166.

[25] Ibid., 168. To equate the "ten commandments" and other laws with a "natural law" is not unproblematic. It is true that some of the commandments happen to coincide with what most human beings would regard as rules for decent human behavior. But first, not even all the ten commandment fall within this category (particularly not the first three), and second, such an approach forgets the prefix of all commandments, i.e., the first word, which inserts them in the frame of a covenantal relationship between God and a particular people now saved (pp. 127ff., 138ff.). Again, it must be stressed that the laws of Moses do not distinguish between ethical, "natural" laws and the more "ritual" ordinances. All are proclaimed as the condition for the relationship between God and his people. "What the Decalogue therefore represents in the building of God's pact-bound people is its cornerstone rather than its capstone," as pertinently expressed by Goldberg, *Jews and Christians Getting Our Stories Straight,* 124.

[26] Luther, "Eyn Unterrichtung," 172–73.

[27] Ibid., 168–69.

[28] Ibid., 173.

[29] Ibid., 173.

CHAPTER 12 (pages 207–244)

[1] Only the order of the objects is different (see p. 265).

[2] See further M. Haran, "The Priestly Image of the Tabernacle," *HUCA* 36 (1965): 191–226, esp. 202–3.

[3] Cf. Deut. 3:11; the end of the verse should be translated literally "according to the cubit of a man."

[4] According to rabbinic tradition (*b. Yoma* 72b), the overlay was solid to the extent of forming a golden box, which was put into the wooden box. This was then put into a larger golden box. This technique is known, for example, from the coffin of Tutankhamun in Egypt.

[5] In 25:17 it is added to the word *epithema,* "cover," as an attributive adjective; thus, a "propitiatory cover."

[6] In a similar way the targum translates the word *devir,* another name for the holy of holies, as *beth kappore* in 1 Kgs. 6:5, 19–20.

[7] Sarna, *Understanding Exodus,* 21ff. For an extensive and richly illustrated description, see O. Keel, *Jahwe-Visionen und Siegelkunst* (SBS 84/85; Stuttgart: Verlag Katholisches Bibelwerk, 1977); and M. Metzger, *Königsthron und Gottesthron: Thronformen und Throndarstellungen in Ägypten und im Vorderen Orient* (AOAT 15/1–2; Neukirchen-Vluyn: Neukirchener, 1985).

[8] Josephus calls them "winged creatures . . . in form unlike to any that man's eyes have seen" (*Jewish Antiquities* 3.137; cf. 8.73). Nonetheless, pious fantasy has tried to depict them. The classical icons try to do justice to the biblical description. Only in the Renaissance did the pink-cheeked and chubby cherubim appear. However, it is not improbable that this figure is originally based on a talmudic tradition, according to which the word "cherub" is linked to the Aramaic word for "child," *rabya*ʾ; thus, according to popular etymology the word "cherub" is read as *ke-rabya*ʾ = "like a child" (*b. Hagigah* 13b; *b. Sukkah* 5b). The real etymology of the word is uncertain. The corresponding word in Akkadian, *kāribu*, is to be linked to the verb *karābu*, which means among other things "pray" and "bless."

[9] For the footstool as a symbol of power at the royal court, see Sarna, *Exploring Exodus*, 210–11. An extensive presentation of the cherubim and their function is given by Metzger, *Königsthron und Gottesthron*, 91ff., and T. N. D. Mettinger, *The Dethronement of Sabaoth: Studies in the Shem and Kabod Theologies* (Coniectanea Biblica, OT Series 18; Lund: Gleerup, 1982), 19ff.; 87ff., with further references.

[10] Mettinger, *Dethronement of Sabaoth*.

[11] For the same reason, the cupboard in which the Torah scrolls would later be kept in the synagogue is called ʾ*aron ha-qodesh*, "the ark of holiness."

[12] Sarna, *Exploring Exodus*, 209, with further references. See also 134–39 for his extensive investigation of covenants and treatises in the ancient Near East.

[13] See further M. Haran, "The Disappearance of the Ark," *IEJ* 13 (1963): 46–58. For a survey of the various ancient sources, see G. Larsson, *Jom ha-kippurim* (ed. G. Mayer; Rabbinische Texte, Die Tosefta, Übersetzung und Erklärung, 2; Stuttgart: Kohlhammer, 1997), 222–23. This tradition has sparked several efforts to discover the ark. It also inspired the film, "Raiders of the Lost Ark."

[14] *m. Menahoth* 11; *b. Menahoth* 94a–b; 96a–97a; see also Josephus, *Jewish Antiquities* 3.139–43, 255–56.

[15] This arrangement of the bread in two stacks is confirmed by archaeological discoveries. On a sarcophagus from Byblos (ca. 10th century B.C.E.), a table can be seen with u-formed bread. See further L. Yarden, *The Spoils of Jerusalem and the Arch of Titus, a Reinvestigation* (Skrifter utgivna av Svenska Institutet i Rom 8.16; Stockholm: Svenska Institutet i Rom, 1991), 96–97, fig. 53–55.

[16] *b. Menahoth* 97a.

[17] See the richly illustrated descriptions in Yarden, *Spoils of Jerusalem*, 38–70; E. R. Goodenough, *Jewish Symbols in the Greco-Roman Period* (New York: Pantheon Books, 1954), 4:72–77, and L. Yarden, *The Tree of Light: A Study of the Menorah, the Seven-branched Lampstand* (Ithaca, New York: Cornell University Press, 1971). A copy of an ancient Jewish coin appears on a modern Israeli coin (10 agoroth). For an extensive presentation of the menorah in the pious Jewish tradition, see F. Gottlieb, *The Lamp of God: A Jewish Book of Light* (Northvale, N.J.: Aronson, 1989). Models of the menorah are as rare as depictions of it are common. Out of reverence for the objects of the temple, objects similar to these could not be manufactured (*b. Rosh*

Hashanah 24a–b; *b. Avodah Zarah* 43a; *b. Menahoth* 28b). While seven-branched candleticks are common in churches, in the synagogue the candlesticks usually have more or fewer than seven branches. See also pp. 236f. regarding the oil and the incense.

[18] The Star of David *(Magen David)* became a specifically Jewish symbol only in the Middle Ages and has no biblical background. See G. Scholem, "The Star of David: History of a Symbol," in *The Messianic Idea in Judaism* (New York: Schocken Books, 1971), 257–81.

[19] *b. Menahoth* 28b.

[20] At the Diaspora Museum, *Beth Hatefutsoth,* in Tel Aviv, the history of the Jews is framed by two seven-branched candlesticks, one at the entrance and one at the exit. In fact, it is one and the same menorah: the one on the Arch of Titus in Rome, carried away from Jerusalem, and the one that is Israel's state emblem, restored in connection with the creation of the modern state. Fall and restoration, dispersion and regathering, exile and homecoming—these focal points in the history of the Jewish people become marvelously alive and are beautifully summed up in these two depictions of the menorah.

[21] See Goodenough, *Jewish Symbols;* and Yarden, *Tree of Light.*

[22] Sarna, *Exodus.*

[23] Nogah Hareuveni, *Ecology in the Bible* (Kiryat Ono, Israel: Neot Kedumim, 1974), 41ff., 48–49 (with illustrations).

[24] Goodenough, *Jewish Symbols,* 72ff.; C. L. Meyers, *The Tabernacle Menorah: A Synthetic Study of a Symbol from the Biblical Cult* (ASOR Dissertation series 2; Missoula, Mont.: Scholars Press, 1976), 95–131; Yarden, *Tree of Light,* 35ff. The role of the motif in Mesopotamia is thoroughly dealt with by G. Widengren, *The King and the Tree of Life in Ancient Near Eastern Religion* (Uppsala Universitets Årsskrift 1951/4; Uppsala: Lundequistska Bokhandeln, 1951), esp. 63ff.

[25] Sarna, *Exodus.*

[26] These measures are not explicitly mentioned but can be deduced from the measures of the wooden frames below (Exod. 26:15ff.). Ten cubits in length, they were consequently the height of the tabernacle, and 1.5 cubits broad, thus requiring twenty to make up the structure's length. The breadth, finally, was made up of the six frames at the rear plus the two at the corners, parts of which were hidden by the thickness of the wall. The length and breadth of Solomon's temple were twice as large, and the height was three times as large (1 Kgs. 6:2).

[27] For an extensive description of the tabernacle in general and of this complicated construction in particular, see A. R. S. Kennedy, "Tabernacle," in *Hasting's Dictionary of the Bible* (5 vols.; Edinburgh: Clark, 1898–1904), 4:653–68.

[28] An impressive effort at reconstructing the tabernacle and its utensils has been made by Moshe Levine in Israel. Since the biblical description is incomplete and presupposes a heavenly vision of "the pattern of the tabernacle and of all its furniture" (25:9; cf. 25:40; Num. 8:4; Heb. 8:5; 9:23), any reconstruction will necessarily be partly speculative. Yet, Levine's model helps us to visualize many obscure details in the text. It is published in a magnificent book, *The Tabernacle, Its Structure and Utensils* (Tel Aviv: Soncino, 1969).

[29] Josephus, *Jewish War* 5.225; according to rabbinic sources, the dimensions are smaller (*m. Middoth* 3:1).

[30] Sarna, *Exodus*, referring to Y. Aharoni, "Arad: Its Inscriptions and Temple," *BA* 31 (1968): 19, 25.

[31] *m. Middoth* 3:1; *b. Zebahim* 53a.

[32] Sarna, *Exodus*, 173–74.

[33] See further the extensive monograph by C. Van Dam, *The Urim and the Thummim: A Means of Revelation in Ancient Israel* (Winona Lake, Ind.: Eisenbrauns, 1997), 56ff., 140.

[34] *Jewish Antiquities* 3.162; *Jewish War* 5.233. Josephus deals with the garments of the high priest in *Jewish Antiquities* 3.159–178 and *Jewish War* 5.231–237, and of the ordinary priests (see 28:39–40 below) in *Jewish Antiquities* 3.151–158. A description is also presented in Sirach 45 and the *Letter of Aristeas* 96–99 (both from the second century B.C.E.).

[35] Alternative orders are discussed in *b. Sota* 36a–b.

[36] See Van Dam, *Urim and the Thummim*, 153.

[37] For a survey of the translation of the stones in the Septuagint, the targums and Midrash Rabbah, see "Precious Stones and Jewelry," in *EncJud* 13:1007–13 with further references. Cf. also Josephus's listing in *Jewish Antiquities* 3.168 and *Jewish War* 5.233–234.

[38] Obviously "Urim" provides a negative answer in the Septuagint's version of 1 Sam. 14:41: "If this guilt is in me or in my son Jonathan, O LORD God of Israel, give Urim; but if this guilt is in your people Israel, give Thummim" (see the whole context, where it is the destiny of Jonathan that is at stake); Levine, *Leviticus*, 51; Plaut, *Torah: A Modern Commentary*, 623, n. 4.

[39] Milgrom, *Numbers*, 486; B. Johnson, "Urim und Tummim als Alphabet," *ASTI* 9 (1973): 23–29; Van Dam, *Urim and Thummim*, 15, 20, 31, 190ff. The thesis finds support in rabbinic tradition (see *b. Yoma* 73b).

[40] According to Josephus (*Jewish Antiquities* 3.218), the usage was abandoned two hundred years earlier. He probably refers to the period of John Hyrcanus (135–104 B.C.E.; cf. *Jewish War* 1.69). For rabbinic references, see *m. Sota* 9:12; *b. Sota* 48b; *b. Yoma* 21b. The whole problem is thoroughly investigated by Van Dam, *Urim and Thummim*, 232–55.

[41] P. Friedländer, "Über den Farbstoff des antiken Purpurs aus Murex Brandaris," *Berichte der deutschen chemischen Gesellschaft* 42 (1909): 765–70; Milgrom, *Numbers*, 412; see also n. 43.

[42] *Jewish Antiquities* 3.172; *Jewish War* 5.235; so also *Letter of Aristeas* 98. In *Jewish Antiquities* 20.67, Josephus uses the same word, *tiara*, for a royal crown.

[43] It is also used for ornamentations in the temple (1 Kgs. 6:18, 29, 32, 35). The word used for the "fringes" in Num 15:37–41 (*tsitsith*) comes from the same Hebrew root. The reason this word is used may be the fact that the fringes are regarded as a sign of the covenant, i.e., of the membership in the "priestly kingdom" (Exod. 19:6). As has been pointed out above, the cord of blue—the royal and priestly color—may symbolize a democratization of the royal and priestly dignity to embrace all the people. Another fact points in the

same direction. According to Jewish tradition, the fringes were made from linen, with the exception of the blue cord, which was made from wool (*b. Menahoth* 39b–40a, 43a; see further Milgrom, *Numbers,* 413). This is remarkable, since a woven mixture of linen and wool was otherwise reserved for the priests (see pp. 224f.). It is thus not surprising that the word chosen for these fringes displays a linguistic connection with a word associated with both royal and priestly dignity. The word *tsitsith* may also refer to the form of the fringe as similar to a lock of hair (*tsitsith;* Ezek. 8:3) or to the function of the fringes to be a reminder of God's commandments ("to look upon and remember all the commandments of the LORD"; Num. 15:39). The verb *tsits* means "to blossom" and "to shine"; in Hiphil, "to gaze" and "to look."

[44] *Jewish Antiquities* 3.172 (see also the detailed description in 3.173–178); *Jewish War* 5.235. Even Sirach 45:12 speaks about a crown.

[45] *b. Shabbath* 63b.

[46] *Letter of Aristeas* 99.

[47] *Jewish Antiquities* 3.157–158.

[48] *Jewish Antiquities* 3.154–155.

[49] The comment in Ezek. 44:17, according to which the priests "shall have nothing of wool on them," does not necessarily reflect another view, since the reasoning for this rule is that they shall not wear anything that "causes sweat" (Ezek. 44:18), and the mixture of wool and linen in the sash would hardly have any effect in this respect.

[50] This did not preclude that the workmanship was more costly than that for the ordinary priests; see *m. Yoma* 3:7 and my commentary (n. 13) on *Tosefta Yom Hakippurim* 1:21, 170–71.

[51] In the rabbinic literature, the priests are often called "brethren" (*ʾahim kohanim).*

[52] There is no *sh* sound in Greek. Therefore *sh* is always rendered as *s*. See p. 284, n. 19.

[53] Cf. Isa. 61:1–2; Matt. 11:9; 21:11, 26, 46; Mark 6:15; 11:32; Luke 4:18–19; 7:16, 26; 24:19; John 1:21ff.; 6:14; 7:40; 9:17; Acts 3:20ff. The multiplication of the bread as a renewed manna miracle indirectly depicts Jesus as the new Moses (Matt. 15:32ff.; Mark 6:35ff.; 8:1ff.; John 6:14, 30ff.).

[54] Cf. *The Rule of the Community* (1QS) 2:11–22; *Damascus Document* (CD) 8:20–21; 12:22–23; 13:20ff.; 14:18–19; *Testament of the Twelve Patriarchs: T. Reuben* 6:10ff.; *T. Simeon* 7:1–2; *T. Levi* 18:2–3; *T. Judah* 21:2ff.

[55] For an extensive analysis of the function of the sin offerings, see J. Milgrom, *Studies in Cultic Theology and Terminology* (Leiden: Brill, 1983), 67–84.

[56] In Hebrew this offering is called *shelamim,* which is etymologically linked to the word *shalom,* which explains why it is usually rendered as "peace offering." What lies behind the use of the word *shelamim* in this context remains unclear (see the discussion in Levine, *Leviticus,* 14–15).

[57] *On the Life of Moses* 2.150.

[58] For a thorough investigation of the so-called wave offerings, see Milgrom, *Numbers*, 132–58.

[59] Here also the right thigh is mentioned as given to the priest (Lev. 7:32). However, this is not elevated but is simply called an "offering," or rather a "gift" *(terumah)*. The same word is used for this piece even in 29:27. The thigh was regarded as payment to the sacrificing priest, while the breast was consecrated to the Lord, later to be shared among all the priests present. Both the *tenufah* and the *terumah* designate something set apart for a sacred purpose. In both cases it is transferred from the owner to the Lord. The former word refers to a sacred act in the sanctuary ("before the LORD"), while the latter word refers to an act that can take place anywhere and that merely implies an oral declaration followed by the handing over of what has been set apart for the Lord. Consequently, this means that every *tenufah* has been preceded by a *terumah*. On the other hand, not every *terumah* has to lead to a *tenufah*. See, for example, the material given for the construction of the sanctuary in 25:2 or the half shekel in 30:13ff. See further Milgrom, *Numbers*, 426–27; and Milgrom, *Studies in Cultic Theology*, 159–70.

[60] This is the translation chosen by Milgrom, *Studies in Cultic Theology*, 70–84, to whom I am indebted for the comments below.

[61] This offering was called *minhah*. The word is still used for the afternoon service in the synagogue, which is regarded as a reminder of the *tamid* offering in the temple.

[62] These reasons are succinctly indicated by Sarna *(Exodus)*, whom I largely follow.

[63] Therefore, only priests who had never before performed this duty had access when it was allotted. This made it more likely that every priest would be given the privilege to perform at least once in their lifetime (*m. Tamid* 5:2; *m. Yoma* 2:4; cf. Luke 1:8ff.).

[64] C. Meyers, "Realms of Sanctity: The Case of the 'Misplaced' Incense Altar in the Tabernacle Texts of Exodus," in *Texts, Temples, and Traditions: A Tribute to Menahem Haran*, ed. M. V. Fox ct al. (Winona Lake, Ind.: Eisenbrauns, 1996), 33–46.

[65] Cf. J. Milgrom, *Studies in Levitical Terminology* (Berkeley: University of California Press, 1970), 30–31. For the religious and cultural background, see Cassuto, *Exodus*.

[66] The king was, however, marked with a "crown," probably a circle around the head (*b. Kerithoth* 5a–6b).

[67] Rashi (*Sonciono Humash*, 543).

[68] For an extensive investigation of the ingredients, see Y. Feliks, "The Incense of the Tabernacle," in *Pomegranates and Golden Bells: Studies in Biblical, Jewish, and Near Eastern Ritual, Law, and Literature in Honor of Jacob Milgrom*, ed. D. P. Wright, D. N. Freedman, and A. Hurvitz (Winona Lake, Ind.: Eisenbrauns, 1995), 125–49.

[69] *t. Yom Hakippurim* 2:5–7; *b. Yoma* 38a.

[70] See further *m. Kerithoth* 1:1; *b. Kerithoth* 5a–7a.

[71] *b. Moed Katan* 28a. This punishment (Hebrew *kareth*) is meted out for sins which do not directly affect the fellow human beings (cf. 12:15, 19 and 31:14). See further Milgrom, *Numbers*, 405–8. These sins are regarded as being of such a serious nature that they

defile the whole land (cf. Lev. 18:24–30). The mishnaic tractate *Kerithoth* specifies thirty-six such sins (see especially chs. 1 and 5).

[72] A. J. Heschel, *The Sabbath: Its Meaning for Modern Man* (New York: Farrar, Straus and Giroux, 1951), 21.

[73] This is clearly expressed in the Jewish thanksgiving prayer *(berakhah),* said when particular commandments are obeyed, i.e., when the gift of a covenantal sign is received: "Blessed are you, Lord our God, King of the Universe, who has sanctified us through your commandments and commanded us to. . . ."

[74] Only holiness of life takes precedence over the holiness of the Sabbath. Hence it is an obligation to set aside the Sabbath commandments to save life *(piquah nefesh);* cf. Mark 3:4; Luke 6:9; John 7:22–23; *Mekhilta Shabbata* 1 (Lauterbach ed., 3:197ff.).

[75] To be sure, the conclusion of the construction of the tabernacle demonstrates striking verbal parallels to the creation story. Compare "In this way all the work of the tabernacle of the tent of meeting was finished" (39:32) with "Thus the heavens and the earth were finished" (Gen. 2:1). Compare "When Moses saw that they had done all the work just as the LORD had commanded, he blessed them" (39:43) with "God saw everything that he had made, and indeed, it was very good" (Gen. 1:31) and "God blessed the seventh day" (Gen. 2:3). Compare "So Moses finished the work" (40:33) with "God finished the work that he had done" (Gen. 2:2). See Fox, *Now These Are the Names;* Leibowitz, *Studies in Shemot;* and Sarna, *Exploring Exodus.*

[76] The Hebrew word for "moon" *(yareah)* is thus linked to the word for a lunar month *(yerah).* Similarly, the word for new *(hadash)* is like the word for month *(hodesh),* which originally designated the day on which the new moon appeared. Since there are only about 29.5 days between every new moon, an extra "leap month" is inserted during some years—in a cycle of nineteen years every third, sixth, eighth, eleventh, fourteenth, seventeenth, and nineteenth year—in order to make up for the missing days. Otherwise, the feasts would not follow the seasons and eventually Passover, for example, would be celebrated in the winter or the fall. Different from the Jewish year, the Muslim year only follows the moon, which means that, for example, the fasting month of Ramadan can occur at any time of the year.

[77] *m. Shabbath* 7:2; *b. Shabbath* 49b; *b. Bava Qamma* 2a. We should bear in mind that what we regard as "work" is not necessarily what is forbidden. A particular Hebrew word is used for the forbidden activities, *mel'akhah.* This stands for creative work, since the Sabbath marks the end of creation, and its observance implies returning creation to God after six days as God's cocreators. Physical strain is thus not immediately forbidden (like weightlifting), while turning on the light—parallel to igniting a fire, the source of energy—is certainly forbidden.

[78] *Mekhilta Shabbata* 1 (Lauterbach ed., 3:198); *b. Yoma* 85b.

[79] Denis Janz, *Three Reformation Catechisms: Catholic, Anabaptist, Lutheran* (Texts and Studies in Religion 13; New York and Toronto: Edwin Mellen Press, 1982), 189ff.

[80]This insight was formulated by the Jewish philosopher Achad Ha'am (1856–1927 C.E.): "More than Israel kept the Sabbath, it is the Sabbath which kept Israel" (quoted by Pinchas Hacohen Peli, *Shabbat Shalom: A Renewed Encounter with the Sabbath* [Tel Aviv: World Wizo Department of Education, 1984], 5).

[81]*The Hirsch Siddur,* 294–95.

CHAPTER 13 (pages 245–267)

[1]Rabbinic tradition speculates how long it actually took after Moses had left them until they turned away from God. The answers vary from one single day up to eleven (*Exodus Rabbah* 42:7).

[2]A Christian oral tradition, however, labels Noah "a herald of righteousness," which would indicate that Noah was not as silent as may be concluded from the Hebrew text (2 Pet. 2:5). Moreover, some early Jewish and Christian traditions hold that Noah warned his contemporaries (see J. L. Kugel, *The Bible As It Was* [Cambridge, Mass.: Harvard University Press, 1997], 114–15).

[3]Genesis 6:9 states that Noah was blameless "in his generation." What does this indicate? Rabbinic interpretation often opines that it means that in another generation he would not be given as positive an evaluation, i.e., that he was only relatively good. Again, in comparison with other servants of God, such an understanding of the text is not too farfetched as will be demonstrated below. See also Kugel, *The Bible As It Was,* 116–17.

[4]From *Kether Malkhuth (The Royal Crown)* 38 (in *Ibn Gabirol,* trans. R. Loewe [New York: Grove Weidenfeld, 1990] 155–56).

[5]Fox, *Now These Are the Names,* 181.

[6]There are contemporary legal documents, where the expression "to break the tablets" means to invalidate or repudiate a document or agreement (see *ANET,* 167; Sarna, *Exploring Exodus,* 219).

[7]*Exodus Rabbah* 36. A similar thought is expressed in Rom. 5:13, "sin is not reckoned when there is no law." See also the difference between the death penalty for adultery within a marriage (Deut. 22:22) and the less severe punishment for unmarried people (22:16–17; Deut. 22:28–29). This mercy was probably what motivated Joseph to quietly divorce Mary, his betrothed, when she became pregnant and could be taken to have been unfaithful (Matt. 1:18–19).

[8]Leibowitz, *Studies in Shemot,* 2:613. In this context it is relevant to refer to John 1:1 concerning the Word. According to most translations, it is stated that "the Word was God." John makes, however, a clear distinction between the Word and God. In the expression "the Word was with God" (John 1:1, 2), God has a definite article, while this article is missing in the expression "the Word was God." The meaning is therefore rather that the Word was "godly" or "divine." The Word is the revealed God, which means that God limits himself for our sake (see pp. 140f., 144, 209f.).

[9]A similar ritual for the annihilation of a god is known from a document from the second millenium B.C.E. from Ugarit in

northwestern Syria. The god is burnt and crushed, and afterward the dust is scattered (Sarna, *Exploring Exodus,* 219).

[10] *Mekhilta Bahodesh* (Lauterbach ed., 2:262–63). The expression "a great sin" *(hata'ah gedolah),* which is referring to the sin of the golden calf (32:21, 30, 31), has parallels in both Akkadian and Egyptian documents, where it refers precisely to adultery (Sarna, *Understanding Exodus,* 220).

[11] A survey of different interpretations is found in Childs, *Exodus,* 574ff.

[12] For a critical exposition of the relation between this tent and the tabernacle, see Milgrom, *Numbers,* 386–87.

[13] The Hebrew verb translated by "so that we are distinct" means "marked." This same Hebrew root, *plh,* is found in the word *tefillin,* usually translated by "phylacteries," the covenantal signs commanded in Deut. 6:8 (cf. Matt. 23:5).

[14] *b. Rosh Hashanah* 17b; *Midrash on Psalms* 93:8 etc. The number thirteen is the sum of the two different names of God in 34:5, *YHWH* ("the LORD") and *El* ("God")—representing different aspects of God (mercy/judgment)—plus the different attributes applied to God, plus the three different terms for sin (since God takes them away in different ways).

[15] For the etymology, see G. Gerleman, "Das übervolle Mass: Ein Versuch mit *haesed,*" *VT* 28 (1978): 151–64. In modern Hebrew, the word *hesed* can still be used to express something received for free. The basic meaning of the word has thus survived throughout the centuries from the market in Beer-Sheba in the time of Abraham to a supermarket in modern Jerusalem.

[16] In a typical rabbinic way John refers to 34:6–7 by merely quoting two key concepts. Since there was no division of the text into chapters and verses he could not quote in a modern way. Moreover, he could assume that the Torah was known more or less by heart. Therefore, a mere hint was enough to make clear what he was referring to, at least when it comes to such a central passage as this one. This way of alluding to a whole passage by just rendering a few words is frequently found in the Bible itself. We have seen this use of the phrase "I am the LORD" in 20:2 (see pp. 138ff.).

[17] *Epistle of Barnabas* 4:6–8; cf. 14:1–6, where the following point is further made: "The Lord himself has given it (i.e., the covenant), after he had suffered for our sake. He was revealed in order that they would be complete in their sins and we receive the covenant through the heir, the Lord Jesus."

[18] In *Barnabas* 14:1–6 the record significantly ends with the smashing of the tablets of the covenant, linked to the new covenant.

[19] Ephraem, *Sermon* 3.421 (Corpus scriptorum Christianorum orientalium 135.84).

[20] See the monograph on this topic by P. C. Bori, *The Golden Calf and the Origins of the Anti-Jewish Controversy* (South Florida Studies in the History of Judaism 16; Atlanta: Scholars Press, 1990), with an extensive bibliography.

[21] *Against the Jews* 1.2 (Patrologia graeca 48.846); quoted by Bori, *Golden Calf,* 40.

[22] *Shavu‘oth*—Pentecost—is celebrated by the Jews to commemorate the first revelation on Sinai; it is therefore called *mattan Torah* ("the giving of the Torah"); see pp. 126f., 133ff., 184ff. The Day of Atonement is also called *kabbalath Torah,* "the reception of the Torah." Only at this point do the people of Israel really receive the Torah.

[23] *b. Berakhoth* 8b; *b. Baba Bathra* 14b.

[24] The verb expressing that Moses' skin was shining, *qaran,* appears also in the noun "horn," *qeren.* Based on this, Aquila's Greek translation (second century C.E.) and the Vulgate (Latin translation; fourth century C.E.) understand the text to mean that Moses had horns. This explains why Michelangelo on his famous statue depicts Moses with horns, a motif that frequently recurs in art.

Glossary

Abrabanel, Isaac ben Yehudah Abrabanel (1437–1508 C.E.). Portuguese Jewish statesman, philosopher, and Bible commentator, active also in Spain, and, after the expulsion of the Jews in 1492, in Italy. Among other things, he wrote commentaries on the Torah and the *Passover Haggadah.*

Apocalypse. The name is derived from a Greek word meaning "disclosure, uncovering" and refers to texts claiming to reveal secrets received in a vision or a dream. These revelations pertain to the past (creation, historical events), the present world (cosmos, the nature of man), and the future (the end of this era). As examples of apocalypses, the book of Daniel in the Old Testament, Revelation in the New Testament, and several of the Pseudepigrapha deserve mention. Even the Qumran literature contains apocalyptic material.

Apocrypha. The name is derived from the Greek, meaning literally "from hidden things" (cf. English "crypt, cryptic"), and designates a collection of Jewish writings from the time between the Old and the New Testaments, the oldest ones from ca. 200 B.C.E. In the Septuagint they are interspersed with the books of the Old Testament, and they were accepted by the early church as canonical Scriptures. However, when they were excluded from the Jewish canon, they were given secondary importance even in the Christian Bible. Today, they are usually excluded from Protestant Bible editions. They contain historical, prophetic/apocalyptic literature and didactic material of the kind found in the Wisdom literature. The most well-known books of the Apocrypha are *Maccabees, Sirach* or

Ben Sira, Wisdom of Solomon, Baruch, Judith, and *Tobit.* Cf. *Pseudepigrapha.*

Avot de-Rabbi Nathan. Like the mishnaic tractate *Pirqe Avot (Sayings of the Fathers),* this text contains a number of ethical sayings and proverbs from renowned rabbis. The collection of sayings is ascribed to Rabbi Nathan, who lived in Babylonia in the second century C.E.

B.C.E. This abbreviation for "before the Common Era" corresponds to B.C.E. ("before Christ"). Modern historians and theologians have increasingly used B.C.E. and the corresponding C.E. to designate the historical eras.

C.E. This abbreviation for "Common Era" corresponds to A.D. ("anno Domini"). See B.C.E.

Dead Sea Scrolls. See *Qumran.*

Ibn Ezra, Abraham (1089–1164 C.E.). Jewish scientist, philosopher, poet, and Bible commentator from Spain. Through numerous travels, he gained influence in wide circles. He wrote a commentary on the whole Torah, but the one on the book of Exodus is the most extensive.

Ibn Gabirol, Solomon ben Yehuda (ca. 1020–1057 C.E.). Spanish poet and philosopher. Even though no Bible commentary of his is known, he is quoted by other Bible commentators (for example, Ibn Ezra).

Josephus, Flavius (ca. 38–100 C.E.). Jewish commander, historian, and Bible commentator of noble priestly descent. Up to the destruction of Jerusalem in 70 C.E. he lived in Jerusalem. Then he followed the Roman conquerors to Rome, where he wrote his extensive works *The Jewish War (Bellum judaicum)* and *Jewish Antiquities (Antiquitates judaicae).* He is an invaluable witness of the political, social, and religious life of Judea in the first century C.E. As a priest he documents the temple and its worship from his own experience. He also provides important insights into the interpretation of the Bible in the time when the New Testament was being shaped.

Jubilees, book of. See *Pseudepigrapha.*

Kosher (Yiddish) or *kasher* (Hebrew). The word means literally "fit," and is best known from the context of the biblical and

Jewish dietary laws. It applies to foods prepared according to these rules, thus being "fit for consumption."

Letter of Aristeas. See *Pseudepigrapha.*

Luzatto, Samuel David (1800–1865 C.E.). Jewish scientist, philosopher, and Bible commentator from Italy. Among his numerous works is a commentary on the Torah that is largely based on the medieval Jewish tradition of interpretation.

Maimonides, Moshe Ben Maimon, or *Ramban* (1135–1204 C.E.). Jewish physician, philosopher, Bible and Talmud commentator from Spain, later active in Cairo. Through his comprehensive Bible commentaries, an immense systematization of the Jewish law *(Mishneh Torah),* and his extensive philosophical and medical writings, he counts among the greatest scholars throughout the ages.

Mekhilta. The oldest rabbinic commentary on the book of Exodus. The material goes back to the time before 200 C.E. but received its present shape only some hundred years later. The commentary begins with the ordinances regarding Passover in chapter 12.

Midrash. A Jewish Bible commentary. The word is derived from the Hebrew verb *darash,* "to seek, inquire, expound, research," in this case searching out the meaning of Scriptures (cf. the expression "study the law of the LORD," *lidrosh eth torath YHWH,* in Ezra 7:10). The word *midrash* (plural *midrashim*) is used for any interpretation of a verse or section in the Bible, as well as for a special Bible commentary as a literary composition, such as *Mekhilta, Midrash Rabbah,* and *Midrash Tanhuma.*

Midrash Hagadol. A thirteenth-century C.E. compilation of midrashim on the Torah, some of which go back to the mishnaic period.

Midrash Leqah Tov. A collection of midrashim from various times on the Torah and the books of Ruth, Esther, Song of Songs, Ecclesiastes, and Lamentations (called the five *Megilloth,* "Scrolls") by Rabbi Tuvia ben Eliezer (1036–1108 C.E.).

Midrash on Psalms. A collection of mostly homiletical midrashim, probably compiled between the eleventh and thirteenth centuries C.E.

Midrash Rabbah. A generic name for a series of midrashim on the Torah and the books of Ruth, Esther, Song of Songs, Ecclesiastes, and Lamentations (called the five *Megilloth,* "Scrolls"). *Midrash Rabbah* does not emanate from one commentator or school of commentators but is a collection of commentaries from different times. *Exodus Rabbah* dates to the eleventh century C.E. but contains material much older.

Midrash Sekhel Tov. A collection by Menahem ben Shlomo (twelfth century C.E.) of midrashim on Genesis and Exodus from various times.

Midrash Tanhuma. A generic name for various compilations of homiletic midrashim on the Torah. The oldest Tanhuma collection is quoted in the Talmud.

The Mishnah. The first collection of the interpretations and applications of the mosaic laws. The name is derived from the Hebrew verb *shanah,* which means "to repeat," thus also "to study, learn." Even though much narrative material is included (*haggadah;* see pp. 190ff.), the application of the laws in real life is in focus (*halakhah;* see pp. 190ff.). The Mishnah received its present shape around 200 C.E., but the material is usually considerably older. Hence, sages from the beginning of the first century C.E. are referred to, for example, Hillel and Shammai. The laws were systematized into six main "orders" (Hebrew *sedarim*), which in turn were divided into 63 tractates. The first order, *Zeraim* ("Seeds"), contains mainly ordinances that are applicable only in the land of Israel, such as the sabbatical year. Often the temple worship is the precondition for the fulfillment of these laws, for example, tithes and first fruits. The second order, *Moed* ("Appointed Times"), deals with the feasts and the third order, *Nashim* (Women"), involves primarily the marriage laws. The fourth order, *Neziqin* ("Damages"), is a criminal and penal code dealing with crimes and misdemeanors and the prescribed punishments and restitutions. The fifth order, *Qodashim* ("Holiness," Sacrifices"), contains the sacrificial laws and the sixth order, *Toharot* ("Purities"), comprises laws regarding ritual impurity and its removal. The systematization of the content is only partially accomplished. Therefore, every order also contains material that would fit better thematically into another order or does not belong to any of the six main categories.

Nachmanides or *Moshe Ben Nachman* (1194–1270 C.E.). Jewish philosopher, mystic, and Bible commentator from Spain. In 1263, after a successful disputation with the church, he left for Palestine, where he advocated the return of the Jewish people to the land of their fathers. He wrote among other things an extensive Torah commentary.

Passover Haggadah. Literally "the Passover narration," the ritual for the Jewish Passover meal and the telling of the Exodus story during the Passover night. To tell of the exodus is an explicit commandment (Exod. 13:8). The *Passover Haggadah* contains Bible texts, midrashim, blessings, hymns, and regulations regarding the various ingredients in the Passover meal. It received its present shape in the tenth century but essentially goes back to the first centuries C.E. See further pp. 86ff.

Pesiqta de Rav Kahana. A collection of homiletic midrashim (sermons) named after Rabbi Kahana (third century C.E.) not because the sermons were given or compiled by him but because he is mentioned in the beginning of the collection in some manuscripts. The collection was probably not finalized before the fifth century. The name *"pesiqta"* is Aramaic for "section" or "portion," referring to the weekly portion of the Torah and the reading from the prophets *(haftorah)*.

Pesiqta Rabbati. Like the previous one, a collection of homiletic midrashim for the festivals and special Sabbaths. The final compilation was probably made some centuries later, but like most midrashim it contains material from different times.

Philo (ca. 20 B.C.E. – 50 C.E.). Jewish philosopher and Bible commentator from Alexandria. Together with Josephus, he is incomparably the most productive Jewish writer of the Second Temple period. Deeply influenced by Greek philosophy, he is more interested in the spiritual and symbolic dimensions of the Bible than their historical and literal meaning. Through his method of interpretation (allegory and typology), he became very popular among the early fathers of the church, to whom Jewish history and the laws and ordinances of Moses were reinterpreted to refer to Christ and the church. The following writings deal particularly with the book of Exodus: *On the Life of Moses (De vita Mosis), On the Decalogue (De decalogo), On the Special Laws (De specialibus legibus),* and *Questions and Answers on Exodus (Quaestiones et solutiones in Exodum).*

Pirqe de Rabbi Eliezer. Midrashic rewriting of the biblical history, probably from the ninth century C.E.

Pseudepigrapha. The Greek name literally means "a false epigraph," namely, "the falsely ascribed." This collection of writings from roughly the second century B.C.E. to the second century C.E. contains several texts that claim to be written by biblical figures, such as Adam, Enoch, the patriarchs, Moses, Solomon, Baruch, and Ezra. Unlike the Apocrypha, they have never received canonical status. They contain primarily apocalyptic material. Among these writings are the *Letter of Aristeas,* written in Egypt in the first century B.C.E., which describes how the Greek translation, the Septuagint, came into being, and book of *Jubilees,* written in the land of Israel in the same time period, which claims to be a revelation to Moses of the biblical history from creation to exodus. Other well-known works of the Pesudepigrapha are the *Testaments of the Twelve Patriarchs, Psalms of Solomon, Enoch, Apocalypse of Baruch, Assumption of Moses, Ascension of Isaiah,* and *Sibylline Oracles.*

Qumran and the *Dead Sea Scrolls.* Scrolls and fragments from the first century B.C.E. and the first century C.E., found along the western shore of the Dead Sea, particularly at Qumran in the north, from 1947 on. The texts contain fragmentary manuscripts to all the books of the Old Testament (except the book of Esther), and to the Apocrypha and Pseudepigrapha, commentaries on biblical texts, rules for the community (probably Essenes), hymns and prayers, and apocalypses describing the final—mostly bloody—events leading up to the end of this era.

Rabbinic. The term usually refers to the period of the Jewish sages which extends from the destruction of the temple in 70 C.E. to the Islamic conquest of the Middle East in the seventh century. The literature that emerged during this time is called rabbinic literature.

Rashbam. Abbreviation of Rabbi Shmuel (Samuel) ben Meir (ca. 1080–1174 C.E.), Bible and Talmud commentator, grandson of Rashi.

Rashi. Abbreviation of Rabbi Shlomo (Solomon) ben Yitzhak (Isaac), (1040–1105 C.E.). Jewish Bible and Talmud commentator, active in Germany and France. Rashi commented on most biblical books and talmudic tractates and is—together with

Maimonides—regarded as one of the greatest Jewish sages throughout the ages and is widely studied up to this day.

Saadya Gaon (882–942 C.E.). Jewish philosopher, grammarian, Bible and Talmud commentator from Egypt, active in Babylonia. One of the greatest of the *ge'onim,* the leaders of world Jewry for five hundred years following the completion of the Talmud.

The Second Temple period. Solomon's Temple was destroyed in 586 B.C.E. The Second Temple was inaugurated in 518 B.C.E. and destroyed in 70 C.E. This era is consequently called the Second Temple period.

The Septuagint. The first translation ever of the Hebrew Bible, made for the Jews in the Diaspora, whose mother tongue was Greek and whose knowledge of Hebrew was limited. The name, derived from Latin, means "seventy" and comes from a legend according to which seventy-two scholars from Jerusalem gathered in Alexandria for the translation of the Torah. Each one was confined to a cell, yet finished simultaneously with an identical translation. This allegedly took place around 200 B.C.E. Through the Septuagint, the Bible for the first time became known in wide circles outside the Jewish community. Since any translation is always an interpretation of the text as well, the Septuagint is a valuable testimony to the Bible's history of interpretation.

The Talmud. A rabbinic commentary on the *Mishnah.* The name comes from the Hebrew verb *lamad* ("to learn") and is actually an abbreviation of *Talmud Torah,* meaning "the teaching of the Torah." The Talmud contains both the Mishnah and the continuous commentaries on the Mishnah, called *Gemara.* The Talmud is organized into the same orders and tractates as the Mishnah. There were two talmudic collections. One emerged in Israel and is called the Palestinian Talmud, *Talmud Yerushalmi* or *Talmud Erets Yisrael.* It was concluded in the first half of the fifth century C.E. The second one emerged in the Jewish Diaspora of Babylonia and is consequently called the Babylonian Talmud or *Talmud Bavli.* It was concluded in the middle of the sixth century C.E. The two versions of the Talmud have much material in common. When "Talmud" is used without further definition, the Babylonian Talmud is usually meant, since from the eleventh century on it became normative within Judaism. It contains 6,000 folio pages totaling 2,500,000 words.

Tanhuma. See *Midrash Tanhuma.*

Targum. The word means "translation" and refers to Aramaic Bible translations and paraphrases. As Hebrew became increasingly replaced by Aramaic as a spoken language in the land of Israel and in Babylonia during the Second Temple period, translations of the scriptural readings in the synagogue became necessary. Originally these were presented orally, but eventually they were written down. There are targums on most books of the Bible. On the Pentateuch, or Torah, the following targums have survived: *Targum Onqelos* from the first century C.E.; the later *Targum Pseudo-Jonathan* (or *Targum Yerushalmi I*) which, in spite of interpolations from medieval times, contains material as old as that of *Targum Onqelos; Targum Neofiti,* which is probably contemporary with or somewhat older than *Targum Onqelos;* and the *Fragmentary Targum* (or *Targum Yerushalmi II*) on about 850 verses from various parts of the Pentateuch. While *Targum Onqelos* is a fairly literal translation, *Pseudo-Jonathan* and *Neofiti* are more paraphrasing and therefore provide more insight into the history of biblical interpretation. *Targum Jonathan* on the prophets should not be confused with *Targum Pesudo-Jonathan* on the Pentateuch.

Torah. The word is a noun etymologically related to a Hebrew verb, *yarah* ("to teach"). The most common translation of *Torah* is "the law," which goes back to the translation of the word in the Septuagint (see above) with the Greek word *nomos.* As long as this word was read by Jews who knew their Bible, it was linked to the Hebrew concept of *Torah* with all its rich connotations. When Gentile Christians took over the Septuagint from the Jews, only the literary understanding of the Greek word remained, which led to a misunderstanding of the concept of *Torah* as exclusively commandments, regulations, or decrees—"law." More specifically, *Torah* stands for the first five books of the Bible, namely, the Pentateuch.

It is true that *nomos* often means "law," but like *Torah* it also means "teaching," "instruction," as in "astronomy" (teaching of the stars), "agronomy" (teaching of the field), etc. However, neither "law" nor "instruction" does justice to the Hebrew concept *Torah,* particularly as frequently used in Christian theology as a contrast of "grace" or "gospel." In the Bible, *Torah* refers both to single laws and ordinances and to God's Word in general (see, for example, Ps. 119). In Jewish tradition, *Torah* in a narrow sense may be used for the first part of the Bible, namely, the five books of Moses, as distinct from the latter two parts, namely, the Prophets (Hebrew *Neviim*) and the Writings (Hebrew *Ketuvim*). The most common usage, however, refers to the entire revelation of God. In this way Jesus obviously uses it, as clearly demonstrated, for example, in John 10:34, where he refers to the book of Psalms as "law." The same applies to Paul when he quotes from the Prophets but refers to "the law" (1 Cor. 14:21). In an even wider sense, Jewish tradition uses the concept not only for the whole Bible, but for the entire religious tradition of the Jewish people as well, that is, "Judaism."

In most cases the translation "law" is not only inadequate but downright false and misleading. In the New Testament the word rather refers to promises than to laws—what Christians would normally term "gospel" (see further pp. 137ff., 257ff., 260ff.). The word should be left untranslated (like *Amen* and *Hallelujah*), but if it is translated, the most appropriate translation would be "the Word of God."

Tosefta. A collection of interpretations and applications of the Mosaic laws closely related to the Mishnah both in content and arrangement. The name means "addition," namely, addition to the Mishnah. Even though it was compiled almost two hundred years later and is about four times larger than the Mishnah, the material is not later than that of the Mishnah.

Selected Bibliography

Braude, William G., and Israel J. Kapstein, trans. *Pesikta de-Rab Kahana*. Philadelphia: JPS, 1982.

Brichto, H. C. *The Names of God: Poetic Readings in Biblical Beginnings*. Oxford and New York: Oxford University Press, 1998.

Buber, M. *Moses: The Revelation and the Covenant*. Atlantic Highlands, N.J.: Humanities Press International, 1988.

Buber, Salomon, ed. *Midrash Leqah Tov*. Reprint, Jerusalem, 1959.

_____. *Midrash Sekhel Tov*. Reprint, Tel Aviv, 1963.

_____. *Midrash Tanhuma*. Reprint, Jerusalem, 1963.

Cassuto, U. *A Commentary on the Book of Exodus*. Jerusalem: Magnes Press, 1967.

Childs, B. *The Book of Exodus: A Critical Theological Commentary*. Philadelphia: Westminster Press, 1974.

Daube, D. *The Exodus Pattern in the Bible*. London: Faber and Faber, 1963.

Epstein, N. Y., ed. *Mekhilta d'Rabbi Shimon ben Yochai*. Jerusalem: Mekitse nirdamim, 1955.

Fox, Everett. *Now These Are the Names: A New English Rendition of the Book of Exodus*. New York: Schocken Books, 1986.

Friedlander, Gerald. *Pirqe de Rabbi Eliezer*. 4th ed. New York: Sepher-Hermon Press, 1981.

Glatzer, Nahum N. *The Passover Haggadah*. 3d rev. ed. New York: Schocken, 1979.

Goldberg, Michael. *Jews and Christians Getting Our Stories Straight: The Exodus and the Passion-Resurrection*. Nashville: Abingdon Press, 1985.

Greenberg, M. *Understanding Exodus*. New York: Behrman House, 1969.

Hertz, J. H. *The Pentateuch and Haftorahs.* 2d ed. London: Soncino Press, 1979.

Hirsch, Samson Raphael. *The Hirsch Siddur: The Order of Prayer for the Whole Year.* Jerusalem: Feldheim Publishers, 1997.

_____. *The Pentateuch.* 5 vols. Gateshead: Judaica Press, 1976.

Horovitz, H. S., ed. *Sifre Zuta.* Lodz: Masorah, 1929.

Kees, Hermann. *Der Götterglaube im alten Ägypten.* Berlin: Akademie-Verlag, 1977.

Lauterbach, J., ed. *Mekhilta de-Rabbi Ishmael.* 3 vols. Philadelphia: JPS, 1933.

Leibowitz, N. *Studies in Shemot (Exodus).* 2 vols. 6th ed. Jerusalem: The World Zionist Organization, 1986.

Levenson, J. D. *Sinai and Zion: An Entry into the Jewish Bible.* San Francisco: Harper & Row, 1987.

Levine, B. A. *The JPS Torah Commentary: Leviticus.* Philadelphia: JPS, 1989.

Margulies, Mordecai. *Midrash Haggadol on the Pentateuch: Exodus.* Jerusalem: Mosad Haraw Kook, 1956.

Milgrom, J. *The JPS Torah Commentary: Numbers.* Philadelphia: JPS, 1990.

Muffs, Y. *Love and Joy: Law, Language, and Religion in Ancient Israel.* New York: Jewish Theological Seminary of America, 1992.

Nachmanides. *Ramban, Commentary on the Torah.* Trans. C. B. Chavel. 5 vols. New York: Shilo Publishing House, 1971–76.

Plaut, W. G. *The Torah: A Modern Commentary.* New York: Union of American Hebrew Congregations, 1981.

Rashi. *Pentateuch with Targum Onkelos, Haphataroth and Rashi's Commentary.* Trans. M. Rosenbaum, A. M. Silbermann. 5 vols. Jerusalem: Routledge and Kegan Paul, 1973.

Redford, D. *Egypt, Canaan, and Israel in Ancient Times.* Princeton: Princeton University Press, 1992.

Sarna, N. M. *Exploring Exodus: The Heritage of Biblical Israel.* New York: Schocken Books, 1987.

_____. *The JPS Torah Commentary: Exodus.* Philadelphia: JPS, 1991.

Sperling, S. D. *The Original Torah: The Political Intents of the Bible's Writers.* New York: New York University Press, 1998.

Tacitus, Cornelius. *The Histories and Annals.* 1937. Trans. C. H. Moore and J. Jackson. 4 vols. LCL. Cambridge, Mass.: Harvard University Press.

Walzer, M. *Exodus and Revolution.* New York: Basic Books, 1985.

Zakovitch, Y. *"And You Shall Tell Your Son . . .": The Concept of Exodus in the Bible.* Jerusalem: Magnes Press, 1991.

Subject Index

Scripture Index